BEYOND VIETNAM

A volume in the series

CULTURE, POLITICS,
AND THE COLD WAR

Edited by Christian G. Appy

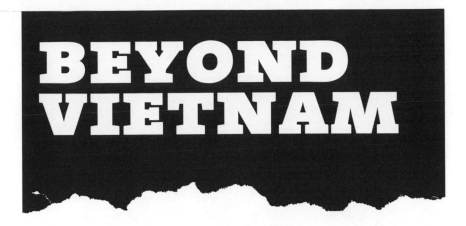

THE POLITICS OF PROTEST IN
MASSACHUSETTS, 1974–1990
ROBERT SURBRUG JR.

UNIVERSITY OF MASSACHUSETTS PRESS

Amherst and Boston

LC 2009030041
ISBN 978-1-55849-712-2 (paper); 711-5 (library cloth)

Designed by Richard Hendel
Set in Quadraat and The Serif types by House of Equations, Inc.
Printed and bound by The Maple-Vail Book Manufacturing Group, Inc.

Library of Congress Cataloging-in-Publication Data

Surbrug, Robert, 1964–
    Beyond Vietnam : the politics of protest in Massachusetts, 1974–1990 / Robert Surbrug, Jr.
        p. cm. — (Culture, politics, and the Cold War)
    Includes bibliographical references and index.
    ISBN 978–1–55849–712–2 (paper : alk. paper) — ISBN 978–1–55849–711-5 (library cloth : alk. paper)
    1. Protest movements—Massachusetts—History—20th century.   2. Antinuclear movement—
Massachusetts—History—20th century.   3. Solidarity—Political aspects—Massachusetts
History—20th century.   4. Solidarity—Political aspects—Central America—History—20th century.
5. Peace movements—Massachusetts—History—20th century.   6. Human rights
movements—Massachusetts—History—20th century.   7. Massachusetts—Relations—Central
America.   8. Central America—Relations—Massachusetts.   9. Massachusetts—Social
conditions—20th century.   10. Massachusetts—Politics and government—1951–   I. Title.
    HN79.M4S87 2009
        322.409744´09048—dc22   2009030041

British Library Cataloguing in Publication data are available.

CONTENTS

ACKNOWLEDGMENTS

First and foremost, I owe deep gratitude to Kevin Boyle, who not only helped me focus and shape this work in its early stages but offered his personal support and encouragement during difficult times as well. I know few people whose lives are better expressions of their social democratic values than Kevin, and I am proud to be associated with him.

I wish also to thank those who gave important feedback and criticism over the years, most notably Ronald Story, Daniel Horowitz, Veronica Wilson, Van Gosse, and Mary Wentworth. Several people from the greater University of Massachusetts community also deserve thanks for their support, especially David Glassberg and Larry Owens. Chistian Appy was immensely important in the development of the manuscript. Robert Cox, director of Special Collections and University Archives, was also of great assistance in the final stages.

Special thanks go to Rob Weir, whose advice, support, and collegiality (as well as a few desperately needed rides) have been more important to me than he probably knows. I also want to acknowledge important friends and colleagues who traveled the road with me: Matt Crocker, Christoph Strobel, Marian Mollin, Leo Maley, Brad Paul, and John Lund.

The staff at the University of Massachusetts Press has been a delight to work with. I especially want to thank Clark Dougan and Carol Betsch. I would also like to express my appreciation to Joan Vidal for her important editorial work. As always with such projects, I am hugely indebted to the many librarians and archivists over the years who helped guide me through the maze of resource material, especially those at Smith College, Northeastern University, the Tamiment Library and Robert F. Wagner Labor Archives at New York University, and the University of Massachusetts. Of special note are the tireless Joe Heimann and Beth Campbell of the University of Massachusetts Microform Collections.

I owe a huge debt to Frances Crowe, who during the earliest stages of this work allowed me free access to her personal papers, then located in her legendary basement (a veritable time capsule of decades of activism). And a warm *merci beaucoup* to Lionel Delevingne for his gracious permission to use one of his many iconic photographs from the 1970s "No Nukes" era for the cover.

I also want to thank my valued friends and colleagues at Bay Path College who have made my years there a joy: Brenda Hardin Abbott, Ginna Freed, John Jarvis, Ellie Long, Lisa Ruch, Tom Schorle, Sandy Burns, James Wilson, and Dave Wallace. My life has largely been divided between New Jersey, where I was born and raised, and my adopted home of Massachusetts. For treasured friendship and support from the Garden State I wish to acknowledge Dave Roskos, Beth Borrus, Tom Obrzut, John Richey, Chris Aubry, Jeff Maxchi, and Joel Bertin. And from the Bay State, Patty McGill, Jason Simon, Paul Bailey, and Rich Thomas.

I also wish to acknowledge my brother Jeff Surbrug and sister Chris Surbrug. Most of all, I wish to thank my mother, Georgianna Surbrug, and my father, Robert Surbrug Sr., for their enduring love and support.

ACRONYMS

ABM	Anti-Ballistic Missile Treaty
ACLU	American Civil Liberties Union
ACRS	Advisory Committee on Reactor Safeguards
AEC	Atomic Energy Commission
AFL-CIO	American Federation of Labor–Congress of Industrial Organizations
AFSC	American Friends Service Committee
AID	Agency for International Development
AIFLD	American Institute for Free Labor Development
AFSCME	American Federation of State, County and Municipal Employees
ANC	African National Congress
ANDES	National Association of Salvadoran Educators
ARENA	National Republican Alliance (Alianza Republicana Nacionalista)
CASA	Central American Solidarity Association
CAWG	Central American Working Group
CDAS	Clams for Direct Action at Seabrook
CIA	Central Intelligence Agency
CISPES	Committee in Solidarity with the People of El Salvador
COINTELPRO	Counterintelligence Program
CLW	Council for a Livable World
CORE	Congress of Racial Equality
CRP	Crisis Relocation Planning
EFE	Environmentalists for Full Employment
EIS	environmental impact studies
EPZ	Emergency Planning Zone

ERAP	Economic Research and Action Project
FBI	Federal Bureau of Investigation
FDR	Democratic Revolutionary Front (Frente Democrático Revolucionario)
FEMA	Federal Emergency Management Agency
FMLN	Farabundo Martí National Liberation Front (Frente Farabundo Martí para la Liberación Nacional)
FOIA	Freedom of Information Act
FOR	Fellowship of Reconciliation
FRG	Federal Republic of Germany
FSLN	Sandinista National Liberation Front (Frente Sandinista de Liberación Nacional)
HUAC	House Un-American Activities Committee
IAM	International Association of Machinists
IBEW	International Brotherhood of Electrical Workers
IDDS	Institute for Disarmament and Defense Studies
INS	Immigration and Naturalization Service
ISO	International Socialist Organization
LNS	Liberation News Service
LTBT	Limited Test Ban Treaty
MAES	Medical Aid for El Salvador
MASSPIRG	Massachusetts Public Interest Research Group
MfS	Mobilization for Survival
MIT	Massachusetts Institute of Technology
MUSE	Musicians United for Safe Energy
NATO	North Atlantic Treaty Organization
NECAN	New England Central America Network
NEST	New El Salvador Today
NFZ	Nuclear Free Zone
NGA	National Governors Association
NISGUA	Network in Solidarity with the People of Guatemala
NNSNP	National Network in Solidarity with the Nicaraguan People
NOPE	Nuclear Objectors for a Pure Environment
NRC	Nuclear Regulatory Commission

NU	Northeast Utilities
NWFC	Nuclear Weapons Freeze Campaign
OPEC	Organization of Petroleum Exporting Countries
OXFAM	Oxford Committee for Famine Relief
POR	Pledge of Resistance
PSE&G	Public Service Electric and Gas
PSNH	Public Service Company of New Hampshire
PSR	Physicians for Social Responsibility
ROTC	Reserve Officers' Training Corps
RSU	Radical Student Union
SALT	Strategic Arms Limitation Treaty
SANE	Committee for a SANE Nuclear Policy
SAPL	Seacoast Anti-Pollution League
SCANN	Student Coalition against Nukes Nationwide
SDI	Strategic Defense Initiative
SDS	Students for a Democratic Society
SNCC	Student Non-Violent Coordinating Committee
SSD	Special Session on Disarmament
SWAT	Special Weapons and Tactics
UAW	United Autoworkers
UFW	United Farm Workers
UE	United Electrical Workers
UNO	United Nicaraguan Opposition
VVAW	Vietnam Veterans against the War
WILPF	Women's International League for Peace and Freedom
WRL	War Resisters League

INTRODUCTION

A TALE OF TWO SIXTIES

In 1999, during a meeting of the World Trade Organization, radical protest against corporate globalization shook Seattle, Washington. The relatively small number of young anarchist militants who smashed windows and battled riot-control police drew world media attention to a protest that comprised tens of thousands of nonviolent participants. Among their ranks were environmentalists, proponents of indigenous people's rights, labor unionists, and Third World solidarity activists. Suddenly the U.S. press and media focused on the growing anti–corporate globalization movement. Media coverage of the Seattle protests almost universally framed them as the largest since the 1960s. From the news accounts of the "Battle of Seattle," it appeared that, after a thirty-year hibernation, leftist grassroots political activism had just reawakened.

Within a few short years, the devastating attacks of September 11, 2001, ushered in the chain of events that would lead the administration of George W. Bush to launch the 2003 invasion of Iraq. In the months that led up to the war, mass peace marches were held around the world in an impressive demonstration of global opposition to the impending war. The new peace movement quickly eclipsed the anti–corporate globalization movement, and—as they had with the Seattle protests—the U.S. press and media heralded the new wave of protests as a phenomenon unseen since the Vietnam War era.

These not-since-the-sixties accounts of turn-of-the-century protest movements testify to the strength of the dominant historical interpretation of the 1960s: "The Movement," in this paradigm, is a comet that trails brilliantly across the idealistic sky of the 1960s only to burn out upon reentry into the sober gravitational pull of the 1970s. In this view the descending arc of 1960s radical activism intersected around 1968 with the ascending arc of the conservative Right; thus, the story of the subsequent decades has largely entailed the national repudiation of the 1960s and the embrace of the new conservatism. By examining the rich activist history of the U.S. Left between 1974 and 1990—tracing the political continuity through the movement against nuclear energy, the nuclear weapons freeze movement, and the Central American solidarity movement—I challenge the prevailing view of the post-1960s Left as fragmented splinters of the Vietnam

War–era movement defined solely by the politics of identity. In fact, by helping to reconfigure post-1960s liberalism (which itself underwent important transformations at this time), post–Vietnam War era activism played an important role in shaping the political landscape of the 1970s and 1980s. A brief review of the politics of the 1960s highlights the continuity between the activism of that seminal decade and the decades that followed.

———

The 1950s movement for racial freedom and equality was the spark that set off the chain reaction that swept across the United States in the 1960s. The civil rights movement awoke an idealism and commitment to democratic change that intersected with a swelling "baby boom" generation and rising prosperity to create a decade of almost unprecedented cultural and political transformation.[1] The civil rights struggle helped awaken a radical pacifist movement against the cold war, the arms race, and nuclear testing. A student New Left emerged from remnants of the Old Left, which handed down a radical tradition from the 1930s.[2] In an age of affluence, the New Left sought to de-emphasize the orthodox Marxism and labor focus of the Old Left in favor of a more existential search for authenticity and commitment. White college students returned from their participation in southern sit-ins, freedom rides, and voter registration drives to lead a rebellion against in loco parentis rules on college campuses and to organize the low-income population of the northern slums.

By the second half of the 1960s, Black Nationalism and other minority-empowerment movements grew alongside a rising tide of opposition to the war in Vietnam. Increasingly, the political movements of the sixties generation fused into what contemporaries called simply the Movement—a sweeping challenge to what many saw as the materialism, racism, cultural repression, alienation, and social disconnectedness of modern American life. The Movement also led a frontal assault on U.S. cold war ideology and policies, which it denounced as militarist and imperialist. Running parallel to the overtly political Movement was a rapidly expanding counterculture, which promised personal and social transformation through experimentation with sex, drugs, music, meditation, communal living, and other radical changes in lifestyle. As the 1960s progressed, political and cultural movements increasingly merged in a utopian assault on the "old order."[3]

By 1968—as the United States became polarized over the stalemated war in Vietnam, campus unrest spread, and five summers of urban disorder exploded in the riots that followed the assassination of Martin Luther King, Jr.—the old order seemed to be teetering on the verge of collapse. Abroad, anticolonial revolutions in the Third World and rebellion on both sides of the Iron Curtain in Europe generated global hope among activists that they might sweep away the racism, exploitation, and social repression of the old order and usher in a new epoch of freedom and equality.[4]

When the revolution failed to materialize, the Movement seemed to shatter. Some activists joined militant underground guerrilla groups, such as the Weathermen, whose extremism appeared to grow in proportion to the diminishing prospects for revolution. Others adopted an increasingly nihilistic drug lifestyle that seemed to lose sight of the earlier countercultural ideals of positive personal transformation. Some who were burnt out by the political failures of the Movement turned "from slogans to mantras," embracing various forms of eastern mysticism and in some cases joining authoritarian religious cults. The 1968 election of the Republican candidate, Richard M. Nixon, on a law and order platform appeared to herald a new era. For many, the killings at Kent State University and Jackson State College and the national student strike of 1970 signaled the end of the movement that once promised triumph.[5]

The contemporary narrative of discontinuity between the 1960s and the decades that followed owes much to the early epitaphs of the 1960s. Often pronounced during the late 1960s and early 1970s by those who had believed most deeply in the promise of world revolution and were most disillusioned by its failure to materialize by the change in tide that occurred in 1968, obituaries for the Movement, and thus the sixties, poured in. The journalist Michael Herr, who covered the war in Vietnam, wrote this of the cultural exhaustion of the decade: "Out on the street I couldn't tell the Vietnam veterans from the rock 'n' roll veterans. The Sixties had made so many casualties, its war and its music had run power off the same circuit for so long they didn't even have to fuse. . . . The year [1968] had been so hot that I think it shorted out the whole decade."[6] Perhaps the most memorable postmortem for the decade was that of the counterculture journalist Hunter S. Thompson. In his 1971 novel, *Fear and Loathing in Las Vegas*, Thompson described the existential mood shift from the mid- to late sixties: "You could strike spark anywhere. There was a fantastic universal sense that whatever we were doing was right, that we were winning. . . . And that I think was the handle—that sense of inevitable victory over the forces of Old and Evil. . . . We had all the momentum; we were riding the crest of a high and beautiful wave. . . . So now, less than five years later . . . you can almost *see* the high-water mark—that place where the wave finally broke and rolled back."[7]

Ironically, these obituaries came at a time when—in the wake of post-1968 disillusionment (1969–1971)—the movements of the 1960s, both political and cultural, were making their deepest inroads into American culture. As the Vietnam War slowly subsided, activists streamed into new movements that—as direct and conscious descendants of the activism of the 1960s—would define the 1970s. Yet the "death of the sixties" narrative, implying the dissolution of the impulse for radical social and political transformation, was now clearly established. According to this view, while environmentalism, feminism, and gay liberation soldiered on as the last surviving heirs of the Movement, the rest of America sank into the drift, apathy, and narcissism of the "Me Decade" until the conservative ascendancy that had begun with Nixon's election in 1968 (and was temporarily interrupted by the Watergate scandal) resumed in 1980 with the election of Ronald Reagan.[8]

POST–VIETNAM WAR MOVEMENTS

In many ways, in the 1970s much of the country was only beginning to feel the political and cultural rebellion of the 1960s. The impact of the movements was like a concentrated ink drop on a napkin, whose circle expands ever wider as the ink dilutes. Opposition to the war in Vietnam and reevaluation of cold war premises did not move into the mainstream of American society until the end of the 1960s and into the 1970s. As the 1970s progressed, the clothing, hairstyles, music, sexual experimentation, and drug use of the counterculture spread into small towns across the United States. Television programs such as *All in the Family*, *The Jeffersons*, and *Good Times* took up racism, feminism, the sexual revolution, and other progressive themes in a way that had only rarely been seen in the 1960s on shows such as *The Twilight Zone*, *The Smothers Brothers*, and *Laugh-In*. The persistent antiwar theme of the most popular television program of the 1970s, M*A*S*H, indicates the degree to which the changed attitudes of the 1960s continued to permeate the popular culture of the 1970s.

The new movements of the 1970s and 1980s, which also derived inspiration and a sense of legitimacy from the movements of the 1960s, sought to adapt lessons learned from the previous era to their changed environment. By the mid-1970s, the feminist and environmentalist movements had converged into the movement against nuclear power, which sought to employ New Left ideas of direct action and participatory democracy but also elevate the role of women in a way that the antiwar movement never had.[9] The No Nukes movement also pursued a community strategy that continued the trajectory of the antiwar movement in the late 1960s, attempting to move it from college campuses to mainstream communities. The movement against nuclear power rejected the violent rhetoric and vanguard politics of the antiwar movement in favor of a return to the grassroots organizing and bottom-up approach of the early years of the Student Non-violent Coordinating Committee (SNCC), the Economic Research and Action Project (ERAP) of Students for a Democratic Society (SDS), and the 1967 nationwide student antiwar organizing campaign Vietnam Summer. The movement against nuclear power also sought to incorporate the communal, agrarian lifestyle of the counterculture in an effort not only to stop nuclear power but also to create new forms of community and democracy.[10]

Many antinuclear activists of the 1970s were veterans of the civil rights and antiwar struggles of the 1960s. Activists saw the new technology as part and parcel of the impersonal corporate technocracy that had created the war in Vietnam and subordinated the welfare of the people and citizen democracy to the imperatives of power, profit, and an ever-expanding consumer society.[11] The movement against nuclear power that began to grow around 1974 reached critical mass in 1977, when 1,414 members of the antinuclear Clamshell Alliance were arrested during an occupation of the site of a proposed nuclear power plant in Seabrook, New Hampshire.[12] One of the largest mass political arrests of the 1960s and 1970s, it surpassed the eight hundred–plus protestors arrested during the Berkeley Free Speech Movement in 1964 or the seven hundred–plus arrested during Columbia University uprising of 1968. Indeed, only the mass arrests of the Birmingham, Alabama, protests, exceeding two thousand during the spring of 1963, and the detention of more than ten thousand antiwar radicals in Washington, D.C., during the May Day protests of 1971 surpassed the arrests at Seabrook.[13]

The movement against nuclear power continued to sweep the nation, peaking in 1979 when the near meltdown at the Three Mile Island Nuclear Power Station in Pennsylvania effectively ended the era of nuclear expansion in the United States. Although the crusade against nuclear power began to wane, it had helped reawaken the next of the mass movements of the post–Vietnam War era: the movement against nuclear weapons. Like the movement against nuclear power, the effort to freeze the arms race of the 1980s was deeply rooted in the activism of preceding decades. After the 1963 Limited Test Ban Treaty, the disarmament movement that had grown so dramatically in the late 1950s and early 1960s had largely gone into abeyance, only to be further eclipsed by the escalating war in Vietnam.[14] By 1980, however, the nuclear weapons freeze movement had been reborn and—with the breakdown of détente during the late years of the Jimmy Carter administration and the arms buildup under the Republican administration of Ronald Reagan creating fears of Armageddon—the movement took the nation by storm.

Freeze activists pursued a moderate political strategy that downplayed the countercultural influences so prominent in the movement against nuclear power. In a campaign reminiscent of Senator Eugene McCarthy's "Clean for Gene" presidential campaign of 1968, freeze activists (many from old-line radical pacifist organizations) sought to make ending the nuclear arms race as mainstream as apple pie. Within a few years, polls revealed that an overwhelming majority of Americans supported a nuclear weapons freeze by the United States and the Soviet Union. In June 1982, more than 750,000 Americans attended a nuclear weapons freeze and disarmament rally in Central Park in New York City. The numbers surpassed all but those of the November 15, 1969, march against the war in Vietnam in Washington, D.C.[15] The movement won passage of a freeze resolution by the House of Representatives in 1983 and challenged the dominance of the martial cold war rhetoric of the Reagan administration.[16] Although the freeze movement fell short of accomplishing its stated goals, it managed to shift the terms of debate. This shift not only forced the Reagan administration to downplay the strategy and rhetoric of limited nuclear war emanating from the "war winners" in his administration but also helped lay the groundwork for the serious negotiations that took place in the age of Mikhail Gorbachev.[17]

The Central American solidarity movement, which grew in the shadow of the freeze movement in the early 1980s, exploded as the freeze movement declined in late 1983. The year 1979 saw revolutionary movements sweep across Central America, as the leftist Sandinistas of Nicaragua overthrew Anastasio Somoza (the Nicaraguan dictator supported by the Untied States) and the Farabundo Marti National Liberation Front (Frente Farabundo Martí para la Liberación Nacional [FMLN]) threatened to topple the military junta and right-wing oligarchy of El Salvador (also supported by the Untied States). Reagan campaigned for president on a promise to push back what conservatives saw as a rising tide of Communist-backed revolution in Central America. As president, Reagan set out to overthrow the Sandinista government in Nicaragua, and he dramatically increased U.S. military aid to El Salvador.[18]

For those on the U.S. Left, events in Central America portended a replay of Vietnam and an effort to resurrect early cold war ideology. A vigorous and eclectic opposition to U.S. policies emerged and grew throughout the 1980s. Young militants gravitated toward groups such as the Committee in Solidarity with the People in El Salvador (CISPES), hearkening back to the Third World revolution advocates of the late 1960s. Like their predecessors, who traveled to Cuba as part of the Venceremos Brigade in the late 1960s and early 1970s, the Central American solidarity activists of the 1980s journeyed to Nicaragua and El Salvador to show their solidarity with the efforts of Central American revolutionaries to build new egalitarian societies.[19]

Many church organizations became deeply involved in efforts to stop U.S. intervention and to support popular movements in Central America. In the wake of the Second Vatican Council in the early 1960s—with its call for peace and social justice—a growing number of Catholics spoke out in opposition to the war in

Vietnam and remained politically active in subsequent decades. The emergence of "liberation theology" (which drew on both Marxist and Christian doctrine) as a driving force in the revolutionary movements in Central America assured the political participation of North American Catholic activists in the Central American solidarity movement, alongside members of other historically active peace denominations, such as the Quakers, Mennonites, and Unitarians. The highly visible role of faith-based activists continued a trend begun by the civil rights movement in the 1950s, which expanded with the growth of clerical activism against the war in Vietnam and the nuclear arms race.[20]

Central American solidarity activists worked to prevent U.S. invasions of Nicaragua and El Salvador, lobbied Congress to cut U.S. military aid to conservative forces in the region, and launched "material aid" campaigns to help Central Americans affected by war and poverty. The faith-based wing of the movement undertook a "sanctuary" campaign by providing church asylum to Central American refugees fleeing persecution in El Salvador and Guatemala. Many activists joined "internationalists" from Europe and Canada in Nicaragua to help with the coffee harvest. The movement pursued a national campaign to have universities become "sisters" to universities in Central America and to have U.S. cities declare themselves "sisters" to cities in Central America. Others joined a national Pledge of Resistance, a pledge to take part in massive civil disobedience if U.S. military forces invaded a Central American country. Much like the movements against nuclear power and nuclear weapons, the Central American solidarity movement was a direct outgrowth of the political movements of the 1960s. Keeping alive the specter of Vietnam, the movement aimed to resist the resurgent cold war doctrines of the Reagan administration.[21]

The post–Vietnam War movements against nuclear power, the nuclear arms race, and U.S. intervention in Central America are the focus of this book. One succeeded another in an undulating wave that saw a new movement emerge as the preceding movement peaked and then waned. These were by no means the only heirs to 1960s radicalism and activism. Joining them were post-1960s movements such as the campaign for divestment from the apartheid government in South Africa, the powerful movement to promote AIDS awareness and combat government apathy to the epidemic, a nationwide campaign to fight homelessness, and the efforts of the Reverend Jesse Jackson to bring minorities and white progressives together in a national Rainbow Coalition. Thus, contrary to the black hole between Kent State University and Seattle depicted by the media, the 1970s and 1980s constituted an age of ongoing activism, rooted in the 1960s but transformed by the changing economic and political landscape of subsequent decades. What made these activist movements so relevant in the post–Vietnam

War era was their strong impact on mainstream liberalism, which—like radical and left-leaning activism—underwent significant transformations that were rooted in the politics of the 1960s.

LIBERALISM: THE 1960S AND BEYOND

The early to mid-1960s witnessed the apex of post–World War II liberalism. Rooted in the New Deal coalition of urban ethnic groups, labor unions, African Americans, liberal academics, and the white South (decreasingly so, as the 1960s progressed), the Democratic Party of the John F. Kennedy and Lyndon B. Johnson era implemented much of the leftover Fair Deal agenda of Harry S. Truman and went on to expand the New Deal social welfare state and advance the cause of civil rights. The pinnacle of 1960s liberalism came with the avalanche of Great Society legislation signed by Johnson in the years between 1964 and 1966, running roughly parallel with the peak years of post–World War II economic prosperity. With many middle- and working-class Americans enjoying unprecedented affluence, Johnson was able to take the proposed legislation on poverty and civil rights proposed by his predecessor and expand it to his ambitious War on Poverty and the historic Civil Rights Act of 1964 and Voting Rights Act of 1965. In the election of 1964, the American public endorsed the liberal direction of the Kennedy-Johnson years by handing Johnson a historic landslide over his conservative Republican challenger, Barry Goldwater.[22]

The War on Poverty and civil rights bills of the Great Society were, in many ways, driven by activist politics on the Left, particularly the civil rights movement in the South. The civil rights and New Left movements helped reenergize the social democratic elements of the Democratic Party, especially among organized labor, which bridged the grassroots activism of the Left with the institutional powers in the Democratic Party to produce the flurry of social transformation and liberal legislation of the mid-1960s.[23]

The alliance between the activist Left and mainstream liberalism was, however, tenuous. For example, SDS, always critical of the speed and scope of mainstream liberal reform, supported Johnson against Goldwater in 1964 under the slogan "Part of the Way with LBJ."[24] The tenuous Left-liberal alliance was strained first by the speed with which implementation of the civil rights agenda was pursued.[25] Tensions surfaced during the 1964 Democratic Convention in Atlantic City, when the Democratic leadership refused to replace the segregationist Mississippi delegation with the integrated delegation from the Mississippi Freedom Democratic Party.[26]

The breach between the activist Left and mainstream liberalism that had opened in Atlantic City widened dramatically after Johnson's election in 1964, with his rapid expansion of U.S. military involvement in the Vietnam War. Radical politics spread across U.S. campuses as protests swelled year by year. By 1967, the radical wing of the antiwar movement had announced a shift from protest to resistance, which led to confrontational actions at the University of Wisconsin, the Pentagon, and the Oakland, California, draft induction center. As the police and the National Guard increasingly turned to the use of tear gas in response to campus and street demonstrations, the student wing of the New Left—heavily influenced by the militant shift in the civil rights movement toward black power— turned its focus to calls for revolution. Antiwar radicals were now denouncing "corporate liberalism" and "cold war liberalism" as the prime engine behind "U.S. imperialism," class inequality, and the war in Vietnam. By 1968, many on the Left had come to consider mainstream liberalism to be a worn-out institution of the old order that must be swept away by the rising tide of revolution.[27]

Like civil rights in the early 1960s, antiwar activism had a profound impact on late 1960s liberalism. Only two members of Congress had opposed the 1964 Gulf of Tonkin resolution, but by 1968, the Democratic Party had become deeply divided over the war in Vietnam. At the 1968 Democratic Convention in Chicago, the divisions came to a head. While Mayor Richard Daley's police teargassed antiwar radicals in the streets of Chicago, fistfights broke out between Democratic "hawks" and "doves" inside the convention hall.[28]

The divided Democratic Party limped out of Chicago to confront a united Republican Party and an increasingly disaffected U.S. electorate. The white South had already abandoned the Democrats over civil rights, and now some feared that the ethnic and urban base of the party would begin to hemorrhage. The increase in campus unrest, urban riots, and cultural rebellion incensed many middle- and working-class Americans. Although the concerted efforts of organized labor kept most union workers in the Democratic fold, many middle-class voters who had helped hand Johnson his landslide victory in 1964 abandoned the Democrats for the law and order platform of Richard Nixon. Many southern whites and some northern urban ethnic groups contributed to the 13.5 percent share of the popular vote held by George Wallace, the conservative third-party candidate who gained national prominence as the segregationist governor of Alabama in the early 1960s.

Even so, Nixon's presidency hardly ended liberal politics in America. As Johnson's war became Nixon's war, many once-hesitant Democrats began to join the ranks of the antiwar movement. Opposition to the war grew in Congress throughout the Nixon years. Congress also turned back Nixon's efforts to put conservative former segregationists on the Supreme Court, and Nixon signed important pieces of liberal legislation, including the Environmental Protection

Act, the Endangered Species Act, and the legislation that created the Occupational Safety and Health Administration.[29]

The major issue of the early Nixon years remained the war in Vietnam. Antiwar activism exploded in late 1969 and—as witnessed by the October moratorium and November mobilization against the war—made wide inroads into mainstream America.[30] A few months later, Nixon's April 30, 1970, invasion of Cambodia, ignited an unprecedented number of campus protests, with hundreds of schools going on strike. Although public demonstrations declined somewhat as Nixon began to withdraw U.S. troops and move toward détente with the People's Republic of China and the Soviet Union, in 1971 and 1972 other large demonstrations took place.[31] In 1971, polls indicated that the vast majority of Americans opposed the war in Vietnam.

It was during the Nixon presidency that the convergence of elements of the activist Left and the liberal establishment reshaped U.S. liberalism. Many radical activists slowly dropped back into mainstream politics as elements of the Democratic Party embraced aspects of the New Left perspective. This new Left-liberal politics culminated in the presidential campaign of Senator George McGovern from South Dakota in 1972. The groundwork for the McGovern campaign had been laid at the 1968 convention: A system of proportional representation had been created for the next convention, which set aside a percentage of seats for minorities, youth, and women. Thus, the Miami convention experienced a stark changing of the guard. Alongside hawks such as Senator Henry ("Scoop") Jackson from Washington and George Meeney, the president of the American Federation of Labor and Congress of Industrial Organizations (AFL-CIO), were assembled feminists, environmentalists, peace activists, civil rights crusaders, gay rights advocates, and counterculture libertarians. Although some unions, such as the United Auto Workers and the American Federation of State, Municipal, and County Employees, embraced the changes, Meeney fumed as he surveyed the decidedly liberal New York delegation, "What kind of delegation is this? They've got six open fags and only three AFL-CIO people on that delegation.... Representative? This party seems to have an instinct for suicide."[32]

Nixon's landslide victory over McGovern in 1972 struck some commentators as a repudiation of 1960s activism and a consolidation of the conservative backlash begun in 1968. Yet, once again, the backlash proved tentative. Nixon's coattails remained short, and Republicans made little headway in Congress. Then in 1974, liberal Democrats exploited the aftermath of the Watergate scandal (which began with the break-in at the Democratic National Committee headquarters at the Watergate Hotel in Washington, D.C., and ended with the resignation of President Nixon), racking up impressive gains in Congress. During the 1970s, Democrats in Congress challenged what they saw as the excesses of the national security state—which were revealed during the Vietnam War, when the War Powers Act was passed and Frank Church conducted the Senate hearings that not only led to significant restrictions on the ability of U.S. intelligence agencies to conduct a shadow foreign policy but also outlawed assassinations by U.S. agencies. As the United States entered the post–Vietnam War era, many Democrats were determined to move beyond the cold war ideology that they believed had led to the war in Vietnam. Moreover, they brought the influences of environmentalism, feminism, and minority empowerment into the mainstream of U.S. political discourse.[33]

The influence of the activist Left within mainstream liberalism during the post–Vietnam War era coincided with an uneven but growing ascendancy of the New Right in U.S. politics. The roots of this conservative ascendancy can be traced to Goldwater's 1964 campaign, when the moderate wing of the Republican Party lost control to the right wing, which called for the rollback of the New Deal social welfare state and more aggressive conduct of the cold war. In 1966 Reagan was among the first to capitalize on 1960s backlash politics by winning the California governorship in a campaign that blasted Berkeley radicals, the Watts riot, and the emerging San Francisco counterculture. Supreme Court decisions regarding school prayer, classroom Bible reading, and abortion helped mobilize a politicized evangelical Christian movement.[34] In the 1970s, neoliberals centered at the hard-line conservative Committee on the Present Danger challenged the direction of détente and called for a renewal of all-out cold war.[35] The cold warriors, free marketers, and religious conservatives of the New Right made inroads throughout the 1960s and 1970s by exploiting the backlash politics of social alienation. By 1980, a decade of economic decline, deindustrialization, waning U.S. power evidenced by the Iranian hostage crisis, and the drift (lack of focus) of the Carter administration created the opening for the New Right to bring about a major shift in U.S. politics.[36]

There can be no doubt that the rise of the Right and the partial realignment of U.S. politics that it engineered constitute a historical event of mammoth importance.[37] The emphasis on the rise of the Right, however, has tended to downplay the importance of post–Vietnam War activism and liberalism as at best an irrelevant postscript to the 1960s and at worst the fuel that fired the right-wing ascendancy by further alienating the Democratic Party from mainstream U.S. society. Yet by holding forth an alternative vision and vigorously contesting the rightward trajectory of the country, the activist Left and Democratic liberals of the 1970s and 1980s played an important role in defining the terms of debate and the course of history in the post–Vietnam War era.

Although antinuclear activists did not end our national reliance on nuclear power, by the end of the 1970s, the movement had raised so many questions in the public mind and had contributed so much to the rise in the costs of nuclear industry growth that the near meltdown at the Three Mile Island plant would spell the end of the age of nuclear expansion. In addition, the nuclear freeze movement energetically contested the reemergence of cold war tensions in the early Reagan years. Although the movement failed to halt the arms buildup, it revealed the deep anxiety of the American public with respect to the arms race.

In addition, the movement helped blunt the trajectory of the cold war policies of the Reagan administration and, I would argue, paved the way for a new détente in the latter half of the decade. Finally, the determined movement against U.S. intervention in Central America kept alive the Vietnam syndrome (the fear of having U.S. troops bogged down overseas) and constrained the ability of the Reagan administration to intervene more directly in Central American affairs. Indeed, the efforts of the administration to circumvent congressional limitations on its covert war against the Sandinista government in Nicaragua led to the series of illegal arms sales to Iran intended to fund the Nicaraguan Contras that would soon become known as the Iran-Contra scandal.[38]

Mixed though the record may have been, activism and liberal politics in the post–Vietnam War era were far more dynamic than they have often been depicted, and they represented far more than speed bumps on the conservatives' road to political ascendancy. A more accurate portrayal of the 1970s and 1980s reveals it as a period of political bifurcation, when the cold war consensus that had defined the postwar United States shattered and—in a reflection of the deep changes that had taken place in the U.S. populace—the center of gravity of both parties shifted toward their respective Goldwater and McGovern wings. Although the conservatives gained dominance in the 1980s, much of their blueprint for transforming U.S. policy at home and abroad was circumscribed by the liberal wing of the Democratic Party, which was being pushed into more vigorous opposition by the post–Vietnam War activist Left. During the 1970s and 1980s, no state in the union represented a more energetic counterweight to the conservative ascendancy than Massachusetts.

MASSACHUSETTS: CRADLE OF THE AMERICAN REVOLUTION

As the Watergate scandal unraveled Nixon's presidency in 1973 and 1974, a bumper sticker that read, "Don't Blame Me; I'm From Massachusetts" began to appear on vehicles in the state. Implicit in this reminder that Massachusetts had been the only state to vote for McGovern in 1972 was a reproof of the rest of the country for having taken the wrong fork in the road. The sense that the United

States was straying from the right path seems deeply ingrained in Massachusetts politics in the decades after the assassination of John F. Kennedy. The idea that Kennedy's death interrupted the promise of a national trajectory toward a brighter future (ushering in the disastrous detour into the Vietnam War led by Johnson) remains a powerful part of the national psyche—and that of Massachusetts in particular. The myth of aborted promise, of the road not taken continued to give post-1960s Massachusetts liberalism a sense of legitimacy as the executor of the legacy of Kennedy and the unfulfilled hopes and ideals of the 1960s.

Massachusetts liberals frequently invoked Kennedy's name in support of policies that were far to the Left of anything embraced by the president while he was alive. None laid claim to the title of heir to the martyred president's legacy more than his younger brother Edward, the senator from Massachusetts, who for the nation as a whole became the embodiment of Massachusetts liberalism. Many other Massachusetts liberals invoked the legacy of the late president, from Thomas P. ("Tip") O'Neill (who became Speaker of the House in 1976) to the three-term governor Michael Dukakis (who frequently sought to associate himself with the Kennedy administration during his own ill-fated presidential campaign) to John Forbes Kerry (a Vietnam veteran turned lieutenant governor turned senator who sought to strike a Kennedyesque pose throughout his career). As the political center drifted to the Right in the wake of the 1960s, Massachusetts liberals associated themselves with nostalgia for "Camelot" to put themselves forward as the trustees of the unfinished journey of John F. Kennedy.

The post-1960s liberalism of Massachusetts politicians may have sought legitimacy by association with John Kennedy; however, in many ways during the post–Vietnam War era it was the radical activism of the 1960s that most shaped Massachusetts liberalism. The civil rights and antiwar movements were especially strong in Massachusetts. Massachusetts colleges and churches, powerful incubators for the civil rights movement, produced a disproportionate share of northern civil rights activists who headed south as the "new abolitionists" for SNCC and the Congress of Racial Equality (CORE). Although the campus-based wing of the New Left and antiwar movements had its origins in the Midwest (the "Third Coast") and in the San Francisco Bay area, by the late 1960s Massachusetts had become a stronghold of the Movement. Counted among the largest demonstrations in the nation were the 1967 draft card burning in Boston and the October 15, 1969, moratorium against the war in Vietnam (which attracted more than 250,000 participants) that took place in the Boston Commons. By 1970, the inroads of the New Left into mainstream liberalism were highlighted in Massachusetts when the state legislature became the first in the nation to pass a resolution that called for the immediate withdrawal of U.S. military forces from Vietnam.

Massachusetts radicalism had grown from the same baby boom, prosperity, and cold war dynamics that had produced the youth rebellion nationwide, but the roots of radical activism in the state could be traced well beyond John Kennedy to the revolutionary heritage of the commonwealth—from the Boston Massacre of 1770, the Tea Party of 1774, the Daniel Shays rebellion of 1786, the abolitionist movement and utopian politics of the nineteenth century, and the campaign to save Ferdinando Nicola Sacco and Bartolomeo Vanzetti in the 1920s all the way up to the modern civil rights and peace movements. A close examination of Bay State activism in the 1960s and beyond reveals the degree to which Massachusetts radicals sought to lay claim to the revolutionary heritage of the nation.

In 1974, when the anti–nuclear energy activist Sam Lovejoy toppled a weather tower in Montague, Massachusetts, to protest the planned construction of a nuclear power station there, he chose February 22, George Washington's birthday, as the date of action. When Randy Kehler, Judith Scheckel, and other Massachusetts activists launched the nuclear weapons freeze movement in 1980, they repeatedly invoked the legacy of nineteenth-century abolitionists, pro-claiming that just as their predecessors had abolished slavery, they would abol-ish nuclear weapons. In the 1980s, moreover, Massachusetts Central American solidarity activists repeatedly compared Central American revolutionaries to the (North) American revolutionaries of 1776. Massachusetts radicals were not alone in laying claim to symbols of the American revolutionary past, but such rhetoric was inextricably woven into the discourse of Bay State activists and seemed to give them a unique sense of historical continuity and legitimacy.[39]

Although Massachusetts was not the only state with a special sense of identity, it played a disproportionately influential role in the national politics of the 1970s and 1980s. It was the birthplace of two of the major post–Vietnam War activist movements to sweep the United States. The first, the direct action campaign against nuclear power, began in western Massachusetts in 1974, when the antiwar activist Sam Lovejoy committed a dramatic act of sabotage by toppling the weather tower of a proposed nuclear power plant. This action sparked a mass movement against nuclear energy, which spread throughout New England in the span of a few years and culminated in the mass protests in Seabrook, New Hampshire, in 1977 and 1978. By the late 1970s, Massachusetts was exporting activists such as Sam Lovejoy, Anna Gyorgy, and Harvey Wasserman to the rest of the country to help mobilize a national movement. In 1980, western Massachusetts peace activists took the idea of a nuclear weapons freeze and put it on the ballot in three western Massachusetts counties as a nonbinding referendum.

Massachusetts freeze activists became apostles of the new movement through-out the United States. Within two years, the freeze movement had swept the

United States to become the largest peace movement of the post–Vietnam War era. The third major post–Vietnam War activist movement to sweep the United States was the opposition to U.S. intervention in Central America. Although this movement had originated on the West Coast, the Bay State had quickly become one of its strongholds. The first Witness for Peace mission to the Nicaraguan-Honduran border in 1983 included a disproportionate number of Massachusetts activists. During the mass civil disobedience that swept the country in 1985 to protest the Reagan administration embargo against Nicaragua, the single largest number of arrests (more than five hundred) occurred in Boston.[40]

The pioneering role of grassroots radicalism in Massachusetts percolated up (as the national freeze movement activist Randall Forsberg described it) to shape the mainstream politics of the commonwealth, mirrored in the profound influence of state politicians on national politics in the 1970s and 1980s. Foremost among the Democratic heavyweights from Massachusetts was Senator Edward ("Ted") Kennedy. Unlike his brothers, John and Robert, Ted did not see the Senate as a stepping-stone to the White House. Ranking among such masters of the Senate as Lyndon Johnson and Daniel Webster, Ted has deftly used his power in the Senate to advance the liberal agenda. In Massachusetts, Kennedy was able to straddle the blue-collar, union, ethnic "Old" Democratic Party of the New Deal and the activist, college-educated, middle-class "New" Democratic Party.[41] Kennedy became an early critic of nuclear power; in the 1980s he drafted a Senate freeze resolution and coauthored a book with the maverick Republican senator Mark Hatfield of Oregon: *Freeze! How You Can Help Prevent Nuclear War.*[42] One Massachusetts antinuclear activist commented about Kennedy, "He has defined what is legitimate. His presence did not allow anyone to move the political center to the right. . . . I think the stability and direction he has provided has given an umbrella under which a lot of things could be done [on the Left]."[43]

Another titan of Massachusetts politics, Speaker of the House Tip O'Neill, magnified the influence of Massachusetts liberalism. His Cambridge district embraced both the activist elements of academia and the old ethnic neighborhoods of the city. Like Ted Kennedy, Tip O'Neill, who moved rapidly from whip to majority leader to Speaker of the House in the 1970s, was a master parliamentarian who bridged the gap between New Deal Democrats and the younger generation of "New Democrats" who grew from the activist politics of the 1960s. O'Neill helped set the agenda in the House, and in the 1980s the burly Irish American became for many the personification of liberal opposition to Reagan. O'Neill's position in the House ensured the influence of Massachusetts liberals in the national debate on the nuclear weapons freeze and U.S. policy in Central America.[44]

The influence of young Bay State firebrands complemented that of Massachusetts powerhouses such as Kennedy and O'Neill. In the early 1980s, Congressman Gerry Studds, from the district that encompassed Cape Cod, became the icon of outspoken opposition to Reagan administration policies in Central America. His 1980 "Studds Report" was influential in its delineation of a left-liberal congressional position on Central America. By mid-decade, the newly elected senator John Kerry, a Vietnam veteran and former antiwar activist—who traveled to Nicaragua on a peace mission in 1985 and later in the decade conducted a series of hearings into drug smuggling by the United-States–supported Contras—had taken up the mantle of opposition to Reagan's Central American policies.[45] Another of the Young Turks from Massachusetts was Congressman Edward Markey, who represented a mixed blue-collar and professional district north of Boston. In the late 1970s, Markey developed a reputation as an ardent opponent of nuclear power and was the only member of Congress invited to speak at a mass rally against nuclear power in New York City in 1979. In the 1980s, Markey spearheaded the congressional campaign to pass a nuclear weapons freeze resolution, making the same name for himself in the nuclear freeze movement that Gerry Studds had made for himself in the Central American solidarity movement.

The influence of Massachusetts Young Turks such as Markey and Studds and party stalwarts such as Kennedy and O'Neill was further enhanced by the influence of lower-profile veteran politicians such as Senator Paul Tsongas and Congressman Edward Boland from western Massachusetts. Both enjoyed national reputations for integrity that helped cement Massachusetts influence in Congress. As chairman of the House Intelligence Committee, Boland lent a great deal of legitimacy to efforts to contain the more adventurist policies of the Reagan administration with respect to Central America. In 1983 and 1984, Congress passed a series of Boland amendments designed to end covert U.S. support for the right-wing Contras, who were trying to overthrow the Sandinista government in Nicaragua. It was the illegal efforts of the Reagan administration to circumvent the Boland amendment that led to the worst scandal of the Reagan years: The covert arms for hostages deals made by the administration exploded in the Iran-Contra affair.

Finally, the lone Massachusetts Republican in Congress, the moderate Silvio Conte from the western part of the state, greatly augmented the influence of the Massachusetts delegation. Elected to Congress in the 1950s, Conte had a reputation for independence. In 1968 he was one of the first members of Congress from Massachusetts to speak out against the Vietnam War. His good nature and earthy sense of humor made him a popular member of Congress with influence in both parties. By the 1980s, Conte represented one of the most activist districts in the nation, western Massachusetts, which had been a pioneer of both the movement against nuclear energy and the freeze movement and a stronghold of Central American solidarity activism. Conte thus became an advocate of the nuclear weapons freeze and a defender of human rights in Central America, lending a bipartisan imprimatur to the work of the state delegation on these issues.

By the early 1980s, the Massachusetts delegation had become the congressional flagship in the fight for a nuclear weapons freeze and the fight to oppose U.S. intervention in Central America. Whereas other states, such as New York and California, boasted immensely influential liberal members of Congress, no state, liberal or conservative, boasted as unified a delegation as the eleven Democrats and one moderate Republican who constituted the delegation of Massachusetts. Through this united and unusually effective unit, Bay State activists held a special influence over mainstream national politics. That influence was often felt first at the state level. In the 1980s, Massachusetts freeze, antinuclear, and Central American solidarity protestors were particularly active in state politics, which they viewed as the springboard to national influence.

Massachusetts activists had a strong impact on Governor Dukakis, especially during his two terms in the 1980s. More a good government progressive than a New Deal liberal or post-1960s "McGovern" Democrat, Dukakis nevertheless embraced causes dear to the activist Left. In 1977 Dukakis was the only New England governor to refuse the New Hampshire authorities' request to send state police to assist in the arrest of the 1,414 protestors who occupied the Seabrook nuclear power plant site. By refusing to submit a federally mandated evacuation plan for Massachusetts communities that fell within the ten-mile Emergency Planning Zone (EPZ), Dukakis delayed the Seabrook nuclear power station from going on-line. He also refused to participate in Crisis Relocation Planning (CRP), a civil defense measure pushed by the Reagan administration as part of its efforts to prepare the nation for possible nuclear war. An early advocate of the nuclear weapons freeze effort, Dukakis commissioned a state group to study the impact of the arms race on Massachusetts and to find ways for the commonwealth to promote disarmament. In 1985 Dukakis became one of the first governors to refuse to allow the state National Guard to participate in military exercises in Central America. He later joined other governors in fighting the Honduras exercises in federal court.

During his 1988 presidential campaign, the Republican candidate, George H. W. Bush, sought to make the election a national referendum on Massachusetts liberalism by tying Dukakis to his past support for activist causes. By 1988, the two issues that had helped breathe so much life into the Left in the early 1980s—

war in Central America and the nuclear arms race—had faded from the national radar screen. The Bush campaign worked to distance the Republican candidate from the unpopular Central American policies of the Reagan administration, and the Reagan administration pursued serious nuclear weapons negotiations with President Mikhail Gorbachev of the Soviet Union. The ugly but effective campaign to tar Dukakis as an unpatriotic member of the American Civil Liberties Union who furloughed convicted black rapists and allowed schoolchildren to refrain from reciting the Pledge of Allegiance set the stage for a resounding defeat.

To many, the 1988 Dukakis presidential campaign was a swan song for post-1960s Massachusetts liberalism, which paved the way for the emergence of the centrist southern Democrat Bill Clinton.[46] Although some Massachusetts politicians indeed moderated in the 1990s, the state nevertheless continued to play a disproportionate role in national affairs, through John Kerry's 2004 bid for the presidency and beyond. As the first decade of the twenty-first century marched on, Massachusetts would remain a stronghold of activism on the Left.

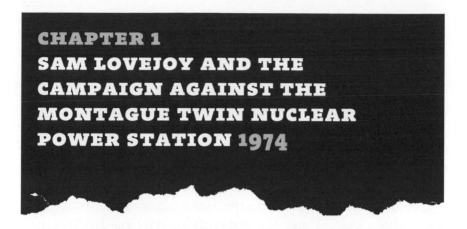

CHAPTER 1
SAM LOVEJOY AND THE CAMPAIGN AGAINST THE MONTAGUE TWIN NUCLEAR POWER STATION 1974

CROSSROADS: FEBRUARY 1974

In February 1974 the United States seemed to be slowly falling apart. Americans had become familiar with a new word, stagflation, which described the bizarre combination of inflation and unemployment. The nation entered its fourth month of the oil embargo of the Organization of Petroleum Exporting Countries (OPEC), compounding an already serious energy crisis. As automobiles formed lines at gasoline stations—sometimes more than a mile long and often in near freezing temperatures—indictments and convictions in the Watergate crisis kept pace, with new revelations of abuses by the Richard Nixon administration. Nixon, who had won one of the largest electoral landslides in U.S. history just two years earlier, saw his poll numbers continue to drop.[1]

The oil embargo and the ongoing Watergate saga were joined that February by a news story that seemed to confirm the sense of exhaustion. An obscure underground revolutionary group, the Symbionese Liberation Army (SLA), had kidnapped the newspaper heiress Patricia Hearst from her home in Berkeley, California. The press and media hung on the tape-recorded communiqués of the SLA, which invariably ended with the slogan "Death to the fascist insect which preys upon the life of the people!" Accompanying lengthy denunciations of U.S. "imperialism" and "fascism" was a series of demands, the most prominent being that Patricia Hearst's wealthy father, Randolph Hearst, set up a free food program for the poor in Oakland. Americans were gripped by this revolutionary throwback to the late 1960s and early 1970s. Even the Weather Underground, the best-known of the violent groups to grow out of the revolutionary dreams and frustrations of the Vietnam War era had been quiescent for some time. If the SLA heightened the sense of helplessness, vulnerability, and drift that pervaded the country, however, few feared—or hoped—that the self-styled guerrillas would spark the revolution that was their avowed aim.[2]

On February 22, 1974—the same date that the ill-fated food distribution demanded by the SLA ended in riots in Oakland—a former antiwar activist named Sam Lovejoy took radical political action of a different sort in the small town of Montague, Massachusetts. To protest a proposed nuclear power station in his New England hometown, Lovejoy sneaked onto the site in the middle of the night and, using assorted farm tools, managed to topple most of a 550-foot weather tower. Lovejoy then hitchhiked a ride from a passing police car, turned himself in to the local police chief, and issued a four-page statement explaining his actions. He took "full responsibility for sabotaging that outrageous symbol of a future nuclear power plant."[3]

Both the SLA abduction of Patricia Hearst and Sam Lovejoy's sabotage were rooted in the radicalism of the 1960s. Whereas the SLA represented the movement at its burnt-out extreme, however, Lovejoy's action melded various tendencies from the 1960s and put them to work in the changed environment of the mid-1970s. His sabotage—which incorporated the militancy of the New Left, the notion of moral witness and civil disobedience from the civil rights movement, and the alternative communal lifestyle of the counterculture—attempted to make 1960s qualities relevant through a grassroots localism that would come to define 1970s activism.

The SLA had envisioned an apocalyptic, utopian, and violent revolution that would wipe out capitalist structures of repression and exploitation in one fell swoop. Following the most revolutionary, vanguard dreams of the 1960s to their terminus, they eventually self-destructed in a hail of gunfire. Lovejoy, in contrast, took the more democratic radical visions of the 1960s and helped to transplant them into the new soil of the 1970s. If the SLA represented the end of the road for the revolutionary fervor of the 1960s, Lovejoy and the movement he helped to mobilize formed a bridge from the 1960s to the 1970s and beyond. Speaking of the 1960s Movement in an interview published in Studs Terkel's *American Dreams: Lost and Found*, Lovejoy stated, "The media is selling us on the notion of apathy and paralysis in the country. Bullshit. The movement did not die. It did the most intelligent thing it could do: it went to find a home. It went into the community. It's working, unnoticed, in the neighborhood. They're starting to blossom and make alliances, connections. I've been all over the country, and I have not been into one community where I did not meet people exactly like me. If there's ever gonna be change in America, it's gonna be because every community in America's ready for it and—boom!"[4]

Lovejoy's action not only generated a good deal of local and regional news coverage but also won national coverage in the *New York Times*. His protest quickly became a lightning rod for the nascent local antinuclear movement. Over the course of the next year, Lovejoy's sabotage resulted in a highly politicized trial and a regional referendum to ban nuclear power. A documentary film titled *Lovejoy's Nuclear War* soon circulated among the antinuclear groups proliferating around the country. In 1976 and 1977, antinuclear activists shook the region with mass protests in Seabrook, New Hampshire, resulting in thousands of arrests. By 1979, the antinuclear movement had grown into the largest mass movement of the late 1970s, with a massive No Nukes! rally in Washington, D.C., the star-studded "No Nukes!" concert at Madison Square Garden, and the eerily prophetic film, *The China Syndrome*, released just months before the near nuclear meltdown at Three Mile Island, Pennsylvania.[5]

Lovejoy's action would also provoke a backlash and counteroffensive by the nuclear industry and organized labor, with the former viewing the dawning anti-nuclear movement as a threat to profits and the latter viewing it as a threat to jobs. In western Massachusetts this circumstance resulted in an unusual corporate-labor alliance to combat the antinuclear referendum that grew out of Lovejoy's action. The corporate-labor strategy forged in western Massachusetts became a model for opposition to similar antinuclear campaigns, especially the 1976 California referendum on nuclear power. The western Massachusetts antinuclear movement galvanized by Lovejoy also put John Olver (the local liberal Democratic state senator) on the spot, leaving him torn between his loyalty to organized labor and his solicitation of the growing environmental vote. By forcing the issue, Lovejoy revealed a fault line in the Democratic Party that would confront liberals nationally throughout the decade.

THE SABOTEUR

Lovejoy's sabotage came in the wake of a massive shift toward nuclear energy throughout the United States. The increasingly severe energy crisis and the con-comitant fear of dependence on foreign oil spurred the Nixon administration to accelerate the construction of nuclear power plants. At the time of Lovejoy's action, there were 42 nuclear plants running in the United States, 56 under construction, and 101 on order.[6] On December 31, 1973, the Connecticut-based Northeast Utilities (NU) announced its plans to build twin nuclear reactors in the quiet, rural town of Montague, Massachusetts. New England, which endured severe cold in the winter and had few indigenous sources of coal, natural gas, or oil, was more dependent on foreign oil than any other area of the United States. As a result, the region led the way in the development of nuclear power plants, receiving 20 percent of its energy from nuclear power compared to the 5 percent received by the nation as a whole.[7]

When NU announced plans to build its $1.5 billion, 1,150-megawatt twin nuclear reactors in Montague, the company was hardly new to the business of nuclear power. NU customers received 33 percent of their energy from nuclear power, and NU investments in nuclear energy spanned the New England region. In 1974, NU already owned 34 percent of the Yankee Rowe plant in Massachusetts, 44 percent of Connecticut Yankee, 15 percent of Yankee Maine, 12 percent of Vermont Yankee, and 100 percent of Millstone I in Connecticut. Moreover, NU was in the process of constructing a Millstone II nuclear reactor in Connecticut and had plans for a Millstone III. In addition, NU and other New England utilities were investing in the proposed nuclear plants at Plymouth, Massachusetts, and Seabrook, New Hampshire.[8] Still, NU deemed the New England constellation of nuclear power plants insufficient to meet regional energy needs. Taking note of the national energy crisis and the cold winters, heavy industry, and dearth of energy sources in New England, Dr. Harold Lurie, the NU director of research, stated, "The only conclusion you can draw, based on the logic of the situation, is to build more nuclear power plants in New England and to build them as fast as you can."[9]

NU wasted no time in disseminating what it saw as the benefits of nuclear power. In pamphlets and bulletins such as "The Way It Is: Talking about Nuclear Power" and "Montague Nuclear Station Fact Sheet," NU made its case that nuclear power would produce abundantly cheap energy, was a cleaner source of energy than fossil fuels, and involved a negligible safety risk. One of the pamphlets that extolled the virtues of nuclear power had an inner flap that showed a photograph of children wading in the ocean, silhouetted by the Millstone I nuclear power station. The back flap showed a photograph of a softball game and picnic across the Connecticut River from the Yankee nuclear plant in Haddam, Connecticut. The message was clear: Nuclear power was a benign source of energy, clearly no threat to such wholesome family activities as a day at the beach and a Sunday softball game.[10]

Enticed by the prospect of huge tax cuts (the Yankee Rowe plant, just twenty-five miles north, paid 90 percent of the taxes in that town) and racked by an unemployment rate of 8 percent (compared to 6 percent for the state as a whole), roughly two-thirds of the eighty-five hundred residents of Montague supported the construction of the plants in their town.[11] Interviews with local residents conducted by the alternative weekly the *Valley Advocate* in the fall of 1973 showed that they were generally receptive to the NU plants. Responses included, "They wouldn't build 'em if they weren't safe"; "Why they're talking about work for 4,000 people!"; and "Why our taxes would go way down with something like this!"[12]

Not all residents supported the plants, however. Dr. David Ingless, a science professor at the nearby University of Massachusetts in Amherst, voiced concerns that soon became hallmarks of the antinuclear movement: "I consider it irresponsible to go ahead building new nuclear plants. . . . Of the many dangers, the three that concern me most are the likely diversion of plutonium to make atom bombs for terrorists, the possibility of disastrous accidents at nuclear plants, and the unsolved problem of permanent storage of high level radioactive wastes."[13]

Still, opposition to the plants was small in 1973 and focused narrowly on legal interventions. The Massachusetts Public Interest Research Group (MASSPIRG) expressed skepticism over the ability of legal interventions to stop the Montague plants. In a report issued a mere month before Lovejoy toppled the towers, MASSPIRG declared, "Citizen groups, which have entered the debate as nuclear interveners in plant licensing processes, have gained, in general, only slight concessions in plant design, or short delays in their construction."[14]

Although mainstream antinuclear groups seemed to be making little headway, opposition to the plants soon arose from another quarter. Rural western New England had undergone many changes in the decade before 1974. In the late 1960s and early 1970s, many young people involved with the counterculture had headed for the countryside to escape the bustle of the cities and an increasingly nihilistic drug culture that was losing any connection to earlier counterculture ideals. These "hippies" sought to live out their communitarian visions in harmony with nature in the deserts of the Southwest (especially around Taos, New Mexico), the woodlands of the Northwest (now populated by constituents of the exodus from the San Francisco Bay area), and the farmlands of New England.[15] Rural western Massachusetts—with its rolling hills and Berkshire Mountains, vast woodlands, open fields, and fertile farms lining the Connecticut River valley—comprised small towns, several colleges, and a few aging rust-belt cities, such as Springfield, Holyoke, and Chicopee. Like Vermont to the north, the area was a magnet for the new communes of the late 1960s.

Communes in New England tended to be disproportionately populated by members of the New Left. In western Massachusetts and southern Vermont, three sister communes played a key role in shaping the antinuclear politics of the 1970s. The largest was the Montague Farm, also known as the Old Ripley Farm or the Chestnut Hill Farm, whose fluid population ranged between twenty and thirty people. A commune of people associated with the people of Montague Farm formed in neighboring Wendell. Both Massachusetts communes had close ties to the Packers Corner Farm, just over the border in southern Vermont.

These communes grew from a split in the Liberation News Service (LNS), the radical New Left news outlet founded by Marshall Bloom and Raymond Mungo in the summer of 1967. The LNS had grown rapidly, attracting talented New Left journalists such as Harvey Wasserman and Marty Jezer to its staff, and by the fall of 1967 it had acquired an enthusiastic national following. In the wake of the April 1968 riots that followed the assassination of Martin Luther King, Jr., the LNS—which was originally located in Washington, D.C.—had decided to relocate to New York, a city that had become more central to New Left activity. In New York, the LNS joined forces with radicals associated with Students for a Democratic Society (SDS) at Columbia University. Before long, however, the new LNS broke into Washington and New York factions, with the former moving in a countercultural direction and the latter moving in a sectarian Marxist direction. In the summer of 1968, the Washington faction, led by Bloom, undertook a daring heist of the LNS printing press and left for rural western Massachusetts. Others, including Mungo and Jezer, relocated to Vermont.

Weary of urban life and New Left infighting, the rural refugees ushered in the New Age by focusing on personal transformation and the creation of a new communal society far removed from the corruptions of the old. Wasserman later described the LNS split as one between "the belief in magic crowd" and "people who were more explicitly ideological."[16] The split became acrimonious when an article that spread through the underground press accused Bloom of having been planted by the Federal Bureau of Investigation (FBI). Later, using the Freedom of Information Act, the investigative journalist Angus Mackenzie discovered that it was the author of the article—not Bloom—who was an FBI plant. At the time of the article, however, the accusation hit Bloom hard, compounding a depression that led to his tragic suicide. Slowly, the rural LNS ceased publication and removed itself from activist politics.[17]

The communes that grew out of the LNS fallout developed a strong sense of community that would help provide a solid base for antinuclear activism in the mid-1970s. Randy Kehler, an activist who had recently moved to western Massachusetts and would later lead the national nuclear weapons freeze movement, described the people at Montague, Wendell, and Packers Corner as "one family with three locations."[18] According to Vince O'Connor, another activist who had just moved to the area, "The [Montague] farm was the spiritual organizational center of things."[19]

By 1974, as these communes continued their focus on organic farming, they had begun to emerge from their nonactivist slumber with a growing interest in the environmental movement. In western Massachusetts the communes would soon overshadow mainstream organizations such as the Montague Nuclear Concerns Group to become the cutting edge of the antinuclear movement. Lovejoy, who moved to the Montague Farm in 1969, recalled, "We were living in a commune...and living communally, I thought, was a political statement. The dynamic was from 1969 to 1972; we were building fences, repairing barns, insulating houses, organizing [the use of] tractors, growing food. It took three solid years, three growing seasons, to get the rhythm down, and it was truly 1973 [when for] the first time we could sit back and say, 'O.K. We sunk our roots. We got our economic base in place. Now what's gonna happen?'"[20] As Wassermann observed, "There's only so long you can watch organic carrots grow." Commenting on the merger of the countercultural lifestyle and political activism that would come to define the Montague Farm, Wasserman added, "Psychedelics played a role in our political strategy.... [T]hat was the magic. We had a sense of humor; we learned that from Abbie Hoffman."[21]

The New Age communes of western Massachusetts put down roots in an area with a strong tradition of religious activism that stemmed from the historic peace churches in the area, including the Quaker, Unitarian, and Congregationalist churches. Western Massachusetts had a history of rural resistance to centralized power that reached back (long before New Left activists and hippies had migrated to the region) to the Daniel Shays rebellion of 1786.[22] The region had also been a stronghold of nineteenth-century abolitionism and efforts to form utopian communities led by the likes of Sojourner Truth.[23] Moreover, the area was home to numerous colleges and universities, many of which had become highly politicized in the late 1960s and early 1970s.

The combustible combination of the headlong rush to develop nuclear energy in New England and the many political radicals in the region made western Massachusetts the first major U.S. battleground over nuclear power. Commenting on the fact that NU had placed the Montague reactors in the midst of such a large group of experienced activists, O'Connor said, "They had no idea what a hornet's nest they stirred up.... [It was] the worst corporate decision an industry has ever made. They put it in the wrong place."[24] Lovejoy remembered, "I didn't go after the nuke. The nuke came to me.... [T]here was this throbbing energy available that just needed a trigger."[25]

Despite the potentially broad radical base in western Massachusetts, prior to Lovejoy's sabotage the opposition to the Montague reactors was relatively small. The mantle of opposition was carried largely by the respectable Montague Nuclear Concerns Group, which comprised mostly members of academia and centered largely on a conventional strategy. In the fall of 1973, this group was joined by Nuclear Objectors for a Pure Environment (NOPE), which was formed by a handful of activists on the Montague Farm.[26] Although vastly different in style, both groups expressed concerns about the environmental impact of low-level radiation, the transportation and storage of nuclear waste (which had a radioactive half-life of more than a hundred thousand years), the susceptibility of nuclear generators to terrorist attack, and—most crucially—the danger of nuclear reactor core meltdowns and the related problem of evacuation. In January 1974, in the first of a series of articles titled "Twin Nuclear Plants: Blessing or Curse?" the *Springfield Union and Springfield Republican*, a leading local newspaper, stated prophetically, "No one seems sure whether the nuclear debate in Montague will become a full-fledged controversy before the year is over."[27]

Twenty-seven-year-old Sam Lovejoy was determined to make sure the issue did become a full-fledged controversy. Lovejoy had grown up and spent most of his life in western Massachusetts. As a promising high school student in the post-Sputnik era, he had won a National Sciences Foundation award. He had gone on to graduate from Amherst College with a degree in political science. During the 1960s, Lovejoy had become deeply involved in the movement against the war in Vietnam. In the late 1960s, he was the New England regional coordinator of SDS and a member of the first Venceremos Brigade contingent to Cuba. He also felt a great affinity for Chile and the rising socialist movement led by Salvador Allende. He went to Cuba with the Venceremos Brigades in the hope that he might improve his Spanish and make contacts that would help him move to Chile to take part in the socialist struggle there.

While he was cutting sugar cane in Cuba, Lovejoy became disillusioned with many U.S. leftists. Having grown up on a farm, he was struck by how few of his fellow *brigadistas* seemed to have ever worked any hard labor. The experience with middle-class North American activists who seemed out of place in tropical Cuba helped move Lovejoy from an internationalist focus toward a concentration on the local activism being embraced by much of the antiwar movement, which sought to "bring the war home." He recalled, "What happened in Cuba was I really did believe that all politics is local, which Tip O'Neill said, but I think that's ultimately true. If you can't talk to your neighbors about political issues, then how are you gonna ever change national policies?" Lovejoy decided to shift his focus. "While I was there, I changed my mind about going to Chile and decided [to] stay at the communal farm I had moved to and sink my roots here."[28]

In late 1969, Lovejoy became a full-time resident of the Montague Farm, growing organic vegetables and marijuana. For Lovejoy, the "social rules rebellion" and the personal transformation of the 1960s counterculture was as political as civil rights or antiwar organizing: "There was the cultural revolution. Sex, drugs, and rock 'n' roll was a true other liberation that occurred, and [it] affected people immensely and cannot be downplayed.... That shared [generational] experience did reinforce a shared [political] base."[29]

By February 1974, Lovejoy had lived and worked on the farm for nearly five years. His friends included a nucleus of activists who would play major roles in first the regional and later the national antinuclear movement. One was Anna

Gyorgy, an antiwar activist who went on to publish *No Nukes: Everyone's Guide to Nuclear Power* (1979), an encyclopedic guide to local antinuclear movements around the country, which became an antinuclear bible for the movement. Also included among Lovejoy's associates was Harvey Wasserman, a husky, good-natured journalist (known to friends as Sluggo because of his resemblance to the character in the *Nancy* comic strips), who was active in the New Left.

After graduating from the University of Michigan, Wasserman had attended the University of Chicago as a Wilson Fellow, where he had become one of the feature journalists for LSN.[30] After teaching at a high school in a low-income area of New York in 1968, Wasserman, like his comrades, made the transition to rural life. By 1976, he had emerged as the premier activist-journalist for the antinuclear movement. His series of frontline reports for *The Nation* during the Seabrook protests of 1976–1977 and his numerous articles for the *Village Voice*, *WIN*, *New Age*, and other left-liberal journals formed the basis of his 1979 book, *Energy War: Reports from the Front*. Wasserman, who was also a major spokesperson for the movement throughout the 1970s, was frequently sought out for comment by such mainstream members of the press as the *New York Times* and the *Boston Globe*.

Lovejoy also became friends with Randy Kehler, who had spent eighteen months in prison for draft violation from 1970 to 1971, became active in anti–nuclear energy politics in the mid-1970s, and later used lessons learned from that movement to launch the nuclear weapons freeze movement in 1980.[31] Thus, as Lovejoy contemplated taking action against the Montague Twin Nuclear Power Station, he was surrounded by individuals who later became some of the most vocal, visible, and active members of the movement.

Despite his association with such dedicated activists, Lovejoy has always insisted that he acted alone in toppling the tower. During his trial, Lovejoy testified that others knew he was planning something, and may have even been aware that he was considering toppling the tower, but that they were never sure whether he was serious about following through with his plans. Lovejoy spent three months prior to the event researching nuclear energy, writing and rewriting a statement to release to the police and the press after the action, and surveying the construction site. He was planning an act of moral witness designed to galvanize the loose-knit regional antinuclear movement and move it toward more militant opposition to the twin reactors. Lovejoy recalled, "Environmental groups [had] no civil disobedience psychology. . . . I wanted to get the movement off the ground in this area. But I also wanted to talk to people nationally."[32]

Lovejoy planned his action for February 22, 1974, to correspond with George Washington's birthday. As the date approached, Lovejoy's thoughts focused less on the broad philosophy behind his action and more on the practical questions raised by his intended sabotage. Having found scattered beer bottles and discarded condoms when he had scoped out the area on several occasions, Lovejoy was concerned that the site was a popular late-night rendezvous point for local teenagers. He was also anxious about any possible police presence, which would put at risk both the safety of the police as the tower came down and the completion of the action. Looking back a year later, Lovejoy told an interviewer, "I was really worried that someone would get hurt, other than myself. I was worried about getting hurt but I didn't want, under any circumstances, anybody else to get hurt. I was really worried about the idea that in the middle of working, say, the cops walked in on foot... for some routine security check or for some weird reason. And I would have to like yell to them to get out of the way, because something might happen that I didn't have fully in control."[33]

Beyond practical considerations, Lovejoy was unsure how friends and others in the community would react to his destructive and militant form of protest. "I was worried about all the hippies and all the radicals in the area," he recalled. "I was worried about all the communes in the area. I was worried about all the antinuclear people. I was worried about people who basically got along with me but were 'straight' and I was worried about losing friends because I had done something that they would not be able to deal with."[34] Despite these concerns, Lovejoy decided he would go through with the action.

By the eve of his sabotage, Lovejoy was fully prepared. "I had mulled it through so much that basically the doing of the act was like just doing a rehearsal all over again," he explained. His plan to topple the 550-foot weather tower that collected meteorological data involved releasing the taut 750-foot suspension-cable wires that anchored the tower to the ground. This required loosening well-tightened turnbuckles and removing tight-fitting pins. "Of course, the biggest problem I had was thinking about myself getting cut in half... like a pound of butter with a hot knife if these cables let go and sprang back at me; you know there would be no Sam Lovejoy," he remarked.[35]

Having worked through the logistics one more time, Lovejoy set out for the tower on the cold, crisp fifteen-degree night of February 22. Although a recent snow had melted on the streets, there were still six to eight inches of snow in the woods through which he trekked to the construction site. Lovejoy dressed in dark brown pants and a black windbreaker and carried with him an assortment of tools in a tightly tied leather bag. The penlight he had brought to guide him through the darkness proved unnecessary, as the moon illuminated the snow-covered landscape. Lovejoy was surprised by the loud noise that reverberated through the woods as his boots trod through the crusty snow, raising fears of premature discovery. After a long march through the "scrubby and tangly" woods, he reached the site, scaled a metal fence that surrounded the base of the weather tower, and went to work loosening the turnbuckles to undo the suspension-cable wires in the hope that the tower would come crashing to the ground.[36]

The strobe light atop the meteorological tower blinked on and off, alternately illuminating the area around Lovejoy and returning it to darkness, causing a surreal effect as Lovejoy banged to loosen the buckles. "It was hypnotic," Lovejoy remarked. The banging "made so much noise I couldn't believe it."[37] He recalled, "It was so noisy out there on the Montague Plains for a minute, I'm surprised the entire [town of] Montague didn't wake up."[38] After twenty minutes of banging, the first cable was loosed, unleashing a loud metallic twang as it snapped free. Breathing hard from the exertion, Lovejoy took a break. "I sort of bunkered down," he recounted, "and sat there for a minute waiting for anybody to come and nobody came and that totally blew my mind. No dogs barked, nothing. It was like all this noise, [a] really clear night, [when] you can hear incredibly long ways. If someone was out there, they would have heard it for sure, miles away they would have heard it."[39] Lovejoy lit up a cigarette, composed himself, and took stock of the situation. He pocketed the cigarette filter "so that no one could find out the saboteur smoked Kools."[40] Lovejoy wanted to leave no evidence that connected him to the tower, so that he alone could prove that he had committed the sabotage.

Then he returned to work. Once again the sounds of banging and clanging echoed through the crisp night air. After twenty to thirty minutes, the second cable broke free. After another short break, he went to work on the final cable. When the last cable snapped free, the top half of the tower wobbled precariously back and forth. Lovejoy's heart sank as the top lurched back into place. Then suddenly the strobe light at the top of the tower went dark and the top of the 550-foot structure came crashing down into the nearby woods. It made "a thunderous roar," Lovejoy recalled, and "the thing came down!"[41] (The next day, when police and workers examined the fallen tower, the clock on the meteorological recording box was stopped at 2:50 a.m.)[42] Lovejoy surveyed his handiwork with mixed feelings. Having hoped to bring down the entire tower, he felt disappointed as he turned his gaze from the wreckage in the woods to the 140-foot stump that remained solidly planted in the ground. Still, the 410-foot structure that lay mangled in the woods conveyed his point.[43]

A year later, Lovejoy recounted the night in an interview with a University of Massachusetts graduate student. He repeatedly described his feelings leading up to the action as romantic. He felt, he noted, like an "environmental Viet Cong." Lovejoy explained, "I had set out on a mission. I was the Viet Cong. I was an American revolutionary. I was the saboteur. I was a romantic idealist that was in this utopian action thing." If Lovejoy's trek to the tower was imbued with a romantic aura, his retreat after toppling the tower was more of a comedy of errors complete with a touch of Keystone Cops. He walked briskly from the site and stashed his bag of tools in the woods about two miles away. With his statement in his pocket, he continued to hike through the woods toward the nearby town of Turners Falls. Soon he heard aggressive barking coming from two dogs in the distance. From out of the forest thicket into the small clearing where he stood, emerged two snarling German shepherds, who branched out and flanked Lovejoy to his left and right. He froze with the thought "German Shepherds. Bad Vibes!" His mind raced: "Oh my God! I've done this giant political stunt; I've taken on this whole political-criminal reality; I've attacked this nuclear power plant thing in this total direct-action-civil-disobedience [way;] . . . I got this political statement I've been formulating for months[;] . . . and [now] these dogs are chasing me, man." What an anticlimax it would be, he thought, if his action ended with two German shepherds mauling him in the middle of the woods. He fantasized, as he recalled, "dragging myself to the street and waving down a car, exclaiming, 'ahhh, dogs attacked me, and [by the way] I tipped over the tower.'" He found himself alternately mollifying the dogs by saying, "nice dogs" and intimidating them by growling back, but both tactics only elicited more growls. Lovejoy continued to stand motionless, until—having made their point or become bored—his canine antagonists retreated into the woods.[44]

Finally, Lovejoy reached the road to Turners Falls, where he planned to turn himself in at the local police station. Hitchhiking on a dark country road in the middle of the night proved difficult. There were few cars, and the first two passed him by. He had better luck with the third car—a police cruiser. The time was 3:55 a.m. Lovejoy prevailed on the hesitant officers inside to give him a lift to the Turners Falls police station. The Montague area was so sparsely populated that locals knew most of the police officers who patrolled the area. Lovejoy recognized one of the officers from a marijuana bust at the Montague Farm in 1971. He recalled that eleven officers—in his words, "pigs," who were "really sick"— burst onto the commune grounds, guns drawn, and impounded not only their homegrown marijuana but also large quantities of legal organic herbs that the police mistook for cannabis. He recognized the other as the officer who—in the first Montague shooting since 1959—had shot a seventeen-year-old boy several weeks earlier.[45]

The police cruiser deposited Lovejoy at the Turners Falls police station at 4:00 a.m. On overnight duty was Sergeant Richard H. Cade, one of the few police officers Lovejoy respected. In a later comment about Cade, Lovejoy said, "[He] doesn't have a militant, sick fascist vibe to him. He's not a 'pig'; on a level, you know, he's just a real decent guy who happens to be a policeman." Lovejoy explained to Cade that he had just toppled the tower and was now turning himself in. Cade responded that he did not believe him. Taken aback, Lovejoy continued to insist that he had committed the crime. Cade then radioed the officers who had dropped Lovejoy off at the station, who radioed back that they had just been by the construction site and had seen the lights on the tower blinking. Exasperated, Lovejoy explained that this was impossible, since he had toppled the tower well over an hour before. Largely as a gesture to Lovejoy, Cade radioed back and instructed the officers to drive by the site to double-check. Ten minutes later the officers radioed Cade that the lights were indeed out. Cade told them to proceed by foot to get a closer look, and moments later the officers reported by walkie-talkie, "My God! Looks like an airplane hit it about halfway up."[46]

If Lovejoy thought he had finally proven his culpability, he was mistaken. Cade, doubtful that one man could have caused so much damage, phoned local airports to see whether any missing planes had been reported. At his wit's end, Lovejoy submitted that if an airplane had hit the tower halfway up, surely the wreckage of the craft would be nearby. When local airports reported that all planes were accounted for, Cade finally placed Lovejoy under arrest and accepted the typed statement justifying his destruction of the weather tower. As they waited for Lovejoy's lawyer to arrive, Cade conjectured how he would have felled the tower himself. Lovejoy retorted that Cade's proposals were all impractical. Cade then chided Lovejoy, touching on the most sensitive issue: "I'd be awfully disappointed if I didn't get the whole thing down."[47]

Lovejoy's lawyer, Thomas Lesser, arrived near dawn. Like Lovejoy, Lesser was a product of the counterculture. With long, pony-tailed black hair and a thick black beard, Lesser looked the part of "a hippie lawyer" with an "Eastern mysticism orientation." After consulting with Lovejoy, Lesser asked Cade to let him borrow Lovejoy's prepared statement so that he could make copies. He would return the statement to Lovejoy, who would then return it to Cade. Cade put Lovejoy in a cold cell that held an intoxicated local youth. When Police Chief Edward W. Hughes arrived, he sharply criticized Cade for having relinquished the statement—the only tangible evidence that linked Lovejoy with the destruction of the tower—but Cade responded that Lovejoy could be trusted to return the statement to the police. Later that morning, when Lesser brought the statement to his client, Lovejoy defiantly refused to hand it over to the police chief, asserting that he would surrender the document only to Sergeant Cade.[48]

Around 8:00 p.m., Lovejoy was transported from the Turners Falls police station to the district court in nearby Greenfield. The judge, William Ball, berated Lovejoy at length, comparing his action with the recent terrorist acts of the SLA.

"When I walked into court for the arraignment," Lovejoy recalled, "the judge absolutely flipped out. He actually...insinuated I was a terrorist.... And the analogy between the kidnapping of Patty [Hearst], and [the actions of] Sam [Lovejoy] was a pretty disturbing thought."[49] The district attorney pressed Lovejoy to name accomplices, hoping to lodge a conspiracy charge. Lovejoy, in his own words, "went ballistic." He insisted that although he had bandied about certain actions (even toppling the tower) with his friends, they were never quite sure "whether that was just Sam fantasizing a little bit too much."[50] After failing to obtain a conspiracy charge, the court proceeded with the original charge—willful and malicious destruction of personal property—a circumstance that would play a crucial role in Lovejoy's acquittal. As he later noted, he could have been charged with trespassing, breaking and entering, burglary, and tampering with utilities: "Basically they screwed up on a lot of levels. I could have been charged with eleven years' worth of crimes. They could have thrown the book at me. Instead they went for broke.... If you really want to be 'law and order,' they blew it."[51]

By the time Lovejoy was asked how he pled, many of his friends had gotten wind of his arrest and had converged on the Greenfield District Court. When Lovejoy answered the charge by pleading "absolutely not guilty," a cheer went up from his supporters in the courtroom.[52] Finally, after a long and eventful night, Judge Ball released Lovejoy on his own recognizance, and Lovejoy went home, where he "bullshitted with about 8,000 fucking reporters and then went to bed."[53]

News of Lovejoy's action electrified western Massachusetts, polarizing the region into pro- and anti-Lovejoy camps. The toppling of the tower had brought to the surface not only the political differences over nuclear energy but also the fissures between more traditional residents and the growing group of young people in the area who were leading a countercultural lifestyle. In a front-page Greenfield Recorder essay titled "Freedom Threatened," which came out later that day, Lovejoy was compared to Adolf Hitler and his sabotage was denounced as an act of "savagery" and "terrorism."[54] Selectman Donald Skole of Montague declared Lovejoy "a nut" and wondered "what Mr. Lovejoy would feel like if I decided to burn down his house because I didn't like his way of living?" He went on to say, "I think they should lock him up and throw away the key. This seems to be the whole psychosis of the country. If you don't like something, you take the law into your own hands and blow it up."[55] The Greenfield Recorder columnist Neil R. Perry, referring to Lovejoy as Strangelovejoy, denounced him as a "self-appointed savior of the people" and compared his action and his justification to those of the SLA, asking, "Isn't someone called 'Cinque' in the Symbionese Liberation Army uttering similar thoughts as he tries to explain the kidnapping of 21-year-old daughter of Randolph A. Hearst—that alleged symbol of fascist corporatism?"[56]

Lovejoy's action similarly alienated the local mainstream antinuclear movement. Speaking for the New England Coalition on Nuclear Pollution, Portia Weiskel of Leverett stated, "This is not a tactic that we in any way approve. We were shocked to hear about this and feel the place for debate on nuclear power is in the press, debates, lectures and in the courts."[57] A month later, Ralph Nader commented on Lovejoy's action during an antinuclear speech at the University of Massachusetts at Amherst, stating, "[The sabotage was] not my style.... It was not the way I would have handled it."[58] Lovejoy later observed, "Nader had a very difficult time for a short period ... trying to figure out how to deal with us direct action types, but he's got a creative mind and started figuring out ways he could assist us informationally.... He was a little bit nervous [regarding] me; he didn't want to get dragged down in the media by hanging out with antiwar saboteurs."[59]

At the same time, just as Lovejoy had hoped, his action galvanized much of the local activist Left. According to Frances Crowe, a longtime Northampton resident and American Friends Service Committee (AFSC) activist, the antinuclear movement "really exploded after Sam cut the tower down.... It sent a message to everybody that this was serious business and we better get to work.... [Sam] unleashed an awful lot of energy."[60] Lovejoy called Randy Kehler the next day. "Notice anything different over the horizon?" Lovejoy asked. For many, the tower—visible for miles away, especially at night when its lights blinked—had become an eyesore. As it was daytime, Kehler had not yet noticed the change. "C'mon, man! Look out the window!" Lovejoy prodded. After Kehler still registered a blank, Lovejoy exclaimed, "The tower's down! I knocked the tower down!"[61] Almost thirty years later, Kehler noted, "[It was] not until Sam knocked over the tower that I woke up to nuclear power.... [That was] true for a lot of people."[62] The New York Times reported, "Sam Lovejoy's act has made him somewhat of a celebrity among many of the young people in the communes sprouting up here along the Connecticut River Valley and in nearby college and university towns"; however, "it has elicited a certain queasiness among ecology groups opposing the nuclear plant, who quickly disowned his deed."[63]

Lovejoy was pleased to learn that his militancy resonated with much of the local political Left and counterculture. In a piece titled "Tower Toppler Tells Why" for the Valley Advocate, Lovejoy described his action as an effort to bridge the 1960s and 1970s: "This is the beginning of a re-awakening. What's really happening is that the radicals of the late 60s and 70s split to the country, to their own lives in search of a spirituality. We have now established a community base after being inward for a couple of years and are moving out again." Describing his act as intended to spark a movement, not stop the reactor in one fell swoop, Lovejoy compared the coming antinuclear movement to the antiwar movement: "That's not the point of radical action. When no one else was against the Vietnam War, radicals were saying it was absurd and were being called treasonous. But only several years later, these radicals were vindicated and the vast majority of Americans, I do believe, feel now that the war was bad."[64] Lovejoy also articulated his philosophy in terms of a nonorthodox Marxism that was rooted in the 1960s New Left: "I am a commune-ist. I'm not a Russian authoritarian communist, but I definitely believe that people got to share their shit. Because that's the only way [human] life's gonna survive."[65]

Lovejoy's colorful countercultural language might have struck a chord with many of the young people in the region, but it also lent itself to misuse by others. The *New York Times* treatment of Lovejoy's sabotage offered a somewhat bemused look at the activist, making liberal use of his colorful quotes and stringing them together in a way that marginalized both Lovejoy and his concerns. The *New York Times* reporter wrote, "Mr. Lovejoy's plethora of objections to the nuclear power plant—including what he described as 'the safety rap,' 'the background radiation and eco-system rap' and the 'whole Madison Avenue dance'—led him to conclude that 'it was tower-tippin' time.'"[66]

In truth, however, Lovejoy's countercultural rhetoric masked an abiding commitment to the U.S. political tradition. Unlike Lovejoy's interviews, which were replete with countercultural slang, his prepared statement was carefully thought out and written in formal prose. He dated his statement "George Washington's Birthday" and quoted extensively from the Declaration of Independence and the Massachusetts Bill of Rights. The statement began:

> The Declaration of Independence rightfully legislates action "...whenever any form of government becomes destructive of these ends...of safety and happiness." The Massachusetts Bill of Rights further states "...The people alone have an incontestable unalienable, and indefeasible right to institute government; and to reform, alter or totally change the same, when their protection, safety, prosperity and happiness require it." With the obvious danger of a nuclear power plant...a clear duty was mine to secure for my community the welfare and safety that the government has not only refused to provide, but has conspired to destroy.[67]

In his book *Working Class Americanism*, the historian Gary Gerstle describes traditionalist and nationalist elements of Americanism that have lent themselves to the political values of conservatives as well as a progressive element that holds up symbols of American radicalism and egalitarianism, which was embraced by elements of the Old Left ("Communism is Twentieth Century Americanism").[68] Much of the New Left also embraced progressive Americanism in the 1960s. Beyond the use of such imagery on the part of the civil rights movement—especially notable in the speeches of Martin Luther King, Jr.—many radicals, often seen as anti-American flag burners, also used symbols of America's revolutionary past. The yippie activist Jerry Rubin appeared before the House Un-American Activities Committee (HUAC) dressed in the clothing of a revolutionary-era minuteman, and antiwar radicals often spoke of Ho Chi Minh as "the George Washington of Vietnam." The countercultural film *Easy Rider* featured two hippies, Captain America (Peter Fonda) and Billy the Kid (Dennis Hopper), who embodied the true spirit of American freedom (throughout the film Captain America wears a jacket with a U.S. flag sewn to the back).

Lovejoy carried out the New Left and countercultural brand of Americanism in what might be described as a type of counterpatriotism. Linking the New Left and the progressive tradition of Americanism, Lovejoy (as noted) often referred to himself as "the Viet Cong... an American revolutionary." His choice of George Washington's birthday—with its obvious allusions to the mythical chopping down of the cherry tree—to topple the weather tower at the nuclear construction site is also significant. According to the *New York Times*, "Mr. Lovejoy... said he had selected George Washington's Birthday for 'symbolic reasons.'"[69] Lovejoy observed, "I'm sure George is up there in heaven smiling down and saying 'That's solid.'"[70]

Lovejoy's statement repeatedly returned to the theme of democracy and local community control, both of which he believed were being trampled by larger outside powers. He accused the nuclear industry of "preying on the weakness of the local citizenry," choosing economically depressed communities in which to locate their plants, and using tax cuts as "bribes" in what ultimately constituted "social blackmail." Lovejoy wrote, "When even the most learned physicists in the country continue to disagree... the citizens of the town were supposed to make a definitive judgment in a very few months on an issue that would radically alter their lives forever."[71]

Finally, Lovejoy's statement addressed the issue that largely spawned the dramatic rise of nuclear plant building in the 1970s, the ongoing energy crisis. Criticizing a corporate-dominated society guided by the imperative of growing public consumption, Lovejoy wrote, "The energy crisis, so-called, is an obvious signal for the need for immediate and nationwide introspection and re-evaluation. We must give up those false and selfish notions of individual freedom where they impinge on the freedoms necessary for a wholesome and balanced community life. We must bring to an end the greed of the corporate state. We must see that profit, as the modus operandi of our society, is defunct."[72]

Linking the various themes in Lovejoy's statement was a line of argument that would form the basis of his necessity defense at trial. Lovejoy argued that the principles of community democracy had been traduced by the powerful nuclear industry. The government had become, in his view, an active conspirator with the nuclear industry in usurping the democratic rights of the community. Given this circumstance and the potential dangers of the twin nuclear reactors, Lovejoy argued, he had no choice but to violate the law to protest what he believed to be a greater evil. This thinking was very much informed by the philosophy of nonviolent civil disobedience that had formed the core of the civil rights movement in the first half of the 1960s. When his case went to court, he would put nuclear energy on trial. His defense would hinge on convincing a jury of his peers that his criminal act was necessitated by the greater danger to the community that the nuclear reactors posed. Lovejoy ended his statement with these words: "Love and affection to all my fellow citizens."[73]

THE TRIAL OF SAMUEL HOLDEN LOVEJOY

The movement against nuclear energy grew dramatically in the Pioneer Valley during the months between Lovejoy's arrest and his trial. The high profile of the upcoming trial proved to be invaluable to the movement. An antinuclear group called the Alternative Energy Coalition (which, parodying the Atomic Energy Commission, was also referred to as the AEC) fanned out across the valley, securing enough signatures (thirty-eight hundred) to put a nonbinding referendum question on the November ballot in Hampden, Hampshire, and Franklin Counties about whether construction of the Montague twin nuclear reactors should be stopped.[74]

Members of the Montague Farm were the driving force behind the Alternative Energy Coalition, which started with twenty members and, within a matter of months, had grown to more than one hundred, spanning Franklin, Hampshire, Berkshire, and Hampden Counties.[75] Kehler, a member of the coalition, recalls that it was Wasserman who came up with the name for the group in order "to whimsically confuse people."[76] Wasserman, Gyorgy, Lovejoy, and others in the coalition disseminated the views of the group in the publications the *AEC News* and the *Montague Muse*. The LNS background of many of the commune members played an important role in making them some of the most visible and articulate antinuclear activists of the 1970s. The first issue of the *Montague Muse* included an editorial by Lovejoy that indicated that the early focus of the group was to reach members of the local counterculture:

The tower ecotage episode was a catalyst for awareness and action. But it also surfaced an inevitable social collision between the progressive-enlightened and the stagnant forces in Franklin County, in the United States, and the world. The background, lifestyle, the entire mindset of myself, and countless other brothers and sisters, see the locally proposed nuke as the...microcosmic symbol for an enormous political-social system so corrupt and so in need of change [that we should all thank] Northeast Utilities for its focusing efforts in this regard.[77]

Early on, the Alternative Energy Coalition encountered skepticism about its referendum strategy. In response, Robert Strachota, a coalition member, circulated a letter among activists in the three-county area that made the case for the efficacy of the referendum campaign: "First, we could force NU to reconsider their plans by the vote itself. Secondly, a referendum vote means that the Senator from this district must work against the plants.... Thirdly, the national media are ready and waiting to cover our campaign and this means both national education and additional pressure on NU.... To pull this off is going to take a big effort. NU is going to spend a lot of money to beat us."[78]

The campaign got off to a good start in the spring of 1974 when residents at town meetings in three communities voted for a moratorium on the construction of the twin plants. In May the town of Wendell became the first western Massachusetts community to vote for a moratorium. The towns of Leverett and Shutesbury soon followed suit.[79] Public Information Officer Bill Semanie of the NU attempted to play down the growing opposition to nuclear energy by sounding a theme that would become more common as debate over nuclear power heated up in western Massachusetts: that opposition to the plants came from elements of academia and the counterculture, both of which were outside the mainstream of American life. Semanie declared, "We'd frankly be surprised if these particular communities voted against the moratoriums—they are heavily loaded now with people from the academic world around Amherst."[80] Ironically, at a town meeting in the local bastion of liberalism, the town of Amherst narrowly voted down a moratorium on the Montague reactors. As debate progressed over the coming months, however, Amherst—home to Hampshire College, Amherst College, and the flagship campus of the University of Massachusetts—would become a stronghold of the antinuclear movement.[81] The campaign gathered steam in the fall as returning students enlisted in the campaign, especially members of student environmental groups such as MASSPIRG.

The Montague Farm became the base for both the referendum campaign and organization for Lovejoy's fall trial. Frances Crowe, a longtime Northampton resident and Quaker antiwar activist, recalled sitting on bales of hay in a barn with (as the conventionally dressed, fifty-four-year-old activist later described them) "alternative-type people" and "vegetarians."[82] The veteran activist Mary Wentworth, then in her forties, remembered, "The Quakers didn't quite know what to make of Sam. . . . He was a trip."[83] Despite the many cultural differences between the old-guard religious pacifists represented by Crowe and the new radicals of the hippie communes, their philosophies and their commitment to nonviolence overlapped considerably.

Preparing for his defense, Lovejoy was intent on putting NU, the Atomic Energy Commission, and nuclear energy itself on trial. Furthermore, Lovejoy was determined to represent himself at the trial. He spent days scouring law books and meeting with Judge Kent Smith, who—although impressed by Lovejoy's ability to learn the law and prepare a defense—urged him to retain council.[84] Lovejoy succeeded in obtaining two high-profile witnesses to testify on his behalf during the trial. John Gofman, a University of California professor and former Manhattan Project scientist, whose book on nuclear energy, *Poisoned Power*, had become an important source of information for members of the growing anti-nuclear movement, was the most important witness. In his work, Gofman drew attention to the underreported problems that had plagued the nuclear industry throughout the years: the dangers of low-level radiation; the underestimated threat of a reactor core meltdown; the risk to future generations of spent radiation, which would have to be buried and would then remain radioactive for more than a hundred thousand years; and the undemocratic decision-making processes of the Atomic Energy Commission.[85]

Lovejoy's other star witness was the radical activist-historian Howard Zinn of Boston University. A veteran of the movement against the Vietnam War, Zinn was assigned the role of reviewing the history of civil disobedience in America and placing Lovejoy's action in the tradition of Henry David Thoreau, nineteenth-century abolitionism, the women's suffrage movement, the labor movement, and the civil rights and antiwar movements. Together, the testimonies of the scientist and the historian would make the case for a "necessity defense." They would claim that Lovejoy had no meaningful legal recourse and that this crime was committed in an effort to prevent a more egregious crime.[86]

The trial was a major spectacle. It began on September 17, 1974, at the Franklin County Superior Court in Greenfield and proceeded to electrify the Pioneer Valley, garner a great deal of local publicity, and earn coverage by the *New York Times*. As hoped, the courtroom, which was packed with Lovejoy supporters, had a very politicized atmosphere. Judge Smith commented, "This is one of the strangest trials ever held in Franklin County."[87] District Attorney John Murphy led the prosecution, whose case was simple: Lovejoy had intentionally destroyed the weather tower, causing more than fourteen thousand dollars in damage and had confessed to the crime. Dismissing civil disobedience as an arbitrary and unacceptable form of opposition to nuclear energy, Murphy argued that Lovejoy's personal motivations were immaterial.[88] After the prosecution presented its case, the defense began to lay the groundwork for its "necessity defense" argument.

On the witness stand, Lovejoy began by telling the story of his life, emphasizing his deep ties to the region. Turning to his destruction of the tower, he declared that because legal channels were blind alleys, he believed that he had no other choice. Lovejoy argued that the public hearings held by the Atomic Energy Commission, where "interveners" could make their case against a proposed nuclear power plant, were nothing more than a sham. Noting the dubious role of the Atomic Energy Commission as both promoter of nuclear energy and regulator of the nuclear energy industry, Lovejoy called it "a kangaroo court...a panel that acts as promoter and regulator, judge, jury and thief all rolled into one."[89] He asserted, "There is no [meaningful, legal] recourse.... We do have recourse, but not through established means."[90]

Lovejoy made the now familiar arguments against nuclear energy before he personalized the act of toppling the tower. He described doubting himself and agonizing over his decision. He recounted how he wondered who he was to take on such a major decision on behalf of others. He explained, "The existence of Sam Lovejoy means nothing compared to future generations... and all those people who are gonna be hung under a cloud, a dismal cloud." Lovejoy's attorney then asked him, "Was there one single thing personally or in writing that influenced you the most in your decision to topple the tower?" In some of his most moving testimony, Lovejoy answered, "Yes... [a] little girl named Sequoia.... [I]t was impossible for me to not tip over that tower and live in a house with two young children who had no control over their own lives."[91]

The defense then called its first witness on Lovejoy's behalf, John Gofman. Given the unusual nature of the defense witnesses' testimony, Judge Smith decided to withhold the subsequent testimony from the jury. Gofman began by stating that he felt "a moral and social obligation" to testify on Lovejoy's behalf. He reiterated many of the arguments against nuclear energy that he had included in his book. To reinforce the "necessity defense" argument, he also contended that the nuclear industry was involved in a conspiracy to promote nuclear power through a concerted media campaign while it effectively limited public debate through its power over the corporate media.[92]

After Gofman's technical testimony regarding the health and environmental risks of nuclear energy, Howard Zinn took the witness stand. He reviewed the tradition of civil disobedience in American history and argued that Lovejoy's action fell well within that tradition. Zinn contended that laws were often made by people who represented special interests, especially corporate interests, and (in an allusion to the Nuremberg defense) he argued that often more harm was done by those who obeyed unjust laws than by those who broke them. Zinn recounted the history of corporations running roughshod over local communities and people. He described a hundred years of almost unchecked pollution and numerous industrial accidents that began to be curtailed only with the emergence of the organized labor movement, which had also engaged in tactics of civil disobedience. Whereas Lovejoy had invoked children and the future to justify his actions, Zinn argued that Lovejoy also acted on behalf of those generations in the past that had suffered at the hands of the powerful without any recourse. After the trial, Zinn stated, "If my trial testimony had an essence . . . it was the necessity of civil disobedience in times of danger to life and liberty and health and how historically in the United States we've seen many, many times how the . . . institutions of government are really very inadequate in protecting us."[93]

Betty Bell, a librarian from Gill, Massachusetts, appeared as a character witness for Lovejoy. An older woman who dressed conventionally, Bell said that she was opposed to nuclear energy but had felt uncomfortable with civil disobedience. She spoke highly of Lovejoy as a person and described how his sabotage of the tower and the subsequent publicity around the case had led her to reconsider her views on civil disobedience. Now, Bell said, she viewed Lovejoy's destruction of the tower as akin to the Boston Tea Party, the Daniel Shays rebellion, and Rosa Parks's refusal to move to the back of the bus. She told the court that in her view Lovejoy's action bought the community time to reconsider something that would have repercussions for generations to come. In an interview after the trial, Bell stated, "If the tower were toppled, it would give us a year to think it over, to learn, to educate ourselves, you know, have our eyes open to what the dangers were."[94]

In the end, however, it was a technicality that gained Lovejoy's acquittal. In order to discredit NU, the prosecution, and the police, Lovejoy had brought in Robert Sulda, a Montague tax assessor, who testified that the weather tower had been assessed as "real property" rather than "personal property."[95] Whereas the destruction of personal property was a felony, destruction of real property was a misdemeanor. As a result, Judge Smith ordered the case thrown out on the grounds that Lovejoy had been charged with the wrong crime.

Many of Lovejoy's supporters were euphoric, but Lovejoy was not. He pleaded with Judge Smith to allow his case to be sent to a jury, which had been his objective all along, but the judge (who seemed relieved to find a way to dispense with the case) refused. In the most politicized local trial in recent history, Smith found himself buffeted by countervailing pressures. Established business and labor interests, especially the giant NU, and many of the more conservative local residents wanted a conviction. Meanwhile, the Pioneer Valley was aflame with antinuclear activism, and the case had gained not only regional but also nationwide significance.

The fact that Smith had a reputation as a liberal judge, Lovejoy later speculated, might have influenced his decision. Lovejoy also believed that the arguments made by the defense were beginning to resonate with the liberal judge. Zinn attributed the judge's decision to the "moral pressure" he felt and the politicized atmosphere in the court.[96] Whatever Judge Smith's personal reasons were for tossing the case out, Lovejoy walked out of court a free man. Once again, Lovejoy was left with mixed feelings about what he regarded as a partial victory. Just as he had failed to topple the full weather tower, he had won his case without a jury verdict. From the beginning, he had seen a jury verdict on his behalf as the symbol of an indictment of the nuclear industry that would put the industry on the defensive both locally and nationally.

Despite the somewhat anticlimactic end to a highly charged case, Lovejoy and his supporters had a great deal to celebrate. After the trial, several jurors stated that the jury was leaning toward acquittal. Since Judge Smith had withheld Gofman's and Zinn's testimonies from the jury, an acquittal would have been based almost exclusively on Lovejoy's personal testimony. Many of Lovejoy's supporters felt confident that the jury was leaning in that direction. According to Crowe, "Everyone knew he would have been found not guilty."[97] Apparently, Lovejoy's demeanor at the trial, his emphasis on the community and future generations, and his willingness to risk a long jail term impressed jurors. Shortly after the trial, James O'Neill, one of the jurors, told a documentary film crew that the jury was inclined to acquit because the "Commonwealth didn't prove the point that he [Lovejoy] was malicious when he did it." O'Neill continued, "That's the reason why I think the jury would have acquitted him. . . . I don't think he was malicious. I don't think he's that kind of man. He figured he would sacrifice his own life . . . for the existence of the community in this area. In other words he was going to be the sacrificial lamb. He didn't care what happened to him. All he cared about was just the community at large, the generations and generations to come." Commenting on Judge Smith's decision to dismiss the case, O'Neill stated, "I was really glad he did what he did."[98]

The trial of Sam Lovejoy not only energized the antinuclear movement of western Massachusetts but also worked as a springboard for local activists to address a national audience. Green Mountain Post Films, a film cooperative based at the Montague Farm, made the documentary *Lovejoy's Nuclear War* to record the sabotage and trial. The documentary begins with a 1946 quotation attributed to the physicist Albert Einstein that states, "To the village square we must carry the facts of atomic energy. From there must come America's voice." The film gives a short background on the history of nuclear power from President Dwight Eisenhower's Atoms for Peace program through President Richard Nixon's pronuclear Project Independence speech of November 7, 1973, in which Nixon proposed reducing the plant start-up time from ten to six years. The documentary goes on to review the history of the proposed Montague reactors leading up to the toppling of the tower and the life of Sam Lovejoy.[99]

The film focuses primarily on the trial and includes numerous interviews with Gofman, Zinn, and Lovejoy. Standing against the backdrop of the Connecticut River, Lovejoy says, "I had to hunt around for some recourse, some way I could stop this disaster from occurring in my area, and maybe stop it around the country or even the world." Although the documentary is openly sympathetic to Lovejoy, it seeks a semblance of balance by giving a good deal of voice to those who favor nuclear energy. It includes several extended interviews with Charles Bragg (the vice president of NU) and local residents who favored nuclear energy. What emerges, perhaps unintentionally, is the degree to which the debate over nuclear energy in western Massachusetts was being defined in cultural terms. The film shows snippets of local residents who express anger at Lovejoy for standing in the way of progress and especially for breaking the law and destroying private property. Many of the more traditional residents of the Pioneer Valley, it becomes apparent, saw Lovejoy's sabotage as a terrorist act more reminiscent of the actions of the SLA and the Weather Underground than of those of Martin Luther King or Mahatma Gandhi. Lovejoy responds, "I found out how hung up, literally, people are on property.... They tend to protect property more, in many ways, than they are willing to protect liberty, sometimes more than they are willing to protect life."[100]

Bragg repeatedly sounded the cultural themes that permeated so much of the debate over nuclear energy, portraying those opposed to nuclear energy as part of an extremist fringe. Arguing that people must take into account not only an individual's arguments but his or her background, Bragg states, "You try to weed out those who are perhaps anti-technology.... They'd be as much against an electric toothbrush, if you will, as against nuclear power plants. It's a lifestyle with them. You have, I think, to take their opinions in context [and weigh that against] the background of science and Western civilization."[101]

A good portion of the documentary centers on the question of civil disobedience. Lovejoy and Zinn spend a great deal of time discussing the philosophy and history of civil disobedience. In response, Bragg dismisses civil disobedience as a formula for anarchy in which a self-anointed minority can run roughshod over the will of the majority as expressed through the democratic process. Bragg makes the case that civil disobedience can be used by the Right as well as by the Left and is ultimately coercive and undemocratic. He argues that perhaps civil disobedience is acceptable when used by a Gandhi but not when it is used by a Hitler. Others describe how Lovejoy's act forced them to reevaluate their views and see civil disobedience in a new light. Stanley Bell (Betty Bell's husband and constable for the town of Gill), for example, states that the Montague Twin Nuclear Power Station "was not just detrimental to Sam, but to all mankind." He goes on to say, "I had a completely different view of civil disobedience after the trial."[102]

Lovejoy's Nuclear War became a powerful organizing tool for the antinuclear movement in the 1970s. It was screened at antinuclear group gatherings and at independent film festivals. In 1975 the producers of the film, Daniel Keller and Charles Light, asked Randy Kehler, who was getting ready to travel to Europe for the international War Resisters Conference, to screen *Lovejoy's Nuclear War* for antinuclear groups overseas. Kehler and his life partner, Betsy Corner, found themselves at the massive twenty-five-thousand-person antinuclear occupation at Wyhl, West Germany. According to Kehler, "tons of people came out" to see the film as it was "simultaneously translated." Kehler and Corner also showed the film to enthusiastic crowds in Freiburg, Bonn, and several other West German locations.[103] In 1976 Lovejoy and Gyorgy took the film on a West Coast tour to promote the antinuclear referendum.[104]

Although Lovejoy's trial would become known both nationally and internationally, its immediate impact was felt most intensely in western Massachusetts. Within weeks of the end of the trial in late September 1974, residents of Hampden, Hampshire, and Franklin Counties would head to the polls to vote on whether to halt the construction of the Montague Twin Nuclear Power Station and whether to dismantle existing nuclear plants in Vernon, Vermont, and Rowe, Massachusetts.

COUNTERATTACK

During the months that led up to Lovejoy's trial, the Alternative Energy Coalition fanned out across the Pioneer Valley and collected thirty-eight hundred signatures to put the question of nuclear energy on the November ballot in three western Massachusetts counties. Hampden, Hampshire, and Franklin Counties constituted the state senatorial district then held by the Democrat John Olver. The first of the two nonbinding referenda read, "Shall the state senator from this district be instructed to oppose the building of nuclear power plants in Montague, Massachusetts?" The second question asked voters, "Shall the state senator for this district be instructed to sponsor and support a resolution calling for the closing and dismantling of nuclear power plants in Rowe, Massachusetts, and Vernon, Vermont?"[105]

As Lovejoy's trial approached, the ballot questions became the battleground in an intense debate that involved more than forty towns in the three-county area. The regional battle over nuclear energy was closely observed by the national nuclear industry and by organized labor, both of which saw the referenda as a worrisome challenge to nuclear power with national implications.

As the energy crisis and high unemployment took its toll on U.S. workers, many unions, especially those in the construction trades, viewed nuclear energy as a potential source of jobs. Although, once operational, nuclear power plants employed only 200 to 300 skilled technicians, the construction of the plants, which took about four years, employed between 2,000 and 3,000 workers. NU estimated that, at its peak, construction of the Montague twin reactors would employ 2,450 workers, including 100 boilermakers, 350 electricians, 200 iron workers, 300 pipe fitters, 150 welders, 250 carpenters, 50 asbestos workers, 50 operating engineers, 60 bricklayers and cement finishers, and 300 general laborers.[106] In the face of high unemployment both nationally and regionally, residents could not easily dismiss the prospect of more than 2,400 jobs that would benefit not only workers and their families but local businesses as well. For organized labor, the Montague plants represented a needed shot in the arm in a recession-plagued economy.

Both locally and nationally, the International Brotherhood of Electrical Workers (IBEW) spearheaded the labor campaign on behalf of nuclear energy. In western Massachusetts, the point man in the pronuclear labor campaign was George O'Brien, a former electrician and Navy veteran. O'Brien had worked his way up the labor movement from a journeyman electrician to business manager for IBEW Local 34, president of the Northampton Labor Council, and president of the Berkshire-Hampshire Building Trades Council. A tough Irish American with a bawdy sense of humor, O'Brien declared, "I was a Democrat since I was born."[107] An old-style, lunchbox labor liberal, O'Brien had little patience for the new environmentalist, civil rights, antiwar, and feminist activists who streamed into the Democratic Party in the 1970s.

"When Sam Lovejoy was kicking up his heels and knocked the tower down," recalled O'Brien years later, it "upset me to no end. I was concerned with workers, with people." For O'Brien, the unemployment of the 1970s was "heartbreaking": "I always felt bad for the poor guy that wasn't working. . . . When I ran that outfit [IBEW 34,] . . . I knew each man by his first name. I knew his wife by her first name. I knew how many kids he had and some of them by their first names." Witnessing some of his members go through divorces that he attributed to the "frictions" of unemployment, O'Brien "called up anywhere and everywhere to get [his] men work."[108]

Thus, the November nuclear energy referenda quickly became a struggle between two grassroots movements. Organizing in college classrooms, peace churches, and barns at local communes were the advocates of a nuclear moratorium; from the union halls came the moratorium opponents. Both sides spread out across the Pioneer Valley in search of supporters. O'Brien recalled, "We did what we did best: leafleting, going door to door."[109] Often enlisting the help of their children, union members (according to one estimate) reached more than twenty thousand homes.[110] Especially active in opposing the Alternative Energy Coalition campaign was the newly formed IBEW Nuclear Committee, which distributed thousands of pamphlets, some urging that residents "Vote NO!" on the moratorium. The Montague plants, the committee argued, "will not release harmful amounts of radiation. They will be built and operated with the most rigid safety requirements of any technology ever developed. They will provide needed electricity, far cheaper than any available alternatives. They will provide jobs for the construction crafts and material suppliers in this area."[111]

Local colleges provided the forum for much of the debate over the referenda. Referring to the popularity of the antinuclear movement at the University of Massachusetts at Amherst, O'Brien recalled, "They enlisted half the university."[112] At one university debate, organized by MASSPIRG, O'Brien declared, "If this group [MASSPIRG] is so concerned for your safety and mine, then I submit that the [question] to appear on the November 5th ballot should read as follows: 'Instruct the state senator from the Franklin-Hampshire district to do everything in his power to have the state legislature declare a ban on the use of all motor vehicles in the Commonwealth of Massachusetts.'"[113] Attempting to personalize the issue for the students, O'Brien asked, "What would the University of Massachusetts do with a 36% reduction in power? Half the students would have to attend classes one week and then go home for a week while the other half of the student body attend classes on the alternate week."[114]

Although the labor campaign had many of the hallmarks of a grassroots campaign, behind the scenes representatives of the nuclear industry were advising O'Brien. As O'Brien put it, "NU embraced me."[115] At every stage of the debate, two public relations men from NU—Montague Nuclear Project Officer Robert Barrett and Public Information Manager Bill Semanie—who saw in the labor leader a more human face for the nuclear industry, coached O'Brien. Barrett and Semanie sent O'Brien a constant stream of memorandums and articles. "They would fill me in. I wasn't the brainiest type, but I could read. We'd sit down with them [and] we'd take an anti-[nuclear] argument apart," recalled O'Brien.[116]

O'Brien described doing a lot of "soul searching" about his cooperation with NU, saying that he was not "overly enthused to side with the nuclear industry."[117] The nuclear debate in western Massachusetts was a microcosm of a strange corporate-labor alliance that was being forged at the national level as the controversy over nuclear energy heated up in the mid-1970s. As a trade journal for General Electric gushed, "Organized labor has gone to bat for nuclear power." The journal approvingly quoted Paul Snoop, international representative of the IBEW Utility Operations Department, who stated, "Across the bargaining table the adversary style prevails. [But] at this time there is no table between us. Our friends need help."[118]

Both the nuclear industry and the national labor unions that stood to benefit from nuclear power took a keen interest in the fight being waged by NU and O'Brien against the antinuclear movement in western Massachusetts. Snoop wrote O'Brien, "Your approach to the anti-nuclear groups is the correct one. The obstructionists have taken to the ballot and pose quite a serious threat to the nuclear industry. If they are successful locally (and they have a good chance of success), it will encourage them to seek a statewide moratorium on nuclear construction. Our efforts must be directed toward preventing this."[119] Charles Pillard, international president of the IBEW, wrote in the *IBEW Journal*, "Presently the industry is under great pressure from a small group of intelligent, articulate prophets of doom, who claim they, and only they, have the knowledge and capability to determine the direction of this nation.... However, THEY DO NOT SPEAK FOR THE IBEW!... In short, what they seek is to retard or halt progress, which stimulates economic growth.... This is not doomsday! [We] will not knuckle under to intimidation by word or deed of obstructionists. We will support our God, our Nation, our Union!"[120]

The NU and IBEW use of the term "obstructionist" to describe opponents of nuclear energy highlighted a fundamental division between environmentalists—who spoke frequently of the need for Americans to reconsider unchecked consumption and who advocated conservation—and those who believed that new technology held the key to unlimited economic growth and prosperity. At a debate held at an area high school, O'Brien sought to underscore this difference with a touch of humor: "I am amazed at the effort here to stop progress. Has anybody here ever stopped to think what would happen...if they scuttled Ford and the first automobile and we were still using the horse and carriage? How could [we] ever get rid of all that horse shit?"[121]

For advocates of nuclear energy, the new power source held the key to maintaining the economic growth and prosperity that had lifted much of the working class toward the ranks of the middle class in post–World War II America and that was now threatened by the energy crisis and stagflation. Lelan Sillin, the president of NU, warned of a "de-industrial revolution" that would impoverish working- and middle-class Americans.[122] Robert Murphy, business manager for Local 64 of the United Association of Plumbers and Steamfitters, sounded a similar theme: "If these environmentalists and anti-nukes don't get their act together with the rest of the people here in New England, then the six New England states will become a national park."[123]

For the opponents of nuclear energy, whose views were in many cases informed by the antimaterialism of the counterculture, Americans had to reject the view that nature existed merely to be exploited to maintain a lifestyle based on ever-expanding consumption. Speaking of the energy crisis and its impact on U.S. workers, Lovejoy declared, "So it's a short-term riff. For the workers it's a burn. And so what the workers need is . . . constant construction projects and so therefore, constant development, right? Evermore, Evermore, Evermore. . . . Well, then you start studying the electrical consumption of the country and how much juice this country consumes in comparison to other countries. And you realize this country really is the peak of gluttony and that we're just living this illusion."[124]

Thus, the debate over nuclear energy increasingly became a battle between those who sought to maintain a lifestyle that they knew and loved and those who believed that Americans must radically alter their thinking and their way of life. Like the corporate representatives of the nuclear industry, O'Brien consistently accentuated the cultural chasms that had developed in the 1960s and persisted in the 1970s. Whereas the New Left and the counterculture of the 1960s had represented a threat to traditional American values, however, in the recession-plagued 1970s many saw the Left, and especially environmentalists, as a threat to their standard of living.

O'Brien repeatedly invoked the environmentalist threat to the ultimate symbol of middle-class life: the television. In one speech, he asked, "Has the thought ever occurred to you that we might have to ration electricity? Can you imagine unplugging the TV set? What a horrible thought!"[125] In another paean to the comforts of middle-class life, O'Brien declared, "We can all agree that coming home after a hard day's work . . . there is nothing like a nice cold beer from the electric refrigerator, a refreshing hot shower, a good home-cooked meal from the electric stove and whatever the season, a little heat or air conditioning when you sit to unwind with a good book or watch a little TV."[126] Such appeals were meant not only to invoke fears of brownouts but also to identify nuclear energy with Middle America and as distinct from the hippies and radicals who posed a threat to Americans' standard of living and way of life.

Antinuclear activists, meanwhile, criticized their labor opponents as reactionary. In 1970, construction workers had attacked peaceful antiwar protestors in New York City in what became known as the Hardhat Rebellion. From this incident grew the image of the hardhat that conservative politicians embraced and many liberals and radicals ridiculed. This image was excellently portrayed by the protagonist of the 1970 film *Joe* and by the character Archie Bunker in the television series *All in the Family*. Both Joe and Archie came to symbolize the presumed narrow-mindedness and bigotry of the average blue-collar American.[127]

Years later, the activist Frances Crowe, speaking of labor, conceded that at the time the antinuclear movement just "wrote these people off."[128] Vince O'Connor, however, recalled that the movement went to great lengths to separate the technology and the industry from the workers: "We attacked the industry and not the people who worked in the plants.... [A]ttack the guys in the suits but not the workers in the plant."[129] Nevertheless, as the debate over nuclear power intensified, O'Brien became increasingly defensive about the popular image of working-class Americans. In one speech, he declared, "It is interesting to note that the environmentalists consider the construction workers a bunch of rowdies who come into the area and disrupt a whole city or town."[130] In another speech, O'Brien exclaimed, "The misnomer about the construction worker willing to build anything for a job is a lot of crap. We have families and we are just as concerned with their future as anyone could be. Let's give them a break."[131]

O'Brien continued to develop this theme as he remained on the front line of the nuclear debate into the late 1970s. At a debate at Hampshire College in 1978, O'Brien gave his most spirited and memorable defense of blue-collar workers, linking economic fears with a sense of cultural siege:

> I am one of the rowdy construction workers—Joe or Johnny six pack—or one of the many names that construction workers are called. But you ought to understand where we're coming from.... We are the target of many groups. It is small wonder we get uptight. For years now, multinationals have been raising havoc with the American worker. We in the labor movement have helplessly seen industries disappear from the U.S. as the huge multinationals have moved out of our country... and as ... imports of foreign-produced have spelled doom for many domestic industries. Environmentalists have taken their toll, multinationals have taken their toll and the high cost of energy has taken its toll.[132]

As the debate over nuclear energy continued into the 1970s, environmentalists increasingly came to sympathize with the plight of blue-collar Americans and sought to build bridges between the green movement and the labor movement.

Lovejoy's friend Wasserman, for example, became involved with a Washington, D.C.–based group called Environmentalists for Full Employment (EFE). EFE accused corporations of engaging in "environmental blackmail" by threatening layoffs in retaliation for environmental protection measures. EFE noted that workers were often those who suffered the most from industrial pollution, which they encountered in the workplace.[133] Wasserman conceded, however, that "unfortunately, environmentalists have often been insensitive to working-class needs and have been late to make the case that fighting pollution can also create jobs." He continued, "As a single-issue campaign, environmentalism still lacks the in-depth clout to make a lasting impact. What could tip the balance is a working alliance with organized labor."[134] Despite these efforts, labor-environmentalist cooperation remained the exception to the rule throughout the 1970s.

During the final days before the November 5 vote, lobbying by the antinuclear movement, NU, and labor reached a fever pitch. The results of the vote came as a stunning surprise to many involved. Although the moratorium on the Montague reactors met with defeat, the narrow margin surpassed even the expectations of the heavily outspent antinuclear movement. Fifty-two percent of the voters supported building the twin reactors, and 47 percent opposed it.[135] Less than one year after Lovejoy's assault on the weather tower, the antinuclear movement in western Massachusetts had succeeded in dividing the region almost down the middle. Given the dearth of public discussion before 1974, it was a major accomplishment. The issue of nuclear energy had been elevated dramatically, and the debate in western Massachusetts had drawn the attention of a national audience.

Speaking of the time before he toppled the Montague weather tower, Lovejoy said, "In my opinion, even the hippies around here in the area weren't getting their back up in the air and asking, 'Well, how are we gonna fight this?'"[136] The transformation that took place in the region over the course of 1974 was remarkable. Fred Zapinski of the Alternative Energy Coalition crowed that for a group operating with "a shoestring $700 budget using volunteers—we felt we did a damn good job."[137] O'Brien, however, dismissed such claims of moral victory, comparing them to "the politician who finds some sort of solace in the vote no matter what the margin of defeat."[138] More soberly, Lelan Sillin, the president of NU, noted a "deterioration in the public climate" and warned against "making energy policy a victim of partisan politics [and] encouraging a public vendetta against the energy industry."[139]

Although the vote on the Montague reactors invigorated the antinuclear movement and caused NU representatives concern, it was ambiguous. Unlike the referendum on the Montague reactors, the referendum that called for the dismantling of Yankee Rowe and Vermont Yankee received only 33 percent of the three-county vote, which—with respect to a quarter of those who had voted for the Montague moratorium—may have reflected more a "not in my back yard" sentiment than an across-the-board opposition to nuclear power.[140] Vince O'Connor, however, who had campaigned for the referendum, was among those who saw the second vote as a victory: "One-third of the people, which is astounding, thought we should close Vernon. I think it was the second vote [that was significant]. I mean you can always be against something that hasn't happened yet, but to be for closing a nuclear power plant that's already there and employs people and so forth [means] we had been very effective."[141]

The referendum had perhaps its biggest impact on the liberal state senator John Olver. A Pennsylvania native gifted with extraordinary academic skills, Olver completed an accelerated program to graduate high school at the age of fifteen, received a bachelor's degree from Rensselaer Polytechnic Institute at the age of eighteen, earned a master's degree from Tufts University in a year, and then went on to earn his doctorate in chemistry from the Massachusetts Institute of Technology (MIT) in 1961. From Cambridge, Olver and his wife, Rose (who earned a doctorate from Harvard), moved to Amherst, where he became a professor of chemistry at the University of Massachusetts and she became a professor of psychology and later a professor of women's studies at Amherst College. In 1968 Olver moved into public service when he was elected to the Massachusetts House of Representatives and quickly earned a reputation as a consummate liberal. In 1973 Olver won the state senate district that encompassed Hampshire, Franklin, and parts of Hampden Counties. Still, the aura of academia clung to him, and his aloof, intellectual demeanor prompted many who knew him to comment that he seemed more comfortable in a classroom than on the campaign trail.[142] Frances Crowe made the following statement about Olver: "He was a follower, not a leader. He wasn't very courageous."[143] Vince O'Connor recalled, "John Olver . . . was a very bright guy . . . [but] not much of a windmill tilter."[144]

Prior to the vote, Olver had supported nuclear power, arguing that scientists and experts could be trusted to determine the safety of nuclear energy. Certain that the referendum on the Montague reactors would go down in a sizable defeat, Olver had declared that he would follow the wishes of the voters.[145] The surprising percentage of voters opposed to the Montague reactors took Olver by surprise. After the vote, Olver made this statement about the narrow defeat of the moratorium: "[It] indicates more concern about nuclear power issues in this district than I had expected. This vote shows how quickly anti-nuclear feeling has grown in this area during the past six months."[146] Olver was also quoted as saying, "Three months ago, I would have suspected the whole thing would lose by a 2 to 1 or 3 to 1 margin. . . . [The vote] is certainly a tribute to the work done by many groups on the nuclear issue—a great many questions have been raised in the public's mind."[147] Henceforth, Olver attempted to straddle the divisive issue by supporting nuclear power in general while opposing the building of the Montague twin reactors until questions concerning the reprocessing, transportation, and storage of nuclear waste had been adequately answered.[148]

The polarization of the heavily Democratic district foreshadowed a division that increasingly confronted many Democrats throughout the 1970s. Environmentalists and organized labor formed two core constituencies for many Democratic politicians. In the 1960s, the Democratic Party had been wrought with divisions over civil rights and the Vietnam War. In the 1970s, nuclear energy and environmentalism became the new challenge for Democrats. Senator Edward Kennedy of Massachusetts had assiduously courted both labor and environmentalists. After the Montague vote, Kennedy intensified his support for the antinuclear movement. He proposed an amendment to the new law that replaced the Atomic Energy Commission with the Nuclear Regulatory Commission (NRC)—the law made the NRC a strictly regulatory body, separating nuclear regulation from nuclear advocacy—which would require the federal government to provide funds for the usually outspent antinuclear "interveners" at nuclear regulatory hearings.

The year following the 1974 referenda was relatively quiet in western Massachusetts. Although local groups were permitted to testify against nuclear energy before the Advisory Committee on Reactor Safeguards (ACRS) as interveners, public participation was largely limited at the pro forma hearings.[149] Meanwhile, Thomas Lesser and other movement attorneys advised activists to focus their efforts on the state rather than on the federal government, noting with reference to the Nuclear Regulatory Commission that "no utility proposal has ever been rejected by the federal agency." Rather, they argued, the movement should focus its efforts on the recently created Massachusetts Energy Facilities Siting Council, which included environmental representatives and was not beholden to the nuclear industry. They noted, "The fact that Governor [Michael] Dukakis has announced his opposition to the proposed Montague plants will certainly not be without influence."[150]

As the political climate deteriorated, NU—beset with economic difficulties—announced the first in a series of deferrals of the Montague reactors in the fall of 1974. Originally the twin reactors had been slated to be operational in 1981 and 1983, respectively.[151] In September 1974, NU announced the deferral of the first plant to 1982. Then, in February 1975, Sillin announced a deferral of both plants to 1986 and 1988, respectively. Citing double-digit inflation, high interest rates, a decline in investor confidence, and the first reduction in electricity sales in twenty-five years, Sillin stated, "Even Millstone Unit No. 3 [in Connecticut] could become [a] victim of the present climate."[152] NU remained committed to building the Montague reactors, Sillin continued, "provided public and regulatory support were forthcoming for that level of utility rates necessary to attract capital investment.... [M]eanwhile the clock ticks on and conditions grow more threatening.... I assure you that we remain committed to the construction of these units at Montague... for what is at stake is more than the deferral of planned construction. It is the deferral of all of our mutual plans and hopes for the development of this region and the prosperity of its people."[153] For the IBEW, the deferrals were disappointing. The IBEW international leadership issued a statement reading, "The impact of zero electrical growth is felt by many IBEW members. The delay and cancellation of projects have forced us on the unemployment rolls."[154]

On March 28, 1979, nuclear energy advocates suffered a devastating blow as the world learned of the near core meltdown of the Unit 2 nuclear reactor at Three Mile Island, Pennsylvania, and the attendant evacuation of more than a hundred thousand people. For NU, as for the entire U.S. nuclear industry, Three Mile Island meant public relations damage control. On May 14, 1979, NU took out a full-page advertisement in the *Daily Hampshire Gazette*, which began, "In the wake of the Three Mile Island accident, there have been public expressions of doubt, of fear, of concern over Northeast Utilities' reliance on nuclear power.... [W]hile it may not yet be possible to answer all the questions that are in people's minds, we urge you to seek out facts and to avoid the emotionalism which obscures truth and impedes the making of rational decisions." The piece went on to argue that no one at Three Mile Island had received more radiation than an average annual exposure to medical x-rays and assured readers that the plant designs at Connecticut Yankee and Millstone differed from that of Three Mile Island. NU argued that it continued to examine alternatives but that coal produced pollution and mining accidents, oil was expensive and unreliable, hydroelectric power was limited, and solar power was decades away. The advertisement concluded, "It is our firm belief that the decision to pursue the nuclear alternative was the correct one for this region.... We continue to have faith in nuclear energy."[155] In 1981 NU announced the "temporary cancellation" of the Montague reactors.[156]

In an interview with the *Valley Advocate*, Wasserman proclaimed victory: "The fact of the matter is we succeeded in Montague. If there hadn't been citizen opposition, there would be a plant there, or there would be construction there." Again, the Vietnam War analogy loomed large. "Throughout the Nixon years in the war, I am convinced that the extension of the war in Viet Nam was solely designed to confuse any possible feeling on the part of the antiwar movement that it was responsible for ending the war. . . . I am sure the same thing is true with the Nuke. . . . It has taken them all this time to organize their orderly withdrawal. The last thing that Northeast Utilities wants to do is admit that their defeat has been at the hands of a citizen movement. I think it's important people realize this."[157] Ultimately, the Montague Twin Nuclear Reactor Power Station was never built.

The degree to which Lovejoy's sabotage and the subsequent movement against nuclear energy led to the deferrals is difficult to gauge. As the 1970s progressed, many energy companies sought rate increases from consumers to build the plants that had been ballyhooed as capable of producing energy "too cheap to meter." The questions raised by the antinuclear movement certainly played an important role in the erosion of public confidence so necessary for nuclear expansion. In addition, the growing participation of the public as interveners at ACRS hearings in Massachusetts and around the country bogged down many nuclear industry representatives, which resulted in further industry expenses and delays.

As 1974 came to a close, the antinuclear movement in western Massachusetts could look back on a year of tremendous growth. The movement had established a pattern that became evident in the later movements against nuclear weapons, U.S. intervention in Central America, and apartheid. Radicals employing direct action had forced the issue of nuclear energy to the fore, mobilizing grassroots participation, galvanizing more mainstream groups into action, and thus forcing politicians to address the new issue of concern. Meanwhile, the western Massachusetts antinuclear movement had produced several new national leaders, most notably Harvey Wasserman, Anna Gyorgy, and Sam Lovejoy, who went on to play major roles in the national antinuclear movement. The same pattern would repeat itself with the nuclear weapons freeze movement six years later. Following the opening battle over Montague, many western Massachusetts antinuclear activists would throw themselves into the most dramatic confrontation to take place over a nuclear power plant in the 1970s: the 1976–1979 showdown in Seabrook, New Hampshire.

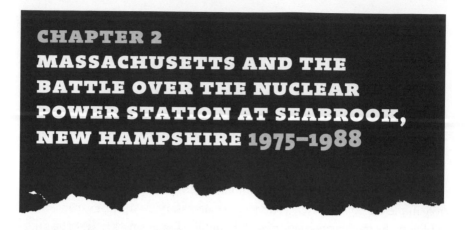

CHAPTER 2
MASSACHUSETTS AND THE BATTLE OVER THE NUCLEAR POWER STATION AT SEABROOK, NEW HAMPSHIRE 1975–1988

THE ANTINUCLEAR OCCUPATION AT WYHL, WEST GERMANY: 1975

In February 1975, frustrated by the lack of legal recourse, antinuclear activists in the upper Rhine town of Wyhl, West Germany, occupied the site of a proposed nuclear reactor. Twenty-eight thousand participants soon joined the action, which lasted ten long months. The occupation at Wyhl was for many U.S. antinuclear activists a protest model that embraced values and tactics that Sam Lovejoy and his allies hoped to bring to the U.S. antinuclear movement: It had both a local base and an international perspective that embodied the 1970s slogan "Think Globally; Act Locally."

Beginning with local environmentalists, farmers, vintners, and members of the Protestant clergy, the Wyhl occupation soon attracted activists not only from all corners of West Germany but also from France and Switzerland. The movement, which embraced a philosophy of local grassroots democracy, was heavily influenced by the growing European environmentalism that the more militant sectarian groups of the West German New Left had dismissed until that time as bourgeois. With the virtual tent city that it erected on the site, the Wyhl occupation took on a countercultural sensibility that meshed well with its rural local base.[1] The communal, nonviolent protest resonated strongly with the rural counter-cultural U.S. Left, which was then emerging as the driving force of the direct action antinuclear movement in New England. According to Anna Gyorgy, "The action [at Wyhl] inspired nuclear opponents throughout the world."[2] Over the coming years—as the protest against the proposed nuclear site at Seabrook, New Hampshire, grew—leading U.S. activists would refer frequently to the example of the Wyhl occupation, which ultimately succeeded in stopping construction of the proposed nuclear power plant in West Germany.

Over the long term, the Wyhl occupation helped plant the seeds that would grow into the West German Green Party in the 1980s. In important ways, however, it had a larger immediate impact on U.S. than on European antinuclear activists. The growing antinuclear movement in West Germany was gradually appropriated by more sectarian Marxist groups (known in West Germany as the C-Groups because of their communist orientation) and later by urban anarchist groups (known as the Black Block), which attempted to steer the movement in an antistate direction.[3] Contrary to the peaceful occupation at Wyhl, the West German antinuclear movement became involved in a spiraling cycle of violence in which activists temporarily blinded police with mirrors, made use of slingshots and other weapons, and were met by the full weight of state power.

The pitched battles between helmeted antinuclear militants and West German police in riot gear reached an apex in 1977, when unrelated acts of left-wing terror by the West German Red Army Faction (a group whose violence far exceeded that of the Symbionese Liberation Army [SLA] and the Weathermen in the United States) reached an all-time high. Under siege by the aboveground C-groups and the underground Red Army Faction, the West German government responded with severe restrictions on civil liberties that bordered on martial law and constituted one of the most serious constitutional crises in the nation. The shift to revolutionary violence, which precipitated the government crackdown, squandered the positive image that the antinuclear movement had earned with the West German public at Wyhl.[4] The West German antinuclear movement would not recover until the late 1970s and early 1980s, when the countercultural and environmental wings began to reassert themselves.[5]

In contrast, the U.S. antinuclear movement that exploded at Seabrook attempted to maintain the values and tactics that had proved so successful at Wyhl, Germany. Lovejoy's sabotage had helped begin the redefinition of the U.S. Left. That trend accelerated rapidly with the protests at Seabrook, as the antinuclear Left continued to define itself in terms of moral witness, the philosophy of nonviolence, the counterculture, participatory democracy, feminism, and especially grassroots localism. In the latter half of the 1970s, the U.S. Left came full circle, returning to the roots of the early 1960s New Left and civil rights movement (the philosophy and tactics of which had been eclipsed by the revolutionary militancy of the late-1960s antiwar movement).

It was this shift that increasingly attracted activists to the nonviolent movement at Seabrook. As the activist and historian Barbara Epstein notes in *Political Protest and Cultural Revolution* (her important study of the direct action movements of the 1970s and 1980s), the founders of the Clamshell Alliance, who led the opposition to the Seabrook plant, were mostly in their late twenties and early thirties. Many were "the younger brothers and sisters" of the antiwar generation, who were infected by the idealism of the 1960s yet disillusioned by the New Left shift to violent confrontation.[6] The prevailing nonviolent trend of the Seabrook movement would be challenged from within by a minority that wished to return to the more militant style of the Vietnam War–era New Left and to emulate the more confrontational style that dominated the European antinuclear movement of the day. For the U.S. Left in the 1970s and 1980s, Seabrook was a defining movement. In the words of Epstein, "The non-violent direct action movement of the late 1970s and 1980s began in 1976 with the formation of the Clamshell Alliance."[7]

THE BIRTH OF THE CLAMSHELL ALLIANCE

In 1969 the Public Service Company of New Hampshire (PSNH) announced plans to build twin nuclear reactors in the seacoast town of Seabrook, New Hampshire. PSNH would be a majority shareholder in the project, with the remainder to be funded by eight other New England utilities (including Northeast Utilities). PSNH, which provided 90 percent of the energy for New Hampshire, planned to use energy generated from the twin reactors to supply power not only to New Hampshire but to the entire New England region. The quiet town of Seabrook, a beach resort along the eighteen-mile New Hampshire coastline, had a small off-season population of fifty-three hundred. During the summer months, however, the population of the town swelled, as residents from greater New England flocked to Seabrook to enjoy its beaches and scenery. PSNH chose Seabrook because of its proximity to the ocean, which could supply the hundreds of thousands of gallons of water needed to run the cooling systems for the plant.[8]

From the beginning, a small number of Seabrook residents expressed concern about the impact that the proposed plant might have on both the local ecosystem and—with its looming, gray nuclear generating station towers—the aesthetic value of the idyllic beach-front resort scenery. Prior to the 1970s, there had been interventions in various parts of the nation at Atomic Energy Commission licensing hearings, which raised safety concerns and in some cases prompted safety improvements in proposed plants. Because the interventions always came late in the process, when the plants were near completion, however, they were restricted by law to narrow technical objections.[9]

These limited grounds for public intervention expanded greatly after the 1970 Environmental Protection Act, which mandated environmental impact studies (EIS) for all proposed federal projects. Subsequent court decisions broadened the possible grounds for citizen interventions by ruling that the EIS required by the act applied to the Atomic Energy Commission and its successor, the Nuclear

Regulatory Commission (NRC). By the early 1970s, there had been a dramatic increase in citizen interventions using the Environmental Protection Act. Most commonly these interventions challenged nuclear power plants that were under construction, on the grounds that low-level radiation would be emitted into the atmosphere and thermal pollution—a rise in temperature in bodies of water (often as much as 40°F) caused by the return of cooling water to its source—would occur.[10]

In the early 1970s, a small group of New Hampshire residents responded to these changes by forming the Seacoast Anti-Pollution League (SAPL). SAPL focused much of its attention on challenging the PSNH request for a licensing permit for the Seabrook plant on the grounds that thermal pollution in the waters around Seabrook would affect local marine life, especially the numerous clam beds in the area. SAPL hoped to repeat at Seabrook its success of a few years earlier, when it had stopped Aristotle Onassis's construction of an oil refinery along the upper coast of New Hampshire.[11]

In 1975 SAPL elected as its president thirty-one-year-old Guy Chichester, a self-employed carpenter from Rye, New Hampshire, a town just outside Seabrook. Born and raised in Queens, New York, Chichester was the son of a fireman and a telephone operator. He had eventually relocated to Long Island, served four years in the navy, and in the early 1970s moved to Rye with his wife, Madeleine, and their children.[12] Chichester brought to SAPL a more militant personal style than the presidents who had preceded him. As 1975 progressed, Chichester came to believe that the narrow legalistic focus of SAPL needed to be broadened. His increasingly vehement denunciation of the heads of PSNH and members of the New Hampshire political elite during public forums dealing with the Seabrook issue were making many SAPL members uncomfortable.[13]

In March 1976, working to employ new means of challenging the Seabrook plant Chichester succeeded in having a nonbinding referendum about the Seabrook Nuclear Power Station put to the year-round residents of the town. Unlike the result in Montague, where two years earlier residents had voted for nuclear power, the vote among Seabrook residents—who were mindful of the potential impact on the local environment and tourism—was 768 to 632 to "ban transportation or storage of nuclear materials associated with the [nuclear] plants."[14] As in Montague, the referendum in Seabrook set off a wave of similar referenda and town meetings, which resulted in eight nearby towns voting their opposition to the plant.[15] PSNH, the NRC, and the conservative New Hampshire governor Meldrim Thomson, however, all remained adamantly committed to building the Seabrook Nuclear Power Station.[16]

As 1976 progressed, Chichester became even more disillusioned with the legal intervention process, which he now condemned publicly as impervious to public opinion. Chichester later recalled, "Our time and energy were going into the hearings presentations. And what we thought was that our little lawyer there, who everyone was going around scraping up bucks for, that he's able to do it. But on the right side of him there was a bank of lawyers that were getting $1,000 a day. And on the left side of him was a bank of lawyers that were getting $900 a day. It was a total gang-up picture."[17]

Chichester began to speak of the need to employ the tactics of nonviolent civil disobedience (about which he knew relatively little). At the same time, he came to believe that opposition to Seabrook needed to focus less on environmental impact and more on the dangers of full-scale catastrophe: the potential for a nuclear reactor core meltdown. Soon Chichester was criticizing his own membership as too white, middle-class, legalistic, and cautious, which set off rumblings of discontent throughout the group, much of which was now thoroughly alienated from him. Moderates within the organization openly denounced Chichester's vociferous style and accused him of running roughshod over the wishes of group members.

Meanwhile, Chichester had begun making contact with more radical New England antinuclear activists, including the New Hampshire Quakers and those who had led the fight against the proposed nuclear plant in Montague (such as Lovejoy). Chichester screened *Lovejoy's Nuclear War* at a SAPL meeting and argued for a Montague-style movement. "That was about all I needed," recalled Chichester. "I had been thinking about how do we get people in the streets? I didn't really know how. I was not quite ready yet."[18] With Chichester's networking with New England radicals further accelerating his radicalization, by the end of the year he had broken his ties with SAPL.[19]

While Chichester was undergoing his transformation from legal intervener to more confrontational opponent of nuclear power, other New Hampshire residents, already grounded in the counterculture and more militant environmentalism, shot the first radical salvo in the fight against the Seabrook Nuclear Power Station. As many late-1960s hippie radicals fled the cities for rural Vermont and western Massachusetts, a few chose rural New Hampshire as their home. Among these was a group of radical pacifists who set up a commune called the Greenleaf Harvesters' Guild in Ware, New Hampshire, not far from Seabrook. The members of the guild sought to integrate Gandhian political and spiritual principles with a 1960s countercultural lifestyle and a focus on environmentalism. On January 4, 1976 (in an act reminiscent of Lovejoy's action at Montague almost two years earlier), twenty-two-year-old Ron Rieck, an apple picker at the collective, climbed up a 175-foot weather tower on the Seabrook construction site and announced that he would remain there as a protest against the plant.

Rieck camped out at the top of the tower for thirty-six hours, while friends brought him food and supplies. Among those who came to support Rieck were Suki Rice and Elizabeth Boardman, two members of the Cambridge (Boston) American Friends Service Committee (AFSC) who were among the earliest Massachusetts residents to become involved in the Seabrook debate. Finally, authorities persuaded Rieck to climb down from the tower, where local police awaited him with hot tea. PSNH never charged Rieck with trespassing, and Rieck was later acquitted of the charge of "creating a public nuisance." Nevertheless, his action was a harbinger of events to come.[20]

By the spring of 1976, Chichester and other opponents of the Seabrook plant had established ties with other activists from New England, especially from Massachusetts. Meeting at Chichester's home in Rye, they began plans that resulted in the founding of the Clamshell Alliance. At a larger meeting of fifty people a few weeks later, the principles of the Clamshell Alliance were ratified. A number of Massachusetts activists were among the Clamshell founders—among them, the Boston-based veteran AFSC activists Rice and Boardman, who became the main advisors for Clamshell on the principles of nonviolence, the Quaker practices of affinity groups, and consensus decision making. By the end of the year, Lovejoy and Gyorgy—who were crisscrossing the country as antinuclear ambassadors, giving talks and encouraging the formation of locally based anti-nuclear movements—had also joined the organization.[21]

A number of other western Massachusetts activists were on hand from the beginning. Especially prominent were those with pacifist and civil rights experience—among them, Mary Wentworth (a former Philadelphia civil rights activist) and Wally and Juanita Nelson (an African American couple who had moved to western Massachusetts in the early 1970s and had become close friends of Randy Kehler's). Wally Nelson had been one of the original Congress of Racial Equality (CORE) members in the early 1940s, a conscientious objector during World War II, a member of the pacifist group the Peacemakers, and a lifelong war tax resister. Wally had met Juanita in prison in the 1940s, when she had arrived to interview him for a magazine article, and the two had been active in civil rights and antiwar struggles since. Soon other pacifists with civil rights experience joined, including the former CORE activist Randy Kehler and the former Student Non-violent Coordinating Committee (SNCC) organizer Vince O'Connor, both of whom had spent eighteen months in prison for draft resistance during the Vietnam War.[22]

The organizational skills that core activists brought to the early Clamshell Alliance helped shape the new antinuclear movement. "People brought this enormous reservoir of organizational experience," recalled O'Connor. "Their organizing methodology was the SNCC organizational methodology, which is you go into the community and you organize people about issues . . . grass roots organizing." To a large degree, the Clamshell organizers looked to the Montague movement as a model. "I would say the genesis of this came out of Sam Lovejoy and his friends because of the Montague plant. . . . We had sunk the Montague nuclear project with the referendum," recalled O'Connor. Speaking of the Montague group, O'Connor explained:

> It became very clear to me not very long from moving [to western Massachusetts] in July 1974 . . . that this group had community roots. They had identified nuclear power with harm to the community. And they successfully said these things were dangerous to us. And they were extremely effective at community organizing. . . . I had the instinct from working with SNCC that I could see this wasn't just a bunch of hippies; this was a real smart group of people that had great connections with the community, which all the radicals didn't have [in the 1960s]. They had all these organizations, they were doing all this stuff, but none of them [after SNCC] had a community base.[23]

With organizational experience reaching back sometimes decades to pacifist and civil rights activism (bolstered by the Montague model), members of the Clamshell Alliance—or Clams, as they came to be known—mapped out their long-term strategy for putting a stop to the proposed Seabrook plant. The members decided to start a campaign of civil disobedience that would begin small, including only local New Hampshire residents, and grow incrementally, bringing in activists from around the New England region. Prior to any action, all participants were to be trained in the principles of nonviolence and passive resistance. Anyone who took part in civil disobedience would have to join a small affinity group, numbering from five to fifteen additional activists, with whom they would be required to stay in contact during any occupation or imprisonment. The affinity groups would also act as decision-making bodies during any action, passing the group consensus up through a "spoke" to a meeting of representatives of all the affinity groups. Activists who engaged in civil disobedience were also expected to adhere to certain rules, including abstaining from drug or alcohol use during any action and refraining from destroying property.[24]

In a strategy reminiscent of SNCC methodology during the early civil rights movement and modeled on the Montague movement, the Clamshell Alliance also decided that close ties with local Seabrook residents were imperative. Connection with the local community would not only give the movement legitimacy beyond its countercultural base but also prove crucial logistically, as local residents availed Clamshell activists of access to their property for groups of up to five hundred activists to convene, organize, and camp out in preparation for acts of mass civil disobedience. As the movement against the Seabrook Nuclear Power Station grew into the thousands and activists from throughout New England joined the cause and pushed for more militant resistance, however, tensions arose: On one side were those who believed that increased militancy would alienate the more conservative local base of the Clams, and on the other side were those who believed that because a nuclear catastrophe would affect all New Englanders, locals must not be given a privileged position within the movement.[25]

Having grown from the experiences of the 1960s civil rights and antiwar movements, the principles and tactics of the Clamshell Alliance were tailored to build on the successes of their predecessors and avoid repetition of their failures. The return to the nonviolent philosophy of the early 1960s civil rights movement was especially attractive for many. One Clam activist recalled, "The nonviolence is what really appealed to me. This is what I missed during the Vietnam War days. Though I was younger then, I wanted to get involved. But all I saw was the violence, and I did not want to get my head bashed. I was terrified of that. So here was that non-violent group, the Boston Clamshell, and I thought now I am home."[26]

The Clamshell was also heavily influenced by the environmental, countercultural, and feminist movements, which injected a more interpersonal and consensus-based approach to progressive politics than had been present in the male-dominated antiwar movement. Epstein captures the evolution of the Clams from the late 1960s: "[The Clamshell Alliance] continued the New Left impulse toward a politics of living out one's values and rejected the anti-war movement's machismo and authoritarianism. For many of its members the Clamshell was a realization of the hope that seemed to fade in the late sixties for a movement based on shared commitments and mutual trust."[27]

Harvey Wasserman and Cathy Wolff would emerge as the two principal designated spokespeople for the Clamshell Alliance. Wasserman highlighted the importance of nonviolence to the new movement in the preface of his 1979 book, *Energy War: Reports from the Front*: "The adoption of disciplined, non-violent mass action by late-seventies activists has indicated a maturity and staying power born of the work of Gandhi, Martin Luther King and Cesar Chavez. These tactics could carry the seeds of a new social order in the country rarely dreamed possible during the raucous, polarized days of Vietnam."[28]

Although a majority of Seabrook residents had voted against the nuclear plant, the countercultural attire and lifestyle of Clamshell members caused many local residents to view the activists with suspicion. Over time, nevertheless, the Clamshell Alliance began to realize its vision of a radical movement against nuclear power rooted in the local community. Slowly the group built bridges to the growing minority of more conventional, traditional, and frequently older residents of Seabrook, some of whom even reached out to the Clams. Such was the case for Tony and Louisa Santasucci, who contacted the Clamshell Alliance after they read a blistering editorial against the Seabrook nuclear plant by Guy Chichester in one of the local papers. For the Santasuccis, the issue of the Seabrook plant was literally a matter of "not in my backyard."

Unbeknownst to the Santasuccis, PSNH planned to buy a swathe of their four-acre property, which abutted the site of the nuclear power station. Tony Santasucci stumbled upon these plans when he stepped into a drill hole that had been dug in his yard, spraining his ankle.[29] In one of his contemporary articles on the Seabrook movement, Wasserman described Tony Santasucci—a sixty-two-year-old veteran of World War II and a truck mechanic by profession—as "a folk hero in the saga of the Seabrook nuke."[30] Throughout the mass actions of the Clams during 1977 and 1978, the Santasuccis—who frequently offered their four-acre property as a staging area and campground for Clam direct actions—were the most reliable of the more traditional local supporters.[31] On one occasion, Tony Santasucci proclaimed, "We don't need that plant and if you ask me, the Public Service is a bunch of liars. They'll never kick me out of here. They'll have to drag me out first."[32] When a real estate agent with ties to PSNH told Louisa Santasucci that their home would be bulldozed if they did not sell, Louisa snapped back, "You bring that bulldozer in and I'll sit right in front of it."[33]

The feistiness of the Santasuccis was just the image of local opposition that the Clamshell Alliance wished to emphasize. The Santasuccis appeared in numerous local television interviews and were featured prominently in *Seabrook '77*, a documentary film created by western Massachusetts activist and filmmaker Robbie Leppzer, and in *The Last Resort*, another documentary film about the early Seabrook struggle created by the makers of *Lovejoy's Nuclear War*.[34] For the early, predominantly countercultural members of the Clamshell Alliance, the support of stalwart locals not only gave the movement a sense of legitimacy but also highlighted the post-1960s grassroots vision.

ROUND ONE—AUGUST 1, 1976, SEABROOK OCCUPATION: 18 ARRESTS

Before the Clamshell Alliance was officially formed, protest against the Seabrook nuclear plant had already been growing. From Rieck's January tower occupation through an April 1 rally by about three hundred antinuclear activists outside the Seabrook site, opponents of the Seabrook plant felt a growing momentum.[35] Early members of the Clamshell Alliance, who wanted to build on this momentum, planned their first site occupation for early August. The intention was to hold a small occupation that comprised New Hampshire residents and to then follow with larger occupations, each one increasing tenfold over the last. By starting slowly and limiting arrests to local residents, the Clams could give their roots time to take hold before the movement was swamped by people from out of state.[36]

Although the Clams had agreed that New Hampshire residents would carry out the first occupation, on August 1 more than six hundred antinuclear activists—hailing, according to Wasserman, from every state in New England—arrived in Seabrook to show their support. The day began with speeches, chants, and singing outside the Seabrook site. Some of the slogans that would become hallmarks of the antinuclear movement nationally were scrawled on signs: "Hell No! We Won't Glow!"; "Split Wood, Not Atoms"; and "Better Active Today than Radioactive Tomorrow!"[37]

Evincing early media savvy, Clamshell organizers of the event succeeded in arranging for more than forty journalists and reporters from both mainstream and alternative outlets to cover the event. As the rally ended, the eighteen predesignated occupiers, all having undergone nonviolence training, broke away from the crowd to cheers and marched onto the plant site with some thirty journalists, media reporters, and film crews in tow.[38] Because the Seabrook police station did not have room to accommodate the eighteen arrested protestors, they were all booked at the nearby Hampton Falls police station—the first of several Seabrook spillovers that would engulf New Hampshire in less than a year.[39]

The first Clamshell occupation had garnered significant coverage from not only local and regional media but also the national alternative press. The early media success of the Clams continued throughout the week, as members protested the August 5 ground-breaking ceremony for the Seabrook Nuclear Power Station hosted by the Republican governor Meldrim Thomson and the heads of PSNH. Police had to clear out several older Seabrook residents who had parked themselves on chairs along the route of the dignitaries' motorcade. The streets outside the site became the stage for scattered protests and other street blockages, which resulted in three arrests, including that of Chichester. At the Exeter Inn, police removed twenty-four-year-old Gretchen Siegler for disrupting Governor Thomson's speech. Meanwhile, in a public relations boondoggle, a photograph of the governor's photo at the August 5 ground-breaking ceremony appeared on the front page of several local newspapers the following day, juxtaposed with headlines about the thirty-first anniversary of the atomic bombing of Hiroshima—thus inadvertently linking nuclear power with nuclear war.[40]

As Clamshell activists were waging their nonviolent guerrilla street campaign against Governor Thomson's Seabrook ground breaking, the Seabrook antinuclear movement struck media gold. In nearby Manchester, Jimmy Carter, the Democratic presidential nominee, was celebrating his New Hampshire primary victory earlier that year. Following the Georgia governor was the Vermont-based Green Mountain Post Films Co-op, which had produced *Lovejoy's Nuclear War*, then being screened at antinuclear events around the country.[41] Members of Green Mountain Post Films were able to get close enough to the future president to ask him about his thoughts on the August 1 Seabrook occupation. Since any words spoken by the presidential contender were national news, Carter's answer gave the Clamshell Alliance publicity before a national audience.[42]

Carter had already evoked cautious optimism among the growing national antinuclear movement by declaring that he would make NRC appointments that would "be acceptable to Ralph Nader."[43] His reply to the Green Mountain Post Film questions about civil disobedience would encourage antinuclear activists further. Carter, a former nuclear engineer, answered, "I've always felt that anybody who disagrees with the civil law in a matter of conscience has a right openly to express that [through civil] disobedience. At the same time, under our societal structure, it's necessary that they be willing to take the consequence of their disobedience. I believe that there's a place for nuclear power in our future. It ought to be minimized; it ought to be a last resort."[44]

After its first week of active nonviolent protest, the Clamshell Alliance had fortuitously intersected with the bicentennial presidential campaign, gaining national attention. The momentum that had been building throughout 1976 now began to snowball.

ROUND TWO—AUGUST 22, 1976, SEABROOK OCCUPATION: 180 ARRESTS

Except for its scale, the August 22 occupation was a rerun of the August 1 occupation. Again the occupiers began their trek to the plant site after a large legal rally, this one attracting more than 1,500 protestors. The rally took place at Hampton Falls, near the Seabrook site, and once again the occupiers set off with an entourage of reporters in tow. The 180 site occupiers consisted of many New Hampshire residents, but now the Clamshell Alliance opened the door to out-of-state activists. Many of the August 22 occupiers had come from the Boston area and from western Massachusetts.[45]

Like the 18 occupiers from the August 1 action, all 180 trespassing Clams were arrested. This time they were taken to Portsmouth Armory, more than twenty miles away, where they were held overnight. The next day most were released on personal recognizance after being charged with criminal trespass[46]; however, 10 who had been arrested at the site previously (soon known as The Seabrook Ten) were taken to jail and charged with contempt for violating an earlier Superior Court injunction. The Seabrook Ten were held until trial in early September. In a somewhat irregular move, they were scheduled to be tried by Maurice Bois, the same judge who had issued the injunction. When Thomas Lesser, the Massachusetts attorney who had played such an important role in the Lovejoy case, attempted to withdraw from the case to comply with the desire of some of the defendants to represent themselves, the court ordered him to stay on as legal advisor to The Seabrook Ten.[47]

Massachusetts activists were now playing a growing role in the movement against the Seabrook nuclear plant. Suki Rice and Elizabeth Boardman of the Boston AFSC were the main advisors to the Clams on matters of nonviolence and consensus; Thomas Lesser from Northampton was the—albeit reluctant—legal advisor to The Seabrook Ten; Sam Lovejoy and Anna Gyorgy had interrupted their cross-country antinuclear proselytizing to focus on Seabrook; and now Harvey Wasserman worked tirelessly to publicize the Seabrook struggle in the national alternative press (from The Nation to New Age) and in regional newspapers (such as the western Massachusetts Valley Advocate).[48]

Describing the injunctions as "fishy" and the trial of The Seabrook Ten as a "railroad," Wasserman argued that Judge Bois—who had been appointed by Governor Thomson and was a close associate of William Loeb, the conservative editor of the pronuclear Manchester Union Leader—was acting as a tool of the pronuclear establishment of New Hampshire. Describing the constant personal tête-à-têtes between Judge Bois and the defendants, Wasserman wrote, "The judge . . . conducted a game of psychic jujitsu with the defendants, browbeating them whenever possible . . . [including having] a tiff with defendant Medora Hamilton over her wish to be addressed as 'Ms.'" The trial concluded with the defendants' final statements on the moral imperative of opposing the plants, after which Judge Bois declared all the defendants guilty and sentenced them to six months in jail without bail pending appeal.[49]

The draconian sentences offended many New Hampshire residents, who saw the judge's behavior during the trial and during his sentencing as strong-arming. By order of the New Hampshire Supreme Court, the ten defendants were released after six days of imprisonment. Describing what he saw as the use of the law for political objectives, the Democrat John Durkin, a New Hampshire senator, proclaimed in disgust that Judge Bois had made New Hampshire look like "the Mississippi of the North."[50] Wasserman described Senator Durkin's statement as "a comment that should have offended the people of Mississippi."[51] After the trial, Wasserman wrote, "The trial of the Seabrook Ten made it clear . . . that the stakes were going to be very high in New Hampshire, and that somebody was taking these protests very seriously."[52] After the trial, members of the Clamshell Alliance hunkered down for the winter and began to organize their third and largest occupation for the following spring. The floodgates would be opened, and activists from all over New England would be actively encouraged to join the Clamshell Alliance. Meanwhile, Governor Thomson was preparing for what promised to be a major showdown.

"THE MISSISSIPPI OF THE NORTH": MELDRIM THOMSON AND NEW HAMPSHIRE POLITICS

New Hampshire had long been the most conservative of the six New England states. As their state motto, "Live Free or Die," implied, New Hampshire voters were renowned for their independent, small-government conservatism and their opposition to virtually any form of taxation (the state had no sales tax or income tax). The limited New Hampshire tax base was partly responsible for the relatively underdeveloped state infrastructure, especially relative to that of its neighbors (particularly Massachusetts to the south). Many New Hampshire residents saw this situation as merely preserving the rustic New England charm of the state and harbored a particular disdain for Massachusettsespecially for the greater Boston area, which they regarded as a prolabor bastion of big government and cosmopolitan liberalism.[53] The New Hampshire electorate also had a well-earned reputation for unpredictability and independence, however—most dramatically underscored in the 1968 Democratic primary when Eugene McCarthy, the antiwar candidate, nearly outpolled Lyndon Johnson, the incumbent president.[54] Southeastern New Hampshire, where Seabrook was located, fell within the greater Boston media area and represented the most liberal section of New Hampshire; by Massachusetts standards, however, even this part of the state was conservative.[55]

The symbol of New Hampshire conservatism in the 1970s was the Republican Meldrim Thomson, who had won the governorship in 1972 on a strongly antitax platform. Raised in Georgia, Thomson had worked in the publishing industry and had eventually settled in the Granite State. According to Wasserman, Thomson ran the state like "his personal fief."[56] In his study *Seabrook Nuclear Power Station: Citizen Politics and Nuclear Power*, the historian Charles Bedford wrote, "Governor Thomson [believed that] no problem had two sides and . . . relished his bull-in-a-china-shop image."[57] Throughout the 1970s, Thomson had sought to bolster his conservative reputation for a national audience in anticipation of a possible bid for the presidential nomination, hoping to run to the right of Ronald Reagan in the 1980 Republican primaries. To that end, Thomson had visited the Republic of South Africa and lauded its racial policies, and he had ordered all state flags lowered to half-mast when Taiwan was ejected from the Olympics in favor of the People's Republic of China.[58]

Thomson, one of the most outspoken U.S. political advocates of nuclear power, saw the completion of the Seabrook Nuclear Power Station as a personal crusade. As governor he ordered a gag rule, forbidding any state employee to express public criticism of the Seabrook project. When a suspiciously large percentage of local Clamshell supporters in the Seabrook area reported various forms of harassment, many believed it was part of Thomson's pronuclear crusade. According to Wasserman, "Thomson's hand had already been evident throughout the town. Tax assessments for local nuclear opponents had jumped far higher than [for] those who supported the plant. Known Clamshell sympathizers found themselves with zoning hassles, threatening phone calls, tax problems, and an escalating atmosphere of intimidation and potential violence."[59]

Thomson's firm grip on the apparatus of state power was augmented by his close alliance with William Loeb, the archconservative publisher of the *Manchester Union Leader*, a nationally read outlet for ideological conservatism. Loeb used his newspaper as a booster for the Seabrook nuclear plant and as a mouthpiece for Thomson to denounce the Clamshell Alliance. Throughout the struggle over the Seabrook nuclear plant, Thomson accused the movement of being run exclusively by "outsiders" and employed polemical invectives reminiscent of those used by Spiro Agnew in the late 1960s. He referred to Clamshell activists as "a filthy, foul, un-American minority...a gurgling, spurting bunch of unproductive individuals."[60]

Thus, as the May 1, 1977, date approached for what clearly would be the largest of the Clamshell site occupations, both the alliance and the governor hoped to use the event to address a national audience. Each became the other's perfect bête noire, and as the showdown approached, tensions escalated. In an article for *The Nation*, Wasserman wrote, "Together Thomson and Loeb used the week prior to the [spring 1977] occupation to create an environment absent from this country since the days of Vietnam... [l]abelling alliance members 'Communists' 'perverts'...and a 'cover for terrorism.'"[61] Governor Thomson seemed prepared to wield the full weight of state power against the Clamshell Alliance. The degree to which he did so shocked even his most ardent detractors.

SHOWDOWN—"THE BATTLE OF SEABROOK": MAY 1977

In the days leading up to the April 30 to May 1 occupation, the Clamshell Alliance held workshops on nonviolence and passive resistance in churches and classrooms throughout New England. Those who planned to commit acts of civil disobedience met with members of their affinity groups. The Clamshell

Alliance distributed its "Handbook for Occupiers," which instructed the activist to take food, blankets, and medicine with them. Many occupiers arrived with their lawyers' phone numbers inked onto their hands. Several local Seabrook residents, including the Santasuccis, opened up their land to some five hundred Clams, who congregated and camped out there in preparation for the occupation that would take place the next day. Massachusetts Quakers opened up meeting houses as weigh stations near the New Hampshire border, where a large number of western Massachusetts Clams spent the night before the action. Clamshell activists carpooled and chartered buses that streamed into the Seabrook area, many from greater Boston and western Massachusetts colleges.[62] Some came from Connecticut and Rhode Island, and others came from as far away as New York City. Signs all over the Seabrook area that read, "Welcome Clams" greeted them. The atmosphere was one of excitement and anticipation as the preparations took on the air of a large-scale, nonviolent military campaign. Wasserman told John Kifner, a *New York Times* reporter, "This will be our Bunker Hill—the first serious resistance."[63]

Vince O'Connor drove to Seabrook in a large vehicle with a group of younger college students from Amherst and a pacifist deserter from the Czechoslovakian military who had swum across a river to Austria to defect. O'Connor had attended San Francisco University, a Jesuit school, and had been an organizer for SNCC in Arkansas in the mid-1960s. Later he had become active in the San Francisco War Resisters League, where he got to know Randy Kehler, and sometime after that he had spent eighteen months in prison for refusing to be inducted into the military.

As with many affinity groups that trained and traveled together to Seabrook, a strong esprit de corps developed among the members of O'Connor's group. They shared stories and sang; some of the older, veteran activists shared stories of the U.S. civil rights struggle, and the Czechoslovakian participant told how he had escaped his communist nation. O'Connor warned the younger activists that despite the thorough organizing, situations might be unpredictable: "I told people, 'Look, this could be dangerous: the governor is a nut; the police have guns....' I told them stories of Mississippi about how this one woman said, 'No one should come to the South unless you're prepared to die.' ... You don't want to tell people, 'Don't worry about it; it's completely cool; there's no problem here,' when, in fact, that's not the truth, so I said, 'This could get pretty dangerous.'"[64]

Despite bellicose rhetoric from the governor and fears of official violence, the police hoped to avoid conflict. The Clamshell Alliance members, for their part, sought to establish cordial relations with the local police. Two days before the occupation, Clamshell organizers met with Colonel Paul Doyon, who would be in charge of the police during the occupation, and informed him of their plans. The Clams emphasized to Doyon their intention to maintain complete nonviolence. Relations between the Clamshell and both the police and the New Hampshire National Guard would remain generally peaceful throughout the event.[65]

Two days prior to the occupation, a small delegation of Clams also succeeded in gaining a personal audience with Governor Thomson, who had referred to the Clams as everything from "sexual deviants" to "terrorists." The meeting produced very little, but some members of the delegation believed they saw a slight softening on Thomson's part. Two Clamshell delegates, Cathy Wolff and Robin Read, emerged from the meeting with an upbeat attitude: Read declared, "I think the meeting blew the governor's mind. He suddenly had to confront the fact that we are also human beings, and that we were, in fact, committed to non-violence."[66] Such congeniality would prove short-lived, however, as the governor managed the state response to the occupation in the manner of a general commanding his troops. Meanwhile, the Loeb press went into overdrive villainizing the Clams. One cartoon in the *Manchester Union Leader* depicted an invading army of clams, each with a hammer and sickle on its shell. On April 29, the headline read, "Leftist Groups Hope for Violence."[67]

On the afternoon of April 30, 1977, the Clams converged on the Seabrook site from three main staging areas. Most arrived by land, but some were ferried to the site by local lobstermen, who—believing that the nuclear plants threatened their livelihood—were among the strongest area supporters of the movement. More than two thousand activists—not all of whom stayed to be arrested—and more than two hundred members of the press and media poured onto the site. Colonel Doyon had decided to let the Clams enter the property, instead of blocking them at the periphery, to prevent any violence from spilling onto the streets (especially Route 1, the main highway into Seabrook).[68] Describing the scene sometime later, Wasserman wrote, "There was an air of good feeling and self-assurance among both the police and occupiers that made events seem more like a ballet than a traditional political confrontation."[69]

Robbie Leppzer, a Hampshire College graduate, captured the event in his documentary film *Seabrook 1977*. Leppzer's film shows hundreds upon hundreds of Clam activists peacefully strolling onto the site. Although older, white-haired Quakers (such as Elizabeth Boardman and Frances Crowe) and others who were dressed conventionally are seen, the overwhelmingly countercultural nature of the movement is abundantly clear in the documentary. On first sight, in fact, the footage greatly resembles a scene from Woodstock in 1969. Waves of activists with long hair, tie-died shirts, sandals, and other accoutrements of the counter-culture are seen backpacking onto the site. The occupiers appear determined and in good spirits and display a good deal of camaraderie. By all accounts, the Clamshell Alliance stricture that protestors refrain from bringing any drugs or intoxicants onto the site was respected.[70]

John Kifner of the *New York Times* wrote, "The demonstrators intended to set up a camp site on the grounds modeling their action after a demonstration in western Germany [Wyhl] in which protestors seized a plant site and stopped construction of a nuclear plant."[71] Once on the site, the occupiers dug in, pitching tents, setting up latrines, and creating what amounted to a small village on the Seabrook site, which the Clams took to calling Occupation City. Occupiers clustered with their affinity groups, and several distinct "neighborhoods" took shape.[72]

The police decided that they would allow the occupiers to camp out and would make their arrests the following day (May 1, or "May Day"). The occupation, which was far larger than Governor Thomson had anticipated, was beyond the capacity of the 140 New Hampshire state troopers. On May 1, the governor called up the New Hampshire National Guard, which converged on the Seabrook site, bringing with them scores of buses for the mass arrests.[73] Still, state resources were insufficient. Declaring a state of emergency, Governor Thomson put out a call to all New England governors for police backup. Every New England governor except one complied, dispatching a total of 65 state police to Seabrook. The notable and conspicuous exception was the governor of Massachusetts, Michael Dukakis.

Elected in 1974 as an unabashed liberal reformer, Dukakis was the antithesis of the openly reactionary New Hampshire governor. Each made little secret of the contempt in which he held the other. In response to Governor Thomson's call for police assistance from Massachusetts, Dukakis declared that because there was no threat to public order, he would not send Massachusetts state police to New Hampshire.[74] (In the 1980s, Dukakis would follow suit by refusing to send the Massachusetts National Guard on military maneuvers in Honduras.) Dukakis was no doubt mindful of the numerous Massachusetts activists camped out at Seabrook, whose support he would court in his bid for reelection the following year. Beyond that fact, however, although Dukakis had never advocated dismantling existing nuclear plants in Massachusetts, he had become increasingly unenthusiastic about nuclear energy: "I don't view nuclear as a particularly promising or desirable source of energy for the nation and for New England in the future," he had declared. "Given both the environmental problems and also the cost problems, I don't see much of a future for nuclear in the energy picture for this country. I think alternative sources are where we ought to be moving."[75]

(In the 1980s, the Bay State governor could be credited more than any other single individual for keeping the Seabrook Nuclear Power Station from going on-line.)[76]

As a virtual army of New Hampshire police, National Guard, and police from Maine, Rhode Island, Connecticut, and Vermont amassed outside the nuclear plant site on May 1, Governor Thomson dramatically arrived by helicopter to take charge of his troops, with two American flags protruding prominently from his jacket pocket. At approximately 3:00 p.m., Colonel Doyon walked to the edge of Occupation City and announced over a loud speaker that those who did not immediately vacate the premises would be placed under arrest. After a brief interval to allow the few who chose to do so to leave, the arrests commenced, with some occupiers going limp, as they had been trained at the preoccupation seminars. Most walked to the waiting buses, where they were photographed and identified. As the mass arrests got under way, one occupier played "We Shall Overcome" on a bagpipe.[77] Wasserman described the scene for The Nation: "The arrests proceeded smoothly, if slowly. Piling people onto chartered school buses and into National Guard troop carriers, the patrolmen took more than twelve hours to haul everyone away. Some of the occupiers who had packed up their gear in the afternoon unpacked it again and re-opened their tents to wait through the long hours of the night. Many were not arrested until dawn."[78]

A total of 1,414 Clamshell activists were taken into custody, taxing New Hampshire resources and its infrastructure to the core. The occupiers were transported to National Guard armories at Concord, Manchester, Portsmouth, Dover, and Somersworth. Some of those arrested were held for more than twelve hours on the buses without access to toilets. Many supporters of those who were arrested despaired, as they frantically tried to ascertain where their friends and relatives had been taken. Gyorgy observed, "It was a classic police-state situation. . . . It was like 1,400 people had been 'disappeared' by the state."[79] The situation was chaotic. Many of the arrestees were unable to telephone outside supporters or their attorneys for up to three days. Hundreds went as long as three days without beds.

Meanwhile, Governor Thomson helicoptered back and forth across New Hampshire, from the Seabrook plant site to the armories and to the courts where the first occupiers were being arraigned. Early on, arrestees at some sites were released on personal recognizance; others were released on one hundred dollars' bail. After being apprised of this situation, Thomson helicoptered to the Hampton County District Court and ordered the clerk to put away all personal recognizance forms. Most releases stopped throughout the state.[80] Clearly, Governor Thomson believed that detainment, which few Clams had expected to last more than a few days, would be a deterrent to future actions at Seabrook and would bolster his hard-line law-and-order reputation nationally.

Most of the arrestees ended up spending at least a week in National Guard armories, and almost 1,000 would be held for two weeks. Bail, originally set at one hundred dollars, seemed to rise arbitrarily, first to two hundred dollars and then to five hundred dollars (Thomson wanted bail set at fifteen hundred dollars.) Application of the law was erratic throughout. To divide the movement, the state pursued a policy in which it allowed only New Hampshire residents to be released on personal recognizance; the courts argued that bail was needed to ensure that people from out of state would show up for trial.[81] Those who had already posted a one-hundred-dollar bond were told before they were released that their bail had been increased. One Clam activist exclaimed in exasperation, "At Portsmouth we were told we would be released on personal recognizance. Then it turned into $100. This morning it was $200 and this afternoon it's $500. What's next?"[82]

Lawyers for the Clamshell Alliance charged the state with "punitive detention," arguing that the bail was not only excessive but also unnecessary, since all those who had been arrested at previous Clamshell actions had, in fact, appeared on their court dates. The attorney Emanuel Krasner complained, "It was a travesty. The state violated just about every right in the Constitution."[83] The ACLU soon launched an unsuccessful civil suit against Governor Thomson.[84]

The detained activists at all the armories responded by embarking on a course of "bail solidarity": They collectively refused to post bond and demanded to be released on personal recognizance. Thomson dug in his heels in what the *New York Times* described as a "battle of wills."[85] Gyorgy told one reporter, "It's Meldrim. It's showdown in Meldrimville."[86] The showdown quickly became the focus of national attention, receiving coverage from the major television networks, from *Time* and *Newsweek*, from the major U.S. daily newspapers, and from the international press. To a national audience, Governor Thomson declared, "We are winning the battle of Seabrook."[87] The governor was wrong.

Each day that the Clams were detained resulted in more press and media coverage that became increasingly critical of the governor and sympathetic to the Clams. O'Connor recalled, "Meldrim Thomson was a lunatic, and he played into our hands by arresting us, which was a terrible mistake on his part, because it gave us enormous publicity and created solidarity among people that exists to this day."[88] Moreover, the imprisonment of the activists was costing fifty thousand dollars a day in a state with little tax base. Rumblings of discontent emerged even among New Hampshire residents who were unsympathetic to the Clamshell Alliance. (The Loeb press was a notable exception.)

The commissioners of Rockingham County, whose courts would have to try all those who had been arrested, openly denounced the governor and declared that they not only refused to shoulder the massive legal expenses but also planned to sue the governor if he tried to pass on the costs of the armory detentions to the county. (Further infuriating the frugal New Hampshire voters, the costs of the arrests would soon be compounded by PSNH utility rate increases to pay for the escalating "construction work in progress" costs in Seabrook. This turn of events would cost Meldrim Thomson his bid for reelection in 1978.)[89]

A few days into the detentions, Thomson sought to turn the huge expenses to his advantage by portraying himself as a frontline defense against a radical antinuclear movement that threatened to sweep the country. He put out a national call to "corporations, labor unions and rank-and-file citizens throughout America" to send contributions to defer the huge debt being incurred in New Hampshire. "All Americans should know," declared Thomson, that "our battle of today can become theirs tomorrow."[90] State Attorney General (and future Supreme Court justice) David Souter argued that if the Clams were released, they would immediately reoccupy the site. Wasserman, whom much of the national press now looked to for comment, described the governor's call for contributions as "a cheap publicity stunt" and Souter's fears of reoccupation as "absurd."[91]

Meanwhile, those detained in the armories replicated the communal democracy they had established at Occupation City. Many sang at the site, during their arrest, and at the armories. When decisions needed to be made, the Clams met with their affinity groups, as they had been taught, and passed the group consensus up to elected affinity group representatives. Initially, this system frustrated the police and National Guard, who sought conventional spokespersons. Because men and women were held in common in most of the armories, many romances bloomed there. Guards at the Manchester Armory responded by threatening to segregate the men and women. Because this would have broken up most of the affinity groups, near rebellion broke out at the news.

In an interview with Epstein some years later, Boardman described an instance in which the National Guard pulled her aside and confronted her about the liaisons that were taking place: "It was evidently my role as an older woman to be shocked about this. I said . . . 'If you separate us from our affinity groups, we are not going to be responsible for what hell breaks loose.'"[92] The National Guard relented, with the stipulation that barriers be erected for couples. A move to segregate males and females at the Portsmouth Armory was also abandoned after the detainees all tied their shoelaces together and piled their shoes in the middle of the armory. Other armories, such as Concord, however, followed through with the segregation of men and women.[93] O'Connor recalled that this was something of a joke in the gay- and lesbian-friendly movement: "They separated men and women, but they didn't quite get the idea that might not accomplish their goal of suppressing sexual activities."[94]

Gradually, many Clamshell detainees worked to forge positive relationships with the National Guard and to sound them out about their views on nuclear power. Rennie Cushing, a highly visible local Clam, recalled, "We treated them [the National Guard] like fellow human beings. A lot of the Guard were against the nukes to begin with, and a lot more were against it by the time the occupation was over."[95] The *New York Times* described the relationship between the Clams and the National Guard as "strikingly cordial."[96]

O'Connor recalled one poignant story that occurred in the Concord Armory:

The real dramatic moment was on May 4.... [It was] the anniversary of the killings at Kent State, and so people decided we were gonna hold hands around the armory, circle the armory and have some minutes of silence, ten or fifteen. We did it, and the [National Guard], who were cooking, kept making noises... and the silence just became overpowering. People didn't tell them to "Shish"; we said, "We're doing our thing; we'll let them do what they think is appropriate." And, of course, who killed the people at Kent State but the National Guard? You know, this is who is taking care of us. So finally everything stopped. No one made any noise throughout the last few minutes. It was very remarkable. Then someone sang us out of it with the Holly Near song "It Could Have Been Me."[97]

The intimacy was stronger in smaller armories, such as Concord, than in Manchester, the largest, which held more than six hundred people. O'Connor recalled, "Everyone could know each other [at] Concord.... [I]t had two hundred people in it, and I mean you could know everybody by sight and feel comfortable with them."[98] Beyond meeting with their affinity groups and fraternizing with the National Guard, many Clams held informal seminars on various topics, convened to sing, met in small prayer groups, or read. On the few occasions when the Clams were allowed outside, games of Frisbee, soccer, and jumping on makeshift trampolines passed the time. Talent shows were held in some of the armories.

At Portsmouth, some Clams found and prominently displayed a National Guard sign that read, "As a prisoner I will keep faith with my fellow prisoners."[99] O'Connor commented, "Jails are the university of the revolution; you just created four universities at Manchester, Concord, Dover, etc."[100] Many Clams would later remember this time as the golden age of the Clamshell Alliance, a time of euphoria and solidarity that would be sorely missed a year later when the group factionalized. O'Connor observed, "The atmosphere in the Concord Armory was so good that people stayed there instead of going back to school, like 'This is the first place in the real world I feel comfortable outside my family.'"[101]

Many attributed the spirit of mutuality and unity to what the Clam activist Richard Asinof (writing for the *Valley Advocate*) described as "the strong impact that women in key leadership roles exerted on the events."[102] By 1977, the role of women had greatly evolved from the earlier campaign against the Montague plant, in which Mary Wentworth later described herself as a "feminist in a movement that wasn't feminist."[103] According to Wentworth, "Many men simply learned to accommodate the women's movement by paying lip service to it, but had not changed their underlying attitudes toward women. . . . Too many men still dropped out mentally when one of us began to talk, waiting until we finished so they could get on with 'their' meeting." Wentworth described being disappointed by some women on the Montague Farm, who, in her view, "preferred not to ruffle any of the roosters' feathers."[104]

By 1977, women were redefining the antinuclear movement. Elizabeth Boardman, Suki Rice, and Anna Gyorgy were among the leading women who were working for the cause. Cathy Wolff became co-spokesperson for the movement. Although Wolff found that, at first, the reporters (who were predominantly male) instinctively sought out Harvey Wasserman, she asserted herself and began to take on a more visible role. According to Wolff, the good feelings and unity among the Clams were largely thanks to the role that women played in forging a politics that departed from the machismo of the late 1960s antiwar movement. "Women have been important in holding the Clamshell together between actions," she noted. Women helped the movement transcend male egotism, what Wolff called the "my dog's bigger than your dog" syndrome. "That tone is set when you must be competitive. Women have helped the men get over this hurdle in the movement."[105] Describing this woman-directed movement, Asinof wrote of the plans for the occupation: "There was very little ego battling in the decision-making bodies, hardly any of the typical behavior associated with academics, bureaucrats and radical groups, of people speaking just to listen to themselves talk. When Sam Lovejoy started monopolizing the phone and information at Clamshell headquarters, he was quickly banished for the next day at the Portsmouth office."[106]

Clamshell women further sought to make the connections between the antinuclear movement and feminism. At one Clam gathering, Anna Gyorgy and Nesta King, a doctoral candidate in feminism and ecology, conducted a seminar on women and energy, which they described in the program as follows: "The connections between feminism and stopping nuclear power. Why the issue is relevant to women. Nuclear power as a manifestation of male domination and exploitation of the earth. Women's concerns as bearers of future generations."[107]

Despite the high spirits and camaraderie between men and women in the armories, concerns arose. As the detentions dragged on, lawyers for the Clamshell Alliance worried aloud about health conditions. They took their case for release to federal court, where they described the armories as "ideal for transmission of epidemic diseases." The effort failed. A slow stream of Clam activists trickled out of the armories, as some decided to pay their bail so that they could return to their jobs or to college final examinations. By May 10, however, the New Hampshire armories still held 737 Clamshell detainees.[108]

Finally, after two weeks of detention, Carlton Eldridge, the Rockingham County prosecutor, entered into negotiations with the remaining detained Clamshell activists. Eldridge offered to release the Clamshell detainees on personal recognizance in exchange for an agreement to hold mass trials (which would save the county enormous expense). Breaking into their affinity groups, the detainees at the Somersworth, Dover, and Portsmouth Armories accepted the deal; however, objections arose at the Manchester and Concord Armories, forcing the Clams and Eldridge back into negotiation. The dissenting Clams demanded that some of the detainees receive public trials and at least one jury trial (the purpose was to allow the Clams to attempt to put nuclear energy on trial in a public forum as Sam Lovejoy had done in western Massachusetts). They also demanded refunds for those who had already bailed out.

With the prolonged detentions causing national embarrassment for the state and with the spiraling costs of the mass detainment, Eldridge agreed to most of the Clamshell demands, and on May 13 the detained Clams approved the deal. The processing and release of the last 541 detained Clams went on throughout the night, taking more than fourteen hours, but by May 14 (two weeks after the occupation had begun), all Clamshell occupiers were free.[109] Commenting on the agreement, the Clam negotiator Charles Light declared, "I guess the weight of all those people was just too much for the state to carry."[110] O'Connor observed, "The meter was running, [and] they just couldn't handle the bills."[111]

Six months later, in November 1977, the public trials that the Clams had demanded commenced in Rockingham County Superior Court. According to the agreement, sixty-four Clam activists were to have public trials. Twenty-six-year-old Carter Wentworth, an artist from Kensington (not far from Seabrook), was the focus of the jury trial. Wentworth was represented by the Boston attorney Eric Blumenson. On Wentworth's behalf, Blumenson announced that he would employ a "competing harms" defense similar to the "necessity defense" used by Lovejoy in 1974. As in Lovejoy's trial, the defense stated that it would call experts on nuclear energy and civil disobedience, such as Dr. Helen Caldicott and the Boston University historian Howard Zinn, in order to "put the nuclear industry on trial." The presiding Judge, Wayne Mullavey, denied both motions.[112]

Wentworth sought to persuade the jury that it had been necessary to occupy the site in order to protect others from the potential harm of nuclear energy: "I went to Seabrook to protect my life and my neighbors' lives. . . . I was acting under the freedoms given to us in our Constitution and the Declaration of Independence."[113] With instructions from Judge Mullavey to disregard the "competing harms" defense, the jury found Wentworth guilty. The county prosecutor asked the judge to pass down a sentence of fifteen days and a fine of one hundred dollars. Surprising even the prosecution, Judge Mullavey sentenced Wentworth to four months in prison. Describing the occupation of April 30 as a "mob action" and mindful that Clamshell was planning another occupation in the spring of 1978, Mullavey proclaimed, "This is one of the few cases since I've been on the bench in which sentencing may serve as a deterrent to future crimes of this type."[114]

As the other public trials plodded along, similar sentences of three to four months—far longer than most sentences imposed by New Hampshire courts for "criminal trespass"—were meted out. Meanwhile, the mass trials of the vast majority of the occupiers, which had been agreed to in the May 13 accord, were delayed so long that charges were eventually dropped. Some speculated that the disproportionate sentencing, like the early distinctions made between New Hampshire and out-of-state Clams, was intended to drive a wedge into the movement.[115]

In mid-May 1977, however, the Clamshell Alliance had no knowledge of the harsh sentences that lay ahead for a fraction of the occupiers. Upon the release of the last detainees, the mood was euphoric, and Clamshell activists felt an increasing sense of momentum. Within the short space of one year, the Clamshell Alliance had indeed grown dramatically. By generating a great deal of national press and media coverage—much of it sympathetic—the April-May action had successfully linked nuclear power at Seabrook with a growing nuclear debate nationally. (Even so, many Clams complained that much of the press and media coverage focused on the arrests and detainments, ignoring the underlying dangers of nuclear energy that had prompted so many to risk so much by occupying the Seabrook site.)

The direct action militancy of the Clamshell Alliance now became a model for new antinuclear groups—such as the Abalone Alliance (California), the Palmetto Alliance (South Carolina), the Oyster Shell Alliance (Louisiana), the Crabshell Alliance (Washington), and the Conch Shell Alliance (Florida)—which began to emerge around the country.[116] With the immense publicity and growing sense of momentum that the Clamshell Alliance had achieved, few doubted that the organization would continue its exponential growth. Looking ahead, Wasserman wrote, "Now, in the wake of its third tenfold increase in size, the alliance faces a critical period. Direct-action environmentalism has clearly accelerated from a small assembly of local groups to a full-scale movement, and with that must inevitably come all the growing pains of factionalism and organizational strain."[117]

In 1978 Wasserman's forecast would prove far more accurate than he had realized, as the Clamshell Alliance became increasingly divided over goals and strategy. Two major factions emerged: the Soft Clams and the smaller, more militant Hard Clams. Before the Clamshell Alliance had to deal with the dissension within its own ranks, however, it had to brace itself for a major pronuclear counteroffensive.

CORPORATE-LABOR PRONUCLEAR COUNTEROFFENSIVE

In the fall 1976 elections, environmental activists had put antinuclear initiatives on the ballot in six states. The initiatives did not seek to ban nuclear energy outright; rather, they sought to establish requirements for nuclear waste disposal, added safety requirements, or the empowerment of state legislatures to regulate the nuclear industry. Many of these ballot initiatives were complex; all were geared toward putting significant brakes on the growth of the nuclear industry. Most contested was Proposition 15 in the state of California, which sought to give the California legislature wide-ranging power to set standards for the nuclear industry or even impose a nuclear moratorium. Environmentalists working for the California campaign, like those working for many ballot initiatives that year, were heavily outspent by the nuclear industry. Taking advantage of the complexity of the initiative, the nuclear industry urged voters, "If you're confused, vote no."[118]

What ultimately worked best to defeat the ballot initiative, however, was a massive pronuclear campaign run by organized labor in close coordination with the nuclear industry. Organized labor fanned out across California, making arguments similar to those made by George O'Brien in the 1974 western Massachusetts referenda debate. When the California antinuclear initiative was defeated, a representative for the California Public Service Electric and Gas Company (PSE&G) gave most of the credit to California workers: "The very fact of the visibility of neighborhood campaign workers in so many communities acted as an offset to the 'it's the little people vs. the giant corporations' argument being used by the proponents [of the antinuclear initiative]."[119]

In New England the corporate-labor alliance was once again mobilized, this time against the Clamshell Alliance. The New Hampshire PSNH, the largest shareholder in the Seabrook nuclear project, organized a putative citizens' group called New Hampshire Voice of Energy, which (although largely funded by the utility company) sought to put organized labor front and center. O'Brien and scores of New England labor leaders attended a Northeast Nuclear Advocates Workshop in early 1977, where attendees were instructed how to make the case for nuclear power in television interviews and debates: "When asked a tough question, ask, 'Are you sure of your facts?'"; "Try to end on an upbeat note"; "Never apologize on the air."[120]

As the Seabrook struggle heated up, O'Brien again took up the pronuclear cause. At a locally televised debate at Hampshire College in western Massachusetts, he sought to highlight what he saw as the hypocrisy of the Clamshell Alliance: "How many gallons of fuel were wasted on the trip to Seabrook to protest and demonstrate? Surely, everyone didn't walk to Seabrook. How much fuel was used to light the armories and courtrooms in Manchester? How much fuel was used to police and transport the demonstrators from Seabrook to Manchester? Who's kidding who when they urge conservation of fuel?"[121]

A few weeks after the last Seabrook detainees were released, New Hampshire Voice of Energy staged what Wasserman described as "the nation's largest pro-nuclear rally."[122] More than three thousand workers from New England and some from as far south as Philadelphia and New Jersey held a boisterous rally for nuclear power in the Manchester John F. Kennedy Arena. Many took up the chant, "Nukes! Nukes! Nukes!"; others held banners that read, "Nuclear Power: The Pollution Solution" and "Nuclear Power: Safer than Sex." Many in attendance wore hardhats as they listened to Governor Thomson praise them as "good Americans [who] came together, obeyed the law, and made [their] point." Continuing his approbation, Thomson told them, "You're much better than what I saw May first. By comparison, you're beautiful."[123]

Also speaking was Norman Rasmussen, a Massachusetts Institute of Technology (MIT) professor, who had conducted a report for the Atomic Energy Commission in the early 1970s, which had concluded that the likelihood of a nuclear catastrophe was negligible (the report was hotly contested by other, more skeptical scientists). To cheers, Rasmussen denounced Clamshell activists as "irrational and illogical." The conservative Massachusetts Democrat Ed King (soon to defeat Michael Dukakis in his bid for renomination in the 1978 Democratic gubernatorial primary) proclaimed, "This really is the death struggle against the no-growth advocates."[124] Looking back, Wasserman observed, "The demonstration underscored ongoing support for the Seabrook project, and further reminded antinuclear organizers of the urgency of building ties with the union movement."[125]

Wasserman joined a growing number of national environmentalists who worked to forge ties between the antinuclear movement and organized labor. He became active in Environmentalists for Full Employment—which sought to mobilize environmentalists behind labor actions, such as Full Employment Week—and he won the support of some unions for the prosolar Sun Day celebrations in 1978.[126] The Clamshell Alliance had also worked to win support from labor. In a Clamshell newsletter titled "Workers, Energy, and Jobs," the Clams quoted the United Auto Workers (UAW) representative Leo Goodman, who had campaigned against a Detroit nuclear plant in the 1950s and continued to oppose nuclear energy in the 1970s: "There is no ecology-job conflict. We must have a common goal to improve the quality of life. It is our right, not a privilege, to have meaningful, safe and healthy jobs."[127] The newsletter also declared, "If ALL Federal buildings were required to use solar and conservation methods (400,000 federal buildings), look at all the jobs that would be created. WOULDN'T WORKERS AND UNIONS SUPPORT THAT?"[128]

In the late 1970s, antinuclear activists succeeded in forging some alliances with labor. Sheet metal workers were enthusiastic about the prospects for solar energy, and more socially activist unions—such as the UAW and the Oil, Chemical, and Atomic Workers Union—forged tenuous ties with the antinuclear movement. These alliances were, however, the exception. At its 1976 convention, the American Federation of Labor and Congress of Industrial Organizations (AFL-CIO) endorsed a strongly pronuclear platform and throughout the 1970s continued to work strenuously to hasten the construction of nuclear plants.[129]

CRACKS IN THE CLAMSHELL:
THE DEBATE OVER A FOURTH OCCUPATION

The spring 1977 occupation had catapulted the Clamshell Alliance into the national spotlight and had made the Seabrook nuclear plant a symbol of the growing national nuclear debate. In the months after the occupation, new recruits from throughout New England poured into the Clamshell Alliance. As the Clamshell Alliance sought to absorb the mass influx, it continued to hold legal demonstrations and prepare for the trials of those who had been arrested at the April–May action. Until the spring of 1977, the Clamshell Alliance predominantly comprised like-minded members, and the slow consensus process plodded along smoothly. During the winter of 1977 to 1978, however, as the Clams planned for a fourth occupation for the coming spring, tensions were growing from both without and within the Alliance.

By the winter of 1977, the Clams had increasingly found themselves entering a siege mentality. Numerous worrisome reports came to the fore: police infiltration, double-ringing telephones (indicating phone taps), and mysterious vehicles parked outside Clam meeting places (which would pull out when approached and which had license plates that turned out to be untraceable).[130] Local Seabrook supporters of the Clamshell Alliance complained of property tax increases disproportionate to those of their neighbors and growing zoning problems. Tony Santasucci and at least one other local Clam supporter complained of low-flying helicopters buzzing over their homes.[131] Compounding the sense of siege was increasingly bellicose rhetoric from Governor Thomson, which made some in the movement fear that he intended to turn Seabrook into another Chicago 1968 if the Clams went ahead with a fourth occupation. The potential for violence had escalated now that PSNH had fenced in most of the Seabrook nuclear construction site. Because the Clamshell Alliance had worked so hard to cultivate cordial relations with law enforcement, the prospects of violent confrontations with the police and National Guard were unnerving.

The biggest problems for the Clamshell Alliance, however, came from within. Some members seemed more interested in the movement for its sense of community and as a vehicle for their nonviolent beliefs than for putting a stop to the construction of the Seabrook plant. These Clams, who seemed more attracted to the form of the movement than to its substance, often downplayed the importance of pragmatic tactical questions. O'Connor observed a cleavage between the leadership and the rank and file: "People had been through enough organizations that they knew how organizations worked and they . . . were [there to] to accomplish goals; for some people, the first time around they're a way to express who you are."[132] Was nonviolence a lifestyle or a tactic? In his comparative study of the U.S. and West German antinuclear movements, Christian Joppke wrote that for these Clams, "opposing nuclear power was only the negative folio against which the movement project of empowerment and community building unfolded."[133]

More worrisome than those who saw the movement as a way of life were those who entered the movement as a way to launch a full frontal assault on the capitalist state. Several small but highly organized and ideologically committed anarchist organizations joined the Clamshell Alliance and turned their affinity groups into platforms for more militant action against the Seabrook plant. The anarchist groups were based mostly in Cambridge, particularly MIT, but enjoyed support from some of the more radical antinuclear activists in Vermont and elsewhere. Black Rose and Hard Rain, among others—who introduced a sectarian style into the Boston Clamshell Alliance that was alien to the early spirit of the organization—believed that the Clamshell Alliance must embrace a more openly radical critique of the corporate state and adopt more militant strategies to shut down the Seabrook plant.

The anarchist groups were the most visible of the members who now called themselves Hard Clams or the Action Faction. These Clams had nothing but contempt for what they saw as a bourgeois fetishism for symbolic nonviolence in the movement, which they believed alienated the predominantly white, middle-class movement from the working class. The Hard Clams argued vociferously that rather than occupy the Seabrook site to generate publicity and elevate the national debate on nuclear power, the movement must, following the European example, move to make it physically impossible for the plant to go on-line. Black Rose, Hard Rain, and the other Hard Clams that they appealed to sought to radical-ize the Clamshell in much the same way that Students for a Democratic Society (SDS) had worked to radicalize the antiwar movement in the late 1960s and West German leftists were working to radicalize the antinuclear movement across the Atlantic.[134]

The influx of these new groups dramatically altered the dynamics of the Clamshell Alliance, making consensus increasingly difficult as the Clams planned the fourth occupation. One question now became the fulcrum on which the divisions in the Clamshell Alliance pivoted: Since the Seabrook site was fenced in, should the Clams cut the fence to gain entrance to the site? From its inception, Clamshell had stated that destruction of property was inconsistent with nonviolence. Some Clams stuck rigidly to this principle and declared that they would take no part in fence cutting. Others, who supported Lovejoy's tower toppling in Montague, believed that fence cutting differed from the nighttime tower toppling, because it would lead to a direct confrontation with police.[135]

The Hard Clams' call for fence cutting and forced entry onto the construction site put the Clamshell Alliance on a collision course with a state government prepared to marshal all its resources and a governor who openly refused to rule out lethal force. Governor Thomson still smarted from the 1977 occupation that had cost the state fifty thousand dollars a day and had generated widespread sympathy for the Clamshell Alliance. Now the Clams threatened to compound the cost to the state by scheduling the late June occupation for the kickoff of the summer tourist season. Thomas Rath, the attorney general for New Hampshire, argued that the line had to be drawn. Sighing, "Seabrook is becoming the spring thing to do," Rath threatened the use of Special Weapons and Tactics (SWAT) police.[136] SWAT units, which had been created in the late 1960s to combat revolutionary left-ists, had fallen out of popularity until 1977, when (according to one SWAT team member) they were "being reactivated because of growing fear that our country may be subject to terrorist organizations and Seabrook-like demonstrations."[137]

Carlton Eldridge, the Rockingham County district attorney, went even further: "Let's just say that we will make their visit to our county as uncomfortable as possible.... The governor has said the same thing. We will use whatever force options we have, from nothing to bullets. Non-violent arrests aren't the only thing in our arsenal. How far are we willing to go? Far."[138] The governor threatened the use of fire hoses and dogs and declared that he was willing to close the Massachusetts–New Hampshire border and declare martial law. "I have never used this power before and I hope I don't have to use it for this demonstration," warned Thomson.[139] Beyond threats by the state were threats of violence by private right-wing groups in New Hampshire. At one small but vociferous anti-Clam rally, pronuclear protestors held signs that read, "Clams Should Be Steamed and Not Heard" and "Clamshell Alliance Are a Bunch of Jewish-Communist Hypocrite Stooges."[140]

With the militancy of the Hard Clams and preparations for martial law by the state threatening to turn their hometown into a war zone, local sympathizers of the Clamshell Alliance began to withdraw their support (including use of their property as staging grounds) for the occupation. Since many in the movement believed that beyond conferring legitimacy on the Clamshell Alliance, local support was crucial logistically, they viewed any acts (such as fence cutting and forced occupation) that jeopardized that support as anathema.[141]

At Boston Clamshell meetings, Black Rose and Hard Rain continued to argue strenuously for fence cutting and en masse occupation of the site, tactics that had been used extensively in the European antinuclear movement. Nonviolent purists were aghast, and many rank-and-file Clams were overwhelmed by the Hard Clams stridency and use of anarchist theory. Those who had lived through the 1960s recalled how small sectarian groups such as the Maoist Progressive Labor had mired down SDS in never-ending sectarian debate. Wasserman described the heated Boston Clam meetings for WIN, a radical pacifist magazine associated with the War Resisters League: "In Boston ... unanimity became impossible. A small but dedicated faction within the Clamshell there found it necessary to continually block consensus on basic issues of non-violence, advocating cutting of fences and prolonging debate over basic guidelines of occupation behavior to the point where meaningful political action became virtually impossible.... It did not take long for Boston meetings to degenerate into unpleasant and unproductive debating matches, which debilitated much of Boston's organizing."[142]

Although Wasserman's description spoke for many (perhaps a majority) of Clams, the Boston-based anarchists' arguments struck a chord with other Clams, especially the farther from Seabrook they were. Many out-of-state Clams were anxious to occupy the site and believed that the core, unofficial leadership, the Soft Clams, was steering the movement into safe, mainstream waters. Charges of "sell out" and "lack of democracy" were heard at local Clam meetings outside the militants' Boston base. Many who resented the high public profiles of Wasserman, Gyorgy, Lovejoy, Wolff, and New Hampshire Clams such as Cushing and Chichester charged them with "star tripping."[143] Although few Hard Clams outside Boston subscribed to anarchist principles, the militancy and charges of movement elitism by Hard Rain and Black Rose rang true for a growing number of Clam activists.[144]

It was in this tense atmosphere that the New Hampshire attorney general, Thomas Rath (who had recently replaced David Souter), astutely handed the Clamshell Alliance an offer that would exacerbate the divisions to the breaking point. Rath approached the thirteen-member Clamshell Coordinating Committee with an offer to allow the Clams to hold a legal three-day rally on eighteen acres of property on the Seabrook site. The only conditions were that the Clams must promise to leave the site at the designated time and engage in no illegal actions. Many believed that the offer was meant to be rejected to make the Clams appear obstinate and to make the state and PSNH appear reasonable by comparison. Although the conservative *Manchester Union Leader* denounced the deal as a "capitulationist" compromise with the Clamshell Alliance, Governor Thomson and PSNH supported the proposal.[145]

"The offer hit the Clamshell like a thunderbolt," Wasserman wrote sometime later. "The Rath proposal was clearly an attempt at cooptation.... Polarization within the Alliance soared sky-high."[146] Soft Clams argued that acceptance of the proposal would neutralize Thomson's and the Loeb press's depiction of the Clams as a militant fringe and afford the Clams an opportunity to stage a legal event in which the antinuclear silent majority, the so-called Closet Clams, would come out into the open. Hard Clams shot back that the governor and PSNH would never make such an offer if it did not serve their interests, that it was an effort to bottle up the growing militancy of the antinuclear movement, and that acceptance would be a blatant sellout.[147]

Because the offer was made only a few weeks before the planned June occupation and at a time when the Clamshell Alliance had little hope of reaching a consensus on how to occupy the site, a response had to come quickly. The Clamshell Coordinating Committee replied with a series of demands for safety requirements and plans for nuclear disposal, which, if accepted, would have, in effect, shut down the plants. Rath rejected these counterproposals. With time running out, the committee accepted Rath's proposal without sending the question down through the "spokes" to the Clamshell affinity groups for approval. The committee announced, "The Clamshell has decided to hold a completely legal action and to not transgress the fenced in construction area. Anyone who does so is not a member of the Clamshell Alliance."[148] To make such a unilateral decision was virtual heresy in an organization that had always worked by consensus and claimed to run without leaders. The deal was reported in the press before the committee had time to notify local Clam chapters, making it a fait accompli and compounding the outrage.[149]

Acceptance of the Rath proposal set off a storm within the Clamshell. Members denounced the committee members as sellouts and accused them of betrayal, subversion of process, and elitism. Harvey Halpern, an outspoken representative of the Boston Hard Clams, called a legal rally "an ineffective symbolic act." He added, "I have nothing against legal rallies, but we can't stop there. I would like to have direct action rather than moral witness."[150] Boston Hard Clams announced the formation of Clams for Democracy and talked openly of carrying out civil disobedience on their own at the legal rally. Others begrudgingly accepted the deal. Of the Clams who pointed out the positive side of the deal, few were convincing or enthusiastic.

In the maelstrom that followed acceptance of the Rath proposal, the fault lines that had been growing in the Clamshell Alliance became clearer. Many discerned a Seabrook–western Massachusetts alliance that advocated the agreement, with Boston Clams divided and most other out-of-state Clams decidedly against the deal. Supporters defended the agreement as necessary to maintain the local base of the Clams and as an opportunity for outreach to the presumed legions of Closet Clams. Detractors replied that locals should not be given a special veto within the Clamshell, since a nuclear catastrophe at Seabrook would affect much of the region and since Seabrook had become a national symbol of nuclear power.[151]

Epstein has argued that the divisions took on the dimensions of a "rural vs. urban" dichotomy: "Many Clamshell activists in northern New England believed that the rural roots of the movement mattered most, that what went on in Boston should not be given undue weight. The view circulated among the rural people (most of whom had recently fled the cities themselves) that the behavior of the Hard Rain people could be put down to urban stress: city life drives people crazy."[152] Singling out the activists from the Montague Farm as representative of this tendency, Epstein states, "If any social form was privileged in the movement it was the collective. The influence of the Montague Farm people was enhanced by the fact that they represented a rural commune."[153] For Hard Clams, however, this was unacceptable; many referred to activists such as Gyorgy, Lovejoy, and Wasserman as the "Montague Farm Gang" or the "Montague Farm Mafia."[154] The divisions between urban militants and countercultural rural activists, which hearkened back to the fissures that had shot through the Liberation News Service in 1968, were a far cry from the harmony, unity, and good feelings of the 1977 occupation.

Throughout 1977 and 1978, Wasserman had been not only the foremost chronicler of but also an official spokesperson for the Clamshell movement. During their coverage of the Seabrook saga, the *New York Times* and the *Boston Globe* had repeatedly sought out Wasserman for comment, frequently juxtaposing his replies with responses from Governor Thomson. In almost all of Wasserman's articles and interviews, he dealt openly with challenges that faced the Clamshell Alliance and divisions in the movement. A notably different tone emerges in Wasserman's piece for *WIN* magazine in June 1978. In an uncharacteristically partisan tone, Wasserman denounced Black Rose and Hard Rain as "a small but persistent minority bent on blocking unanimity without compromise" and practitioners of "minority tyranny."[155]

Wasserman insinuated that the Boston groups were agent provocateurs: "Such infiltration could serve at least two purposes—it could provide police with a constant supply of information, and it could also serve to disrupt the organization from within . . . and promote violence."[156] Lovejoy told a reporter, "It's absolutely true that this organization is paranoid. I've seen some new faces who were pretty suspicious-looking to me."[157] For Hard Clams, in turn, Wasserman and his associates were suspect. Halpern called Jim Garrison, one of the Clam architects of the agreement, "a psychotic liar or a police agent."[158]

As infighting spread through the Clamshell ranks, both Hard and Soft Clams invoked the experience of the much larger European antinuclear movement. For Halpern, the European antinuclear activists had made fence cutting an art form, which Americans would be wise to emulate. Furthermore, the key to the success at Wyhl was the sheer number of participants in the occupation, something that the Clamshell Alliance was now in a position to replicate.[159] For Wasserman, the lessons of Wyhl were different: "The three to four thousand trained occupiers on which the [Clamshell] Alliance knew it could count might have been able to move in from Massachusetts and Maine. But that was contrary to the founding principles that, as at Wyhl, Germany, actions must spring from the local community. No land, no local support—no occupation."[160]

The decision of the Clamshell Coordinating Committee left negative feelings, recriminations, and second-guessing that would last for years. On the twenty-fifth anniversary of the formation of the Clamshell Alliance, Cathy Wolff, a Soft Clam, looked back, still torn: "Perhaps we should have forged ahead with the occupation."[161] In a 1981 interview, Wasserman reflected, "For whatever reason . . . people in New Hampshire decided that politically it was acceptable to break the law, but it was not right to destroy property. Now in Massachusetts it might have been different, I think it would have been different."[162] Ultimately, the decision sapped much of the militancy of the Clamshell Alliance, left significant demoralization in its wake, and depleted the movement of its momentum, which had been its strength.

Had the Clams attempted to enter the Seabrook site by force, however, there is little doubt that the situation would have gotten rough. Governor Thomson was determined to avoid another illegal occupation and had made clear his willingness to use force to do so. A violent confrontation would have altered the nonviolent image of both the Clamshell Alliance and the national antinuclear movement at the time. In West Germany, radical leftists in the antinuclear movement waged furious street battles with riot police, squandering much of the good will that the movement had gained with the West German public after the peaceful mass occupation of Wyhl in 1975.[163] Wasserman described the damned-if-you-do-damned-if-you-don't scenario that faced the Clamshell Alliance: "They made us a middle-ground offer that became very hard to refuse. If we refused a peaceful solution, we'd appear unreasonable and lose the credibility we gained last year. If we accepted, it would look like we were growing soft. It was very well calculated to split the alliance and it succeeded."[164]

THE SEABROOK ALTERNATIVE ENERGY FAIR: JUNE 23–26, 1978

The negative fallout from the Clamshell Alliance decision to accept the Rath proposal obscured some of the positive features of the mid-June legal occupation. With very little time to organize, the Clamshell Alliance was able to put together a three-and-a-half-day event, which was attended by more than twenty thousand people. Approximately six thousand Clams camped out on the site during the event, many acting as "peace marshals" and directing the massive influx of traffic. At the fair held Saturday, June 24, were numerous alternative energy exhibitions, including solar energy collectors, solar ovens, windmills, and geodesic domes. Numerous informational tables were stocked with literature that discussed the dangers of nuclear power and the potential of conservation and alternative energy.[165]

By 1978, the national antinuclear movement was placing added emphasis on conservation and alternatives to coal, oil, and nuclear energy. This effort was, in large measure, a result of the 1976 state referenda campaigns, during which antinuclear activists had concluded that their message must put forth energy alternatives more forcefully. Many concluded that the "jobs vs. the environment" framework of the nuclear debates in the 1976 referenda campaigns had worked to the detriment of the antinuclear movement.[166] A further impetus came with Amory Lovins's 1976 work, *Soft Energy Paths*, in which the respected scientist outlined a new "soft" model of energy production and use that would not only diminish dependence on oil, coal, and nuclear energy but also take energy production out of the hands of huge multinational corporations and disperse it in a decentralized and democratic manner throughout the United States. Lovins's vision of locally controlled energy had great appeal to antinuclear groups such as the Clamshell Alliance, which so highly valued grassroots democracy.[167]

The Alternative Energy Fair offered the Clamshell Alliance an opportunity to showcase soft energy and its potential. Despite the absence of a confrontation between the Clams and the state, the event received a good deal of friendly press and media coverage. The fact that it had the feel of a county fair more than a political rally contributed to the huge crowds of local Seabrook and other New Hampshire residents that attended. Some were the much ballyhooed Closet Clams; others were merely curious. Nevertheless, the Alternative Energy Fair afforded the Clamshell Alliance an opportunity to communicate with many people who would have been deterred by the prospect of a confrontation. Adding to the festive atmosphere were musical performances and speeches on Sunday, June 25, by nationally known performers, including Pete Seeger, Arlo Guthrie, and Jackson Browne. The Sunday rally included speakers such as Dr. John Gofman, who had testified on behalf of Sam Lovejoy in 1974; Dick Gregory, the civil rights veteran and comedian; and Dr. Benjamin Spock, the renowned pediatrician and antiwar activist. Some of the speakers became involved in the Hard Clam/Soft Clam dispute. Dick Gregory told a reporter for the *Boston Globe* that he was shocked to hear about the deal with the state and had second thoughts about attending.[168] In a one-on-one encounter with Halpern, a Hard Clam, Spock said, "If enough people show their opposition to nuclear power, whichever way they do it, it doesn't matter."[169]

As New Hampshire locals milled around information tables and involved themselves with interactive exhibits, Hard Clams—mainly from Boston and western Massachusetts colleges—organized, as Clams for Democracy circulated through the crowd handing out literature that called for another mass occupation of the Seabrook site. One Clams for Democracy flier read, "A large number of people have experienced dissatisfaction with the shallowness of political debate within the Clamshell. The leadership's private dealings with the state in recent weeks ha[ve] aggravated the situation, creating doubts about the Alliance's ability or desire to stop nuclear power through direct action.... How can we mobilize ourselves in solidarity AGAINST the state?"[170]

Some discussed remaining on the site after the hour designated for departure, but no occupation materialized.[171] In an interview for the *New York Times*, Wasserman tried to put the best possible face on the fair: "This demonstration brought out the closet Clams. The vast majority of the people who came here

Sunday were local people who have had doubts about the Clams in the past. I've always thought we'd stop this plant, but at times I've been weary. Now I'm sure."[172]

Cushing reiterated the sentiment: "There are even more closet Clams than we thought."[173] There was a good deal of evidence to support this. The *Boston Globe* noted the large number of families with children at the event. Paul and Shirley Trabucco, of Kensington, New Hampshire, who fit this category, commented, "We're not members of any group. We just believe nuclear power should be stopped. What are you going to do with all that radioactive waste? It's not much of a legacy to leave our kids."[174] Halpern's verdict was much different. He described the event as merely a way "for a few people to play out their frustrations. It's strictly symbolic, not a Clamshell action, and without political effect."[175]

Meanwhile at Manchester, Governor Thomson attended a pronuclear rally and "clambake," during which he declared the Clamshell Alliance to be "regenerated and rehabilitated."[176] Asked if the poor attendance (five hundred people) at his pronuclear rally was a sign of growing doubts about nuclear power, the governor explained that the low turnout was "because supporters of nuclear power are working people." Overall, however, Thomson, who symbolized his sense of victory over the Clamshell Alliance with his "clam bake," acted triumphant. He told one reporter, "I'm going to eat some clams."[177] When the Alternative Energy Fair was complete, Thomson declared victory, gloating in a manner that most certainly rankled those who had decided to accept the Rath proposal: "At no time was there one minute construction time lost by workers, and at no time was any portion of construction halted as a result of either direct or indirect actions by demonstrators. The Clamshell Alliance therefore has experienced what must be to them a very distinct and humiliating defeat."[178]

CLAMS FOR DIRECT ACTION TAKE THE INITIATIVE: THE OCTOBER 6–9, 1979, SIEGE

A new organization, Clams for Direct Action at Seabrook (CDAS) grew out of the 1978 Clams for Democracy movement. Halpern was the driving force and public spokesperson for the new group, which was determined to move on its own and carry out the militant action that its members had envisioned for June 1978. The organization had a large student base from western Massachusetts, Boston, and Rhode Island colleges and universities and enjoyed support from the International Socialist Organization (or ISO, a Trotskyist splinter group) and Boston's Haymarket Fund (an anarchist organization). The *Boston Herald American* wrote, "The Coalition for Direct Action at Seabrook is the black sheep of the Clamshell Alliance."[179]

CDAS announced plans for a forced occupation of the Seabrook site to take place on October 6, 1979. A CDAS pamphlet declared, "By direct action, we mean acting to stop nuclear power ourselves, without appealing to or recognizing the legitimacy of the state or corporate authority.... We will be seriously challenging the authority of the state."[180] Another flier announced that the group would cut fences to gain entrance to the site and then "actively resist arrest" by running, linking arms, and erecting barricades. "Once on the site," the pamphlet continued, "we plan to build a community of people living cooperatively with the goal of preventing construction from continuing. We plan to stay until construction is irrevocably canceled."[181]

Like the original founders of the Clamshell Alliance, the CDAS laid claim to the mantle of legitimacy by comparing its planned occupation to the West German occupation at Wyhl. In one flier by an affiliated group, the Student Coalition against Nukes Nationwide (SCANN), the October 6 organizers declared, "The occupation of Seabrook has the potential to stop its construction permanently. Five years ago, West Germans occupied a nuclear plant site in Wyhl. To date there has been no construction."[182] In the CDAS October 6 handbook, "Let's Shut Down Seabrook!" the group stated, "The people at ... Wyhl found that they could only depend on themselves to make the fundamental changes needed to protect their health and safety."[183] Critics pointed out, however, that the Wyhl occupation had depended on local support, which the October 6 occupation could not count on.[184]

The Seacoast New Hampshire Clamshell put out a statement opposing the October 6 occupation, arguing that it not only ignored the "present political and economic climate of the state" but also promised to unleash state violence that would hurt the local movement. The public letter declared, "We state this as our formal position because, unlike others who may, if they choose to, ignore the action, whatever happens on October 6 will have a direct effect on our lives, our future organizing and our relation to our neighbors. The CDAS proposal is like an electric fan—if we get in front of it, we get blown over, if we get behind it, we get sucked in. We have chosen to stand to the side."[185]

CDAS responded that it was not CDAS members but the folks at PSNH who were running roughshod over the wishes of locals. The organizers further argued that Seabrook was now a "worldwide symbol," adding, "We all live in Seabrook."[186] WIN magazine published a debate between Rudy Perkins, of the Boston Hard Rain affinity group, and Igal Roodenko, a Soft Clam and former chairman of the War Resisters League, who opposed the occupation. Roodenko argued, "The Call for the occupation is full of anger, and anger inhibits clear thinking." He charged the CDAS with having a "macho" style and a "devil theory of politics" that would prove counterproductive. In response, Perkins accused the original Clamshell organizers of being hypocritical and selling out: "In 1976 the Clamshell Alliance was formed specifically to leave the well-worn channels of acceptable protest, because those channels had proven to be dead ends.... It is the worst possible moment for a retreat to pre-Clamshell strategies."[187]

The CDAS handbook stated, "October 6 will be a departure from civil disobedience."[188] Members of the Clamshell Alliance who advocated nonviolence were particularly disturbed by this emphasis on physical resistance, which, they believed, threatened to pit "'demonstrators' against 'workers' and 'police.'"[189] The New Hampshire AFSC issued a statement saying that although it had "no reason to suppose that the Coalition for Direct Action at Seabrook want[ed] to perpetuate violence at Seabrook," such would be the result.[190] A group called Citizens for Nonviolence at Seabrook appeared on October 6 to distribute cards imploring all sides "to refrain from acts of physical violence under any circumstances."[191]

When the showdown came on October 6, 1979, approximately 2,500 hardcore activists heeded the CDAS call, far fewer than the 10,000 hoped for. Although activists of all ages were among the ranks, college students and participants from out of state were especially prevalent. Awaiting them were more than 200 members of the New Hampshire National Guard and 250 state police from all the New England states except Connecticut (where the state police were needed at home to deal with recent tornado damage). Unlike his predecessor, the new pronuclear governor of Massachusetts, Ed King, dispatched the Massachusetts state police to the Granite State as requested.[192] The new governor of New Hampshire, the Democrat Hugh Galen, also took action that differed from that of his predecessor in 1977. Galen kept a low profile and avoided inflammatory statements. Moreover, rather than have protestors bog down New Hampshire armories and courts, Galen ordered the police and the National Guard to repel efforts to enter the Seabrook construction site by whatever means necessary and keep arrests to a minimum.[193]

Three days of assaults on the barbed-wire-enclosed Seabrook site ensued, with the police and the National Guard repelling protestors using a water cannon, mace, fire hoses, smoke bombs, and tear gas (German shepherds were held in reserve but were not needed). Protestors attempted to cut through the fence with wire cutters, while police poked their night sticks through the chain-link fence in response. The police repeatedly maced and tear-gassed both protestors and reporters, more than four hundred of whom were covering the story. On the first day, the protestors managed to break through the fence, but police poured in and aggressively drove them back. For three days the assault continued, with sporadic attempts to break through being repelled and with protestors retreating, regrouping, and going at it again.[194]

The lack of CDAS organizational experience was especially evident. Many of the roving bands of people who attempted to break through the fence were stymied by a lack of coordination, and affinity group meetings became bogged down in tactical disputes. The running battles occasionally became farcical. At one point, a Maine affinity group flying the state flag along with an American flag found itself rushed by members of the Maine National Guard, who charged from behind a gate in the fence, seized the protestors' Maine flag, took it behind the fence, and proceeded to fold it neatly.[195] The heavy rains that fell throughout the three-day action added to the desultory atmosphere, and each day more of the original twenty-five hundred protestors trickled away. Some expressed disillusionment; others felt embittered and radicalized by the aggressive police tactics. One activist declared, "There wasn't enough of us and the police had all the weaponry. I think the cops are inviting terrorism by the way they're handling this." Another commented, "It was like this in the 60s. This is how the Weathermen got started and it could happen again."[196]

After three days, the action was over; the fence had been breached only once, and the attempted invasion had been quickly repelled by the police barricade. Authorities had arrested only twenty-one protestors.[197] There would be no rerun of either the occupation at Wyhl or the militant mass street battles that led to a constitutional crisis in West Germany in the late 1970s. The constituency for late 1960s militancy was not there. The CDAS had hoped that the nuclear disaster at Three Mile Island the previous spring would help marshal recruits for the new confrontational direction that they had envisioned. Instead, the disaster further swelled the national nonviolent movement against nuclear power, hurling Massachusetts activists once again to the center.

THE NUCLEAR ENERGY "TET"—
THREE MILE ISLAND: MARCH 28, 1979

On March 28, 1979, the Unit 2 nuclear reactor at Three Mile Island, Pennsylvania, experienced a series of technical malfunctions and human errors, causing the feed water lines to the cooling system of the plant to be cut off and beginning a reactor core meltdown. As technicians frantically arrived at the site to try to arrest the meltdown, more than one hundred thousand residents in the Harrisburg area were evacuated. With great effort, a full-blown meltdown that would have sent a radioactive cloud across a huge swath of Pennsylvania and New Jersey was narrowly averted. Although similar near-meltdowns had occurred before—most notably at the Enrico Fermi reactor outside of Detroit in 1967—the disaster at Three Mile Island was the closest the nation had come to experiencing a catastrophe of unimaginable proportions.[198]

Throughout the 1970s, antinuclear activists had drawn parallels between nuclear energy and the war in Vietnam. Nader had proclaimed nuclear power to be "this country's technological Vietnam."[199] Gyorgy stated, "Nuclear power seemed in many ways to be the 'Vietnam War brought home.' By aiding the nuclear industry while assuring the public it had nothing to fear, the government was supporting an energy source that could prove as lethal as any war."[200] In 1979 Wasserman was not alone in declaring Three Mile Island to be the "Tet" of the nuclear industry. In his 1979 book, *Energy War: Reports from the Front*, he wrote, "During and immediately after Tet, military officials downplayed the importance of the attack. . . . [W]e saw the same thing during Three Mile Island."[201]

Just as with the Tet Offensive of 1968, the near-meltdown at Three Mile Island in 1979 was a turning point. In the parlance of nuclear physics, opposition to nuclear power was reaching critical mass. The accident at Three Mile Island occurred just days after the release of *The China Syndrome*, a major motion picture starring Jack Lemon, Jane Fonda, and Michael Douglas that depicted a near-meltdown at a fictional California plant.

On May 6, a little more than a month after the accident, the largest antinuclear rally to date took place outside the capitol building in Washington, D.C. It was attended by between 70,000 and 125,000 people and featured nationally known speakers, including Jane Fonda, Dick Gregory, Tom Hayden, and Jerry Brown (the governor of California). Senator Edward Kennedy of Massachusetts sent a message of support, which was read at the rally. *Time* magazine described the peaceful antinuclear rally as "one of the largest marches since the Vietnam era."[202] Lovejoy joined other Montague activists in taking a leading role in the May 6 coalition, which organized the rally, and acted as master of ceremonies. On May 7, six members of the coalition, including Lovejoy, met with President Jimmy Carter at the White House.[203]

The antinuclear movement had high hopes for Carter, beginning with the 1976 encounter in New Hampshire, when he told the press and Clamshell activists that nuclear power should be "a last resort." By 1979, however, the antinuclear movement had become disillusioned with the president, who had done little more than oppose the Clinch River Breeder Reactor Project in Tennessee and whose administration had given the go-ahead for the Seabrook reactors in 1977. At that point, the *Clamshell Alliance News* had blasted Carter, stating, "President Carter seems to be turning the Environmental Protection Agency into a bad joke. . . . Carter has, with this decision, destroyed his credibility with those who supported him in the name of the natural environment."[204] On May 7, 1979, when Carter met with Lovejoy and the other antinuclear activists, the administration asked the press to leave, and the activists confronted the president. "We were trying to flush out Carter's position on nuclear power. I think we did that," said Lovejoy after the meeting. "His position basically was 'we're not going to shut down nuclear power so don't kid around.' . . . I think the man is drowning. He's a technocrat who takes one step at a time. . . . He doesn't think in large terms."[205] In 1981 Wasserman, who had had such optimism in 1976, declared, "[Carter] sold us down the river on nuclear power; there is no doubt about it."[206] Thus, despite inroads made with such politicians as Governor Jerry Brown and Senator Ted Kennedy (both of whom would challenge Carter for the Democratic presidential nomination the following year), the antinuclear movement had little impact on the White House.

The post–Three Mile Island disaster movement continued to gain momentum later that summer, when a group of musicians formed a group called MUSE— Musicians for Safe Energy—and staged a star-studded "No Nukes" concert to raise money and awareness. Thousands attended the five gala concerts at Madison Square Garden, which featured such renowned musicians as Jackson Browne, Bruce Springsteen, Carly Simon, and James Taylor. The event went on to become a motion picture.[207] Once again, Montague activists played a major role. The ubiquitous Lovejoy was the president of MUSE and executive producer of the concert and the film, which he distributed nationally in a contract with Warner Brothers. Wasserman was the spokesman for MUSE. Green Mountain Post Films contributed a twenty-minute documentary titled *Save the Planet*, which aired in the middle of each concert and in the *No Nukes* film.[208]

The five days of concerts ended with an antinuclear rally in Battery Park in New York, which was attended by as many as two hundred thousand people. Speaking at the rally were Tom Hayden, Bella Abzug, the Native American activist Winona LaDuke, and Pete Seeger. The organizers invited only one elected official, Congressman Ed Markey of Massachusetts, the antinuclear firebrand, who told the crowd, "People who are a part of this perhaps can learn from the lessons of the 1960s, that demonstrations alone are not effective, that politicians can ignore mass demonstrations, as occurred with the war in Vietnam, and that the only way of really being effective is to take these demonstrations and then funnel them into the political process. . . . When the music is over, the work has to begin."[209]

The accident at Three Mile Island helped legitimize the antinuclear cause and put the burden of proof on the nuclear industry. The public opinion poll numbers that showed that a majority of Americans still supported nuclear energy began a slow descent until, by 1983, a majority of Americans opposed further nuclear plant construction.[210] Most important, a growing number of liberal politicians experienced an "antinuclear coming out," or—in the case of those, such as Ed Markey, who were already sympathetic to the antinuclear cause—an escalation in their opposition to nuclear power.

ENTER THE LIBERALS: MASSACHUSETTS DEMOCRATS AND OPPOSITION TO SEABROOK

By the turn of the decade, Massachusetts in particular and greater New England in general had become a stronghold of opposition to nuclear energy. Before the Three Mile Island disaster, a number of Massachusetts Democrats had, to greater or lesser degrees, aligned themselves with the antinuclear movement (although they found themselves more comfortable with the legal interveners than with the direct action wing of the movement). When Congress debated the Energy Reorganization Act of 1974, which replaced the Atomic Energy Commission with the Nuclear Regulatory Commission, Senator Edward Kennedy introduced an amendment (S. 2744) that would have required utilities to reimburse antinuclear interveners (for expenses that included "reasonable attorney fees") if their interventions resulted in "substantial contributions" to public safety. Kennedy worked closely with Friends of the Earth (one of the more radical legal intervening groups) in writing the bill, which was defeated with strenuous effort by senators with close ties to the nuclear industry.[211] During Kennedy's bid for the Democratic presidential nomination in 1980, under pressure from Jerry Brown—who was actively courting the antinuclear vote—he announced his support for a nuclear moratorium.[212]

One Massachusetts Democrat who would have an immense impact on the Seabrook Nuclear Power Station was Congressman Ed Markey, who represented the northeast corner of the state, much of which abutted New Hampshire and was within ten miles of Seabrook. By 1980, Markey and Kennedy were both among those members of Congress who were known as the "gatekeepers," or those who were friendly to the antinuclear movement and afforded its members access to the corridors of power. In the wake of Three Mile Island, Markey introduced two bills through his Interior and Insular Affairs Subcommittee. The first called for a six-month moratorium on the issuance of new permits for nuclear reactors; the second required approval of emergency evacuation plans by all towns and states in a given area around a nuclear plant before that plant could go on-line. Although the first bill went down to defeat, Congress passed the second.[213] The NRC then put into effect a requirement for an Emergency Planning Zone (EPZ) encompassing a ten-mile radius around a nuclear plant. Henceforth, until all affected towns and states within the ten-mile EPZ submitted plans for evacuation in the event of a nuclear catastrophe, no nuclear power plant could become operational. More than 130,000 people lived within the Seabrook EPZ.[214]

The EPZ requirement became a powerful tool for opposing the Seabrook plants. In 1985 not only the five Massachusetts towns that lay within the EPZ but also Hampton, New Hampshire (just over the border), refused to submit an emergency evacuation plan. Pointing to the huge traffic jams that affected the area in the summer months, representatives of the towns argued that no feasible evacuation plan was possible.[215] They found a powerful ally in Michael Dukakis, who had made a strong political comeback after four years out of office, defeating the pronuclear governor Ed King in a Democratic primary rematch and becoming elected governor again in 1982. In 1986 Dukakis announced that in support of all the Massachusetts towns in the EPZ, he would refuse to submit an evacuation plan. The previous opponents of PSNH had been the easily outspent legal interveners and the grassroots Clamshell Alliance; now PSNH would have to face the full weight of the Commonwealth of Massachusetts.[216]

The issue came to a head in September 1986, when the first Seabrook nuclear reactor was ready to go on-line. The NRC pressed Governor Dukakis to submit an evacuation plan for the six affected Massachusetts towns, but he refused. At a news conference, the governor stated, "The unshakable truth is this: If a serious accident occurs . . . the combination of conditions at Seabrook . . . create a foreseeable likelihood of high dosages of radioactive intake, against which emergency planning and evacuation cannot adequately protect." Dukakis added that his decision was motivated by the recent nuclear disaster at Chernobyl in the Ukraine. "Chernobyl changed the equation dramatically," declared Dukakis. "We are no longer talking about models and theories." As Dukakis emerged from his office following the press conference, a group of some fifty Massachusetts residents from border towns and antinuclear activists applauded him. An Amesbury selectman exclaimed, "It's a whole new war now."[217]

Michael Dukakis and Mario Cuomo—the governor of New York, who was then leading opposition to the Shoreham Nuclear Power Station on Long Island— became the new symbols of state opposition to the federal government on matters of nuclear energy. The two liberal governors argued that they were acting in the spirit of the New Federalism of Ronald Reagan, in which the president delegated increased authority to the states and declared that he would defer to state and regional leaders in questions that pertained to them.[218]

In early 1987—under pressure from both John Sununu, the governor of New Hampshire, and PSNH, which complained of the financial hardships caused by the delay over the EPZ—the NRC unilaterally reduced the size of the zone to take

Massachusetts out of the equation. Both Cuomo and Dukakis appeared at the mandatory NRC public hearings on the rule change. Cuomo's testimony was an impassioned attack on the way the Reagan administration had undermined its own "federalism." Dukakis—more reserved, as usual—told the commissioners, "The area around Seabrook... could not be evacuated in the event of a serious nuclear accident." Assailing the financial considerations behind the rule change, Dukakis declared that it was "the nuclear equivalent of cutting the number of lifeboats for the 'unsinkable' Titanic [because they would] make the voyage unprofitable." Meanwhile, Congressman Markey sponsored a bill designed to give governors a veto over licensing permits for nuclear reactors, but the bill was defeated.[219]

In 1988 the Seabrook debate became part of the presidential election. The *Boston Globe* stated, "[George H. W.] Bush and Dukakis may well offer the voters the clearest choice ever on nuclear power."[220] Ed Markey charged, "If George Bush is elected, the NRC will try to cut corners and do everything possible to license the [Seabrook] plant."[221] Sununu, co-chairman of the Bush presidential campaign, led the Republican charge against Dukakis. Once again Dukakis found himself in a political grudge match with a conservative New Hampshire governor. Sununu compared New Hampshire favorably to Massachusetts and accused Dukakis of high taxation and misgovernment. Speaking in Boston, Sununu charged, "Energy is the classic example of ineptitude. You are out of additional electrical capacity." In response, a Dukakis spokesperson countercharged, "Governor Sununu's outspokenness about Governor Dukakis is really due to the role that Governor Dukakis played in Sununu's greatest failure, which was Seabrook."[222]

Dukakis campaigned hard in New Hampshire, including in Seabrook, where he spoke out against the plant: "Until we do something about nuclear waste, I can't see how we can construct and license and operate these plants."[223] A Dukakis strategist observed, "Seabrook is alive and well in a presidential contest. ... Of all the Republican candidates, George Bush is the one most likely to bring Seabrook on line."[224]

After the election, in a surprising and arbitrary move, the Reagan administration announced that it was issuing an executive order that would allow the Federal Emergency Management Agency to draw up evacuation plans when local communities refused to do so. Denying Dukakis—then running as the Democratic presidential candidate—a campaign issue, the announcement was withheld until after the 1988 elections.

In early 1989 Sununu became the White House chief of staff for the newly elected president, George H. W. Bush. In 1990 the first Seabrook nuclear reactor went on-line.[225]

"THE PIMPLE ON THE PUMPKIN"

The Clamshell Alliance limped along throughout the 1980s, a ghost of its former self, holding periodic demonstrations at the Seabrook site. The group never recovered from the divisive debate over fence cutting in 1978. In its short life, however, the Clamshell Alliance had elevated the nuclear issue nationally; in fact, it had helped increase nuclear opposition to the degree that the ground was set for the decline of the nuclear industry when the accident at Three Mile Island occurred.

The antinuclear movement came late in the development of nuclear power. Much of the demise of the industry was a result of the escalating costs of nuclear energy. The cost of the Seabrook plant had soared from initial estimates of $500,000 to well over $2.5 billion.[226] PSNH had to sell all of its Seabrook shares when it went bankrupt in the late 1980s. For their part, antinuclear activists— legal interveners, direct action activists, and their liberal sympathizers in government—had worked to increase both the financial and social costs of nuclear energy. Although 103 nuclear reactors remained on-line, no reactor begun after 1975 was ever completed.[227]

If the antinuclear movement failed to bring about a nuclear-free United States, it nevertheless contributed in no small measure to the decline of the growth of the industry. In the mid-1970s, both President Richard Nixon and President Gerald Ford had envisioned more than 1,000 operational nuclear power plants that would provide 50 percent of the energy in the nation by the year 2000.[228] The antinuclear movement took center stage in changing the pronuclear trajectory of the United States.

The movement against nuclear energy, which had grown dramatically in the wake of the disaster at Three Mile Island, declined almost as quickly. Summing up the growing groundswell that would sweep over the movement against nuclear energy in 1980, eclipsing the issue of nuclear power in both the United States and Europe, Dr. Helen Caldicott declared, "Nuclear power is the pimple on the pumpkin; the pumpkin is nuclear weapons."[229]

CHAPTER 3
THE NUCLEAR WEAPONS FREEZE MOVEMENT IN MASSACHUSETTS 1980–1985

THE ELECTION OF 1980

On November 4, 1980, U.S. voters went to the polls to elect a president. The mental climate was angry and impatient, as the various crises of the 1970s came to a head. Earlier, Jimmy Carter, the incumbent president, had described the national mood in terms of a crisis of confidence. For yet another year the nation had endured double-digit inflation, rising unemployment, high interest rates, and long gas lines brought on by the energy crisis. On election day, fifty-one U.S. embassy staffers in Tehran, Iran, observed their one-year anniversary as hostages of militant Islamic students. The Iranian revolution and the ongoing hostage saga remained the major news stories throughout late 1979 and 1980. The crisis not only highlighted the apparent post–Vietnam War decline of U.S. power and prestige abroad but also further eroded the image of the sitting president, who—particularly after a botched military rescue mission the previous October—appeared helpless and adrift.[1]

Carter, the Washington outsider, had entered the White House in 1977 with an air of optimism that—in the wake of Watergate and Gerald Ford's unpopular pardon of Richard Nixon—he would be able to return the nation to the path of integrity and reform. The moderate, pro–civil rights former governor from Georgia appealed to both moderate and progressive constituencies in the election of 1976.[2] Backed by his experience as a nuclear engineer, Carter's campaign promises to make environmental appointments that would be acceptable to Ralph Nader and to reduce the role of nuclear energy evoked hope among anti-nuclear activists. Harvey Wasserman was optimistic: "If Carter is held to his campaign rhetoric, his inauguration should be a landmark in the decline of nuclear power."[3] Before the year was out, however, Wasserman had denounced Carter as "the Lyndon Johnson of the seventies," a president who raised progressive hopes only to dash them.[4]

Others soon felt the disillusionment of antinuclear activists on the left-liberal spectrum. Labor advocates and their supporters in Congress felt betrayed by Carter's belated endorsement and unenthusiastic, half-hearted work on behalf of the Humphrey-Hawkins Full Employment Act. After appointing a record number of women and minorities to federal courts and factoring human rights considerations into U.S. foreign policy more than any president before or since, in 1978 the president's erratic shifts from the center began to move decidedly and consistently to the right.[5] This shift was most evident in U.S.-Soviet relations. Early on, Carter endeavored to continue the policies of détente that his predecessors had followed—working toward negotiation and then ratification of a new Strategic Arms Limitation Treaty (SALT II). By 1978, Carter's policies were under heavy attack from the Right in Congress, whose criticisms of détente were amplified by the rabidly antidisarmament Committee on the Present Danger.[6]

In response to pressure from the Right, Carter moved his foreign policy in an increasingly hawkish direction. In 1978 Carter advocated building the mammoth MX missiles and mounting them on railroad cars that would crisscross the Great Plains. Then, in 1979, he agreed to a decision by the North Atlantic Treaty Organization (NATO) to introduce intermediate-range Pershing and Cruise missiles into Western Europe by 1983.[7] Carter followed by issuing Presidential Directive 59, which declared that the goal of U.S. nuclear weapons policy was not only deterrence but also maintenance of the ability to fight a limited nuclear war.[8] The coup de grace came in December 1979, when the Soviet Union invaded Afghanistan to prop up an unpopular pro-Soviet government in Kabul. In response, Carter removed SALT II from consideration by Congress (although the treaty had already been effectively blocked in the Senate), ordered a boycott of U.S. grain sales to the Soviet Union, and announced a U.S. boycott of the 1980 summer Olympics in Moscow.[9]

In response to Carter's lurch toward the Right, the restive liberal wing of the Democratic Party launched an "anybody but Carter" movement in 1980, with both Senator Edward Kennedy of Massachusetts and Governor Jerry Brown of California competing to take up the flagging liberal banner. With the liberal vote divided, Carter pursued a Rose Garden strategy—avoiding the campaign trail to deal with pressing matters of state—and successfully used the weight of incumbency to win renomination at the Democratic Convention in New York.[10]

Carter lumbered into the election a badly wounded candidate. At times during 1980, Carter's approval ratings sank lower than those of Richard Nixon during the Watergate crisis.[11] As liberals felt abandoned and moderates considered the presidential candidacy of the centrist Illinois Republican John Anderson, conservatives enthusiastically and energetically mobilized behind the most ideologically right-wing candidate ever to run for the presidency of the United States: Ronald Reagan. Reagan's candidacy represented the intersection of a trajectory that had begun with the Barry Goldwater campaign of 1964 and a moment in history that was ripe for a major electoral shift against the party in power. Only two years after Goldwater's rout in 1964, Reagan had won the first of two consecutive terms as governor of the bellwether state of California. Denouncing Berkeley radicals, the hippie counterculture, and Black Panther militants, Reagan sought to link Great Society liberalism and New Left radicalism and move the Republican Party—and the country—farther toward the Right.[12]

Reagan had mounted a formidable challenge of incumbent president Gerald Ford at the 1976 Republican primary. Then, in November 1980, with U.S. hostages being paraded and humiliated before the world; Soviet aggression in Central Asia; and gas lines, inflation, unemployment, and energy shortages ravishing a seemingly rudderless nation, Reagan and the Republican Right smelled blood. Reagan denounced détente as a "one way street" and promised a military buildup, tax cuts, business deregulation, and a return to Judeo-Christian values. His strongest appeal, however, was simply as an alternative to Carter, which he summed up in his most effective campaign line: "Ask yourself, 'Are you better off than you were four years ago?'"[13]

On the evening of November 4, 1980, before polls had even closed in California, President Jimmy Carter conceded the election to Ronald Reagan. As the evening progressed, it became apparent that the nation was experiencing a major electoral shift. Although Reagan garnered only 51 percent of the popular vote to Carter's 42 percent and John Anderson's 7 percent, the Electoral College count was overwhelmingly in Reagan's favor (489 to 49); moreover, the Republicans seized control of the Senate for the first time in more than two decades and added thirty-three members to the House of Representatives. The election also saw the defeat of some of the most shining progressive lights in the Democratic Party, including Senator George McGovern (the 1972 presidential standard-bearer) and Senator Frank Church of Idaho.[14]

Reagan narrowly won even Massachusetts, which had been the sole holdout in Nixon's 1972 landslide. Reflecting the conservative tide that seemed to be sweeping the nation, Bay State voters also passed Proposition 2½, a statewide referendum that lowered and limited property tax rates (the initiative was based on Proposition 13 in California, which had set off the national "taxpayer revolt" in 1978). Surveying the political landscape the day after the 1980 election, those who were of a progressive bent found little that encouraged optimism. On the political radar screen, however, a small dot blinked from western Massachusetts, where, in a nonbinding referendum, voters in three state senatorial districts had voted

59 percent to 41 percent in support of a mutual nuclear weapons freeze between the United States and the Soviet Union. Although these districts had voted Reagan in by a narrow margin, the referendum results seemed to buck a national mood that appeared to be moving in an increasingly militaristic direction.

Over the next few years, the nuclear weapons freeze movement that had first taken root in western Massachusetts would sweep the nation, with six states (including California) voting for the freeze in 1982, more than eight hundred thousand Americans rallying in Central Park in New York City for a freeze that same year, the House of Representatives voting for a nuclear weapons freeze resolution in 1983, and virtually every candidate who ran for the Democratic presidential nomination in 1984 endorsing the freeze.[15] The freeze movement, in short, would soon galvanize disillusioned radicals and liberals into a more cohesive opposition to the Reagan juggernaut. If the election of 1980 signaled that the nation was moving toward the Right, there were also signs that the shift would be energetically contested.

THE PEACE MOVEMENT REBORN

The demise of détente in the late Carter years was accompanied by an increase in disarmament activism that soon coalesced around the nuclear weapons freeze movement. Although various arms control lobbies continued to work in Washington throughout the 1970s, in many ways the reenergized disarmament movement of the late 1970s and early 1980s seemed an awakening of a movement that—after being eclipsed by the New Left focus on the war in Vietnam and racial inequality—had lain dormant since the early 1960s. The historian Paul Boyer has described the period from 1963 to 1980 as the "Big Sleep," part of the ongoing pattern of "activism and apathy" that ran throughout the atomic age in the United States.[16]

The first period of activism went from the end of World War II through 1949, when atomic scientists, world federalists, radical pacifists, and remnants of the U.S. Left worked to bring atomic weapons under international control and preempt a nuclear arms race. With the Soviet detonation of its first atomic bomb in 1949 and the ensuing Red Scare, the movement virtually disappeared until the late 1950s. At that time groups such as the Committee for a SANE Nuclear Policy (SANE) helped reignite a movement to ban the bomb, which soon focused on working for a nuclear weapons test ban. The late 1950s and early 1960s witnessed intense public questioning of the arms race, atomic weapons testing, and civil defense.

Concern about nuclear war permeated the popular culture. Novels such as Nevil Shute's *On the Beach* and Eugene Burdick and Harvey Wheeler's *Fail Safe* depicted the horrors of nuclear war and were made into blockbuster films, including Stanley Kubrick's classic film *Dr. Strangelove: Or How I Learned to Stop Worrying and Love the Bomb*. Anxiety over the arms race reached a climax with the very real showdown between the United States and the Soviet Union during the Cuban Missile Crisis of 1962. The peace movement achieved a partial success with the Limited Test Ban Treaty (LTBT), which was signed by the Soviet Union, the United States, and Great Britain in 1963, ushering in the modest beginning of détente. As the superpowers negotiated the issue of nuclear weapons from 1963 through the 1970s, public concern over nuclear war waned and once again apathy held sway.[17]

Never completely quiescent, the disarmament movement nonetheless seemed to disappear after Nixon's visits to Moscow and the signing of SALT I and the Anti-Ballistic Missile (ABM) Treaty. Slowly, however, the movement revived. "When the Vietnam War ended," commented Frances Crowe, "many of us woke up to the fact that the Pentagon used those Vietnam years to stockpile a huge arsenal of nuclear weapons."[18] During the mid-1970s, disarmament activists such as Dr. Helen Caldicott of Physicians for Social Responsibility (PSR) linked the issue of nuclear weapons with the burgeoning movement against nuclear energy. In 1978, at the behest of nonaligned nations, the U.N. General Assembly held its first Special Session on Disarmament in New York City, as somewhere between fifteen thousand and twenty-five thousand activists joined a rally outside. During the 1979 debate in the U.S. Senate over SALT II, Mark Hatfield, the maverick Republican senator from Oregon, introduced an amendment to the treaty, which called for a freeze in the production and testing of nuclear weapons.[19]

Riding the growing concern generated by the anti–nuclear energy movement, the U.N. Special Session, and the SALT II debate, a Swedish-born woman named Randall Forsberg—who was a member of the Institute for Disarmament and Defense Studies (IDDS), based in Brookline, Massachusetts—proposed a U.S.-Soviet nuclear weapons freeze as a way to bring together the technical experts of the arms control lobby with a popular movement for an end to the arms race. Forsberg had focused on disarmament since the 1960s, when she was active in the Stockholm International Peace Research Institute. The difficulty in slowing the arms race, Forsberg came to believe, stemmed from the public's feeling of helplessness in the face of the technical intricacies associated with arms control negotiations, which left the technical experts in the arms control lobby isolated from the general public.[20] Forsberg noted, "There was no active grassroots support [for SALT II]. . . . I think that's the reason it was shelved."[21]

Outlining what she described as the "percolate up theory," Forsberg hoped to generate a popular movement that would create the political pressure that the expert lobbying groups needed in order to be effective in Washington. A proposal to freeze nuclear weapons deployment, production, and testing was simple and accessible to the lay public. The narrow focus of the proposal, Forsberg believed, could bring together liberals, moderates, radicals, and even some conservatives. In her 1980 manifesto, "Call to Halt the Nuclear Arms Race" (soon referred to simply as "The Call"), Forsberg declared, "The pros and cons of... SALT II... are too technical for the patience of the average person. In contrast, an effort to stop the development and production of all U.S. and Soviet nuclear weapons is simple, straightforward, effective and mutual; and for all these reasons it is likely to have greater popular support."[22]

Believing the American middle class to be the constituency that was the key to breaking through to the mainstream, Forsberg hoped to create a broad-based movement.[23] The freeze could appeal to those who were concerned about the costs of the arms race and the potential for nuclear war but who were not interested in radical social transformation. Conversely, although many radicals criticized the freeze movement for failing to address the sources of the cold war, imperialism, and militarism and for constituting an arms control movement more than a disarmament movement, many nonetheless realized that the freeze offered a springboard for launching a more sweeping critique of U.S. society.

Advocates of the freeze, including the American Friends Service Committee (AFSC), Mobilization for Survival (MfS), and the Fellowship of Reconciliation (FOR), sought to introduce the freeze proposal at the 1980 Democratic Convention in New York. Although progressives such as Congressman Ron Dellums of California and Senator Tom Harkin of Idaho championed the freeze, both Jimmy Carter and Ted Kennedy kept the freeze at arms length. The proposal was defeated by a vote of seventy-eight to fifty-one by the platform committee. The attempt to take the freeze directly to the national level proved to be a false start, underscoring the need for a grassroots base.[24]

What gave the freeze its jump-start was a small group of radical pacifists in western Massachusetts who had watched New England activists build a mass movement against nuclear energy from the bottom up. Acting independently, the group sought to implement Forsberg's "percolate up theory" by planting the freeze movement in the soil of western Massachusetts. Only when local movements took root across the country, they believed, would an effective national movement be launched.[25] The two pillars of the phenomenal growth of the freeze movement were this localist strategy and the fear produced by Reagan's pursuit of massive arms buildup and his Strangelovian pronouncements about "winnable" and "limited" nuclear war.

RANDY KEHLER, JUDITH SCHECKEL, AND TRAPROCK

In 1979 Randy Kehler was a thirty-seven-year-old teacher and organic farmer who lived with his wife, Betsy Corner, and his daughter, Lillian. Kehler, however, was about to embark on a whirlwind odyssey—first in 1980 as leader of the successful freeze referendum campaign in western Massachusetts and then in 1981 as the top official of the national freeze movement (a post he would hold through 1983). Kehler's short, chestnut-brown hair and youthful looks gave him a wholesome "all-American" appearance that belied his radical past and played well to the middle-American image that the freeze movement hoped to cultivate. Born in Scarsdale, New York, Kehler had had a typical white, middle-class upbringing. He told one interviewer, "I was certainly not raised a pacifist. . . . My parents were reasonably patriotic, middle-class citizens."[26]

As a young man, Kehler held views on military service that were far from radical: "When I turned 18 it didn't occur to me not to register [for the draft] and in college I came close to signing up for naval ROTC [Reserve Officers' Training Corps]. It was not until several years later that I decided not to cooperate [with the Selective Service]."[27] Like much of his generation, Kehler was politicized at college during the civil rights era and radicalized during the Vietnam War. Kehler traces his political awakening to 1963: "There was a particular incident that opened my eyes to the deeper problems besetting our country and opened my eyes at the same time to activism." He had taken a train from Scarsdale to Harlem to see a jazz show. Emerging from the subway, Kehler noticed an African American crowd gathered in the street listening to a Black Nationalist orator. A young African American approached the naïve Kehler, and said, "You're in trouble here; this is a dangerous place for a white person to be." Then the young man took Kehler to a local Congress of Racial Equality (CORE) meeting, where members were organizing for the upcoming March on Washington for Jobs and Justice. Meeting the CORE people transformed Kehler's attitude from that of a "removed, elitist, and condescending" middle-class white person who saw civil rights activists as "publicity-seeking egotists" to that of a young man who became committed to raising money for CORE.[28]

Kehler traveled on a CORE bus to the Washington, D.C., march in August, experiencing what he described as a "double whammy": First, Martin Luther King, Jr. made his historic "I Have a Dream" speech, deepening Kehler's commitment to civil rights; second, Kehler sat next to Max Sandine, an "elderly pacifist of Russian birth." Sandine, Kehler said, "introduced me to the concept of nonviolence and pacifism, which was as foreign to me as civil rights."[29]

In the mid-1960s Kehler attended Harvard University, spending a year in Tanzania with a private Harvard-Radcliffe organization modeled on the Peace

Corps.[30] Appalled by the massive violence and destruction caused by the Vietnam War, Kehler gravitated in the direction of absolute pacifism, or what he preferred to call "active non-violence."[31] Although he never subscribed to a particular faith, Kehler objected to war on moral and religious grounds. From 1967 to 1970, he relocated to the San Francisco Bay area, the epicenter of 1960s political and cultural radicalism, where he worked as a regional organizer for the West Coast branch of the War Resisters League.[32]

Kehler's pacifism became so absolute that he refused to register with the Selective Service as a conscientious objector. In a 1980 interview, Kehler recalled, "I had declined to apply for c.o. status because I firmly believed that any form of cooperation with the military would make me a guilty party to the military's chief occupation at that time, aggression and genocide in Vietnam."[33] Convicted of failure to cooperate with the draft, Kehler began serving a twenty-two-month sentence at the federal prison in Safford, Arizona, on February 16, 1970. A war tax resister, Kehler deducted a percentage of his annual tax return that was comparable to the military percentage of the federal budget.[34] (In the 1990s, the federal government confiscated and auctioned off the home of Randy Kehler and Betsy Corner to pay for their back taxes; this became the subject of the documentary film *An Act of Conscience*, by Robbie Leppzer.)[35]

In 1973 Kehler returned to the East Coast and settled down in Franklin County, western Massachusetts. He came with friends who told him about a new alternative school at Woolman Hill in Deerfield, where he soon became codirector.[36] Before long, he was swept up in the antinuclear movement sparked by Sam Lovejoy's toppling of the Montague weather tower.[37] In western Massachusetts, Kehler came into contact with radical pacifists such as the AFSC members Wally and Juanita Nelson and Frances Crowe, and he became active in the growing regional network of war tax resisters. Kehler's experience with the western Massachusetts Left in the 1970s helped make him a confirmed and zealous advocate of grassroots politics.[38] In 1980 Kehler declared, "Every movement has to start somewhere and it has to start small."[39] After the 1980 freeze referendum victory, Kehler proclaimed, "Ours is but a small spark, but it's small sparks that often lead to raging forest fires."[40]

The other driving force in the formation of the Traprock group and the western Massachusetts freeze campaign was Sister Judith Scheckel. Having felt a special calling to work among the downtrodden throughout her life, Scheckel came to western Massachusetts from the School Sisters of Notre Dame in Minnesota for an internship with the local AFSC. Drawn (as many Catholics were) by the social doctrines of Vatican II, which called on the faithful to play a greater role in helping the destitute people of the world, Scheckel worked for a time with César Chávez and the United Farm Workers and then spent several months working with the impoverished population in Honduras in the mid-1970s.[41] According to Scheckel, her pacifism was an outgrowth of her Catholic faith: "There is strong theological and moral support [for a weapons moratorium]. Every pope in the nuclear age has called for disarmament."[42] On another occasion, Scheckel explained, "A person cannot be a Christian and believe in a loving God and at the same time allow for the building of nuclear weapons."[43] Scheckel remained active in western Massachusetts throughout the 1980s, increasing her role in the local peace movement when Kehler moved to St. Louis to head the national freeze movement.

The seeds of the western Massachusetts freeze movement were planted in 1978. As Kehler recalled, "When I started, my focus was still local. The Woolman Hill School had folded in 1978 . . . [and] the Quakers who owned it were trying to decide what to do with it." Harvey Cox of the Harvard Divinity School approached Kehler about making Woolman Hill a center for the study of nonviolence. Consulting with others, who soon formed the core group of Traprock, Kehler recalled, "very soon we decided nonviolence as a subject was too broad. . . . [L]ooking for a more particular focus, we decided on nuclear disarmament." Through local fund-raising and support from the International Seminar on Training for Non-violent Action, Kehler, Scheckel, and other members of the core group were able to purchase not only the hilltop buildings that had recently housed the Woolman Hill School but also one hundred acres of bucolic farmland. Because the local population knew the ridge abutting the hill as Traprock, the activists gave their new peace movement headquarters that name. The twentieth-century peace activists relished their connection with John Woolman, the eighteenth-century abolitionist who had once owned the land on which the Traprock buildings now stood.[44] Soon after the official founding of Traprock in September 1979, Kehler declared, "The time has come for a new abolitionist movement, this time to abolish the institution of war."[45]

Kehler, who had "never heard of Randy Forsberg," became aware of the freeze proposal from a group of Christian pacifists centered on Sojourners magazine in Washington, D.C. Among them was Jim Wallis, who had shared the idea with Senator Mark Hatfield of Oregon at one of their many prayer breakfasts. Hatfield had then tried to insert the freeze proposal into SALT II. "As an organizing tool, the freeze being so conceptually simple and clear was great to organize around," explained Kehler. "Then I heard about Randy Forsberg and talked to her about it."[46]

During the first year, Kehler and Scheckel acted as the two full-time, salaried officials of Traprock. They were joined by several area residents (most of whom were already active in other peace organizations), who constituted the core group

and who, in many ways, foreshadowed in microcosm the national freeze movement to come. The members included Pauline Bassett (Mobilization for Survival),
Harvey Cox (Harvard Divinity School), Frances Crowe (AFSC), Gordon Faison
(Movement for a New Society), Meg Gage (Amherst High School), and Judy Titus
(Woolman Hill Farm Community). The central group consisted mostly of educated, white, middle-class people in their thirties or older, whose activism was
predominantly faith based.[47] Members of the core group espoused localism yet
also encouraged a global perspective. Several traveled abroad in the early 1980s
to participate in the European and Japanese peace movements, and a few went
on peace missions to the Soviet Union and to the Eastern bloc nations.[48]

The central group of Traprock presaged the profile of the national movement
in many ways. Many observed that the freeze had an older constituency than
that of the 1960s antiwar movement; indeed it included many veterans of that
movement. In a 1982 *New Left Review* article titled "The Freeze Movement versus
Reagan," the columnists Alexander Cockburn and James Ridgeway observed,
"The generations who came to active political maturity at the time of the civil
rights drive in the early sixties, and at the time of Kent State nearly a decade
later, still probably remain the active leavening in left and left-liberal organizing
in the United States."[49] At the height of the freeze movement in 1982, *Newsweek*
observed, "Up to now, young people—especially college students, like those who
protested [the] Vietnam [War]—have been conspicuously absent from the antinuclear movement."[50] At the height of the 1980 western Massachusetts freeze
referendum campaign, Kehler told a reporter, "This is an older bunch than the
antiwar groups of the Vietnam era . . . more middle class, more religious, more
professionals in its ranks."[51]

Finally, and perhaps of most significance, Traprock saw the emergence of
women as a leading force in defining the movement. The active members included more women than men, and the women activists frequently put forth
a feminist perspective on the arms race. In an early Traprock newsletter piece
titled "War and Patriarchy," the group asserted, "War is the inevitable product
of a society that teaches aggression, competition and hierarchy. We cannot end
war without taking apart the patriarchal ethos which is at its root."[52] Two of the
most prominent leaders of the national freeze movement, Randall Forsberg and
Helen Caldicott symbolized the growing importance of women in the movement. Echoing the maternalist approach of Women Strike for Peace in the 1960s,
Caldicott, in particular, emphasized what she believed to be the role of male
psychology in the arms race: "Men are full of the negative masculine principles
of egocentricity, competition and killing. Therefore, the world is in the grip of
this negative masculine principle. Women, on the other hand, have a highly

developed nurturing instinct and care about humanity. We have a built-in passion for survival."[53]

In December 1982, more than thirty thousand British women activists camped out at Greenham Common to protest the impending arrival of ninety-six U.S Pershing and Cruise missiles. In solidarity, several thousand American women formed the Seneca Women's Peace Encampment outside the U.S. Army Depot in Romulus, New York, through which the Cruise and Pershings were scheduled to pass in transit to England. Several Traprock women joined the encampment, which emphasized a feminist critique of the arms race.[54]

In February 1980, Traprock (which was officially formed in the fall of 1979) began publication of the *Traprock Report*, a monthly newsletter that provided information about the local activities of the organization as well as news about the global peace movement. The masthead of the *Traprock Report* and many of the fund-raising letters sent out by the group included the following quote from the Reverend Martin Luther King, Jr.: "I refuse to accept the cynical notion that nation after nation must spiral down a militaristic stairway into the hell of nuclear destruction. I believe that unarmed truth and unconditional love will have the final word in reality."[55]

Traprock would engage in many activities over the years, including a summer international peace camp, where young people from around the world would work together on peace issues. Its first project, however, was the campaign to put the nuclear weapons freeze on the ballot in western Massachusetts for the November 1980 election. The idea for a freeze referendum grew out of the recent activist history of western Massachusetts. According to Kehler, "I proposed we put a nuclear freeze on the ballot the same way we put the Montague plants on the ballot." Kehler believed not only that a referendum campaign was a great way to "raise [an] issue, [to] make it legitimate" but also that it provided an excellent "excuse to go door to door to educate people about an issue."[56] Summing up the global vision and local activism of the group was the popular slogan "Thinking Globally, Acting Locally."[57]

"A SMALL SPARK": THE 1980 WESTERN MASSACHUSETTS FREEZE REFERENDUM

In 1946 Albert Einstein wrote, "To the village square we must carry the facts of atomic energy. From there must come America's voice."[58] Like the opponents of nuclear power before them, Traprock activists now took the issue of the atom to the village square. Kehler and Faison summed up the approach: "There will be no shortcuts.... There's only one road and it's the long one, the one that begins in our local churches and synagogues, in our union halls and town halls, in our school auditoriums and on our village greens."[59] The road to Washington, these freeze pioneers believed, would be paved through local communities across the United States. This point was reiterated repeatedly in the pages of the *Traprock Report*: "The main focus is on building public support from a very broad cross section of people around the country, and not focusing on Washington until that public support is large enough to cause national leaders to take heed."[60] Kehler predicted that, mirroring the Clamshell Alliance—whose direct actions at Seabrook rose from 18 arrests to 180 arrests to more than 1,400 arrests—the freeze movement would grow in a "geometric progression."[61] "Clearly," stated Kehler, "our efforts here in western Massachusetts are part of something already large and just beginning to grow."[62]

Kehler and other early members of Traprock were galvanized into action by the failure of SALT II and the simultaneous cold war resurgence that so greatly alarmed national disarmament and arms control organizations. Traprock latched onto the freeze idea, which was then being proposed in Boston by Forsberg's IDDA, as a way to bypass the complexities of arms control negotiations and put the arms race before the general public in a simple, appealing manner. In a 1980 speech, Forsberg declared, "People who are afraid of disarmament are more willing to stop where we are, to stop building more. It's a good first step."[63] Anti–arms control organizations such as the Committee on the Present Danger indiscriminately hurled the charge of "unilateral disarmament" at radical dis-armament advocates and liberal arms control groups alike. By advocating a "mutual and verifiable" U.S.-Soviet freeze of the arms race, the proposal could appeal to those who saw the escalating arms race as dangerous and wasteful but who might shy away from more radical appeals. Kehler emphasized Forsberg's point in an interview with the *Greenfield Recorder*: "We can't say we want complete disarmament tomorrow. The first step toward stopping the threat of nuclear war is to freeze the testing, production and deployment of new thermonuclear weapons.... Since the arms race has never stopped, such a freeze would be a monumental achievement.... It's not a wild-eyed idea."[64]

Although Kehler and his western Massachusetts colleagues viewed the appeal of the freeze proposal much as Forsberg did, their approach to the freeze idea differed ideologically from that of Forsberg. Whereas Forsberg hoped that a freeze proposal would generate the popular, predominantly middle-class move-ment that she believed to be necessary to the efficacy of arms control efforts, the Traprock activists hoped that the freeze would be a first step to dismantling the military-industrial complex, the cold war national security state, and the conser-vative national ideology that perpetuated them. Traprock activists, approaching the freeze predominantly from the point of pacifism, hoped that the movement would lay the groundwork for a more sweeping social and economic transformation in the United States.[65] The second issue of the *Traprock Report*, in early 1980, outlined the more left-wing perspective of the group: "Though reversing the arms race may be the absolute precondition to solving many other pressing social problems—patriarchy, poverty, racism, the destruction of the environment—we do recognize the intrinsic connections between them all."[66]

Throughout the meteoric rise and decline of the freeze movement, Forsberg worked assiduously to keep the proposal simple and uncoupled from other issues (such as nuclear power). She also labored to keep the more left-leaning base of the nascent movement off the public radar screen. At an early national meeting of freeze supporters, Forsberg argued that the "peacenik/radical/religious-pacifist composition [of the movement] . . . might dissuade other middle-of-the-road constituencies from participating."[67] Although pacifists and leftists in the movement hewed to this middle-of-the-road strategy in a general way, on favorable occasions they put forth their more radical vision. Thus, Forsberg embraced what was in many ways a radical proposal in the pursuit of the more limited end of arms control, whereas Kehler and other radicals embraced a campaign whose language and tactics were moderate in an effort to bring about more radical change. The freeze was therefore the fulcrum around which both moderate liberals and more radical liberals would push for their respective objectives. Over time this situation would prove to be the source of both strength and weakness in the movement.

In early 1980, Traprock introduced to area activists the idea of a freeze referendum in western Massachusetts. In the April/May 1980 issue of the *Traprock Report*, the group observed, "The moratorium concept, of simply stopping where we are, should appeal to a broad spectrum of voters. Having the questions on the ballot legitimizes the issue and gives every single voter the opportunity to say 'yes' or 'no' to the most important life-and-death question the human race has ever faced."[68] To the *Valley Advocate*, Kehler explained, "We don't naively believe . . . that we can change the course of the arms race with one referendum in western Massachusetts. We alone aren't going to do anything, but how does anything happen? It begins somewhere. This could be the first of many referendums. This is a historic opportunity to serve as catalyst for the whole country. Massachusetts was the first [state] to vote to end the war in Vietnam and we can begin a national effort to freeze the arms race."[69]

Traprock quickly conducted outreach to the many peace organizations in western Massachusetts, stimulating the activist infrastructure that had sprung to life with such alacrity after Lovejoy's toppling of the Montague tower in 1974. The already legendary organizational skills of Crowe, who was both a Traprock and an AFSC member, and her efforts to procure AFSC funding for the referendum cause were particularly crucial. Groups such as the Amherst Disarmament Coalition soon joined Traprock in co-sponsoring the referendum campaign. Armed with fliers and petitions, local activists—predominantly from area churches but also from the faculties and student bodies of nearby colleges—set up tables in town centers, in supermarkets, at strip malls, and at fairs throughout the region. Their goal was to obtain the twelve hundred signatures needed to place the nonbinding freeze proposal on the November ballot in three state senate districts that comprised Hampshire, Franklin, Berkshire and parts of Hampden Counties in western Massachusetts. The petition drive was accompanied by an arms race education campaign, which consisted of public talks, study groups, seminars, and film screenings (including 1,000 Cranes: The Children of Hiroshima, We Are the Guinea Pigs, War without Winners, and the ever-popular Dr. Strangelove).[70]

The freeze campaign aimed to remain separate from the movement against nuclear energy. Petitioners received instructions to ask people to help them get a "proposal for a freeze on the arms race on the ballot" rather than a proposal for a freeze on nuclear weapons. A memo called "Tips for Petitioners" instructed, "We want to stay away from the word 'nuclear' since it has become such an emotionally charged word and since people don't easily separate it from the nuclear energy issue."[71] Kehler recalled, "Some groups felt nuclear weapons and energy should be joined at the hip.... We needed to keep the focus simple and clear and not take on an issue that divided along some different lines."[72]

Within a short time the movement had procured the requisite number of signatures and the freeze became question 7 on the November ballot. (Advocates actually obtained more than five thousand signatures, far surpassing the minimum number required to put the question on the ballot.)[73] The official referendum question read as follows:

> Shall the State Senator from this district be instructed to introduce a resolution in the State Senate:
>
> Requesting the President of the United States to propose to the Soviet Union a mutual nuclear weapons moratorium by which the United States and Soviet Union agree to halt immediately the testing, production and deployment of all nuclear warheads, missiles and delivery systems, and,
>
> Requesting Congress to transfer the funds saved to civilian use.[74]

Once the question was officially ensured a place on the November ballot, activists stepped up what became a nine-month campaign. While supporters handed out freeze fliers on street corners and sympathetic clergy wove disarmament themes into their services, the Radding Sign Company (a Springfield-based billboard firm) donated six area billboards to the newly formed "Yes on 7" campaign.[75] One large billboard depicted the symbolic silhouettes of a man and woman, each holding one hand of a child between them, with the horizontal silhouettes of nuclear missiles pointed at the family; the lines across the top of the billboard read, "Vote Yes on Question 7."[76] Anywhere that crowds gathered—including the U.S Army exhibit depicting the White Sands Missile Range at the Three-County Fair in Northampton—freeze proponents were likely to be present. Despite being repeatedly told to leave because they had no permit to demonstrate, Crowe and fourteen other AFSC members picketed the exhibit. Crowe told a reporter that the exhibit was part of the "Pentagon's advertising campaign . . . [to] justify a soaring defense budget and to get people to accept the inevitability of a limited nuclear war."[77]

Freeze proponents also fanned out to malls and other public gathering places to conduct a so-called "Arms Race Survey," which was really more an effort to win support for the freeze than to gather information. Volunteers would approach passersby and say something like, "Hi. Do you have a minute to answer four questions on the nuclear arms race?" Then they would fill out a card based on each respondent's answers and follow by giving each respondent the "right" answers. The four questions were designed to dramatize the dangers of the nuclear arms race and the need for a freeze.[78]

In its fliers and other forms of public outreach, the western Massachusetts freeze campaign highlighted religious and economic themes. According to one estimate, the "Yes on 7" campaign boasted more than three hundred volunteers, who handed out an estimated sixty thousand fliers.[79] One flier, titled "A Christian Response of 'Yes' to Question 7," quoted the Reverend Father Leo James Hoar of the Campus Ministry Diocese of Springfield: "We here in western Massachusetts are the first community of people having a referendum which offers the choice to the people as to whether or not they want to live with the Russians in peace or we and the Russians will die at about the same time via a nuclear war."[80]

Many pamphlets quoted the Reverend Billy Graham, a conservative evangelical minister, confidant of presidents, and well-known anticommunist, who surprised conservatives by endorsing the freeze early on: "The present insanity of the global arms race, if continued, will lead inevitably to a conflagration so great that Auschwitz will seem like a minor rehearsal. . . . Is nuclear holocaust inevitable if the arms race is not stopped? Frankly, the answer is almost certainly yes. . . . The nuclear arms race is not just a political issue—it is a moral and spiritual issue as well."[81] Graham's endorsement did a great deal to bestow legitimacy on the freeze among Middle Americans.

Proponents of the freeze also connected the arms race to economic issues, a compelling approach in a country shaken by almost a decade of economic dislocation. (Indeed the national trajectory of the freeze movement would run nearly parallel to the recession of the early 1980s.) In this effort, Traprock activists introduced into the western Massachusetts campaign the national work of William Winpisinger, the president of the International Association of Machinists (IAM),who had become co-chairman of SANE. Seeking to merge the issues of jobs and the nuclear arms race, Winpisinger commissioned a study, whose findings were included in a 1979 report titled "The Impact of Military Spending on the Machinist Union."[82] Based largely on Bureau of Labor Statistics sources, the report concluded that defense spending, especially for nuclear weapons, was capital intensive and that one billion dollars converted from defense to civilian spending would result in the creation of far more jobs. According to the report, on average, for every one billion dollars of defense spending converted to civilian spending, fourteen thousand new jobs would be created.[83] Winpisinger wrote to members of SANE: "For years we've been sold a bill of goods about the 'beneficial effects' of military spending. The arms budget has been viewed as a giant public works program to stimulate the economy and provide jobs and income. We now know the truth. Far from aiding prosperity, excessive arms spending weakens civilian industry and is a major cause of inflation and unemployment."[84]

Kehler and others in Traprock hoped to attract the support of local labor organizations. "We want to work with union locals because these groups are mobilized when they realize that military spending costs jobs," Kehler told a local reporter.[85] The major union support for the "Yes on 7" campaign came from the local United Electrical Workers Union, based in Pittsfield, a longtime leftist union headed by the organizer and activist David Cohen.[86] Despite the jobs focus, the western Massachusetts freeze movement (like the later national freeze movement) ran into ambivalence among members of organized labor, some of whom saw in the movement a threat to defense jobs and heard in its campaign discourse echoes of the movement against nuclear energy of the previous decade. A local reporter noted that "spokesmen for local labor organizations . . . gave the [freeze] proposal mixed reviews."[87]

In concert with the freeze movement focus on jobs was its concentration on the cost of the arms race to human services and other cherished social programs, which the activists sought to make tangible by citing the impact on specific local programs. Crowe asked one local reporter, "Why should we be spending all that money for weapons we cannot use? We need the money for human services—for day care and health care—right here in Northampton."[88] Speakers at a three-day teach-in at the University of Massachusetts at Amherst drove home the economic link between tough times and a runaway arms race. Seymour Melman, the renowned political scientist and Columbia University professor whose life work focused on the military-industrial complex, told the students, "The permanent war economy has become the prime source of the inflation and unemployment we now endure."[89]

In its emphasis on religious and economic themes, the western Massachusetts freeze campaign prefigured the national movement to come. The same was true for a regional tactic that would be employed both across the United States and in Western Europe: the endorsement of the freeze campaign position by professional organizations. After reaching out to doctors and nurses, lawyers and educators, social workers and artists, the "Yes on 7" campaign won endorsements from a host of professional associations, which were often accompanied by paid "signature ads" in local newspapers. Immensely popular and effective, the tactic first introduced the arms race and the freeze proposal to these organizations as points of discussion, making them on-the-job "water cooler topics." The professional endorsements then helped move freeze support deeper into the mainstream, and the "signature ads," which often included hundreds of local names, personalized support for the freeze.

Finally, associations gave their own professional vantage point on the freeze: Educators discussed the impact of the arms race on children, psychologists assessed the impact on mental health, scientists focused on the destructive power of nuclear weapons, and social workers highlighted cuts to social programs. One "Yes on 7" campaign advertisement in the Daily Hampshire Gazette, for example, discussed the medical implications of nuclear war and included the signatures of more than one hundred area health professionals, mostly doctors and registered nurses. Nationally, Dr. Helen Caldicott's controversial lectures had introduced the U.S. public to not only the gruesome medical effects of a nuclear blast and radioactive fallout but also the powerlessness of medical professionals to handle such carnage. Echoing Caldicott's views about the effects of nuclear war, the medical advertisement in the Daily Hampshire Gazette declared, "There is no possible effective medical response except to administer stockpiles of morphine."[90]

The "Yes on 7" campaign conducted a savvy press and media drive that procured a surprising amount of local coverage in a presidential election year during which voters would face a ballot crowded with seven questions, including the hotly debated Proposition 2½.[91] The freeze campaign placed paid advertisements in all the major local newspapers and on all eleven radio stations and received coverage from the three regional television networks. The local press and media covered the campaign regularly, conducted interviews with freeze activists, and published numerous (heavily pro-freeze and sometimes full-page) letters to the editor on the topic. Overall, the "Yes on 7" campaign managed to project a sympathetic image to the public and convey its main points through the press and media.[92] By election day, the "Yes on 7" campaign had won the endorsement of most of the local press, including the *Morning Union*, the *Berkshire Eagle*, the *Greenfield Recorder*, the *Valley Advocate*, and the moderately conservative *Springfield Republican*, which also endorsed Ronald Reagan for president.[93]

Although the western Massachusetts freeze campaign maintained its local focus, at least one national figure was brought in to stump for question 7. Famous for leaking the *Pentagon Papers* in 1971, Daniel Ellsberg had joined David Dellinger and other 1960s activists in the mid-1970s to form MfS, a group modeled on the Vietnam War–era group Mobe (Mobilization to End the War in Vietnam). The organization declared that its mission was "to put back on the political agenda what had been lost in the Vietnam years: an awareness of the threat of nuclear holocaust."[94] (In 1979 Forsberg first proposed her version of a nuclear weapons freeze at a convention of six hundred MfS members.) Although the western Massachusetts campaign was launched independently of the national movement, national figures watched the "Yes on 7" campaign closely, viewing it as a pilot program to test the appeal of the freeze with mainstream voters.[95]

Ellsberg, a popular draw, came to western Massachusetts at the request of Kehler, whom he had known since the late 1960s, when Kehler's willingness to go to jail to oppose the war influenced Ellsberg's decision to leak the *Pentagon Papers*.[96] Ellsberg barnstormed the area in the weeks leading up to the election, telling students at the University of Massachusetts at Amherst, "We can stop setting the example (of) encouraging the reliance on nuclear weapons (as a defense) strategy. . . . We've set the worst possible example for the last thirty-five years and that has kept us from using our weight diplomatically against nuclear proliferation."[97] After sharing the concerns voiced by several students over President Carter's recent reintroduction of Selective Service registration, Ellsberg fielded questions about the upcoming presidential election.

It is interesting—given Reagan's hard-line anti-Soviet stance and call for even greater arms buildup—that the local freeze movement rarely mentioned the right-wing Republican in 1980. Much of the liberal Left in the United States continued to focus anger and betrayal on Carter's hard-line turn in 1978, which only grew more belligerent as the 1980 election approached. Asked by students where he stood on question of the presidential contest, Ellsberg expressed an ambivalence that was common among progressives: "I see a threat going with Carter or Reagan." Nevertheless, he conceded that he would vote for Carter, because at least Carter did not "celebrate the arms race."[98] Ellsberg's main message, however, was for his audience to go out and vote for the freeze: "I hope western

Mass' will show the way. I hope two years from now there will be a referendum on every ballot in every state."[99]

The western Massachusetts freeze movement also confronted an issue that the national freeze movement would encounter in the coming years: anticommunism. The 1980 presidential election was one marked by strident anti-Soviet rhetoric from both the Carter and Reagan camps. Thus, the "Yes on 7" campaign had to promote an end to the arms race in an election year in which anticommunist rhetoric reached peak volume. To avoid charges of pro-Soviet leanings, local freeze activists challenged the basic premises of U.S. cold war ideology while they remained critical of both the United States and the Soviet Union. To one reporter, Kehler declared, "We don't naively believe the Soviets have peaceful intensions."[100] Yet, even as they criticized the Soviet Union, freeze activists worked to deflate the image of the superpower as an inveterately expansionist nation bent on world domination.

Marta Daniels of the AFSC, recently back from a trip to the Soviet Union, told a gathering of Traprock activists, "[A] powerful segment of our population (the military-industrial complex) has a vested interest in the maintenance of the Soviet threat."[101] Earlier in the year, Kehler had stated to a reporter from the *Greenfield Recorder*: "The current saber rattling about a new 'Russian threat' is nothing but election rhetoric. Though the Soviet invasion of Afghanistan must be condemned, thus far the scale and duration of it in no way compare to our own invasion of Vietnam. We forget that Russia and its Eastern European client states are almost completely surrounded by hostile neighbors. . . . In short, Russia is hardly on the verge of taking over Western Europe, overrunning the rest of the Third World or launching a war against the U.S."[102]

The "Yes on 7" campaign sought to address questions about the Soviet Union head on. One pamphlet, titled "Behind the Scenes: The Myth of the Soviet Threat," pointed to corporate profits from defense spending and exposed the role of New Right organizations such as the Committee on the Present Danger in promoting the new "Red Scare."[103] Another pamphlet, titled "But What about the Russians?" equated the respective imperialism of the United States and the Soviet Union, stating, "Both nations are seeking control of scarce world resources. Since World War II, both nations have used military intervention, propaganda and scare tactics to maintain and expand their influence. . . . The recent Soviet invasion of Afghanistan to preserve the shaky pro-Soviet government, far from gaining them leadership in the Third World, has earned the Soviets near universal condemnation."[104]

The freeze movement also worked to humanize Soviet citizens. In the coming years—as part of a campaign promoted by Ground Zero, another U.S. arms control organization—several Massachusetts towns would declare their sister city status with towns and cities in the Soviet Union.[105] Several Traprock activists would visit the Soviet Union, and others would join national letter-writing campaigns, in which they called for the Soviet leadership to release imprisoned Soviet peace activists.[106] On the whole, by maintaining a critical stance toward both of the superpowers and by emphasizing a shared global humanity over an ideologically divided world, the western Massachusetts freeze movement helped keep the focus on the arms race itself and the cost to both societies.

The major element of the national movement that was foreshadowed in the 1980 western Massachusetts freeze campaign was its electoral strategy. Kehler repeatedly emphasized that the goal was to produce a locally based mass movement that would be "large enough to cause national leaders to take heed."[107] Although the movement against nuclear energy made forays into electoral politics, predominantly through antinuclear referenda, it remained focused primarily on direct action or legal intervention. More than most movements of the 1970s and 1980s, the freeze movement worked to influence elected representatives and win their endorsement of the freeze. In the 1980 campaign, the immediate focus was on three state senators, John Olver (Franklin and Hampshire Counties), Martin Reilly (Hamden County), and Peter Webber (Berkshire County), who were to be instructed by the referendum to introduce a freeze resolution in the state Senate. The movement also set its sights on Silvio Conte, a well-liked moderate Republican congressman from western Massachusetts.[108]

Much of the focus in the 1980 campaign was on the Democrat John Olver, whose district encompassed many freeze strongholds, such as Amherst, Northampton, and Deerfield. Early in the campaign, sounding a theme that freeze opponents would hear repeatedly in coming years, Olver stated that although he supported arms control efforts, he doubted that the freeze was "verifiable."[109] Conte also expressed reservations. As the election neared and the freeze movement seemed to garner a growing groundswell of support, however, both politicians endorsed the freeze (although Kehler and Faison would later refer to Conte's belated endorsement as "somewhat reluctant").[110] Within months, nevertheless, Olver would find himself the point man in the campaign to win endorsement of the freeze from the Massachusetts legislature, and Conte would find himself torn between his increasingly conservative national political party and his strongly pro-freeze constituency. Both Conte and Olver were the first Bay State politicians who were swept along by the rising tide of the freeze movement. By 1983, both houses of the state legislature, the governor, and all twelve members of the Massachusetts congressional delegation had endorsed the freeze.

On November 4, 1980, voters in three western Massachusetts state senatorial districts voted 59 percent to 41 percent in favor of a nuclear weapons freeze. In Olver's district, an astonishing 64.5 percent of the electorate endorsed the freeze proposal. The numbers were similarly high in Berkshire County, where 59.2 percent of the voters said "yes" to question 7. In the sections of more conservative Hamden County that voted on the freeze, 50.5 percent voted for the moratorium. Overall, fifty-nine of sixty-two towns that voted endorsed the freeze. Yet in a vote that perplexed many, the same region of western Massachusetts that endorsed the freeze narrowly cast the majority of its votes for Ronald Reagan, with thirty-three of sixty-two towns voting for the conservative Republican.[111] Nevertheless, the freeze garnered a majority of votes in virtually every town that voted for Reagan. Some observers speculated that the mixed message sent by voters stemmed from the fact that, going into the election, Reagan's strength was more on the economic front and that his statesman-like demeanor during his televised debate with Carter a week before the election helped alleviate voter concern about his strident anticommunism.[112]

Days before the November 1980 vote, Kehler confidently predicted, "Our work is going to send a signal around the country about how Americans feel about the arms race."[113] In a 1983 speech, Crowe described a less optimistic feeling: "Election night we gathered to celebrate our work ... but certainly not in expectation of victory. Some of us thought maybe twenty-five percent would vote for the freeze. As the news came in that Reagan was winning, the polls also reported that we were winning!"[114] If many liberals and radicals across the United States were despondent over the results of the presidential election, supporters of a nuclear weapons freeze were elated at the overwhelming popular endorsement of their proposal in western Massachusetts. To the *Nation*, Kehler proclaimed, "This vote in western Massachusetts shows that the American public is indeed receptive to proposals for stopping the arms race. The issue of nuclear arms transcends party lines and liberal vs. conservative divisions.... [N]o one wants a nuclear war."[115]

Just weeks before the November vote, Kehler, Crowe, and other Massachusetts activists met with more than forty national arms control and disarmament advocates on the eighth floor of U.N. Plaza in New York City. Kehler returned to western Massachusetts and told local freeze supporters, "I found that nearly everyone at the meeting had not only heard about the western Massachusetts referendum, but they said they viewed it as the bellwether of the whole moratorium movement, the first real test anywhere in the country of the public's reaction to the moratorium proposal."[116] For Kehler, the "Yes on 7" campaign had tested the political waters and found that Americans were open to ending the arms race.

Kehler and others now sought to ballyhoo the western Massachusetts campaign as a model that could be transplanted across the United States: "Our success in western Massachusetts, an area diverse enough to be fairly representative of the country as a whole, means that the American public is indeed receptive to constructive bilateral proposals for ending the insanely dangerous nuclear arms race despite the electorate's apparent rightward shift."[117]

After the vote, Ellsberg promised to tell "the western Massachusetts story" coast to coast, but it seemed to spread on its own following the November election. Mark Hatfield, a freeze pioneer and senator from Oregon, wrote to Traprock, "I want to send you my congratulations for your successful referendum campaign in Western Massachusetts. . . . I understand that the proposition . . . was approved by a decisive majority. This is greatly encouraging."[118] Within a week Traprock was inundated with requests for information from across the nation, especially from pacifist religious groups. Recalling the aftermath of the vote, Crowe noted, "Then mail came in from all over the country asking how we had done it."[119] Anne Willard, an AFSC member from Seattle, Washington, wrote Traprock, "Congratulations on your hard work and on the very positive results. If you have details of the campaign that you are willing to send, I would appreciate very much receiving them."[120] From Bloomington, Indiana, Ruth Sanders wrote, "Word is spreading of your successful referendum on the arms race . . . [which is] raising much enthusiasm in our local [AFSC] meeting that perhaps some such movement could be started in Indiana."[121]

As the western Massachusetts success story circulated, freeze support spread like wild fire up the Connecticut River Valley, and in the months following the November election, more than fourteen Vermont municipalities voted in town meetings to endorse a nuclear weapons freeze.[122] Town meetings across western Massachusetts soon followed suit, transforming the region into a bastion of solidly pro-freeze sentiment. In the spring of 1981, Cambridge joined the trend with its endorsement of the freeze.[123] As Kehler moved to St. Louis to take charge of a newly formed national freeze movement, organizers in western Massachusetts began their efforts to turn the state of Massachusetts into a nuclear weapons freeze fortress. Traprock, the Amherst Disarmament Coalition, and other groups involved in the "Yes on 7" campaign branched out across the state, making contacts with other local Massachusetts disarmament groups (especially in Cambridge), and formed the Massachusetts Coalition for a Nuclear Weapons Freeze.[124] Working with elected officials in the commonwealth, they would soon turn Massachusetts into the flagship state of the national nuclear weapons freeze movement.

THE PASSAGE OF THE MASSACHUSETTS
FREEZE RESOLUTION: SPRING 1981

A week after the election, the *Traprock Report* proclaimed, "We did it! [Our state senators] have a popular mandate to carry the nuclear weapons moratorium proposal to the State House in Boston."[125] The liberal Democratic state senator John Olver had gone from initial skepticism to endorsement of the nuclear weapons freeze proposal as it gathered strength. After western Massachusetts voters resoundingly approved the freeze in November 1980, Olver transformed himself almost overnight into the chief elected movement advocate on Beacon Hill in Boston. Olver coordinated his efforts closely with Traprock. Weeks after the vote, he wrote Traprock members, "As my aide, Stan Rosenberg, indicated during his visit with you at the Traprock Peace Center, I intend to file with the Senate Clerk by December 3 the Resolution related to Ballot Question #7.... I understand that optimally you would like to see the matter acted upon between the third week of March and the end of April to coincide with other activities of interest to your group. I will do my best to see that it comes before the Senate during that period."[126]

As promised, John Olver and the Springfield Democrat Alan Sisitsky cosponsored a freeze resolution in the Massachusetts Senate in early December.[127] Olver took the freeze movement case to his colleagues in the state capital, saying, "Are we really more secure knowing that we and our adversaries can destroy each other many times over in a matter of hours? . . . I think not. I know of no one who would argue against adequate defense. However, we must ask ourselves, defense at what risks? . . . What have we to lose if both the United States and Soviet Union agree to a verifiable nuclear arms moratorium?"[128]

As the freeze debate evolved, Olver found himself most comfortable with the emphasis on the social costs of the arms race. In a statement that seemed to draw on Winpisinger's IAM report, Olver stated, "The same billion dollars [spent on nuclear weapons] put to civilian use will employ 73,000 police, 76,000 teachers or 85,000 nurses."[129] Olver and his allies in the state senate introduced Senate Resolution 455, which called on the president of the United States to propose to the Soviet Union a nuclear weapons moratorium and to transfer the funds saved to civilian use.[130] Lobbying hard for the resolution were activists from the Massachusetts Coalition for a Nuclear Weapons Freeze, including many veterans of the western Massachusetts campaign. As the debate unfolded, eastern Massachusetts activists increasingly weighed in, with the Cambridge city council endorsing a nuclear weapons freeze on March 16, 1981.[131]

In April 1981 the Federal Financial Assistance Committee, a joint committee of both houses of the state legislature, which handled state relations with the federal government, began hearings on the freeze resolution. In three days of hearings, pro-freeze activists filled the hearing room and conducted what the *Traprock Report* called a "three-day lobbying blitz."[132] Witnesses who spoke at the hearings included Randall Forsberg; David Cohen, from the United Electrical Workers; and Lieutenant Colonel John H. Buchan, a twenty-year Marine Corps veteran and pro-freeze "senior analyst" for the Center for Defense Information. Comparing the November 1980 freeze vote in western Massachusetts to the 1775 battle of Lexington and Concord, Buchan declared that the vote "was heard around the world."[133] Alongside the pro-freeze marine appeared a former deputy director of the Central Intelligence Agency (CIA), Herbert Scoulie, who—charging that the current arms buildup, especially the buildup of the proposed MX missile, gave the Russians a first-strike incentive—endorsed the freeze as a responsible and realistic way to arrest the arms race and promote U.S. security.[134] Scoulie stated, "If nuclear weapons are ever used in a conflict, it will be a catastrophe for mankind."[135] Also speaking for the freeze resolution was Father Robert Drinan, who had been elected to Congress in 1970 as an antiwar candidate and had recently retired.

The Joint Federal Financial Assistance Committee of the state legislature approved the resolutions, which were then passed by the Massachusetts Senate on May 18 and the Massachusetts House of Representatives on June 9.[136] While Olver shepherded the resolution through the senate—aided by numerous pro-freeze lobbyists—William Benson, the Democratic state representative from Greenfield, worked for passage in the House, telling colleagues, "We have to take a serious look at what we're doing and [determine] if, in the long run, it's sane."[137] Thus, only eight months after voters in the western half of the state expressed their support for a nuclear weapons freeze, the Massachusetts legislature became the first state legislature in the country to endorse this new direction for the nation. In a press release, the Coalition for a Nuclear Weapons Freeze drew attention to a historical parallel: "The Coalition is encouraged knowing that in 1970, the Massachusetts Legislature voted for a resolution calling for an end to the Vietnam War. That vote was the first such vote by a state legislature—it helped catalyze public acceptance of opposition to the war. . . . The nuclear freeze vote is another historical first."[138] Freeze activists were elated by their rapid progress on the state level. After the vote, Eugene Angus, a professor of literature at Western New England College and a member of the Amherst Disarmament Coalition, declared, "We are telling Reagan in no uncertain terms that we as a state are serious. . . . It was very gratifying to see the state legislature do this."[139]

THE MASSACHUSETTS STATEWIDE FREEZE
RESOLUTION: NOVEMBER 1982

By 1982, the freeze movement was taking the United States by storm, becoming a nightly topic on the evening news and taking up increasing space in the newspapers, periodicals, and public discourse. In an endorsement of the freeze, the *Boston Globe* declared, "Almost suddenly, a new political movement is blowing in the wind from coast to coast. It's called the 'freeze' movement.... To the amazement of national security specialists and others who have lobbied for years in the dusty bins of arms control, the freeze looks like it's going to be a political heavyweight. A few months ago most observers of the American scene would have said that a responsible, credible, politically effective 'peace movement' was years away."[140] On June 12, 1982, more than 850,000 Americans rallied peacefully for a nuclear weapons freeze in New York City in what many consider one of the largest peace demonstrations in U.S. history.[141]

In the commonwealth, the Massachusetts Coalition for a Nuclear Weapons Freeze worked hard to build on the momentum of the previous two years to keep the Bay State at the cutting edge of the national freeze movement. Members of Senator Edward Kennedy's staff had recently contacted Kehler and were working to align the senator more closely with the freeze movement.[142] The minutes of a Western Massachusetts Coalition for a Nuclear Weapons Freeze meeting at which Frances Crowe, Pauline Bassett, and Judith Scheckel were present reveal that Senator Kennedy was behind the idea to put the freeze on a statewide referendum the following November. The minutes state, "Senator Kennedy had suggested to the group of Massachusetts freeze workers who met with him several weeks ago that Massachusetts have a statewide referendum on the freeze. The Council for a Nuclear Weapons Freeze in Cambridge has been working with the legislature to place the freeze on the November ballot."[143] The movement thus set as its goal for 1982 a freeze referendum to be voted on statewide in the November elections, which would make Massachusetts one of nine states to place the freeze on a statewide ballot that year. Since California would be voting on the freeze, the national movement boasted that more than 30 percent of all Americans would be offered a chance to express their views on the freeze at the polls that November.[144]

Once again, the leader in the state senate was Olver, whose western Massachusetts district remained a stronghold of freeze activism in the state. Olver and the Democrat George Bachrach, his fellow state senator from Watertown, codrafted a circular letter that urged the state legislature to put a freeze referendum on the November ballot that would call on President Reagan, Secretary of State Alexander Haig, and U.S. delegates to the U.N. Disarmament Session to propose a "prompt freeze ... [followed by] scheduled, verifiable, progressive reduction of nuclear weapons arsenals, leading to the eradication and banning of such weapons." The letter declared, "So that they may have their share of nuclear weapons the Soviet people stand in line for food and wait years for housing while their government spends a huge share of their gross national product on nuclear arms.... So that we may have our share of nuclear weapons ... budgets for mass transportation, education, housing and social services are cut."[145]

Unlike during the Massachusetts freeze campaigns of 1980 and 1981, when opposition was disorganized and scattered, by 1982, the Reagan administration was regularly employing the "bully pulpit" to denounce the freeze as "unilateral disarmament" and to red-bait the national movement as inspired by Moscow.[146] This strategy emboldened freeze opponents on the state level, who now geared up in Massachusetts to stop the freeze proposal from reaching voters on the state ballot in November 1982. Although the state Senate acted with dispatch, passing the bill to put the freeze on the ballot thirty-six to one, the bill ran into trouble in the state House of Representatives, where Republicans and conservative Democrats tried to kill the ballot question with amendments that used language designed to alter the question.[147] One representative affixed the wording "unless the president feels it will weaken the United States" to the end of the freeze ballot question passed by the Senate.[148] William Robinson, the Republican state representative from Melrose, added language forbidding freeze negotiations "if militarily disadvantageous to the United States."[149] Marie Howe, the Democratic state representative from-Somerville, proposed an amendment forbidding negotiations until the Soviet Union withdrew from Afghanistan and pulled out of Eastern Europe. As freeze activists stepped up their lobbying to break the logjam before the deadline passed for questions to appear on the November ballot, Bassett sighed in exasperation, "We didn't anticipate this."[150] Given their proximity to the statehouse, the Cambridge Council for a Nuclear Weapons Freeze took the lead in lobbying for the ballot question in the state legislature, making almost daily appearances.[151]

Many charged House Speaker Thomas McGee, a conservative Democrat, with preventing the ballot question from going to a joint conference committee. Michael Dukakis, the Democratic candidate for governor, inserted himself into the dispute, hoping to break the impasse by strongly endorsing the freeze. Speaking before the Kennedy Library in Boston, Dukakis declared, "Here, with the Kennedy Library behind us, we are reminded of President John Kennedy's successful support in 1963 of a treaty banning all nuclear weapons testing in the air, sea and outer space.... Nuclear war cannot be won or survived. It can only be prevented."[152]

The logjam was finally broken when McGee received a letter from the Massachusetts national congressional delegation, including Ted Kennedy and U.S. Speaker of the House Tip O'Neill, both of whom were working to promote a freeze resolution at the national level.[153] The conference committee stripped the ballot question of the conservative amendments added in the House and sent it along to the state secretary of state barely in time to make the printing deadline for the November ballot. The freeze question to face Bay State voters—ballot question 5— read, "Shall the Secretary of the Commonwealth of Massachusetts inform the President and the Congress of the United States that it is the desire of the people of Massachusetts to have the government of the United States work vigorously to negotiate a mutual nuclear weapons moratorium and reduction with appropriate verification, with the Soviet Union and other nations?"[154]

Massachusetts conservatives were not happy. Robert Hall, the Republican state senator from Fichtburg, denounced the freeze ballot question as a liberal ploy "to bring all the fruit loops out in November."[155] Echoing the red-baiting coming out of the administration in Washington, D.C., Royall Switzer, the Republican state representative from Wellesley, inveighed, "The liberals, I sometimes think, are carrying the baggage for the Russians, who want a nuclear freeze because they know how far ahead they are."[156]

A place for the freeze on the statewide ballot was ensured with the signature of Governor Ed King, who many called Reagan's favorite Democrat for his opposition to abortion, support for capital punishment, and pro-business and antitax positions. King was gearing up for his own rematch in the upcoming Democratic primaries, where he would face Michael Dukakis, the former governor who was trying to stage his own political comeback. Although King's conservative streak might have inclined him to oppose the freeze, the popularity of the proposal in the state dictated another course of action. Thus, he wisely avoided handing his more liberal gubernatorial opponent another issue by refusing to sign the bill. King declared simply that he was "against nuclear war, against all war."[157]

The election of 1982 saw the freeze movement hit high tide. Earlier that year, the U.S. House of Representatives had fallen two votes short of passing a freeze resolution (206 to 204).[158] The Democrats picked up a number of seats in the House and Senate that November.[159] Of the nine states that had the freeze on a statewide ballot that year, only Arizona voted it down (59 percent to 41 percent). In California the freeze narrowly passed, with 52.5 percent support. Elsewhere, the margin of victory was greater. The tallies were Michigan, 57 percent; Montana, 57 percent; New Jersey, 66 percent; North Dakota, 58 percent; Oregon, 61.5 percent; and Rhode Island, 59 percent. Twenty-nine cities also passed freeze resolutions, as did Washington, D.C. Not to be outdone, Massachusetts voters approved the

freeze by an astonishing 74 percent, with every single town in the state register-
ing its approval.[160] Surveying the coast-to-coast victories of the freeze proposal,
Scheckel exclaimed, "In 1980, after our small referendum victory in western
Massachusetts, none of us dreamt that two years later 30% of the country would
have an opportunity to vote on the Freeze."[161]

By 1982, Massachusetts had emerged as the most reliable base of the freeze
movement. All twelve members of the Massachusetts congressional delegation
in Washington supported the freeze, the state legislature had given its approval,
and now nearly three of every four voters in the state had cast a ballot in favor of
the proposal. The only weak link in Massachusetts politics vis-à-vis the freeze was
the office of the governor, where Ed King offered only tacit and unenthusiastic
support. That situation was about to change dramatically.

NUCLEAR-FREE ZONES, CRISIS RELOCATION PLANNING, AND GOVERNOR MICHAEL S. DUKAKIS

The breakdown of détente in the late 1970s and the ensuing arms buildup was
accompanied by a revived emphasis on civil defense in the United States. The
Carter administration allocated increased funding for civil defense and called
on the Federal Emergency Management Agency (FEMA) to work with the states
to draw up more detailed emergency plans for moving urban residents to rural
"host" communities known as Crisis Relocation Planning (CRP). As the new
Reagan administration undertook its massive nuclear weapons buildup in the
early 1980s, it placed even greater emphasis on CRP in its plan for waging and
winning a nuclear war. The Reagan administration proposed a record $4.2 billion
budget for FEMA civil defense planning. Not since the days of "duck and cover"
drills and fallout shelters of the 1950s and early 1960s had so much emphasis
been placed on civil defense, and never in U.S. history had so much money been
earmarked for it.[162]

The resurrection of civil defense planning was all the more unnerving to peace
advocates, since it took place in the context of the Reagan administration arms
buildup and heightened rhetoric about fighting "limited" and "winnable" nuclear
wars. The rhetoric was often surreal and frightening. Louis Giuffrida, who headed
FEMA, had this to say about a nuclear war: "It would be a terrible mess, but it
wouldn't be unmanageable."[163] Undersecretary of Defense T. K. Jones gave the
following advice: To survive a nuclear war, Americans should "dig a hole, cover
it with a couple of doors and then throw three feet of dirt on top." American
deaths, Jones argued, could be kept to as low as ten million provided there were
"enough shovels to go around."[164] Secretary of State Alexander Haig spoke of
firing "nuclear warning shots," and Eugene Rostow, who had been appointed

director of the Arms Control and Disarmament Agency by the Reagan administration, proclaimed, "We are living in a pre-war and not a post-war world."[165]

In the early Reagan years, FEMA was officially charged with drawing up plans, in concert with the states, for the relocation of more than 75 percent of the U.S. population to designated "host" communities. This plan presumed one week of notice. Many critics pointed out that the Soviet Union would most likely interpret such a massive population shift as a sign that the United States was preparing for a nuclear war, which would encourage the Soviets to strike first. Nevertheless, the Reagan administration pushed ahead with its civil defense planning, making the talk of planning for winnable nuclear war seem all the more palpable to millions of Americans. Adding to the surreal sense, FEMA announced that it would work to keep U.S. financial institutions running after a nuclear war and advised that relocating Americans take their credit cards with them.[166]

As the people of Massachusetts learned the details of the Bay State CRP, the plans made the arms race all the more tangible. Tentatively, much of rural western Massachusetts was designated as host communities. Amherst, for example, was to take in 160,000 residents from the nearby cities of Springfield, Holyoke, and Granby. Greenfield was to host 158,000 people from Cambridge.[167]

In the early 1980s, a national anti-CRP movement grew side by side with the freeze movement. Once again Massachusetts was at the forefront. Two academic communities led the way: first Cambridge and then Amherst. Cambridge, home to Harvard University, the Massachusetts Institute of Technology (MIT), and other academic institutions, was an upscale town that abutted greater Boston. In 1981 members of the Cambridge Council for a Nuclear Weapons Freeze joined other town peace activists to push for some symbolic action to show their opposition to CRP. As the state legislature debated the freeze resolutions of 1981 across the Charles River, 72 percent of Cambridge voters approved a nonbinding resolution that declared Cambridge a nuclear free zone (NFZ) and stated that the town was opposed to any form of cooperation with the FEMA CRP.[168] "I am proud to be among those who recognize the fallacy of Cambridge citizens grabbing their credit cards and their wills and driving to Greenfield to escape the horror of nuclear war," Cambridge City Councilor Sandra Graham later declared.[169]

The issue quickly merged with freeze activism in western Massachusetts, where the Amherst Disarmament Coalition, the Amherst Ad Hoc Committee on Crisis Relocation Planning, the Committee for a Nuclear Free Amherst, and the Traprock Civil Defense Information project led the campaign.[170] The chairman of the Amherst Board of Selectmen denounced CRP as "a cruel joke to convince people you can survive a nuclear war."[171] At a 1982 hearing with state civil defense officials, Aaron Lansky, a Jewish resident of Amherst, compared the state CRP mentality to the genocide-producing mentality of the Holocaust: "The Holocaust was perpetrated by bureaucrats who forgot to ask why, who watched without comment.... Having lost family and friends to one holocaust, we are not content to sit by and watch a second nuclear holocaust.... We cannot take the one bureaucratic step to accept this plan without becoming complicit in the whole. We cannot accept our assigned stations in the machine of death."[172]

The movement to promote noncooperation with CRP gathered steam as the freeze movement swept across the country. Cities and towns in Europe had begun declaring themselves NFZs in opposition to planned deployment of U.S. Pershing and Cruise missiles, and a growing number of U.S. cities and towns were following suit.[173] Amherst and other towns refused to cooperate with the state CRP. In 1984 Amherst passed one of the most stringent, binding NFZ bylaws in the nation. After two hours of raucous debate, the town meeting voted 101 to 60 to designate Amherst as an NFZ, requiring Amherst to divest all funds from any company involved in the production of nuclear weapons; prohibiting all such corporations from doing business in the town; and banning unclassified research related to nuclear war (the University of Massachusetts had banned all such classified research in 1972).[174] Within a year, the town had sponsored two pamphlets on CRP: one titled "Why There Is No Protecting against the Consequences of Nuclear War" and the other, "Why No Steps Short of Nuclear Disarmament Could Protect the Citizens of Amherst from Nuclear War."[175]

By 1984, fifty-eight U.S. cities and towns, twenty of which were in Massachusetts, had declared themselves to be NFZs.[176] Ironically, in 1983, Cambridge residents voted down an effort similar to the one that passed a year later in Amherst, which would have made the Cambridge nonbinding NFZ proclamation binding.[177] During a petition drive to put the NFZ question on the ballot, Richard Schreuer of the Nuclear Free Cambridge campaign wrote an opinion piece in the *Boston Globe* explaining the campaign to Cambridge voters: "We want work on nuclear weapons to stop in Cambridge now, because allowing it to continue is being complicit in the arms race.... Just as 19th century abolitionists took a step toward abolishing slavery by refusing to recognize fugitive slave laws in their own communities, Cambridge and other nuclear free areas are taking a step toward disarmament by refusing to be complicit in the arms race."[178]

An organized resistance led by John Silber, the right-wing president of Boston University, emerged to oppose the proposed NFZ law. At public meetings, Silber would clap in the face of NFZ supporters, declaring that each clap represented one hundred thousand Afghan refugees. Others argued that the bill would impinge on academic freedom or that the NFZ movement philosophy of defying federal policy was too similar in theory to the philosophy of the white segregationist South during the civil rights era.[179] The proposed Cambridge NFZ would have been the first in the nation to actually disrupt nuclear weapons research. Although the bill would have had to be tested in court, the binding referendum would have not only affected the extensive nuclear weapons research being conducted at Cambridge educational institutions but also impacted Draper Labs, a major nuclear weapons contractor located within the town limits. In one of the first setbacks for anti–nuclear weapons activists in Massachusetts, Cambridge voters rejected the NFZ proposal.[180]

In 1984 a similar fate befell NFZ proponents in Northampton. They failed to win passage of an NFZ bill that would have impacted the Kollmorgen Corporation, which had received a $6.2 million contract to make periscopes for Trident nuclear submarines. Local unions mobilized to defend jobs that they saw as threatened by the proposed NFZ. Trying to put a positive spin on the city council vote, Victoria Safford, and AFSC member, stated, "It's more important to lay the groundwork with the community and unions and management than it is to demand they give up contracts. We're trying to get a dialogue going."[181] Meanwhile, nearby Leverett, Belchertown, and Shutesbury joined the list of towns declaring themselves to be NFZs.[182] It became clear, however, that as the peace movement went beyond symbolic referenda to binding resolutions with real economic consequences, resistance would grow.

The disarmament movement in Massachusetts had its greatest success in opposing state participation in CRP. Individual towns led the way by simply refusing to cooperate with state planners, situating themselves in a legal limbo. Beginning in 1983, however, CRP opponents found themselves a friend in the newly elected Bay State governor, Michael Dukakis, and his lieutenant governor, the Vietnam War veteran John Kerry. During the 1982 gubernatorial campaign, Dukakis had condemned CRP as "a Doomsday scheme" and an "attempt to deceive the public into believing that nuclear war is survivable."[183] The Dukakis/ Kerry campaign promised that if elected they would make available "the resources of our office to expand and coordinate all local efforts to say 'no' to such a plan."[184] In a major political comeback, Dukakis won reelection in 1982 after four years out of office.

First elected to the state legislature in 1964, Dukakis came in as one of the young "clean government" reform Democrats then taking on the Democratic old guard of Massachusetts. Dukakis's 1988 presidential campaign literature later stated, "Angered by the excesses of Joseph McCarthy, and inspired by John Kennedy during his campaign for president, Michael Dukakis became an active participant in state Democratic Party affairs."[185] Once elected to the legislature from his home district of Brookline, Dukakis prided himself on being a progressive, dispassionate technocrat who worked against corruption, special interests, and influence peddling in state government.

In the turbulent sixties, Dukakis made a name for himself by championing automobile insurance reform. Then, he supported the resolution by the state legislature calling for the United States to withdraw from Vietnam in 1970 and had also won the praise of Massachusetts disarmament groups. Dukakis ran for lieutenant governor in 1970 on a ticket with Kevin White, the liberal mayor of Boston, who lost the race for governor to the liberal Republican Francis Sargent. In the early 1970s, Dukakis became a household name in Massachusetts as moderator of the popular political television program The Advocates. In 1974 Dukakis won the Democratic nomination for governor and defeated the charismatic two-term governor with the help of a worsening economic downturn and anger over court-mandated busing in Boston.[186]

Dukakis's first term took place during the worst phase of the 1970s economic crisis. Breaking a campaign promise, Dukakis was forced to raise taxes and make painful cuts in social programs to cover a massive budget shortfall hidden by the previous administration. The raise in taxes infuriated moderates and conservatives, and the cuts in social programs threw liberals such as State Representative Barney Frank into a rage. Some accused Dukakis of balancing the budget on the backs of low-income people. Others attacked his style as aloof and arrogant and criticized his absolute refusal to engage in compromise or patronage. In his first term, Dukakis won some plaudits from the movement against nuclear energy by refusing to dispatch Massachusetts state police to assist in the arrest of protestors at Seabrook (see Chapter 2). In 1978—although the budget was on a sound footing and the Massachusetts economy was improving, and despite the fact that Dukakis had conducted one of the cleanest administrations in memory—voters surprised all observers by electing Ed King, a conservative businessman and former football player, in the Democratic primary. King easily went on to defeat his Republican opponent in November.[187]

By 1982, King had scandalized Bay State voters with the most corrupt and inept administration in decades. As it turned out, virtually all of King's most glaring vices were Dukakis's strongest virtues. During his years out of office, Dukakis had softened his image and worked to repair his damaged relations with members of the business community (who believed he had engaged in overregulation) and liberals (who still rankled at the harsh budget cuts of the first Dukakis administration). Dukakis's second term proved the most successful of his three, as he developed a national reputation for his successful welfare, job training, and tax reform programs. While Dukakis made a national name with his economic experiments, he also opened the doors of his administration to Massachusetts peace activists.[188]

Beginning in 1983, members of Traprock and other Massachusetts peace organizations began to meet with MarDee Xifaras, a Dukakis aide, and Lieutenant Governor Kerry, a former peace activist with Vietnam Veterans against the War. Before being elected to the U.S. Senate in 1984, Kerry had acted as a bridge between freeze activists and the governor. At a June 27, 1983, meeting, activists proposed to Kerry that the new administration rescind a 1956 executive order that made evacuation planning part of the state civil defense policy; withhold state funds from all civil defense activity; create an executive position in the commonwealth to promote prevention of nuclear war; and have the governor lead opposition to CRP at meetings of the National Governors Association (NGA).[189] Activists seemed appreciative of their newfound access. In 1984 the *Traprock Report* described Kerry as a "strong supporter" and an "ardent Freeze advocate."[190]

Within a year of taking office, Dukakis moved on CRP and all the other proposals put to Kerry the previous year. First, he circulated a nuclear weapons freeze petition at the 1983 NGA meeting, procuring majority support; then he sent copies of the petition to all members of Congress.[191] Then, on June 28, 1984, as promised, Dukakis issued an executive order withdrawing the commonwealth from the national CRP. Executive Order No. 242 declared, "The only effective defense against the horrors of nuclear weapons lies in their elimination and in the prevention of nuclear war." It pledged the commonwealth to a policy of promoting peace education and working to influence national policy.[192]

At a ceremony attended by hundreds of activists, Dukakis announced his executive order and spoke to the issue of civil defense: "The notion that we can seriously help reduce the horrors of nuclear war by relocating thousands and thousands of people has always seemed to me a fantasy at best....I don't care how far apart we are with other nations.... [I]t seems to me there is one thing that unites all of us in this small world and that is some sense of humanity."[193] Concluding his speech to rousing applause, Dukakis declared, "Simply and practically speaking, there are no safe havens from nuclear attack.... The existing and potential strength of nuclear weapons is such that nuclear war can neither be won, nor survived, it can only be prevented.... [Therefore] no funds shall be expended by the Commonwealth for crisis relocation planning for nuclear war. God save the Commonwealth of Massachusetts."[194]

Sharing the podium with the governor at the executive order signing was the Amherst activist Nancy Foster, who spoke to the assembled crowd, summing up the past three years of activism around the issue: "Public acknowledgement of our profound and immediate peril, and of the futility of seeking protection through evacuation and shelter, is a tribute to an aroused citizenry, working through the democratic process, and to the responsiveness of their elected leaders, first in the cities and towns, now in the Commonwealth as a whole."[195]

By rejecting CRP, Dukakis joined the governors of California, Maryland, and New Mexico in a growing national movement in opposition to the FEMA civil defense plans, which opponents viewed as an unworkable and unacceptable attempt to promote the idea of "winnable" nuclear war. Less than a year from Dukakis's June 28, 1984, executive order that withdrew Massachusetts from all crisis relocation planning, Russell Clanahan, the FEMA deputy press aide, confirmed, "Crisis relocation planning has been abandoned, no question about it."[196] For freeze and anti–civil defense activists, it was an important victory, marking the end of the dark ages of Reagan's first term, during which the administration sought to return the United States to a 1950s civil defense mentality and foster acceptance of waging, surviving, and winning a nuclear war with the Soviet Union.

Freeze activists and their friends in the campaign against CRP were jubilant over Dukakis's 1984 executive order. The *Traprock Report* informed readers that not only had Dukakis pulled the state out of CRP but he had also appointed a Governor's Peace Commission": "Governor Dukakis has recently agreed to appoint a commission that would make recommendations on how the Commonwealth can advance the cause of peace. This is one result of the work done by the Ad Hoc Commission on Crisis Relocation Planning which developed from a statewide meeting organized by Traprock in February 1983 and which led to the Governor's rejection of CRP in June of this year."[197]

On April 25, 1985, Dukakis issued Executive Order No. 254, which officially formed the Governor's Advisory Committee on the Impact of the Nuclear Arms Race on Massachusetts. The preamble read in part:

> WHEREAS, the Massachusetts members of the United States Congress have repeatedly shown a commitment to halting the ever-escalating nuclear arms race; and
>
> WHEREAS, the Massachusetts legislature by resolution in 1981 and the citizens of Massachusetts by referendum in 1982 have declared their clear desire for a halt to the nuclear arms race,
>
> I, Michael Dukakis, do hereby establish the Governor's Advisory Committee on the Impact of the Nuclear Arms Race on Massachusetts.[198]

Executive Order No. 254 called for fifteen to twenty-five members on the advisory committee, who "shall have a demonstrated commitment to arms control."[199] "Talking Points" put together for the announcement by the governor's staff emphasized the role of peace activists in the formation of the committee: "Today's announcement is the culmination of a lot of hard work by people across the state. Concerned citizens throughout the Commonwealth have requested that we establish this Advisory Committee to consider the impact of the nuclear arms race on Massachusetts. Those on the Committee and those here today represent thousands of individuals in Massachusetts."[200] The advisory committee was chaired by Jennifer Leaning of Physicians for Social Responsibility and Undersecretary of Economic Affairs Eric E. Van Loon. Its twenty-two members included representatives from academia, business, and labor and featured prominent peace activists such as Nancy Foster, Randy Kehler, and the veteran disarmament activist Jerome Grossman of the Council for a Livable World.[201]

The job of the advisory committee was to study the economic impact of the arms race on Massachusetts and find ways to promote peace through education and the advancement of links with people in the Soviet Union. In June 1986, as Dukakis was increasingly proposed as a possible 1988 Democratic presidential candidate, the Governor's Advisory Committee on the Impact of the Arms Race on Massachusetts issued its official—and, as it turned out, controversial—report. Several unidentified members leaked stories to the press that accused the Dukakis administration of trying to block the economic committee from offering recommendations and conclusions that the governor considered to be too strong.[202] Ironically, the report showed that the state that seemed most opposed to the arms race actually greatly benefited from it.

The report found that in fiscal year 1985, Massachusetts defense contractors received $1.5 billion from the nuclear arms race, constituting 1.5 percent of the Massachusetts gross state product. Sixty-six percent of this defense work was for the Reagan administration Trident and MX programs, 99 percent of which went to just nine contractors, 77 percent of them in the Route 128/Interstate 495 technological beltway around Boston and 9 percent in Pittsfield in the western part of the state. The report concluded that nuclear weapons spending created fourteen thousand jobs in the commonwealth, or 0.05 percent of the jobs in the state, and indirectly created twelve thousand additional jobs.[203] The largest defense contractors in the state included Avco, Draper Labs, General Electric, General Telephone and Electronics (GTE), and Raytheon.[204] Critics charged that the "Massachusetts Miracle" being trumpeted by Dukakis in anticipation of a presidential run was largely fueled not by the governor's economic policies but by Reagan's arms buildup.[205]

Despite the economic benefits, the study issued four recommendations to help end the arms race:

1) The state continue its annual reports on the impact of the arms race on the Commonwealth.
2) Use public resources to help individuals and firms make the transition to non-nuclear work.
3) Have the Commissioner of Education convene a working group to develop nuclear arms race curriculum materials for possible use by schools.
4) Establish a formal "sister state" relationship with a Soviet province.[206]

The report concluded, "One state within our nation cannot end the nuclear arms race. A mobilized citizenry and an active state government can, however, give direction, clarity, and voice to a concern that is widely shared."[207] Although the recommendations of the report were not radical, the economic conclusions that found so many jobs in the state to be dependent on the arms race were far from comforting for a governor who was so identified with the freeze. Jennifer Leaning told the *Boston Globe*, "I would not be surprised if the governor accepts our report and says, 'Goodbye folks; you're a little too hot to be around.'"[208]

A week after the advisory committee issued its report, Dukakis's staff put together "Talking Points" for the upcoming meeting between the governor and the committee. The governor was to embrace the report but also finesse some of its implications. He would open by stating, "I greatly appreciate all of the hard work of the members of the Committee. It is obvious from the thoughtful and detailed nature of the report that a great deal of time and effort went into its preparation.... The report and the recommendations are bold, innovative and very thoughtful."[209] The governor would then assert, "We are spending billions of dollars on nuclear weapons which we don't need.... Spending on these strategic weapons provides the economy with a false boost. And no state in the union knows this better than Massachusetts. At the end of the 1960s, there were 25,000 engineers out of work in Massachusetts [due to defense cuts.]" Now, the governor would argue, Massachusetts could avoid these consequences of defense cuts. "Our current economic success," he would explain, "is the result of a diversified economy."[210]

The governor's "Talking Points" anticipated "Potential Criticism of the Report," most of which it saw coming from the Left rather than the Right. The potential criticisms included the following: "Report plays down dramatic growth in nuclear arms race spending"; "economic development recommendation should be stronger"; the report did not "create State Office of Economic Conversion"; "the report's focus on the nuclear arms race obscures Massachusetts economic reliance on overall military spending"; "vulnerability to layoffs exists if the late 60s experience is repeated"; and the "governor should denounce nuclear arms race spending as dangerous, wasteful and immoral and let the business community know it's not welcome in Massachusetts."[211] In response to these anticipated critiques, Dukakis planned to emphasize the diversity of the Massachusetts economy, the use of incentives to promote economic conversion, a strong peace education curriculum, and concerted efforts to forge a sister state relationship with a Soviet Republic. Dukakis would argue, "We have done a tremendous amount already. This Committee is an example of a first in the nation initiative.... Also, the responsibility primarily belongs to Congress and to the President. Our Congressional delegation has taken the lead on this issue and is well aware of the support of the Dukakis Administration in this area."[212]

The advisory committee report marked yet another expression of opposition to the nuclear arms race in Massachusetts and reinforced the position of the state as leading the national search for a new trajectory for the cold war. The report forced Bay State residents to confront the degree to which the military-industrial complex had become interwoven in the state economy. Yet the document was also another example of the politics of symbolism, showing the limits of nuclear arms race opposition in the face of the economic realities of thousands of jobs and billions in corporate profits. Although freeze activism had managed to avoid hard economic realities in the past, eventually (like the movement against nuclear power), it would have to take on powerful economic interests. The state would continue to legitimize freeze activism and even make resources available to the movement, but in the end a new direction for the arms race and cold war would have to come from Washington, D.C.

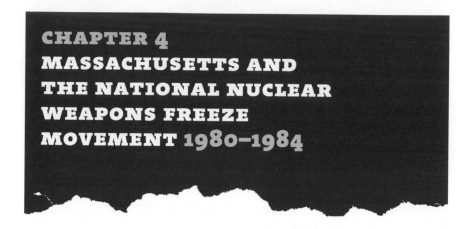

CHAPTER 4
MASSACHUSETTS AND THE NATIONAL NUCLEAR WEAPONS FREEZE MOVEMENT 1980–1984

A TRANS-ATLANTIC PEACE MOVEMENT

The 1979 national election of Margaret Thatcher and the Conservative Party in Great Britain foreshadowed the rightward turn in American politics symbolized by the election of Ronald Reagan in 1980. Like Reagan, Thatcher called for cuts in social spending, decreased regulation of business, reduced taxation, arms buildup, and a harder line toward the Soviet Union. Even Social Democrats such as Chancellor Helmut Schmidt of West Germany, a staunch advocate of détente, called for the North Atlantic Treaty Organization (NATO) to build up its nuclear weaponry. Meeting in Brussels in December 1979, the leaders of NATO nations adopted a decision to deploy U.S. medium-range missiles in Britain, Holland, Belgium, Italy, and the Federal Republic of Germany (FRG) by the fall of 1983. The intent of the NATO nations was to counter the 700 medium-range SS-20s that the Soviet Union had aimed at Western Europe.

To augment the existing independent nuclear capability of Britain and France, the United States would install 464 Cruise and 108 Pershing II intermediate-range missiles in NATO nations, with every Pershing and 96 Cruise missile earmarked for the FRG alone. First, the goal was to create a closer link between the United States and its Western European allies, who feared that the parity in strategic long-range missiles sought by SALT II would leave them vulnerable to the superior conventional forces of the Soviet Union. Second, leaders of European NATO nations hoped to pursue what they called a "double track" policy of building up the intermediate nuclear weaponry of NATO while pursuing parallel negotiations aimed at reducing the number of comparable Soviet SS-20s.[1]

The decision to install U.S. "Euromissiles" in NATO nations (made while Jimmy Carter was in office) was followed only weeks later by the Soviet invasion of Afghanistan. By 1980, the stirrings of a new European peace movement were evident across Western Europe, and especially in the FRG, as concern grew over the emergence of what some called Cold War II. As in the United States, the nascent European peace movement grew exponentially with the election of Reagan, who had campaigned against détente and arms control.[2] If Reagan's loose talk of "winnable nuclear war" disturbed many Americans, it positively rattled many Europeans, who viewed the U.S. president's rhetoric of nuclear war as confirmation of their image of the former actor as a Hollywood cowboy who now had his finger on the nuclear trigger. Unlike earlier presidents—who, regardless of policy, had at least sought to assuage the fear of nuclear war—Reagan seemed to go out of his way to exacerbate such concerns. In a speech at West Point, for example, he proclaimed, "Man has used every weapon he has ever devised. . . . It takes no crystal ball to perceive that a nuclear war is likely, sooner or later."[3]

The freeze movement in the United States, which began before Reagan's election, was, in fact, galvanized into action by the breakdown of détente and the adoption of more hard-line anti-Soviet policies in the late Carter years. For its part, the European peace movement had already begun mobilizing by late 1979. For the political scientist Steve Breyman—who has written about the West German peace movement in the early 1980s and its impact on West German and U.S. cold war policy—it was the NATO decision of December 1979 that constituted the "spark that ignited the dry kindling of [European] peace movement potential."[4] Thus, as Reagan assumed office, the growing trans-Atlantic anti–nuclear weapons movement had already begun to stir. Against the backdrop of the belligerent rhetoric of the Reagan administration, NATO plans to base U.S. Pershing II and Cruise missiles in Western Europe seemed less a part of the "double-track" policy aimed at negotiations than flat-out preparation for waging limited nuclear war. Many Europeans now believed that instead of binding the United States to the fate of Europe, the Euromissiles served to decouple the United States from Western Europe by allowing the option of fighting a nuclear war limited to the European theater.[5]

From 1981 through the final showdown in the fall of 1983, when the U.S. Cruise and Pershing II missiles were installed, Western Europe witnessed the largest peace movement in its postwar history. Anti–nuclear weapons protests attended by tens of thousands and then hundreds of thousands swept across the borders of Western European nations, enveloping large portions of the European middle class. Polls showed that, by 1982, up to 69 percent of West Germans opposed the introduction of the Pershing II and Cruise missiles onto West German soil, with 58 percent of English respondents adopting a similar position with respect to basing U.S. Cruise missiles in Britain.[6] Increasingly, Western Europeans viewed the United States under Reagan's leadership, rather than the Soviet Union, as the major source of instability and possible war in Europe. Members of the

Reagan administration worried about the spirit of what they saw as "neutralism" spreading across Western Europe.[7]

The U.S. freeze and European peace movements blossomed at virtually the same time, ran parallel through most of their respective histories, and shared many similarities. In both, older activists were the driving organizing force, with women such as the West German Green Party activist Petra Kelly playing highly visible, leading roles. Both movements witnessed the mobilization of numerous religious figures—especially Protestant clergy—as leaders. The U.S. freeze and European anti–nuclear weapons movements both sought to achieve as broad a base of support as possible, eventually leading to tensions in each.

Yet for two mass movements that employed similar tactics and consisted of similar bases of support, they often remained remarkably dissociated. Beginning in the fall of 1981, the enormous European peace marches became headline news in the United States. Although West European activists stressed the fact that their protests were directed at the U.S. government rather than at the American people, frequently the marches took on an anti-American tone that became fodder for the U.S. press. Early on, U.S. freeze leaders made the decision to keep the two movements separate. To achieve their goal of winning a mass base of support, freeze leaders wanted to create a wholly individual movement, free of associations with the frequently more militant and sometimes anti-American peace movement overseas.[8] Still, numerous U.S. activists crossed the Atlantic to participate in the Western European mass peace marches, while others engaged in civil disobedience at home to protest the deployment of the U.S. Cruise and Pershing II missiles.[9]

Despite the decision to separate the emerging U.S. freeze movement from the European peace movement, they emerged, grew, peaked, and declined at virtually the same times. Thus, as the freeze movement swept the United States from 1980 through 1983, it had as its backdrop the impending showdown in Europe over the basing of U.S. Cruise and Pershing II missiles, bringing both movements into the fight for a trans-Atlantic cause. The U.S. and Western European movements combined represented the greatest political challenge that Reagan would face during his first term.[10]

RANDY KEHLER AND THE NATIONAL NUCLEAR WEAPONS FREEZE CAMPAIGN

From March 20 to 22, 1981, more than three hundred anti–nuclear weapons activists gathered at the Georgetown University Center for Peace Studies in Washington, D.C., for the National Strategy Conference for a Nuclear Weapons Freeze. Activists representing organizations such as Mobilization for Survival

(MfS), the Council for a Livable World (CLW), the American Friends Service Committee (AFSC), and other mostly radical pacifist peace groups met to map out a long-term strategy for a national nuclear weapons freeze movement. Among the three hundred–plus activists at the conference, who represented thirty-one states, were Randall Forsberg, Randy Kehler, and Frances Crowe of the western Massachusetts AFSC (the keynote speaker).[11] Kehler and Crowe had met with many of the conference attendees at the U.N. Plaza Building the previous October, on the eve of the freeze referendum vote in western Massachusetts. Based on this meeting, Kehler had reported to his Traprock colleagues that national activists were looking to the western Massachusetts referendum campaign as "the bell-wether of the whole moratorium movement."[12]

At the founding conference of the national freeze movement in Washington, D.C., Kehler and Crowe were treated like minor celebrities, repeatedly questioned about the western Massachusetts freeze campaign the previous fall and how its lessons could be applied on the national level. The national strategy adopted at the conference was scheduled to be carried out over a three-year period. The group would embrace the localist strategy advocated most ardently by Kehler and work through existing peace groups across the country. Thus, the national organization would be a coordinating body and an information clearinghouse until the movement was prepared for increased focus on Washington, D.C. The strategy would be to try to reach the broadest possible base of support by emphasizing the freeze as exclusive of other issues and by seeking a least common denominator policy that would allow the movement to grow rapidly (although this would later become a source of tension).[13] The national strategy adopted at the Georgetown conference consisted of four phases:

Phase One: Demonstrate the positive potential of the freeze proposal for stopping the arms race.
Phase Two: Build broad and visible public support for the freeze.
Phase Three: Focus public support on policy-makers so that it becomes a matter of national debate.
Phase Four; Win the debate so that the freeze is adopted as a national policy objective.[14]

The strategy was predicated on past experience with disarmament efforts. The first phase would be dominated by small grassroots efforts similar to the one in western Massachusetts, each designed to show the viability of the freeze proposal on a small scale and begin building the local bases on which the national movement would depend. The early phase was to be as decentralized as possible, giving local activists broad leeway to create the movement to fit local conditions. Building on these small victories, the second phase would seek much greater national visibility, shifting focus (once momentum had been built) onto policy makers in Washington, D.C. Finally, the movement hoped to convert the freeze proposal into reality through its adoption as U.S. policy. The conference presented a "Strategy for Stopping the Nuclear Arms Race," stating that "past efforts at serious arms control ... failed in part because they were not preceded by active educational efforts among the general public by a sufficiently broad spectrum of organizations."[15]

To carry out this national strategy, the conference created the Nuclear Weapons Freeze Campaign (NWFC). The new organization would hold two national conferences a year, during which conferees from across the country would choose a part-time National Committee, which would, in turn, choose a full-time Executive Committee and a Nuclear Weapons Freeze Clearinghouse to disseminate freeze and disarmament information. The National Committee would also elect task forces to deal with issues that included religion, minorities, labor, media, direct action, and fund-raising. The goal was to make the NWFC a loose coordinating body that would map out overall strategy but to encourage as much grassroots organization as possible.[16]

Initially, the NWFC was based in Brookline, Massachusetts, at the headquarters of Randall Forsberg's Institute for Disarmament and Defense Studies (IDDS). Because this situated the movement in the heart of New England (already viewed as far ahead of the rest of the country on the issue) and risked associating the movement with many of the greater Boston area peace groups, however, the decision was made to move the headquarters to St. Louis, Missouri (roughly the geographical center of the United States). This choice, it was hoped, would emphasize the middle-American image that the movement hoped to project.[17] Participants in the national freeze movement elected Kehler as one of its first two national coordinators. Kehler was an ideal choice in many ways: His commitment was beyond question, he had helped lead the first successful local pro-freeze campaign, his physical appearance and dress were conventional, and he was known for his soft-spoken style. Looking back, Kehler stated, "My job was to hold the movement together, to resolve tension, to find a middle road."[18]

Kehler's grand design called for an emphasis on grassroots organizing and the creation of the broadest possible base of support across the political spectrum. At a second national conference in late 1981, he summarized the strategy: "Our challenge in the upcoming months will be to reach out to that wide spectrum of Americans never involved in this type of movement."[19] This focus would put Kehler in the frequent position of advocating moderate positions that belied his radical past and ongoing war tax resistance. Kehler worked hard to bridge the limited immediate goal with the more radical long-term ambitions. In one memorandum, he wrote, "As we are all aware, one of the principal criticisms of the freeze is that it does not go far enough.... This is perhaps a ticklish area, for we don't want to scare people away by seeming to ask for too much too soon.... A very simple approach, I think, is to couple the freeze proposal with a preamble 'Step One' every chance we get."[20]

Beyond those who believed that the national freeze movement did not go far enough were those who believed that it did not go fast enough. As national coordinator of the NWFC, Kehler soon found that many in the national movement seemed eager to take the cause to Washington before the local base had been sufficiently established. Kehler observed, "I think there is a tendency among freeze organizers to look ahead to the Congressional elections of November 1982 with some feeling of panic, a feeling that somehow we must totally reshape our national strategy in order to focus exclusively on these elections. In my view, the primary work ahead of us in '82 is base-building work ... not the Congressional elections."[21] His response was to send out a memorandum to members of the freeze movement urging patience and continued focus on building local grassroots organizations. Signed by Randy Kehler and Gordon Faison (Kehler's colleague at the national headquarters), the memorandum was an impassioned and detailed defense of the local strategy that had proven so successful in western Massachusetts. "Our concern," the memorandum stated, "is that we take this strategy seriously and, specifically, *that we avoid the temptation to go directly to elected officials, at the state or federal levels, without doing our homework*—that is, the work of organizing freeze support at home, in our local communities and local organizations."[22]

Kehler and Faison's memorandum proceeded to make a number of astute observations. First, it noted that a local strategy was a powerful recruitment tool: "The distance between people and faraway capitals and bureaucrats tends to maintain the distancing and numbing that bedevils our psychic and political processes." People who might feel intimidated or alienated by national or statewide campaigns, the memorandum argued, are more inclined to "get their feet wet as organizers if the campaign is local." Eventually, a percentage of such local activists would choose to get involved at a higher level. Furthermore, the scope of a nuclear war was difficult to fathom. A local campaign could personalize the dangers, making them less abstract and thus more persuasive to potential supporters. In a subsection titled "Bringing the Arms Race Home," the memorandum stated, "Rather than try to convince our neighbors that Massachusetts or the country as a whole could never defend itself once a nuclear war had begun, we explain that Greenfield ... would probably be engulfed in a firestorm if a one-megaton bomb fell on nearby Westover Air Force Base."[23] Both recruitment through local organizing and emphasis of the local impact of the arms race became strengths of the movement as it spread across the United States.

The memorandum continued to point out the logistical strengths of a grassroots movement. First, regional organizers would be able to choose "appropriate tactics," suited to regional conditions. Since local activists would not be "anonymous," their influence with their neighbors, local newspaper editors, and local elected officials would have "the most integrity." Finally, regional campaigns would allow the freeze movement to fly under the radar of well-heeled national opposition groups, whose members would be seen as outside intruders if they attempted to intervene in a regional campaign. "We are much less likely to run into well-financed opposition from corporate interests (e.g., defense industries and their lobbying associations) when the campaign is local. The forces most apt to oppose us are usually large and centralized. For this reason, they rarely have much influence in a particular local community."[24] (This was an important lesson, no doubt learned in part from the experience of the statewide campaigns to ban or limit nuclear energy in the 1970s. In all cases, statewide movements for anti–nuclear energy referenda had run into stiff opposition from national utilities, whose pronuclear campaigns outspent anti–nuclear power campaigns up to tenfold.)[25]

The Kehler-Faison memorandum seems to have stanched the rumblings in the national freeze movement. The years 1981 and 1982 saw local movements, all with their own color and flair, sprout up across the nation. The movement took hold most quickly in New England, spreading throughout the Northeast, especially New York and New Jersey. In New York City, more than thirty-four hundred Manhattan residents attended small town meetings to endorse the freeze on May 25, 1982. "This is Jeffersonian democracy in action," declared one participant.[26] In New Jersey, Brendan Byrne, the liberal Democratic governor, proclaimed October 24–31, 1981, Mutual Nuclear Freeze Week in the Garden State.[27] Movements sprang up in the Midwest, throughout the plains states, and across the entire West Coast, taking firm root in all-important California, where, beginning in December 1981, freeze activists began the process of procuring more than five hundred thousand signatures to put the freeze on the ballot in 1982. Not surprisingly, the South and Southwest proved to be the geographical areas that were most difficult for the freeze to breach.[28]

Piggybacking the national media coverage of the European peace movement that began in late 1981, the national freeze movement followed suit. In his important study of the national freeze movement, *A Winter of Discontent*, David S. Meyer graphs the growing press and media attention, showing an explosion of freeze coverage in 1982, which peaked throughout 1983 and rapidly declined in 1984.[29] Meyer found Helen Caldicott and Roger Molander of Ground Zero to be the most commonly quoted activists, with only Senator Edward Kennedy and Congressman Ed Markey of Massachusetts (relative latecomers to the freeze) quoted more frequently.[30]

The freeze movement also spread its message through events organized by other arms control groups. In 1979 Molander, a former National Security Council analyst, founded Ground Zero with his twin brother, Earl, in an effort to close the gap between policy makers and the public. Ground Zero sought to accomplish this primarily through an information campaign, under the slogan "Nuclear War: What's In It For You." Like many, Molander was galvanized into action by the failure of SALT II. "The silence was deafening," Molander told Newsweek. "It was quite clear that you couldn't conduct policy on this issue with a gulf between the people...and the leaders."[31] Ground Zero also promoted arms control through its sister city campaign, which had U.S. cities and towns declare a sisterhood with a town or city in the Soviet Union to underscore the link between those at ground zero in the two nations.

From April 18–25, 1982, Molander organized Ground Zero Week, a nation-wide information campaign modeled on the Vietnam teach-ins that had swept the United States in 1965. An estimated one million Americans participated in the many speeches, film screenings, seminars, and debates held around the country.[32] Although Molander never endorsed the freeze proposal, Ground Zero Week became a major forum for freeze advocates to spread their message. A former member of the U.S. Arms Control and Disarmament Agency, Molander hoped that Ground Zero Week would pressure the Reagan administration into returning to arms control talks. "What we seek is a public active enough in the dialogue about nuclear war that they feel compelled to work with the Government in coming up with solutions, whether it be disarmament, a freeze, or some other option," Molander explained.[33]

By the spring of 1982, the freeze movement had begun to percolate up, as Forsberg had hoped. A number of celebrities—including Martin Sheen, Susan Sarandon, Tony Randall, Stevie Wonder, Yo-Yo Ma, Leonard Bernstein, Meryl Streep, Joan Baez, Pete Seeger, Jackson Browne, Paul Newman, and Harry Belafonte—publicly campaigned for the freeze. The scientist Carl Sagan, of the popular PBS documentary Cosmos, made scores of television appearances on behalf of the movement, becoming one of its most active advocates.[34] The freeze campaign also won endorsements from a number of former national security policy makers, including George Kennan, W. Averell Harriman, George Ball, Warren Christopher, Clark Clifford, Hodding Carter, Henry Cabot Lodge, and

William Colby (the former CIA director). Former military officials who publicly endorsed the freeze included Admiral Gene La Rocque, Admiral Gene Carroll, Admiral Noel Gayler, Major General William Fairbourn, and Admiral Hyman Rickover (a man known to some as the father of the nuclear navy, who now made it a personal crusade to campaign for complete disarmament). In *New Left Review*, Alexander Cockburn and James Ridgeway wrote, "It is remarkable how many out-of-power cold warriors have suddenly seen light on the road to Damascus."[35]

The most potent endorsements of the freeze, however, came from the pulpit. Churches and synagogues across the United States became bases of freeze organizing, and many ministers, priests, and rabbis discussed the freeze with their congregations.[36] The most influential endorsement came in the form of two pastoral letters issued by the National Conference of Catholic Bishops in 1981 and 1982. Titled "The Challenge of Peace: God's Promise and Our Response," the letters contained not only the bishops' endorsement of a nuclear weapons freeze but also their call for severe cuts in nuclear armaments with the goal of the eventual elimination of nuclear weapons. (The Reagan administration protested the first letter in early 1982 only to have the bishops issue an even more adamant letter later in the year.)[37] The National Council of Churches, the Union of American Hebrew Congregations, the United Presbyterian Church, and the American Baptist Churches joined the bishops' plea.[38]

The freeze movement also won the endorsement—and, more important, the financial support—of a number of wealthy businesspeople and well-financed foundations. The Los Angeles millionaire Harold Willens helped finance a large share of the 1982 California freeze referendum campaign. Foundations that funded disarmament and freeze activity included the Rockefeller Foundation, the Ford Foundation, the Carnegie Endowment for International Peace, the Stern Fund, and the MacArthur Foundation.[39] While money streamed in from well-heeled sources, the movement continued its local grassroots fund-raising with traditional bake sales, car washes, and concerts. At one benefit, the Boston Symphony Orchestra raised more than ninety thousand dollars for the movement.[40]

By the spring of 1982, the proliferation of grassroots freeze campaigns and the heightened national visibility of the movement were reflected in public opinion polls. An Associated Press/NBC poll showed 83 percent of Americans supporting the freeze proposal; a *Washington Post* poll showed 79 percent in favor; a CBS/ *New York Times* poll had 77 percent of Americans backing the freeze; and a Gallup poll pegged pro-freeze support at 71 percent.[41] The inroads on the public opinion front were also reflected on the political front. In December 1981, after a little more than a year of freeze activism, 24 members of the House of Representatives and Clairborne Pell, the Democratic senator from Rhode Island, had announced their support for the freeze. By the spring of 1982, there were 169 avowed supporters in the House of Representatives and 25 in the Senate.[42] Noting the shift in public attitude over the course of two years, Douglass C. Waller, a congressional aide to the Massachusetts congressman Ed Markey, wrote, "Just as 1980 was not a good year for a politician to admit he favored arms control, 1982 was not a good year for him to say he opposed it."[43]

In Massachusetts, the positions of politicians were sometimes dramatic. In 1981 Paul Tsongas, the senator from Massachusetts, described the freeze proposal as "on the fringe," adding, "It is not a sophisticated answer to a complex problem."[44] By March 1982, Tsongas had embraced the freeze, and he welcomed Bay State activists to the capital with open arms when they presented to both Silvio Conte and Tsongas eight-foot by twelve-foot postcards filled with signatures in support of the freeze. The minutes of the Western Massachusetts Steering Committee for the Coalition for a Nuclear Weapons Freeze described the moment: "Tsongas loved the card and has put it in his office. Abby [Seixas] came away with the impression that he is involved and sincere, and that she is glad there are politicians of his character. It is interesting to note that he had serious hesitations about the freeze in its ability to get through Congress, and now just a short month later he is sponsoring the resolution in Congress."[45]

Like Tsongas, Conte (a moderate Republican) sponsored the freeze resolution that was making its way through the House of Representatives in 1982. As a result of the incessant lobbying of his western Massachusetts constituents, Conte—once considered a lukewarm supporter—was now leading the push for the freeze. The minutes for another Western Massachusetts Steering Committee reveal how activists lobbied their congressman: "Jeff Ciuffreda, who is the main person in Conte's western Massachusetts office . . . is very supportive of the freeze and will make sure that Conte sees news stories about the freeze when he comes to the area. Our responsibility is to get the articles to him."[46]

On key votes, organizations such as Traprock mobilized freeze supporters to lobby their elected official. In preparation for the September 1982 vote on the MX and Pershing II missiles, for example, Traprock leaders wrote a letter that urged members to focus on Silvio Conte and the Democrat Edward Boland: "They are considered swing votes who could go either way and may be influenced by constituent pressure. Please urge everyone you know to write or call Conte or Boland *immediately* to thank them for their recent support for the freeze (the Zablocki amendment) and to urge them to vote against funding for the MX and Pershing II."[47] (Boland was the only member of the Massachusetts delegation to vote for the Pershing II. All opposed the MX.) Even politicians who strongly supported the freeze could not escape the ceaseless lobbying. Western Massachusetts organizers exhorted freeze supporters to "Birddog Conte, Boland, Kennedy and Tsongas for the purpose of strengthening their commitment to the freeze and disarmament."[48] The national movement also encouraged local groups to continue to lobby supporters. An NWFC memorandum to local organizers urged, "Even if your Congressional Representative supports the Freeze Resolution *and* is a cosponsor, it is still important that he/she receive letters, proxies, and phone calls. This will provide supportive legislators with ammunition for their own lobbying efforts."[49]

In some cases, the politicians sought out the freeze movement. According to Kehler, the staff of Senator Edward Kennedy "very aggressively pursued" the movement: "Kennedy's people came to us. They saw us as a bandwagon they wanted to get their man behind, or in front of, I should say." Kennedy's people attended the 1982 freeze conference in Colorado and quickly developed close ties with the cause, coordinating the push for a freeze resolution in Congress with the national movement. "Ted Kennedy wanted to follow in Jack's footsteps," Kehler recalled. He hoped to pass a freeze resolution to coincide with the twentieth anniversary of John Kennedy's signing of the Limited Test Ban Treaty. According to Kehler, Kennedy, who "sincerely believed in the value of the freeze," had first turned to Mark Hatfield. Kehler believed, however, that Kennedy's solicitousness might have hurt the movement: "[It was] very heady for us to be courted that way by such a national figure; at the same time, it caused us to leap ahead of ourselves before we were ready."[50]

Thus, in a few short years, the movement for a nuclear weapons freeze had exploded across the United States. In western Massachusetts, the *Greenfield Recorder* proudly headlined a May 1982 article on the growing national freeze movement "Seed Planted in WMass Spreads across Nation."[51] To the *New York Times*, Kehler declared, "I feel like I'm on a comet, but I don't know whether I'm leading it or on its tail."[52] As Kehler spoke, the national freeze movement was on the cusp of its most spectacular event, the June 12, 1982, rally for a nuclear weapons freeze in Central Park in New York City.

BREAKTHROUGH—CENTRAL PARK RALLY: JUNE 12, 1982

Following New England, the freeze movement took hold most rapidly in New York, whose State Assembly adopted a freeze resolution in 1981 close on the heels of the freeze resolution adopted by the Massachusetts legislature. New York City had become a particular hotbed of freeze activity. In the fall of 1981, organizers began planning for a huge disarmament rally outside the United Nations to coincide with the Second Special Session on Disarmament (SSD-II). Spearheaded by veteran peace groups such as MfS, AFSC, the War Resisters League (WRL), and Women's International League for Peace and Freedom (WILPF), the march was not originally envisioned specifically as a freeze event. As organizing proceeded, however, the planned New York rally dovetailed with the burgeoning freeze movement and the NWFC became one of the many organizers of the march.[53]

One of the central organizers of what came to be called the June 12 Rally Committee was Leslie Cagan of the Boston MfM. Raised in a left-wing family, Cagan—who had graduated from New York University in 1968—had participated in Ban the Bomb protests and civil rights activities. Cagan later recalled, "It was 1968 and the world was on fire. I was 21 and had spent the last two years of my liberal arts education (primarily) organizing against the war in Vietnam, Cambodia and Laos."[54] That year she had visited Paris in the aftermath of the student/worker uprising, and she had traveled to Prague just prior to the Soviet invasion. She had also attended the World Youth Festival in Sofia, Bulgaria—where she experienced what she described as a moving meeting with members of the Vietnamese delegation—and the following year she had journeyed to Cuba with the Venceremos Brigade. Throwing herself into the growing women's movement, Cagan had gained "fresh revolutionary insights to [her] understanding of oppression." Shortly thereafter she had come out as a lesbian and had become an active participant in the Gay Liberation movement.[55]

Throughout the 1970s Cagan had worked primarily out of Boston. Then, in 1981, representing the Boston MfS, she participated in the planning of the 1982 rally. Cagan helped formulate the focus for the rally, worked to ease tensions between hostile factions, and responded to Reagan administration red-baiting. In an early working paper, Cagan linked the arms race and domestic programs that became a focus of the march: "Poor and working women and men bear the burden of a military and foreign policy geared for war. We believe that the tremendous resources, money and skill that are poured into military expenditures must be re-routed to begin meeting the needs of the people in this country, and throughout the world."[56]

Another important question that Cagan and the organizing committee wrestled with was whether to focus on the United States or on all nuclear weapons states. In the minutes of one early meeting that she chaired, Cagan wrote, "A discussion was held on our emphasis—are we specifically targeting the US and its role in the arms race...and/or calling on all nuclear nations...to engage in disarmament? It was generally agreed that we should seek balance: We need to recognize and articulate the particular role of the US...in escalating the arms race.... [A]t the same time we do not want to ignore or let off the hook other nuclear nations."[57] This early thrust eventually became part of the official "Call to the June 12th Rally," which declared, "Both the U.S. and the U.S.S.R. plan to produce a new generation of nuclear weapons which will dangerously increase the risk of nuclear war."[58]

As the planning gained publicity and momentum, it seemed that almost every political group to the left of center wanted to take part in the march, which increasingly came to be seen as a pro-freeze event. More than 80 national organizations and 150 local New York City groups coalesced into a broader planning coalition. Not surprisingly, the coalition underwent major rifts and divisions. The divisions tended to run between those who wished to connect the arms race with issues such as U.S. policy in Central America and support for apartheid in South Africa and those who wanted to keep the focus of the march on a nuclear weapons freeze followed by reductions in existing arsenals. Radicals believed that the message of the rally was being diluted and lost, whereas moderates believed that if the rally pushed too far, mainstream Americans might become alienated.

Racial divisions also existed, with militant African American organizations such as Harlem Fight Back and the Brooklyn-based Black United Front demanding that connections between the arms race, racism, and poverty be voiced more explicitly at the rally and that African Americans be given greater representation on the June 12 Rally Committee.[59] In an effort to accommodate these demands, Cagan wrote a letter to the Reverend Herbert Dougherty of the Black United Front on behalf of the core organizers, stating, "We will have 1/3 participation from non-white groups. It was also agreed that in the materials that will come out as well as speakers from the platform on June 12th that the issues of racism and intervention will be addressed."[60] Because many of the white, middle-class freeze activists were unaccustomed to working with minority groups, misunderstandings and tensions grew. Furious at what they believed to be an obstructionist attitude by the Black United Front and its allies, some organizations (such as Greenpeace) walked out. More experienced organizations, including the WRL and the AFSC, played crucial roles in holding the bulk of the planning coalition together.[61]

Outside of New York City, Boston became central to the organization of the June 12 rally. The Greater Boston Campaign for the United Nations Second Special Session on Disarmament worked to mobilize local freeze activists behind the rally. In a letter sent out to freeze organizations, the group wrote, "The entire disarmament movement is uniting around [the rally]....The Freeze campaign should not be isolated from such groups." The letter continued, "The Greater Boston Campaign for SSD-II will provide major organizing leadership so Freeze workers do not have to 'drop everything' in order to participate in the event in

New York City."[62] The Greater Boston Campaign for SSD-II included a Feminist Task Force that organized a Memorial Day weekend march against the arms race and drew connections between nuclear weapons and women's issues. In one letter, the Feminist Task Force declared, "As feminists we believe challenging the New Right must be a central focus of the U.S. peace movement. The New Right carries a vision which links militarism to a whole way of life, one that supports the needs of the military—self-sacrifice, unquestioning obedience to authority, conquest, denial of women's rights, and racism."[63]

Boston activists also succeeded in getting the Cambridge City Council to pass a resolution supporting the June 12 rally.[64] Satirizing Federal Emergency Management Agency (FEMA) crisis relocation planning, the resolution read in part, "June 12, 1982 is declared Preventive Evacuation Day and the citizens of Cambridge are urged to join a mass rally for Disarmament in New York City.... [T]he Cambridge City Council urges the United States and all governments ... [to] pledge a prompt freeze on testing, development, production and deployment of nuclear weapons [and] ... progressive reduction of nuclear weapons."[65]

Meanwhile, back in New York City, a last-minute logistical problem emerged. The New York City Police Department, which had been working closely with the June 12 Committee, announced that the area outside the United Nations could not accommodate the hundreds of thousands of participants now expected to converge on the city. Notifying the group that only one hundred thousand people would be able to see the stage at the original location, Police Commissioner Robert J. McGuire called for the rally to be moved to Central Park. Rally organizers agreed, provided that a smaller contingent would be allowed to parade before the U.N. building.[66]

On June 12, 1982, hundreds of thousands of people flooded the streets of New York City, converging on Central Park under sunny, blue skies. Most estimates place the number of attendees at about 750,000, although some argue that the number exceeded 1,000,000.[67] The mood was peaceful and festive, imbued with the wholesomeness that had become something of a trademark at many freeze events. Relations were warm between the crowd and the police, many of whom expressed sympathy with the cause. Amid balloons, tables, exhibitions, and roaming street vendors milled a multigenerational crowd. "It was an intense experience to see the range of people there—from people in wheelchairs to babes at the breast," declared Arthur Westing (a Hampshire College ecology professor) upon his return to western Massachusetts.[68] Westing was one of an estimated 10,000 Massachusetts residents who converged on New York City for the rally.[69] Days before the June 12 rally, Thomas M. Gallagher, the Democratic state representative from Boston, urged Bostonians to attend: "Last fall millions of Europeans came out and demonstrated against the nuclear arms race as totally insane and a danger to the entire planet. . . . [I]t is time for Americans to stand up and be counted this Saturday."[70]

A seemingly endless procession of speakers crossed the podium at the Central Park rally to address the crowd. Among them were Ed Markey, Bella Abzug, Coretta Scott King, Bruce Springsteen, Orson Welles, Pete Seeger, Linda Ronstadt, Seymour Melman, David Dellinger, and Randall Forsberg. Forsberg underscored the social cost of the arms race, asking the crowd, "How can we spend $20 billion a year on these stupid weapons when infant nutrition and school lunches are cut back; student loans are cut back; the elderly [are] forced to go without hearing aids and eat dog food; and 20% of the black population is unemployed?"[71] (At the planning sessions the previous fall, some moderates— concerned about alienating fiscal conservatives who might otherwise support the freeze—went so far as to suggest that the Central Park rally avoid connecting the arms race to its social cost at home. This same strategy was being pursued in the 1982 California freeze referendum campaign, which made no mention of using arms funds for domestic programs in its ballot question—connections that were made repeatedly during the June 12 rally.)[72]

As three-quarters of a million people rallied for a nuclear weapons freeze and disarmament in Central Park, more than fifty thousand people were rallying in San Francisco.[73] Two days later, more than one thousand activists were arrested in front of the U.N. building as they protested the arms race. In an effort to seg-regate civil disobedience from the legal march to avoid alienating moderates, the decision had been made to have direct actions take place on June 14. Among those who attended the Saturday rally and were arrested the following Monday was the Traprock founder Judith Scheckel. Scheckel returned to western Massachusetts ecstatic: "The joy at the rally was intense. We are so bombarded daily by images of violence in the media that it was a moving experience to see so many people who are so loving, patient and peaceful to one another."[74]

For most of those who attended, the June 12 freeze rally was a joyous affirma-tion of life in the cause of preventing nuclear death.[75] There were critics, however; David Dellinger and his radical colleague Sidney Lens charged that the relatively moderate freeze movement had "not yet generated the same kind of idealism of the 60s and 70s on the campuses and among working-class youth. . . . In the Vietnam War, we didn't make progress until we took an absolutist position on withdrawal."[76] For others, the broad base visible at the rally made it an unquali-fied success. Elected officials who had been gradually embracing the freeze were especially pleased. Congressman Markey called the freeze "a middle-class movement," adding, "These are people with real clout in their communities."[77]

In many ways, the June 12, 1982, Central Park freeze rally marked the culmination of two years of rapid growth through grassroots organizing. At the rally, Forsberg had taken up the chant "We'll remember come November."[78] Increasingly, after June 12, 1982, the focus of the national freeze movement shifted from the grass roots to the halls of Congress and the campaign trail.

THE FREEZE GOES TO CONGRESS

From the beginning of the 1980 freeze referendum campaign in western Massachusetts, activists had hoped to win over elected officials to pro-freeze positions. Kehler, who had moved to St. Louis, worked to keep the focus of the NWFC on first building grassroots support and then, when the time was right, using that support to influence Congress. By 1982, the national movement had begun to make the shift. The first member of Congress to feel the pressure of the growing freeze movement was the moderate Republican Silvio Conte of the First Congressional District of Massachusetts, which encompassed most of the freeze stronghold in the western part of the state. During the 1980 referendum campaign, Conte had belatedly endorsed the freeze, and subsequent to the campaign local freeze activists had sought to hold Conte's feet to the fire by confronting him directly at public meetings.[79]

By 1982, Conte had become one of the most visible supporters of a freeze resolution in Congress. He and Mark Hatfield of Oregon had emerged as the main Republican freeze proponents in Congress, giving the campaign the bipartisan appearance that the movement had sought. Conte sponsored the first and second attempts at passing freeze resolutions in Congress in 1982 and 1983, attributing his sponsorship to "the groundswell of public sentiment against the frightening buildup of nuclear weapons."[80] The Oregon senator and the Massachusetts congressman were among the most colorful characters in Washington. Conte had a reputation for flamboyance, especially during his "pork of the year awards," when he would put on a plastic pig nose and—before media cameras—denounce "pork barrel spending" in Congress, highlighting particularly egregious examples. Hatfield was more radical than most Democrats on many issues; he had first proposed a freeze as part of the SALT II accords in 1979 and regularly denounced U.S. intervention in Central America. The freeze was always a personal issue for Hatfield, who had walked through the ruins of Hiroshima as a naval officer in the Pacific in late 1945. Hatfield recalled, "I could not help but be so totally overwhelmed by the utter and indiscriminate destruction. . . . Looking in one direction or any other direction in that city, there was nothing but a mass of rubble and the stench of rotting human life. . . . I had a sense of ambivalence about the kind of power that had been unleashed in the world."[81]

Another Massachusetts congressman who became a driving force behind a congressional freeze resolution was the Democrat Ed Markey, whose district encompassed working-class neighborhoods north of Boston. Viewed by his colleagues as a young firebrand, Markey had made a name for himself as an opponent of nuclear energy in the late 1970s, becoming especially outspoken about the issue after the near meltdown at Three Mile Island. More than any other member of Congress, Markey would work to shepherd the freeze through the House of Representatives. Douglas C. Waller, Markey's congressional aide, who played a major role in Markey's relationship with activists in the freeze movement, recounted the congressional campaign for a freeze resolution in his book *Congress and the Nuclear Freeze: An Inside Look at the Politics of a Mass Movement*. Markey not only shared freeze activists' concerns about nuclear war; he also saw the issue as a way to raise his visibility and recruit supporters. Waller's account describes how Peter Franchot, Markey's administrative assistant, brought Randall Forsberg's "Call to Halt the Nuclear Arms Race" to Markey's attention: Franchot told Waller and Markey, "The freeze is going to sweep this country. I can feel it in my bones. And there's no reason why we shouldn't be in the middle of it."[82]

Most crucial of all was the endorsement by Edward Kennedy, who had remained something of a sleeping giant before he made his overture to the freeze movement. Confirming Kehler's account, one staffer said, "We could all see that the movement was on the verge of a breakthrough. . . . The Senator just wanted to get on top of it, harness all that energy, and bring it to Washington instead of just letting it go on."[83] On March 10, 1982, at a press conference held at the American University Kay Spiritual Life Center, Kennedy announced that he and Hatfield would introduce the Kennedy-Hatfield nuclear weapons freeze resolution in the United States Senate.[84] According to Waller, "For diehard liberals, a wink and a nod from Kennedy were enough to spark a flame under an issue. In the case of the freeze, Kennedy built a bonfire, and the faithful responded in droves."[85] Others were critical, accusing Kennedy of trying to co-opt the movement and make it an appendage of his presidential campaign.[86] Within weeks, however, Kennedy aides working with members of Senator Hatfield's staff had put together a book under the senators' names. Although at times technical in nature, *Freeze! Or How You Can Help Prevent Nuclear War* included a section on the 1980 western Massachusetts referendum campaign and was dedicated to "all members of the nuclear freeze movement who have awakened the conscience of our country and are proving anew that individuals truly can make a difference."[87] The *Traprock Report* described the work as an "excellent handbook."[88]

As Kennedy and his staff worked fellow senators and representatives, his own endorsement led to endorsements by numerous other members of Congress. As a result, Kennedy decided to pursue a joint resolution of Congress rather than a concurrent resolution; this meant that—despite the fact that under the Constitution the measure could be only an advisory resolution—the president would be forced to sign or veto the resolution. In the House, Silvio Conte, Ed Markey, and Jonathan Bingham (the veteran New York Democrat) sponsored the Kennedy-Hatfield resolution. The Kennedy-Hatfield-Conte-Bingham-Markey resolution soon received the cosponsorship of 18 senators and 115 representatives.[89] Kehler and others at the NWFC headquarters in St. Louis believed that Kennedy and Markey were moving too fast in Congress, but Kennedy insisted on forging ahead with or without the endorsement of the national movement.

Jan Kalicki (a Kennedy staffer) and Douglass Waller (Markey's aide) now became full-time liaisons with the NWFC, meeting regularly with its leadership and attending group conventions. Tensions arose as some activists accused Kennedy and Markey of watering down the freeze resolution by taking out the words "immediate freeze" and calling on the president to "decide when and how" to negotiate a freeze with the Soviet Union. Waller and Kalicki informed the movement that these changes were necessary to ensure the support of moderates. The congressional staffers worked to modify other movement demands. Sources of dissent included the NWFC requirements that the freeze resolution target funding for specific weapons systems and oppose deployment of the Euromissiles. Waller and Kalicki generally prevailed in these debates, arguing that these demands would jeopardize moderate support for the freeze resolution.[90]

Congressman Markey's staff spearheaded the professionalization of the freeze movement. Markey formed a pro-freeze political action committee called the United States Committee against Nuclear War. Advising members included such liberal Democrats as Philip Burton of California; Barbara Mikulski of Maryland; Peter Rodino, Jr., of New Jersey; Patricia Schroeder of Colorado; Paul Simon of Illinois; and Morris Udall of Arizona. In a 1983 fund-raising letter for the political action committee, Markey wrote, "We formed the Committee to help ensure the passage of the Freeze resolution I sponsored in the House, and a similar one sponsored by Senators Kennedy and Hatfield in the Senate. . . . For too long, my colleagues in the House have been intimidated by massive New Right war chests."[91]

After the Kennedy endorsement, even the focus of the NWFC shifted increasingly from grassroots activism to congressional lobbying. The *Freeze Newsletter* became *Freeze Focus*, and stories about civil disobedience in the United States and the mass peace marches in Europe gave way to an almost exclusive focus on the campaign in Congress and national elections. Meanwhile, the NWFC took on the feel of a professional organization, hiring experienced lobbyists, researchers, and public relations people.[92] Emblematic of this professionalization was a packet of slick advertisements disseminated by the Nuclear Weapons Freeze Clearinghouse for use as local groups saw fit. Each was designed to address a specific area of concern. The letter that accompanied the packet stated, "This campaign is too important to involve only 'peace people.' . . . Thus we have tried to focus on mainstream Americans who are fearful of nuclear war yet distrust the Russians. . . . Because we don't want to turn people off before they hear the message, we have purposely avoided the traditional movement images of peace doves, missiles or mushroom clouds. . . . Rather we have tried to elicit a *positive* response by connecting the Freeze with agreeable or even pleasant image associations."[93] One advertisement juxtaposed a photograph of Admiral Gene La Rocque with the word "Enough" and a quotation from the admiral on the "Myth of Soviet Nuclear Superiority." Another showed a license plate with fuzzy but discernible numbers, with the caption "We Got Their Number" and a short paragraph that began, "You're looking at an actual Russian license plate as it might appear from a U.S. satellite." The advertisement then made the case that a freeze could be verified with the aid of high-resolution U.S. satellite photography. Others showed mainstream Americans, such as a construction worker and a mother with children, raising concerns about a freeze, which were addressed briefly in the advertisements. Each ended with "Freeze. Because No One Wants a Nuclear War."[94]

The events of that spring—Ground Zero Week, the introduction of the Kennedy-Hatfield resolution in the House and Senate, and the Central Park rally—raised the national profile of the freeze movement to headline status and media saturation. According to Kehler, at this time, "the freeze was hot . . . [with] the media hyping it, to tell you the truth, larger than life."[95] No longer able to ignore the movement, the Reagan administration sent out administration representatives and supporters to challenge the freeze on the airwaves, in print, and on the lecture circuit. Alexander Haig denounced it as dangerous arms control policy that would weaken the United States, while conservative members of Congress accused the movement of promoting "unilateral disarmament." To counter the enormous religious support that the freeze had mustered, the Reverend Jerry Falwell denounced the "freezeniks" and accused the movement of promoting atheism and cold war surrender.[96]

Inevitably, the freeze movement found itself red-baited, as members of the administration now insinuated that the movement was secretly funded and guided by the KGB. Reagan charged that the freeze "was inspired not by the sincere, honest people who want peace, but by some who want the weakening of America and so are manipulating many honest and sincere people."[97] *Reader's Digest* published an article by John Barron in which he claimed that three intelligence officers had told him that the KGB was directing the freeze. Citing the article, Reagan declared that the Soviet Union "saw an advantage in a peace movement built around the idea of a nuclear freeze.... There is no question about foreign agents that were sent to help instigate and help create and keep such a movement going."[98] Passing the president's notice was the fact that one month prior to his charges of Soviet infiltration, Kehler was urging freeze supporters to write to the Soviet government to free Sergei Batrovin, a dissident Soviet peace activist being held in a Soviet mental hospital.[99] Organizers of the Central Park rally that had taken place the previous June issued a press release declaring, "Thirty years ago, this nation experienced the ravages of McCarthyism. The disarmament movement of the '80s will not allow itself to fall victim to red-baiting, nor will we participate in any form of red-baiting."[100] Hatfield responded to Reagan's charges, "I fought the communists in China when I was with the Navy. I fought them on the platforms in a debate on an ideological basis. I just haven't found one in the nuclear freeze movement."[101]

Efforts by the Reagan administration to red-bait the movement seem to have backfired. Congressman Markey believed that the attacks not only served to raise the profile of the freeze but also—because the charges were clearly baseless—solidified its support.[102] Riding the popular momentum of the movement, the House Foreign Affairs Committee, chaired by Bingham, passed a freeze resolution by a vote of twenty-eight to eight on June 23, 1982.[103] The support of Speaker of the House Tip O'Neill ensured that the resolution made its way to the House floor. Before the vote, O'Neill (who, as a congressman in 1953, had witnessed an atomic test) declared, "Anybody that ever saw one of those bombs must wonder why we did not start this freeze long ago."[104] Conte inveighed, "The resolution before us incorporates the mandate of those growing millions to get on with meaningful arms limitation and reduction and at the same time to stop—I say again, stop—the endless nuclear buildup between the Soviet Union and the United States."[105] Markey proclaimed, "I am proud to say that today in the House we are voting on a resolution that says we have learned from the horror of Hiroshima. This resolution says we want to freeze the nuclear arms race so we don't drift closer and closer to a nuclear holocaust that would have the destructive force of one million Hiroshimas."[106]

Republican conservatives such as the Illinois state representative Henry Hyde fiercely attacked the bill as weakening U.S. defenses and locking in Soviet superiority. John Warner (the Republican senator from Virginia) and Henry ("Scoop") Jackson (the hawkish Democrat) introduced a counteramendment in the Senate, calling for a freeze of nuclear weapons, but only after the current buildup by the administration was complete and had resulted in Soviet reductions. Markey denounced the Jackson-Warner amendment, which was introduced into the House debate by William S. Broomfield (the Republican state representative from Michigan), as a "phony freeze." After heated debate, on August 5, 1982, in its first test, the Conte-Markey-Bingham freeze amendment lost to the Broomfield alternative by a razor-thin margin, 202 to 204. Meanwhile, the Senate Foreign Relations Committee rejected Kennedy-Hatfield for Jackson-Warner by a vote of 12 to 5.[107]

Despite the defeat, many freeze proponents were buoyed by a defeat of only two votes on the eve of congressional elections. Kennedy declared, "By the narrowest of margins, the nuclear freeze may have lost in the House of Representatives, but it is winning day by day in the country, and I am confident that it will prevail at the polling places in November and beyond."[108] Kehler responded, "This vote demonstrates the great progress that the Freeze campaign has made since March of this year.... The real vote, however, will come this fall, when millions of freeze supporters, in thousands of communities across the country assess candidates for Congress on the basis of their stand on the Freeze."[109]

The close House vote in tandem with the growing public support for the freeze now focused movement attention on the upcoming congressional elections, in which Democrats hoped to reverse the Republican gains of 1980. The results augured a positive outcome for the freeze movement. The movement won impressive state referendum victories in Michigan, Montana, New Jersey, North Dakota, Oregon, Rhode Island, and—of course—Massachusetts. The campaign won a hard-fought victory in California, where the movement ran into opposition from the aerospace industry.[110] Only Arizona, where Barry Goldwater lobbied hard against it, defeated its freeze referendum. The freeze similarly passed in thirty-six of thirty-eight cities and towns where it had been placed on the ballot.[111] In a press release for the NWFC, Forsberg crowed, "Yesterday's vote on the Freeze sends a clear and unprecedented mandate to the U.S. Government to propose to the Soviet Union an immediate, mutual and verifiable freeze on the arms race. The overall vote count favored the Freeze by a margin of 60% to 40%.... Voters favored the Freeze in industrial states... in rural plains states... and in metropolitan areas."[112]

In November, the Democrats picked up twenty-six seats in the House of Representatives. Although this was, in large measure, due to the recession (which had seen unemployment go over 10 percent), movement leaders believed that they now had the numbers to push the freeze through the House of Representatives.[113]

The movement scored its first victory of 1983 in March, when the House Foreign Affairs Committee once again passed a freeze resolution, this time by a vote of twenty-seven to nine.[114] In June the full House met to consider what was now called the Zablocki resolution (after the Democrat Clement Zablocki, the Foreign Affairs Committee chairman from Wisconsin). In what Markey called a "filibuster by amendment," Congress embarked on fifty hours of contentious debate and numerous attempts by Republicans to substitute amendments favorable to the president's position on nuclear weapons and arms control.[115] Proponents of the freeze fought back seventeen of these amendments.[116] Critics of the Zablocki bill argued that it would lock in the putative Soviet nuclear weapons superiority. In response to the charges being lodged against the freeze proposal in the House, Senator Kennedy responded, "No one in authority, including President Reagan, would trade our deterrent for Soviet forces."[117] As debate dragged on, Markey sighed, "I wanted the Freeze to be the debate of the decade, not a decade of debate."[118]

Finally, exhausted members of the House adopted a pro-administration amendment, introduced by the conservative Democrat Elliott Levitas of Georgia, which supported a freeze but stated that it would be invalidated if no actual weapons reductions occurred shortly after its adoption. Other amendments were adopted that specified that the resolution would not affect current weapons systems or planned deployment of the Euromissiles.[119] The last to weigh in was Speaker Tip O'Neill: "We have concluded a long, and at times trying debate. . . . The freeze issue, in my opinion, has finally been drawn. We are ready to choose a historic course, whether to continue the policies of the past . . . or to chart a new path. The freeze supporters all across the country spoke clearly last November and will now speak through their representatives. They want an end to the arms race. They want the leaders of the superpowers to recognize that the on-rushing train of nuclear weapons must be stopped. That is also my personal desire."[120] The House of Representatives then voted 278 to 149 for the resolution.

Many freeze supporters were crestfallen over the number of amendments, which they believed diluted the message of the resolution. Leon Panetta (the Democrat from California) summed up the elasticity of the resolution: "Whether you are a hawk or a dove or something in between . . . [w]hen you go back home . . . you can say anything you want about this legislation."[121] The ambivalence among freeze activists took a turn toward demoralization when the Senate defeated the Kennedy-Hatfield freeze resolution 40 to 58 on October 31, 1983.

Three weeks later, the House voted 239 to 186 to fund the MX missile. Soon thereafter the Senate followed suit with a vote of 59 to 39.[122]

SHOWDOWN IN EUROPE

The failure of the freeze resolution in the Senate came just weeks before the scheduled November 23, 1983, deployment of U.S. Cruise and Pershing II missiles in Europe. Many freeze and disarmament proponents had hoped to stop deployment of these new weapons, which gave the United States a hair-trigger first-strike capability. The high-velocity Pershing II could reach the Soviet Union in under ten minutes, and the Cruise was designed to fly beneath Soviet radar. Throughout October, Western Europe was rocked by a paroxysm of protest that marked the culmination of three years of demonstrations. More than half a million people convened in Rome, and four hundred thousand people gathered in Amsterdam to protest the impending installation of the Euromissiles. On October 15, more than a million West Germans turned out to protest across the Federal Republic, from Bonn to Hamburg to Berlin. In the Schwabian region of West Germany, more than two hundred thousand demonstrators clasped hands and formed a seventy-mile human chain that surrounded U.S. bases in two cities that were scheduled to receive Pershing II missiles: Stuttgart and Ulm.[123]

In the United States, the national freeze movement had agreed to downplay the Euromissile debate, largely on the advice of Kalicki and Waller, who believed that open opposition to the Euromissiles would be perceived as a call for "unilateral disarmament." Nevertheless, the NWFC continued to lobby Congress to delay installment of the Euromissiles.[124] Some activists, however, had moved to engage in their own, more radical, opposition to the Euromissiles. On July 4, 1983, more than 2,000 women had set up camp at the U.S. Seneca Army Depot in Romulus, New York, to protest the scheduled transport of Pershing missiles through that location en route to Europe. The Women's Encampment for a Future of Peace and Justice remained throughout the summer, swelling at times to more than 6,000 women. At the camp, radical lesbians worked with older, more conventional activists from the historic peace movements, and feminist criticism of the arms race was brought to the fore. Conservative local townsfolk viewed the camp as an invasion of communists and lesbians. Then, on August 1, in a direct action protest of the Pershing II missiles, more than 240 women—among them a number of Massachusetts activists—scaled a six-foot fence only to be arrested at the base. Frances Crowe, who was among those arrested, reported, "It was terribly empowering.... I'd never climbed a fence before. I decided I needed to put my body into the machine that's creating madness."[125] The U.S. Army dropped the trespassing charges but ordered the women to stay away from the base.

The simultaneous campaigns to win Senate approval of a freeze resolution, defeat the MX, and stop the Euromissiles suffered a devastating blow in late August, with the news that the Soviet Union had shot down KAL 007, a South Korean passenger jet, which had crossed into Soviet airspace. The attack, which left no survivors, unleashed a torrent of anti-Soviet hostility in the United States. In a letter to local organizers, the NWFC advised, "The incident of the shooting down of the Korean airliner by the Soviets continues to be a major area of concern.... There seems to be a sense in Congress at the present time that it might be best to let the emotional fervor around the Korean issue die down before getting a vote on the MX or the Senate Freeze resolution. In other words, the further from the airliner movement, the better the possibility there is for a more positive vote on both issues."[126] The NWFC also advised, "To move the nation past its grief and anger... it is important right now to acknowledge the tragedy when doing press work. It is important right now to point to the arms control lessons inherent in the tragedy."[127]

During the period between October 21 and 24, 1983, U.S. peace activists held numerous legal rallies to protest deployment of the Euromissiles. More than six thousand people demonstrated on the Boston Commons, where John Olver was among the speakers.[128] Earlier in the year, western Massachusetts activists had begun to petition Representative Conte under the banner "Support the Freeze. Freeze the Euromissiles." The petition read, "We urge you to support the amendment soon to be introduced, to delay by one year the deployment of the Cruise and Pershing missiles in Europe."[129] In October the petition drive paid off, when Conte wrote a letter to President Reagan, stating, "We believe that a statesman-like initiative to delay the deployment clock is essential at this critical time. In fact, it may be the best hope we have to reverse the direction of the arms race and establish a new momentum for nuclear arms control." Conte's letter was cosigned by Congressman Markey, Senator Kennedy, and Senator Hatfield. Most of Congress, however, remained solidly behind the Euromissiles.[130]

By late October, it was clear that the trans-Atlantic protests would not stop deployment of the Cruise and Pershing II missiles, end funding for the MX, or win Senate support for a freeze resolution. The backlash engendered by the KAL 007 incident was compounded that fall by a suicide attack on a U.S. military compound in Lebanon, which killed 241 marines, and by the U.S. invasion of Grenada a week later, which set off a wave of triumphant nationalism across the nation. In a section of a letter to organizers subtitled "1982 and 1983 Ups and Downs," Kehler discussed the bleak prospects for the movement: "Suddenly, at the end of August, we were all hit with the shocking news of the KAL-007 disaster, which triggered a hurricane of anti-Soviet hysteria. Although U.S. intelligence experts now say that the Soviet fighter pilots probably did not know they were shooting at a civilian airliner, and despite many people's doubts about the true mission of the KAL plane, President Reagan seems to have successfully exploited the incident to pick up additional support for his nuclear arms program in Congress.... Who can help but feel some discouragement?"[131] Anticipating some post-deployment depression in the ranks, Kehler wrote another letter to activists, attempting to boost sagging morale. It read in part, "We will continue to struggle as hard as we can against the deployment. But we must also recognize that if the deployment does take place, a mutual freeze, far from being invalidated by that deployment, will become more urgent than ever.... Missiles deployed now can be undeployed later if there is a will on both sides to do it."[132]

On November 23, 1983, the first nine Pershing II missiles reached the Federal Republic of Germany, soon followed by a steady stream of more Pershing II and Cruise missiles.[133] Coming so closely on the heels of the defeat of the freeze in the Senate and passage of appropriations for the MX (the most politically vulnerable missile pursued by the administration), the deployment of the Euromissiles represented a real nadir for the disarmament movement in the United States. After an exhilarating three years of expansion, accompanied by many emotional peaks, demoralization began to set in on the freeze movement.

The sense of fatigue and despair that began to be felt by some activists in the fall of 1983 was compounded for some by the ABC broadcast of the television movie The Day After. Aired on Sunday night, November 20, 1983, the film, which starred Jason Robards, featured a dramatic depiction of the effects of a nuclear war on Lawrence, Kansas. The movie was in part a breakthrough that helped drive home a message that the freeze movement had been sending out for three years; however, because the film came in the wake of the Soviet downing of KAL 007 the previous September, the defeat of the freeze in the Senate, passage of the MX, and deployment of the Euromissiles, some movement members feared that it would only add to a growing sense of helplessness and fatalism.[134] Local freeze groups organized "How to Avoid the Day After" discussion groups, advised members not to watch the movie alone, offered guidelines about how to discuss the film with children, and generally encouraged members to fight any sense of helplessness the movie might evoke.[135]

DIRECT ACTION IN THE AGE OF THE FREEZE

While the freeze movement worked to build grassroots support and endorsements from elected officials, a number of committed activists continued to carry out direct action protests of the nuclear arms race. The first major action occurred on September 9, 1980, at the General Electric factory in King of Prussia,

Pennsylvania, where a group that called itself the Plowshares 8 hammered on the nose cone of two Minutemen missiles and poured their own blood over blueprints and tools, causing an estimated ten thousand to forty thousand dollars in damage. Among the members of the Plowshares 8 were the Vietnam War–era radical priests Daniel and Philip Berrigan, whose involvement—along with that of their lawyer, Ramsey Clark, a former attorney general—ensured the action widespread publicity. In their first trial in 1981, the defendants were sentenced to three to ten years in prison, but the sentences were thrown out on appeal and the case remained in the news throughout the 1980s, becoming a cause célèbre among U.S. radicals.[136]

Massachusetts freeze activists were especially involved in direct action campaigns of the early 1980s. In the summer of 1981, the Committee for Creative Non-violence organized a Call to Prayer and Resistance, the centerpiece of which was a civil disobedience action at the White House. Seven western Massachusetts activists, including Frances Crowe of the Northampton AFSC, Judith Scheckel of Traprock, and Ruth Benn of the Amherst Disarmament Coalition, joined 124 others who broke away from a White House tour to sit in the White House driveway, praying for the survival of the human race and denouncing recent budget cuts for human services. The group, which included veteran civil rights activist Dick Gregory, was arrested on charges of unlawful entry and taken to separate men's and women's prisons.[137] The arrestees issued a statement, which read in part, "Dr. Martin Luther King stated that non-violent direct action 'seeks so to dramatize the issue that it can no longer be ignored.' We believe that the threat of nuclear war . . . is the most important issue of our time. . . . We call upon the President, in the interest of national security, to initiate a proposal for a mutual U.S.-U.S.S.R. nuclear weapons freeze."[138]

At the hearings in June 1981, the defendants pleaded guilty to unlawful entry, received six-month suspended sentences and three months of probation, and were instructed by the judge (who some observers believed to be sympathetic to the defendants) to stay out of the White House.[139] The case received national attention and helped elevate the profile of Frances Crowe, who—especially skilled at drawing new recruits into various social movements—was already well known as one of the most colorful activists and effective organizers in the Bay State. The speaker who introduced Crowe when she received the New England Award for Excellence in Social Justice Actions in 1981 stated, "I can think of no one who more fully embodies the call of Jesus in Luke 4 to 'set at liberty those who are oppressed.'"[140]

Crowe had played an active and leading role in the movements against the Vietnam War and nuclear energy in the 1970s. During the 1980s, she would also be actively involved with the Central American Solidarity movement and the campaign against apartheid in South Africa. Unlike many in the freeze and disarmament movements, Crowe could date her opposition to nuclear weapons to the dawn of the atomic age. In a 1982 speech on the subject, Crowe recalled the fateful moment: "Thirty-seven years ago, when I heard the news over the radio of the bombing of Hiroshima . . . I was shocked beyond understanding. . . . I was alone . . . a bride in New Orleans waiting for Tom to return from his duty in the U.S. Army. I was overwhelmed with a feeling of shock and grief. . . . The changes that have taken place in my personal life since then and in the society the past thirty-seven years seem more than I am able to absorb."[141]

Crowe can trace her activism back even earlier, to her schoolgirl days in Carthage, Missouri, during the 1930s, where she led a failed petition campaign to have her high school provide a gym class for girls as it did for boys. "My mother gave me a vision," recalled Crowe. "She told me to go places in the world."[142] Commenting on Carthage, Crowe stated, "There was a lot of classism and racism there. The Ku Klux Klan were very strong in our community, and as members of a small Catholic Church we were targeted."[143] After spending two years at Stephen's College, an all-women's institution in Missouri, Crowe earned a degree in psychology from Syracuse University.

During World War II, Crowe experienced important changes. She took on war work at the Sperry and Bell Labs in New York while she worked toward a graduate degree at Columbia University and then the New School for Social Research at night. "I was a 'Rosie the Riveter,'" recalled Crowe, " . . . and then the war was over and we women were told to go home, back to the kitchen and have children."[144] Speaking of her years at the Sperry and Bell plants during World War II, Crowe remembered, "I started to get politicized then." She recalled, "I'd been so idealistic for my country, and then I was seeing all this waste and greed around me. Other people weren't idealistic; they were there to make money from the war. I was getting really turned off. By the time the United States dropped the bomb on Hiroshima, I was ready to be a pacifist."[145]

In many ways, the atomic bombings of Hiroshima and Nagasaki became the guiding motif of Crowe's life. "Spiritual passivity is the first death, nuclear holocaust is the second death," she would later repeat. Crowe gradually gravitated in the direction of the Quakers: "My conscience didn't feel comfortable with Catholic belief." Looking back at her evolution toward radical pacifism, Crowe recalled, "When they dropped the atomic bomb on Hiroshima I became somewhat of a Quaker in belief overnight. . . . I felt [the bombing] was the wrong thing to do. So much killing."[146] After the war, Crowe's husband, Thomas Crowe, shared his expertise as a radiologist with his wife, providing her with a deeper understanding than most Americans of the dangers of radiation.[147]

During the late 1940s and the 1950s, Thomas and Frances Crowe had three children, Caltha, Jareth, and Tom. Frances Crowe described herself as a "traditional housewife and mother"[148] during these years. Because Jareth was born deaf, the family moved to Northampton, Massachusetts, to be near the prestigious Clark School for the Deaf.[149] Crowe gravitated toward the growing Ban the Bomb movement in the late 1950s and became active in Committee for a SANE Nuclear Policy (SANE) during the early 1960s campaign for a nuclear test ban treaty.

Later in the decade, Crowe's activist energies shifted toward opposition of the Vietnam War. Between 1968 and 1973, she organized daily pickets at Westover Air Base in Chicopee and ran the Pioneer Valley Peace Center, which offered draft counseling. At times, more than seventy young men gathered in her basement office. "I feel it was a real crisis in men's lives," she recalled. "People were coming to me desperate, looking for the quickest, easiest way out of military service. I tried to show them how they could respond in a human way."[150] Draft counseling became a crusade for Crowe, who managed to appear at local high schools alongside military recruiters to discuss alternatives to military service.[151] Crowe also frequently drove between Northampton and Amherst, picking up young men who hitchhiked on Route 9 and offering them draft counseling.[152] After becoming a full-time member of the AFSC, she commented about the Quaker religion, "It's a small denomination, but its influence is way out of proportion to its size."[153]

After the war in Vietnam, Crowe became involved in the movement against nuclear energy. With the birth of the freeze movement, however, she came full circle to the issue that more than any other had set her on her activist path. She felt particularly invigorated by the rapid growth of the massive peace movement in Europe, which critics dismissed as "Hollanditis," referring to the strength of neutralist and disarmament sentiment in the Netherlands. Crowe declared, "Well, I have Hollanditis . . . and it's the best disease I've ever had . . . and I caught it from the Europeans. . . . Seeing the pictures of their huge demonstrations . . . talking to people who have been to Europe . . . it's very infectious."[154] For Crowe, Hollanditis was the antidote to the apathy that she believed the arms race created: "If one does not have a future, why struggle?"[155] Quoting a study by the Yale University psychologist Robert J. Lifton in which 80 percent of respondents purportedly said that they believed they would die in a nuclear war, Crowe railed against the "psychic numbing" that she believed pervaded U.S. society: "To endure the thought of possible annihilation of life on this planet results in many people turning to religious cults, drugs, alcohol, entertainment, pornography, excessive self-fulfillment [to] turn it off [and] flip the page."[156]

When the freeze movement began in the 1980s, Crowe was the veteran of many years of activism. She played a central role in the western Massachusetts referendum campaign of 1980 and gave the keynote address at the first national freeze conference. Like Anna Gyorgy and Sam Lovejoy, who took the anti–nuclear energy gospel of western Massachusetts around the country, Crowe lectured for the freeze across the United States.[157]

Crowe also had a long record of direct action experience and accompanying arrests. At five feet, two inches tall and in her sixties, Crowe was frequently amused at the perplexed reaction she encountered from police when they arrested her for civil disobedience: "One gets a lot of mileage out of white hair," she observed.[158] Crowe's civil disobedience at the White House was the first of several high-profile actions that she would undertake in the 1980s. The most spectacular of these took place on October 3, 1983, as the influence of the freeze movement on Congress appeared to be waning. Crowe and seven other women (five of whom were nuns) entered the Electric Boat plant at Quonset Point, Rhode Island (which produced Trident II submarine-based missiles), issued an "indictment" to plant personnel, and then spray-painted "Thou Shalt Not Kill" on several missile casings.[159] Although it was Crowe's fourteenth arrest, the Electric Boat action resulted in her first extended jail time. Crowe and her codefendants were convicted of malicious mischief, sentenced to six months in prison (all but thirty days of which were suspended), and fined approximately $150. Judge Albert DeRobbio ejected from the courtroom in South Kingston, Rhode Island, more than thirty supporters, who showed their solidarity with the defendants by singing.[160]

When she entered the Adult Correction Institution in Cranston, Rhode Island, Crowe was met by quizzical looks from the existing inmates. "I came in and I looked like I could be their grandmother," Crowe told a reporter upon her release.[161] Although she was a vegetarian, she was served only meat while she was in prison. "It was not easy," she recalled. "It was prison."[162] While she served her prison term, she was flooded with letters of support. Because the volume eventually reached the point where the prison could not inspect Crowe's letters, her mail was withheld altogether. The incorrigible Crowe continued her political activity in prison, however, talking politics with the inmates and managing to persuade thirty-eight of them to sign a petition of support for the 1984 bid for the presidency made by the Reverend Jesse Jackson.[163]

Jackson's Rainbow Coalition was a growing force in U.S. politics, and he was anxious to build bridges with the peace movement. He attempted to have Crowe and her fellow activists released early. (When Crowe was released after her mandated thirty days, Jackson mistakenly claimed credit for her "early release.") Upon her release, Crowe made national news by holding a press conference with Jackson at the Olney St. Baptist Church in Providence, where she endorsed him for president: "He's building a Rainbow Coalition, and I don't think we're going to get anywhere on ending the arms race unless blacks are involved. He's really trying to make peace a platform."[164] A photographer who snapped a shot that was reprinted in *Newsweek* and numerous local newspapers captured the moment at the press conference when Crowe and Jackson kissed.[165]

DENOUEMENT: FREEZE VOTER '84, STRATEGIC DEFENSE INITIATIVE, AND THE QUICK FREEZE

Entering 1984, much of the freeze movement was demoralized over the failures of the previous fall, when the Senate had rejected the freeze, Congress had funded the MX missile, and deployment of the Euromissiles had proceeded on schedule. The focus now was on the upcoming presidential elections. The political action committee Freeze Voter '84, formed at the NWFC meeting in St. Louis in late 1983, represented the apex of the professionalization of the movement, employing extensive direct mailing and the "bundling" of individual contributions. The goal was to "change the politicians" by focusing on pro-freeze candidates.

All the Democratic candidates endorsed the freeze in some form, and Freeze Voter '84 circulated a chart with the candidates' positions on major issues, including the freeze, the Euromissiles, the MX, Trident II, and the B-1 bomber. All the candidates except Jesse Jackson and the long shot, George McGovern, had supported at least one issue that the freeze movement opposed. Alan Cranston, the congressman from California, who was the most solicitous of freeze movement support, for example, passed each litmus test but one, his support for the B-1 bomber. Gary Hart, who had endorsed the freeze late in the campaign and was strongly opposed to the MX, supported the Euromissile deployment.[166] Freeze supporters split among the candidates, with some opting for the most viable and others for candidates with the purest records.[167]

In western Massachusetts, an offshoot of the statewide freeze movement, Elect the Freeze in '84, endorsed the freeze activist Democrat Mary Wentworth over the Republican Silvio Conte, who easily went on to reelection. Born in Maine during the Great Depression, Wentworth attended Smith College, where she learned Russian. In 1951 Wentworth's penchant for languages landed her a job with the top secret Armed Forces Security Agency in Washington, D.C., where she translated intercepted messages with the Czech language section. Wentworth left the agency to accompany her new husband to Philadelphia, where she raised her family and was also drawn into civil rights activism through her work with disadvantaged Philadelphia youth. The civil rights movement was the gateway that led Wentworth into the antiwar movement and radical feminism. In the 1970s and 1980s she traveled to the People's Republic of China, Cuba, Holland, West and East Germany, and the war zones of Nicaragua. She was also arrested—and later spent time in jail for—protesting the Seabrook nuclear power plant in 1976.[168]

Wentworth was severely critical of Conte, whom she believed received far too much credit from progressive constituents. She called Conte "a pretender" who by "doing just enough to keep their hopes alive . . . dampened burgeoning dissatisfaction with his tenure." After researching Conte's record and receiving some advice from Shirley Chisholm (then teaching at nearby Mount Holyoke College), Wentworth launched her quixotic campaign as the official Democratic nominee. Although she had once eschewed electoral politics, she was deeply affected by her meetings with Green Party activists in West Germany. She later wrote, "I felt that activists like myself who had protested in the seventies on a variety of single issues now needed to make them part of the platform of a political party and elect people to implement it."[169]

Wentworth hammered away at Conte's support for budget cuts to social programs that benefited the economically disadvantaged, especially women and children. She campaigned as the peace candidate, declaring, "A vote for Wentworth is a vote for jobs, peace and justice." She ran a grassroots campaign that constantly confronted the powerful patronage machine of the "Silver Fox," as many called Conte. Sympathizers were afraid to incur Conte's displeasure by supporting Wentworth, and the state Democratic Party (viewing her candidacy as a long shot) kept her at arm's length. Although she appeared with Governor Michael Dukakis, the senatorial candidate John Kerry, and the vice presidential nominee Geraldine Ferraro before a crowd of twenty thousand at the University of Massachusetts at Amherst, none of the top-billed candidates mentioned her candidacy by name. On election day, Wentworth polled 27 percent of the vote. She believed, nevertheless, that her candidacy had the positive effect of highlighting the shortcomings of the traditionally unchallenged Conte.[170]

It was not only Wentworth who had difficulty in 1984. Across the board, the Democrats and the freeze movement were in for an uphill struggle. By early 1984, the painful recession of the early 1980s had begun to break. Shorn of the inflation that had plagued the economy in the 1970s, Reagan declared success for his economic remedies and proclaimed a new "Morning Again in America."[171] The freeze movement had risen against the backdrop of the recession, which seemed to spread a general pessimism throughout the nation. Moreover, the substantive cuts in social programs that corresponded to defense increases at a time of economic hardship had played into the hands of the freeze movement.

The early Reagan years had seen the "war winners" emerge as the public face of the Reagan administration arms buildup. Their often belligerent rhetoric had done much to scare many Americans into the arms of the freeze movement. Beginning in 1983, Reagan shifted his priorities to a new weapons system, the Strategic Defense Initiative (SDI), a space defense proposal that Reagan contended would stop "mutually assured destruction" and usher in the end of the nuclear arms race. Although disarmament activists recognized that the weapon could be nothing less than destabilizing, was a violation of the 1972 ABM Treaty, and would be likely to foster a new arms race, it served to allow Reagan to change his rhetoric from the belligerent-sounding themes of the "war winners" to the peaceful-sounding theme of ending the arms race through a defensive shield.[172] Speaking of the Republican platform on SDI, Kehler exclaimed, "It was just like ours. It said how deterrence is folly and immoral, and economically the arms race is killing us, and there's no [civil] defense against nuclear weapons anyway."[173]

In her exhaustive study of the SDI program, *Way Out There in the Blue: Reagan, Star Wars, and the End of the Cold War*, Frances FitzGerald argues that the freeze movement tipped the balance that moved the Reagan administration away from its buildup policies to reliance on a proposed defensive shield. By 1982, she argues, "what the debate showed was that in just two years the freeze had achieved rhetorical dominance over the administration."[174] To sound more "reassuring" and "outflank" the freeze, the administration tied freeze rhetoric to its proposed SDI system. Kehler immediately recognized the words of the movement coming back at him from the White House. Commenting on the road to Star Wars (as the SDI came to be known), FitzGerald writes that few administration figures "mention a phenomenon of great importance to them at the time. Once this element is introduced, the story [of SDI] begins to make sense—otherwise it is like the score of a piano concerto with the piano part missing. The phenomenon is, of course, the anti-nuclear movement: the freeze."[175]

With a rebounding economy and the new emphasis on peace rather than war, the Reagan administration was able to move away from the biggest liabilities of its early years: the image of the president as heartless toward the impoverished and the jobless and as a warmonger bent on some sort of nuclear showdown. Going into the 1984 election, Reagan could play to his strengths, and the affable "great communicator" hit his stride, offering an upbeat patriotic message that sounded hollow to some during hard times but that fit the mood of an economic recovery.

Finally, Walter Mondale, the Democrats' standard bearer, failed to catch fire with the U.S. public and especially the freeze movement, which regarded the Minnesotan with ambivalence. Mondale had supported the arms buildup of the late Carter years and continued to embrace deployment of the Euromissiles. He called for a 5 percent military budget increase over inflation, compared to 8 percent by Reagan, and—further alienating the Left—a quarantine of revolutionary Nicaragua.

Dukakis, the governor from Massachusetts, who had endorsed Mondale early in the primaries, sought to energize Mondale's campaign at a Boston Freeze Voter rally in October. He hoped that his own strong freeze credentials would help legitimize Mondale for skeptical freeze advocates. At an October 20 rally, which took place at Faneuil Hall, Dukakis appeared with John Kerry (the lieutenant governor), Barney Frank (the liberal congressman), Gerry Studds, Ed Markey, and Mary Wentworth (the Democratic challenger to Silvio Conte). Invoking the memory of John Kennedy, Dukakis denounced the lack of progress made by the Reagan administration toward arms control and its SDI program: "A little over twenty years ago this month, during one of the most frightening periods of our recent history, President Kennedy got on the hotline to Moscow and ended the Cuban Missile Crisis. The current administration doesn't even know the phone number.... And most disturbing of all, this administration is not content with the tools of destruction here on earth but now wants to circle the heavens with atomic death."[176]

Despite the strong support for the freeze movement in the Bay State, Dukakis's efforts failed to deliver even Massachusetts for Mondale. In November, Reagan was reelected with 59 percent of the national vote, with Mondale winning only the District of Columbia and his home state.[177]

In late 1984, the freeze movement tried one last-ditch effort to get Congress to impose a freeze, by using the power of the purse. Once again, Kennedy, Hatfield, and Markey teamed up—this time with Jim Leach, the Republican from Iowa—to sponsor the Arms Race Moratorium Act, which called for an end to the testing of warheads, long-range missiles, and antisatellite missiles.[178] Known as the Quick Freeze, the bill would have slowed, but not stopped, the arms race. Kehler and the NWFC enthusiastically embraced the proposal, which gained 120 cosponsors in the House and 7 in the Senate. The entire Massachusetts delegation was on board.[179] Still, the bill never made much headway.[180]

Gradually, opponents of the arms race drifted off to other movements. Many focused on opposing the SDI, soon joined by most of the Massachusetts delegation, including Conte. Others moved into the growing Central American Solidarity and anti-apartheid movements.

THE IMPACT OF THE FREEZE MOVEMENT

David Meyer argues that the freeze movement was "notable for its failures."[181] He especially blames the shift in the movement toward political lobbying and professionalization at the expense of the grassroots focus and what he views as excessive dependence on the Kennedy and Markey staffs. According to Meyer, this trend resulted in the "demobilization" and "depoliticization" of the movement.[182] To a great extent, Meyer's assessment is accurate; the situation resembled that of the Clamshell Alliance in 1978, when it opted for a legal energy fair over direct action, a decision that demoralized much of its more committed base. Even so, as Meyer acknowledges, the movement managed to shift the rhetoric in the nation and may well have set the stage for the negotiations with Mikhail Gorbachev that took place in Reagan's second term. According to Meyer, "The movement can also be seen as a political triumph. The freeze effectively forced an extremely popular president to return to long-established bipartisan policies he had consistently eschewed and had vigorously criticized."[183]

The freeze and West European peace movements grew into one of the largest mass movements ever to develop simultaneously on both sides of the Atlantic Ocean. Both moved far deeper into the mainstream established politics of their respective countries than most movements have ever managed to do. They shifted the terms of the debate and highlighted the fact that populations on both sides of the ocean were tiring of the cold war and could not envision it ending in a victory for either side. Although the freeze movement was unable to end appropriations for a single weapons system in the Reagan administration budget, the long-term impact of the effort was to prepare the ground for the negotiations with Gorbachev and for the revival of a new détente that would ultimately lead to the end of the cold war.

The victories of the freeze movement nevertheless remained either symbolic or indirect. According to Kehler, the movement suffered from having a support base that was "a mile wide and an inch deep."[184] In Kehler's view, the shift of focus to Washington, D.C., was premature and fatal: "[The] demise of the national freeze [came when the movement] ran out of things people could do in their local communities. . . . When the focus moved to Washington, it was harder for people to plug in where they are."[185] For Kehler, the major lessons of the freeze movement were "don't go to Washington too soon"; "don't believe your own press"; "have things to do in people's own communities"; and "you can't diversify a movement once it's going [if it isn't] multiracial from the beginning." The long-term lesson that seemed to Kehler to be most important was the power of money in Congress. The freeze, according to Kehler, "underestimated the clout of the nuclear weapons industry."[186]

Between 1980 and 1983 the freeze became the largest countervailing voice to the cold war rhetoric of Reagan. In the fall of 1983, international events such as the downing of KAL 007 and the U.S. invasion of Grenada strengthened Reagan's cold war positions. The economic recovery of late 1983 helped boost Reagan's popularity and further contributed to the decline of the freeze movement. Yet as freeze activists sought to stop nuclear war, another kind of war beckoned closer to home. Throughout the early Reagan years, a growing movement emerged in opposition to the intervention of the administration in Central America, which many Americans feared would lead the country down the path to another Vietnam. The Central American solidarity movement grew in the shadow of the freeze and then exploded in mid-decade.

CHAPTER 5
THE CENTRAL AMERICAN SOLIDARITY MOVEMENT IN MASSACHUSETTS 1980–1990

FOUR CHURCH WOMEN, AN ARCHBISHOP, AND AN AMBASSADOR: 1980

On December 2, 1980, Sisters Ita Ford and Maura Clarke of the Maryknoll Order prepared to take a flight from Managua, Nicaragua, to San Salvador, the capital of El Salvador, and from there return to the small northwestern town of Chalatenango to continue their work. For most of the previous year, they had distributed food and clothing to impoverished refugees who were fleeing the war zone that engulfed ever-larger sections of rural El Salvador.[1]

In 1979 a reform junta had come to power in El Salvador, hoping to address the staggering poverty and inequality in the nation, where for decades a small oligarchy and brutal military had overseen a society in which 1.9 percent of the people owned 57 percent of the land.[2] Within months, however, most left-leaning members of the junta had quit in protest of the refusal by the military to countenance any land reform or democratic change. As popular protest continued to sweep El Salvador, the military intensified its campaign of repression, and in 1980 a divided Marxist guerrilla movement unified into the Farabundo Martí National Liberation Front (Frente Farabundo Martí para la Liberación Nacional [FMLN]).[3] The guerrillas took their name from the leftist leader of a 1932 uprising in which ten thousand to thirty thousand peasants had been killed by the Salvadoran military in what came to be known as la Matanza (the Massacre).[4]

Just six days before Ford and Clarke returned to El Salvador, six civilian politicians from the Democratic Revolutionary Front (Frente Democrático Revolucionario [FDR]), a political coalition that included the mass organizations aligned with the various guerrilla groups in the FMLN, had been murdered by right-wing "death squads" aligned with the Salvadoran military and the ruling oligarchy.[5] According to the *New York Times*, more than eight thousand Salvadorans had been killed in political violence over the previous year, predominantly by the National Guard, the army, and the infamous Treasury Police of the right-wing government.[6]

The atmosphere was quite different in Managua, where Ford and Clarke had just spent several days at a conference of the Maryknoll Order. A little more than a year earlier, a guerrilla army known as the Sandinistas had coordinated a final military offensive throughout Nicaragua, which had toppled the long-time dictator Anastasio Somoza and his National Guard. The Sandinistas had taken their name from the anti-imperialist leader Augusto César Sandino, who had led a peasant army in opposition to occupation by the U.S. Marines from 1926 until 1933, when he was murdered by a dictator installed by the United States. By 1979, the Somoza family had not only ruled Nicaragua for decades but also owned much of the land and resources in the nation.[7] As Ford and Clarke traveled through Managua, much of the city lay in ruins from both the civil war that had brought the Sandinistas to power, claiming the lives of more than fifty thousand Nicaraguans, and the devastating earthquake that had struck the city in 1972.[8]

Nevertheless, in December 1980 Nicaragua was, for many, imbued with a festive air of liberation after long years of oppression. Clarke was especially enthusiastic about the prospects for the Sandinista revolution. Before journeying to El Salvador, the Bronx, New York, native had worked for seventeen years among the impoverished population of Nicaragua.[9] Clarke's years in Nicaragua had coincided with the spread of liberation theology throughout Latin America. Growing out of the Vatican II call for the church to do more to alleviate the suffering of economically disadvantaged people and the impact of the 1959 Cuban Revolution on Latin America, liberation theology drew on many sources, including the Christian Gospel and Marxist ideology. The previous summer, Clarke had told a Church magazine, "I believe very much in non-violence but also we can never judge anyone who has to resort to violence, as in Nicaragua, because of the institutional injustice and violence present in the country for years and years."[10]

Clarke was not alone in her sentiments. Maryknoll was a progressive order; the nuns were not required to wear veils and, in the words of Sister Peg Merker, Ford and Clarke's superior, its members had a mission "to go to other countries to work for the poor and the oppressed and for the promotion of justice."[11] Ford had left her Brooklyn, New York, neighborhood to join the order in 1971. She was then sent to Chile, where in 1973 she witnessed first-hand the United States–sponsored overthrow of the democratically elected socialist president, Salvador Allende. Like Clarke, she had begun work in El Salvador in early 1980.[12]

On the day Ford arrived in El Salvador, a death squad aligned with the leader of the right-wing Nationalist Republican Alliance (Alianza Republicana

Nacionalista [ARENA]) party, Roberto D'Aubuisson, assassinated the archbishop of San Salvador, Oscar Arnulfo Romero. The previous February, the archbishop had written a personal letter to President Jimmy Carter imploring him to cut all U.S. military aid to El Salvador: "I ask that, if you truly want to defend human rights, you: Prohibit military aid to the Salvadoran government: Guarantee that your government not intervene. . . . I hope that your religious sentiments and your sensitivity to the defense of human rights will move you to accept my plea avoiding, with such acceptance, any greater bloodshed in this suffering country."[13]

The day before the archbishop's assassination and Ford's arrival in El Salvador, Romero had made an impassioned plea to the soldiers of the Salvadoran military to stop the bloodshed in that nation: "Brothers, you came from our own people. You are killing your own brothers. Any human order to kill must be subordinate to the law of God, which says, 'Thou Shalt Not Kill.' No soldier is obliged to obey an order contrary to the law of God. . . . In the name of God, in the name of this suffering people whose cry rises to heaven more loudly each day, I implore you, I beg you, I order you: Stop the repression."[14]

As Ford and Clarke returned to El Salvador on December 2, news of the assassinations of six opposition leaders a week earlier was the talk of the capital. Sister Dorothy Kazel (a Cleveland, Ohio, native and member of the Ursuline Order) and Jean Donovan (a Catholic lay worker from Westport, Connecticut) met the sisters at the San Salvador airport. Together, the four churchwomen left the capital in a Toyota van, heading north, to return to their mission in Chalatenango. The previous week, while they were in Nicaragua, several notes had been left on the Chalatenango parish door: One read, "Go to Cuba to finish your Communist work"; another said, "In this house are Communists. Everyone who enters here will die. Try and see."[15]

On December 3, the charred remains of the Toyota van were discovered some twenty-five miles north of the capital. The van was traced back to the churchwomen by the serial number on the engine. The following day, twenty miles from where the vehicle had been deposited, the bodies of Ita Ford, Maura Clarke, Dorothy Kazel, and Jean Donovan were found by local farmers in a shallow, two-foot grave, their clothes torn and their bodies badly mutilated. Autopsies later revealed that the women had been raped and then shot in the head execution style.[16]

On December 4, Robert White, the U.S. ambassador to El Salvador, heard the news and traveled north to collect the bodies of the murdered women. The ambassador had no doubt that this was the work of the Salvadoran military and that no low-level officer would carry out such executions without orders from his superiors. A lifelong professional diplomat, White had been appointed to El Salvador by President Carter, and he took seriously the president's injunction to make human rights a centerpiece of U.S. policy in the region. After the 1979 Sandinista revolution in Nicaragua, however, Central America had become increasingly caught up in the renewed cold war. As the deaths from right-wing violence mounted in 1980, the Carter administration refused to heed Archbishop Romero's plea to cut the recently renewed military aid to El Salvador. Now, in response to the murder of four U.S. citizens, the Carter administration suspended $25 million in military and economic aid to the country. Fearing an FMLN victory, however, the administration reinstated some of the aid only a week later—and all of it within a month.[17]

Ambassador White, an uncommonly decent man with a genuine concern for the welfare of the people of El Salvador, knew that the hopes of the early Carter years to promote human rights throughout the region were gone. The previous month, the people of the United States had elected a man who was determined to make Central America the front line in a resurgent global crusade to contain communism. Charging that Nicaragua and El Salvador could become Soviet outposts in the Western hemisphere, Ronald Reagan vowed to halt the spread of Marxist revolution in Central America by any means necessary. Rightist forces in Central America viewed the incoming administration, with its numerous critics of the Carter human rights policy, as saviors. The Reagan administration promised a massive reshuffling of State Department personnel to reflect the new policy and declared that the first to go would be White, who was fired unceremoniously.[18]

Alongside the renewed arms race, the policies of the Reagan administration with respect to Central America soon became a lightning rod for radical activism and liberal challenges to the new administration. Throughout the 1980s, the unpunished murders and cherished memories of Jean Donovan and Sisters Ita Ford, Maura Clarke, and Dorothy Kazel would hang like a pall over the debate on Reagan's policies in Central America. Responding to a 1993 report by the U.N. Commission on the Truth for El Salvador that concluded that the order for the execution of the churchwomen came from high up the military chain of command, the U.S. State Department issued a statement that read in part, "This particular act of barbarism did more to inflame the debate over El Salvador in the United States than any other single incident."[19]

A NEW ADMINISTRATION AND A NEW MOVEMENT

During 1981, as part of its across-the-board arms buildup and more confrontational policy toward the Soviet Union, the new Reagan administration sought to recast the conflicts in Central America in terms of the global cold war. Although the Carter administration, especially in its later years, had increasingly factored cold war concerns into its own Central American policy, the Democratic administration had continued to see the problems in the region largely as stemming from local causes, such as endemic poverty, stark class inequality, a legacy of military government, and ongoing human rights violations (what conservatives derided as "regionalitis"). Although the Reagan administration occasionally acknowledged such forces, it sought to de-emphasize them, portraying the problems of the region as predominantly the result of outside Soviet and Cuban agitation.[20] Referring to El Salvador (and with the Vietnam War clearly in mind), Alexander Haig, the hawkish secretary of state, privately exhorted Reagan, "Mr. President, this is one you can win."[21]

Reagan quickly worked to triple U.S. aid to El Salvador and increased the numbers of U.S. military advisors in the country to fifty-two. The strategy of the administration was to contain leftist rebels in El Salvador through military aid; bolster the Salvadoran center, especially the Christian Democrats of the junta president, José Napoleón Duarte; gradually reduce the number of death squad killings; hold elections in two years' time; and implement a modest land reform program.[22]

If the policy of the administration was containment in El Salvador, then over time it became rollback in Nicaragua. After the 1979 Sandinista revolution, the Carter administration had hoped to move the new revolutionary government in the direction of multiparty democracy and a market economy. He intended to do so by reinstating and even increasing aid, which had been cut in the last months of the Somoza regime, but also by earmarking large segments of that aid for use in the private sector. Within a year, the Reagan administration had cut U.S. aid to Nicaragua. Soon the administration undertook a covert proxy war using Nicaraguan counterrevolutionaries, later known as the Contras (who had grown out of the remnants of Somoza's National Guard), eight hundred of whom had been secretly flown out of the country to Honduras by the Carter administration with the fall of the Somoza regime in 1979.[23]

The sharp shift in U.S. policy in Central America concerned many liberals. They were outraged that the administration seemed to be giving unconditional support to the Salvadoran junta, which appeared to be unable or unwilling to reign in its armed forces and paramilitary death squads, whose victims averaged more than seven hundred per month throughout 1981 and 1982.[24] The impact was even more electrifying on the Left. Van Gosse has traced radical interest in Latin America back as far as the late 1950s, when Fidel Castro and his band of guerrilla fighters captured the imagination of much of the U.S. Left and, for a time, even many mainstream liberals.[25] Over the next decade, as Che Guevara became an icon of the New Left, a number of young leftists, carrying on a tradition that went back to the Abraham Lincoln Brigades during the 1930s Spanish Civil War, sought to aid the new revolutionary government of Cuba by traveling to the island nation to help with harvests as *brigadistas* in the internationalist Venceremos Brigade. By the 1970s, the hold that Cuba had had on the imagination of the U.S. Left had begun to fade; yet the interest of the Left in Latin America continued, primarily through the influence of liberation theology.[26]

The 1979 Sandinista revolution captivated the North American Left. The Sandinistas recaptured some of the romantic aura of the early Cuban revolution yet seemed to diverge in important ways from the rigid ideologies and bureaucratic governments of the communist bloc nations. The revolutionary movement in Nicaragua appeared to be humanized by the influence of liberation theology: Particularly notable were the absence of a bloodbath after its rise to power, the quick abolition of the death penalty by the new government, and its lenient treatment of former National Guardsmen. The new Sandinista government included poets such as the renowned author Ernesto Cardenal, and—in contrast to Cuba, where the Catholic church was distrusted—the Sandinista government included two priests in its nine-member directorate. The Nicaraguan revolution could be many things to many people. To more-radical leftists who felt disaffected by the less-militant politics of the anti–nuclear energy or freeze movements, solidarity with the Sandinista revolution was a way to identify with an anti-imperialist, Marxist-influenced movement. For those of a countercultural orientation, the agrarian nature of the revolution held much appeal. For religious activists, the revolution held the promise of putting into practice the liberation theology vision of a radical social gospel.[27] Even many liberals saw the Sandinistas as more peasant populists than hardened communists. In the wake of the 1979 revolution, Tom Harkin, the congressman from Iowa, proclaimed enthusiastically, "Yo soy Sandinista!"[28]

Unlike the movements against nuclear power and the arms race, in which New England (especially Massachusetts) was at the forefront, the Central American solidarity movement of the 1980s took root first on the West Coast (particularly in the San Francisco Bay area). Many of the U.S. national solidarity groups, such as the Committee in Solidarity with the People of El Salvador (CISPES), the National Network in Solidarity with the Nicaraguan People (NNSNP), and the Network in Solidarity with the People of Guatemala (NISGUA), grew fastest on the West Coast, an area with both strong demographic and cultural ties to Latin America and a firmly established political Left.[29]

The early solidarity movement was especially attractive to young, more-militant leftists, and tensions with older activists and peace groups often arose. According to Van Gosse, "In those years, CISPES activists acquired a reputation as insistent [red] flag waving partisans of the FMLN."[30] In these divisive early years, many spoke of an anti-intervention movement versus a solidarity movement. Whereas the former focused on opposing U.S. intervention on the grounds of self-determination, peace, and human rights, the latter openly and enthusiastically proclaimed its support for the Sandinistas, the FMLN, and other revolutionary movements in the region. According to Gosse, "The difference was mutual stylistic discomfort. Solidarity activists were committed to a posture of enthusiastic and continual militance on behalf of an anti-imperial revolution. Anti-intervention workers . . . favored persuasion over confrontation and a carefully 'American' humanitarian approach." Gosse, however, calls this a "sterile division" because "as the Right had charged all along . . . the results for Central America are likely to be the same: hindering intervention means 'One, two, many' popular victories in the long run."[31] As the decade progressed, however, the two strands became part of a larger movement, in which the differences at times were difficult to discern (hereinafter referred to as the Central American solidarity movement).

EARLY SOLIDARITY ACTIVISM IN MASSACHUSETTS

Although Massachusetts would emerge as a stronghold of the Central American solidarity movement, the issue of Central America was eclipsed early on by the phenomenal growth of the freeze movement in the Bay State. Despite this overshadowing presence, familiarity with the issues that confronted the people of Central America grew steadily through activist letters to the editor, prayer vigils, speaking tours, and sporadic rallies against U.S. intervention in the region. Much of the early movement was educational in nature. Area churches, including the Congregationalist church, the Unitarian church, and the American Friends Service Committee (AFSC), were especially active in the nascent campaign to educate Massachusetts residents on the issues.

Typical of the community-based rallies against U.S. intervention was an April 26, 1981, protest at Pulaski Park in Northampton, which attracted an estimated fifteen hundred protestors. The featured speakers included Sister Maria Russo of the Maryknoll Order, David Cohen of the United Electrical Workers (UE) Holyoke Local 264, and a representative of the El Salvador FDR (who appeared under the alias "Duran"). Seeking to connect U.S. policy in Central America with U.S. domestic issues, Cohen asserted that many in the U.S. labor movement opposed Reagan's policies, "since El Salvador is a haven for runaway factories and multinational corporations." He continued, "Although the military government declares unions illegal, every major union hall has been bombed or burned. . . . [T]he only reason the U.S. government hasn't sent troops into El Salvador is because of demonstrations like this."[32] As the ragtag band of activists listened, large green military transport planes lumbered overhead, bound for nearby Westover Air Force Base. For many, they symbolized the omnipresent fear that Central America was becoming another Vietnam.[33]

After Cohen, Duran of the FDR spoke to the crowd, emphasizing the indigenous sources of the revolutionary movement in El Salvador: "The press says the conflict in El Salvador is the result of external communist powers rather than internal conditions of poverty... the Salvadorans are a peace-loving people. Our struggle for freedom from (President Jose Napolean) Duarte's oppression has nothing to do with Cuba or Russia, nor can our freedom be determined by U.S. aid to the junta who support a system where 2 percent of the people own 60 percent of the land while 65 percent are landless."[34] Concluding his impassioned remarks, Duran raised a clenched fist and declared to the crowd, "We have been forced to arm ourselves. It is better to die fighting than to live on our knees!"[35]

Massachusetts activists threw themselves into not only rallies but also national material aid campaigns on behalf of war victims in El Salvador. During the decade, Medical Aid for El Salvador (MAES) raised $700,000 for medical supplies; New El Salvador Today (NEST) raised $157,000 in general aid; and CISPES raised $500,000.[36] Because much of the money raised by the material aid campaign was distributed in FMLN war zones considered "zones of control," the campaign was highly controversial and subject to frequent red-baiting. Celebrities such as the actors Mike Farrell of M*A*S*H and Ed Asner of the popular Lou Grant Show played prominent public roles in the national campaigns.[37]

In western Massachusetts, groups such as the AFSC-sponsored Central American Working Group (CAWG), an all-women's organization, worked to bring the successful localist strategy of the freeze and anti–nuclear energy campaigns to Central American solidarity activism. CAWG pursued a multigenerational, highly interpersonal solidarity campaign in an effort to bring the movement into traditionally nonactivist sections of the community. The group often set up stands in public places and went door-to-door to solicit aid for Central American war victims. During these community-outreach campaigns, and at more traditional rallies, the women of CAWG would circulate Polaroid photographs of families from El Salvador, Nicaragua, and Guatemala to personalize the issues of war and poverty in a way that they believed the slick newspaper photographs could not. The goal of such campaigns was not only to raise money for victims of war and poverty in Central America but also (much as the freeze movement had worked to personalize the issues of nuclear war) to forge a sense of personal connection between North Americans and their neighbors to the south.[38]

The Central American solidarity campaign in Massachusetts began to pick up steam in 1983. This was a result of (1) the waning freeze movement, which had pulled so much Bay State activist energy into its vortex and (2) the rapidly escalating Reagan administration proxy war against the Sandinista regime in Nicaragua. Throughout 1982, news reports of a covert military campaign directed by the U.S. Central Intelligence Agency (CIA) and carried out by Nicaraguan counterrevolutionaries against the leftist government in Managua surfaced with increasing frequency. By 1983, denials by the Reagan administration gave way to confirmation of U.S. support for the rebel forces but with the limited aim, the administration contended, of interdicting Sandinista weapons being smuggled to the FMLN in neighboring El Salvador. Thus, although the Reagan administration sought to package its illegal aid to the Nicaraguan counterrevolutionaries as defensive in nature and with specific objectives, to many liberals and radicals the covert aid campaign signaled a dramatic escalation in the efforts to destabilize and ultimately overthrow the revolutionary government in Nicaragua.[39]

In the summer of 1983, the shift in focus in Massachusetts was signaled by the announcement of fifteen Bay State activists that they would be among the first contingent of North Americans to travel to the Nicaraguan war zone as part of Witness for Peace (a national faith-based campaign aimed at raising awareness of the proxy war and ending it through their presence). The Massachusetts delegation to the first Witness for Peace delegation was headed by the Boston Congregationalist minister Frank Dorman and included in its ranks the ubiquitous Frances Crowe, whose focus now began to shift from disarmament to Central American solidarity activism. Crowe, who had just played the leading role in forming the Northampton-based CAWG and only months earlier had been arrested in Rhode Island for painting "Thou Shalt Not Kill" on a several missile casings, now prepared to enter the remote areas of the war-torn Nicaraguan-Honduran border. Before she departed, she told a reporter for the *Boston Globe*, "What we will be doing is putting non-violence to work by putting our bodies in front of violence."[40] The Witness for Peace mission, which gained a good deal of national publicity, was followed by many more such missions to the war zone, with hundreds of North American participants.[41]

By 1985, the Reagan administration proxy war had become increasingly destructive and destabilizing, as the Sandinista government was forced to divert ever-greater resources from popular social programs and to earmark more than 50 percent of its budget to the war against the ever-expanding Contras (as the United States–backed Nicaraguan counterrevolutionaries were now known).[42] Reagan declared the Contras to be "the moral equivalent of our founding fathers." As the U.S. proxy war continued in the mid-1980s, however, the policies of the administration became increasingly mired in controversy. In 1984 it was revealed that the CIA had blown up oil tanks in Corinto, Nicaragua, and had mined the principal Nicaraguan harbor. These actions resulted in a rare ruling against the United States by the World Court in the Hague. The administration responded by declaring the World Court ruling null.[43]

THE SOLIDARITY MOVEMENT AND GOVERNOR MICHAEL DUKAKIS

Like the nuclear weapons freeze movement, the solidarity movement in Massachusetts sought the support of Governor Dukakis. The governor was once again receptive. Dukakis spoke Spanish and had been a student at the University of San Marcos in Peru in 1954, when the CIA orchestrated the overthrow of Jacobo Arbenz, the democratically elected president of Guatemala. Ever since, Dukakis had remained critical of the U.S. role in Latin America. In 1983 Dukakis wrote in response to one solidarity activist, "Both as an individual and as a Governor of the Commonwealth, I have often expressed my disagreement with the policies of President Reagan . . . in El Salvador and Nicaragua. . . . I see those who question the rationale and wisdom of such policies attacked as either naïve or unpatriotic. I am most concerned with the obvious parallels to our unfortunate and costly involvement in Southeast Asia."[44]

Early in Dukakis's term, the Boston Coordinating Council on Central America contacted the governor in the hope that he would declare September 15, 1983, a Day for Peace with Justice in Central America. The Boston Coordinating Council directed cooperative projects by several groups active in solidarity work, such as the AFSC, Mobilization for Survival (MfS), Catholic Connection, the Central American Solidarity Association (CASA), the Maryknoll Center for Justice and Peace Concerns, the New England CISPES, OXFAM (originally the Oxford Committee for Famine Relief) America, and the Unitarian Universalist Service Committee. Dan Petegorsky of the Boston MfS wrote Dukakis, "September 15, the date on which Central American peoples traditionally celebrate their independence from Spain, has been designated as a national day of action for peace in Nicaragua and Central America. . . . We are grateful for the interest that you have shown on Central American issues in the past, and hope that you will join with us and with people across the state and the country on September 15 in voicing our concerns over the direction of the Reagan administration's policies."[45] Dukakis responded by issuing what would be the first of many proclamations at the request of Massachusetts solidarity activists, declaring September 15 a Day for Peace and Justice in Central America and urging citizens to "express their concern over the grave situation in whatever ways they feel are appropriate."[46]

The following year Dukakis once again proclaimed September 15 a Day for Peace and Justice in Central America. At the request of the Massachusetts

Teachers Association, he also endorsed the 1984 East Coast speaking tour of Marta Alicia Rivera—a representative of the National Association of Salvadoran Educators (Asociación Nacional de Educadores Salvadoreños [ANDES]), who had helped initiate a fifty-eight-day general strike in 1968, had been kidnapped and tortured by the Salvadoran National Guard in 1979, and had subsequently fled the country—despite charges by the Reagan administration that Rivera and ANDES sympathized with the Salvadoran guerrillas.[47]

Dukakis also endorsed a referendum question that appeared in thirty-nine state representative districts, calling on the president and Congress to cut all military aid to Central America and withdraw all military advisors from the region. The Central American Referendum Campaign, another statewide coalition of solidarity groups, sought to imitate the success of the freeze movement referenda campaigns by featuring Dukakis's endorsement prominently in the campaign. One flier had emblazoned across the top "Remember Vietnam? Vote 'Yes' for Peace in Central America on November 6." On the bottom was a photo of Dominic Bozzotto, a Massachusetts union organizer, with Rivera; a photo of and quotation by Randall Forsberg endorsing the referendum question; and, in the center, a photo of Dukakis, smiling at his desk, with the following quotation: "The people of Central America want from the American people only those things we ourselves treasure most—respect for self-determination, the peaceful settlement of disputes, and the equitable and democratic sharing of opportunities. We as Americans have an obligation to protect those values and to seek alternatives to intervention and militarism."[48] The referendum question won in most districts, and Dukakis used the results the following spring to proclaim Central America Week.[49] Thus, Dukakis joined the Massachusetts delegation in Congress to make theirs the most visible and unified state in opposition to Reagan's Central American policies. As with the freeze movement, grassroots activism had (to use Forsberg's term) percolated up.

THE 1985 EMBARGO PROTESTS

In the spring of 1985, the Reagan administration imposed an economic embargo on Nicaragua. To many solidarity activists, beyond promising greater hardship for the people of Nicaragua, the embargo seemed to presage war. Over the previous two years, just across the border in Honduras, U.S. Army and National Guard units had been conducting extensive, highly visible military maneuvers known as Big Pine.[50] In response to the escalating saber rattling by the administration, solidarity activists in the United States undertook a national Pledge of Resistance (POR) campaign, in which signatories pledged to conduct massive civil disobedience in the event of U.S. war in Nicaragua or in El Salvador. The hope was to maintain the specter of street protest on the same scale as that of the Vietnam War, as a deterrent to U.S. invasion of a Central American nation.[51]

By the spring of 1985, huge, often boisterous pledge meetings were taking place across Massachusetts. Many activists considered the embargo by the Reagan administration to be an act of war and argued that the pledge should be activated. Yet national leaders of the POR hesitated. Massachusetts activists, both around Boston and in western Massachusetts, pushed for independent regional action. Frances Crowe declared, "More and more people are beginning to think that something has got to be done quickly and it [the POR call for action] should be activated now. Personally, I'm ready now."[52] As a result of this impatience, a number of areas across the U.S. moved to invoke the call to action on their own.[53]

On May 7, 1985, embargo protests took place throughout the United States, all of them targeting federal buildings. More than 300 activists were arrested in San Francisco (cradle of the solidarity movement), more than 500 activists were arrested in Boston, and 135 activists—including Crowe—were arrested at the Springfield Federal Building in western Massachusetts.[54] Again, the issue of self-determination was emphasized. "I feel very strongly that people in that country [Nicaragua] have a right to self-determination," proclaimed Mitchell Gaslin of Amherst after his participation in the civil disobedience.[55] Patrick Sullivan of Faculty for Peace, a University of Massachusetts professor, declared, "The embargo is an act of war and congressional opposition has got to be mounted."[56]

As embargo protests took place in New York City, Seattle, Chicago, New Haven, Denver, Santa Fe, and smaller communities, such as Worcester and Pittsfield in Massachusetts, by far the largest unfolded in Boston.[57] Throughout the day on May 17, Boston-area solidarity activists trickled into the John F. Kennedy (JFK) Federal Building, milling about or eating at the public cafeteria. By late afternoon, more than five hundred activists had converged on the front lobby, had sat down, and had taken up anti-embargo chants, determined to stay past the 6:30 p.m. closing time. Outside the building, between one thousand and two thousand supporters joined the protest of the U.S. embargo. The scene was loud and raucous. Numerous signs, including some that read, "Reagan's Peace Proposal: Drop Dead or We'll Kill You" and "Embargo Reagan," drove home the protestors' message.

The *Boston Globe* declared the protest "reminiscent in its tone and intensity of anti–Vietnam War rallies of the late 1960s."[58] Among the speakers at the energetic rally were the African American community activist Mel King and Senator George Bachrach of Watertown. Bachrach declared, "We can still understand the difference between right and wrong. This is a simple issue. The government of Nicaragua is indigenous. We are the interloper."[59] Also addressing the crowd was Richard Bell, an aide to the Democrat John Kerry, who had been elected to the U.S. Senate seat held by the retiring Paul Tsongas in 1984. Kerry, who (as lieutenant governor) had been the conduit between freeze activists and Dukakis, continued to foster ties with the activist Left by reaching out on the issue of Central America. Bell declared, "Senator Kerry commends [the demonstrators inside] for your moral courage and moral leadership. . . . [C]ivil disobedience is the highest form of political activity."[60]

At 6:30 p.m., police and federal marshals began the process of making mass arrests; most of the protestors walked out, but dozens chose to go limp. The arrestees were transferred in groups of thirty to U.S. District Court for processing, which went on through the night, throughout the next day, and into the subsequent night. Those who cooperated were processed and eventually released on their own recognizance, whereas those who resisted by giving names such as John Doe, Jane Doe, and Sandino were held and threatened with perjury. Among the activists was Frank Dorman, the fifty-eight-year-old reverend from Cambridge who had led the Massachusetts delegation on the first Witness for Peace mission to Nicaragua in 1983. Dorman told a reporter for the *Boston Globe*, "As an ordained minister, [I submit that] it should be recorded that we are here because of acts of conscience."[61] Twenty-three-year-old Ellen Kage of Waltham declared, "What I did was not criminal. What we are protesting is criminal."[62]

As hundreds were arrested in Boston and Springfield, smaller actions took place in Greenfield and Williamsburg, and, after a ninety-minute vigil, one hundred activists in Pittsfield sent medical aid to Nicaragua in a "symbolic embargo-busting action."[63] The embargo protests of 1985 coincided with the fast-growing anti-apartheid movement, which swept U.S. campuses and African American communities, with its call for economic divestment from the white supremacist nation of South Africa. For many, the fact that the United States had imposed an embargo on a developing nation whose government was struggling to help the disadvantaged but refused to divest itself from a wealthy nation that kept the majority of its citizens impoverished and oppressed under a racial caste system underscored the corruption of U.S. foreign policy. The contrast between U.S. policy toward South Africa and U.S. policy toward Nicaragua further highlighted the selective concerns of the administration regarding human rights, which appeared to be dictated more by capitalist imperatives and cold war strategy than by democratic principles. Beginning in the spring of 1985, the solidarity movement increasingly took up the chant "Boycott South Africa, Not Nicaragua!"[64]

In early June 1985, Congress voted 248 to 184 to send $27 million in nonlethal aid to the Contras.[65] The entire Massachusetts congressional delegation, which had played a pivotal role in defeating Reagan's proposed military aid package for the Contras earlier in the year, voted no.[66] Shortly thereafter, however—in a move much criticized as ill-timed and ill-considered—Daniel Ortega, the president of Nicaragua, took a jet to Moscow in search of aid. As a result, Reagan was able to turn around the sagging congressional support for Contra funding, procuring a compromise nonlethal aid package and keeping alive hope of further assistance for the armed Nicaraguan opposition.[67] The vote soon sparked renewed protest across the United States. Civil disobedience resumed on June 12, 1985, when ninety-three activists, led by a procession of drum-beating Buddhists from the Leverett Peace Pagoda, were arrested in Chicopee, outside the Westover Air Base. Many handcuffed themselves to gates, while others entwined themselves with rope to make arrest more difficult.[68]

In Boston, reaction to the $27 million aid package rekindled the militant protests of the previous month. As POR protests erupted in San Francisco; Washington, D.C.; Kansas City; Seattle; and Eugene, Oregon, more than fifteen hundred protestors once again converged on the JFK Federal Building. "We are here to organize an active resistance to war," proclaimed David Truscello, a POR organizer. "We will not permit Ronald Reagan to drag this country into this war. We are going to make sure that we are a significant factor in his decision to wage war. We're going to come back. We will not go away."[69]

Learning from the experience of the May embargo protests, Peter Thomas—the regional administrator of the General Services Administration, which was responsible for running the JFK Federal Building—decided to avoid making arrests. Anticipating the protests, he had had the building barricaded off, and he instructed police simply to remove, without arresting, those who breached the barricade. Nevertheless, daily business was disrupted, since employees entering the JFK Federal Building had to stop and produce identification. "It's not our intention to arrest anyone," Thomas declared. Pleased with the results, he continued, "I must say we came up with a pretty good strategy."[70] Anne Shumway, a POR organizer, told a reporter in response, "We consider this a victory of sorts because we partially closed down the building."[71]

The Contra aid protests spilled over into the next day as hundreds of activists in Boston marched first on the Armed Forces Recruiting Center on Tremont Street and then on the Coast Guard Marine Safety Office on Commercial Street, where a branch of the Immigration and Naturalization Service (INS) was located. The boisterous protestors, who chanted, "No recruiting today!" were held at bay by barricades and mounted police, and more than eighty were hauled away as they breached police lines. "The people here are willing to risk arrest, their jobs, being put in the files of the F.B.I. [Federal Bureau of Investigation] and being trampled by police horses in order to make it clear that the public won't tolerate the killing of innocent people in Central America," declared Shelly Kellman of the Boston POR.[72]

Confrontation between activists and police were not the only source of tension during the 1985 embargo and Contra aid protests. Throughout the first half of the 1980s, there was an undercurrent of disaccord in the solidarity movement between those who had a generally more pacifist orientation and those who were more ardently sympathetic with the revolutionary forces in Central America. Although the groups often shared not only similar interpretations of U.S. policy but also sympathy for popular and leftist forces in Central America, what Gosse referred to as "mutual stylistic discomfort" often surfaced at the POR meetings of 1985.[73] For some, the more strident militancy of some of their fellow activists— whose more outspokenly militant groups tended to be disproportionately male in composition—smacked of a certain machismo. Age also seemed to factor in, as older activists often took an eye-rolling attitude toward the younger, clenched-fisted militants. Lois Ahrens of CAWG, who was in her thirties and forties during the 1980s, recalled disputes with those she described as "more partisan," who had a "much more unshakable, nonquestioning attitude about the infallibility of the Sandinistas."[74] Recalling the large pledge meetings of early 1985, Ahrens commented, "There would be these guys who were the 'revolutionary guys,' that were trying to take a lot of space, and there were those of us who were older than they were, and women, that maybe wanted to be less confrontational." Nevertheless, Ahrens adds, "as a general rule, we won out."[75]

Another cleavage that had come into stark relief by 1985 was a regional rift reminiscent of the division between Boston-based and western Massachusetts activists during the Seabrook protests. Crowe describes the fissure as not so much ideological as organizational. According to Crowe, the Boston-based, largely Cambridge-centered groups, which had closer ties to national organizations, tended to be more "bureaucratic" and "top down," whereas the western Massachusetts solidarity activists were more "grassroots" and "bottom up."[76] Indeed, whereas large national groups, such as CISPES in the early 1980s and New England Central America Network (NECAN) later, played major roles in the eastern part of the state, in western Massachusetts the movement tended to be decentralized and composed of a plethora of small "affinity groups," such as CAWG (which operated independently from not only other groups but even its own parent organization, the AFSC).[77]

Despite the divisions between eastern and western halves of the state, Massachusetts emerged from the 1985 embargo and Contra aid protests with an even higher profile in the national movement. This trend reached its apex in

1986 with the anti-CIA protests that swept college campuses across the country and culminated in the massive April 27, 1987, protests and arrests outside CIA headquarters in Langley, Virginia. Since the role of the CIA in Central America was well known, from its mining of the Nicaraguan harbors to its training of the Contras, the agency had become a lightning rod for militant campus protest by Central American solidarity groups. In 1986 and 1987, the CIA became the focus of militant protest in Massachusetts.[78]

ANTI-CIA PROTESTS AND TRIAL AT
UNIVERSITY OF MASSACHUSETTS AMHERST

In early November, students at the University of Massachusetts Amherst who belonged to the Radical Student Union (RSU) and CASA geared up for the impending arrival of CIA recruiters on campus. During the previous months, the CIA had been met with civil disobedience and large-scale protests on campuses across the country. The student activists argued that since university policy forbade criminal organizations from recruiting on campus, the CIA, which had engaged in illegal activities around the world and especially in Central America, should be banned. On Thursday evening, November 13, 1986, anti-CIA student protestors held a candlelight vigil, which resulted in the cancellation of a CIA informational session. The anti-CIA activists faced counterprotests from pro-CIA students, who argued that efforts to ban the agency from recruiting on campus not only violated the students' First Amendment rights to free association but also undermined national security.[79] The next day, the anti-CIA protestors tried to halt the planned CIA recruitment session, but the agency evaded disruption by quietly relocating and rescheduling. Eleven students, all from RSU and CASA, then occupied the office of Chancellor Joseph Duffey and demanded a meeting to discuss university policy on CIA recruitment. When the students refused to vacate the building at closing time, campus police entered the office and arrested the protestors.[80]

The University of Massachusetts subsequently sought an injunction to limit where students were permitted on campus. RSU and CASA argued that the injunction was an infringement of students' First Amendment rights and an effort to intimidate the movement to ban the CIA from campus. On November 24, 1986, hundreds of University of Massachusetts students, joined by sympathetic "five college" area students and community members, turned out to protest the injunctions and push for a ban on CIA recruitment on campus. The protestors occupied Munson Hall, an administrative nerve center on the campus, holding the building for seven hours. Surrounding the building were forty police officers from the Amherst campus and forty police officers from the Boston campus, the town of Amherst, and—in riot control gear—the state police.[81]

On hand for the protest rally and joining the students in the occupation of Munson Hall was the veteran 1960s activist and Worcester native Abbie Hoffman, who was in the area to promote his idea of a new national student organization.[82] Although at first the students reacted coolly to Hoffman—whom they saw as somewhat of a relic of another era—the Yippie founder succeeded in winning them over. At the occupation, Hoffman declared, "Back to the future. It's 1968 out there!"[83] As the police began to arrest the occupiers, three protestors tried to block a police bus carrying arrested protestors by sitting in its path. Among the three was Amy Carter, the former first daughter, who was an activist student at Brown University.[84]

All told, the police arrested fifty-nine protestors. The students who had occupied the university building were charged with trespassing, and Carter and the other two protestors who blocked the police vehicle were charged with disorderly conduct. Four police officers were injured in the action: a few reported bite marks, and one had a dislocated shoulder. The arrestees were held in handcuffs for more than seven hours. Chancellor Duffy ordered Hoffman banned from the campus, declaring, "If Hoffman wants to have a trial on the C.I.A., that's fine. But to bring a public institution to a halt so he can do that is unjust."[85]

Although most of those who were arrested for engaging in civil disobedience accepted suspended fines, fifteen protestors—including Hoffman and Carter—decided to challenge the charges against them at the county court in nearby Northampton by pleading not guilty using the "necessity defense." The case was taken up by a national organization called the C.I.A. on Trial Project, which hoped to turn it into a national cause célèbre and use the trial to expose what it regarded as the crimes of the CIA, especially those in Central America.[86] The Hampshire District Court judge Richard F. Connon agreed to permit a necessity defense on the condition that the fifteen be tried together in order to streamline the process.[87] (After the trial, Judge Connon told a reporter that presiding over the politicized case "didn't upset" him. "Variety is good," he added. "It breaks up the monotony of hearing all those drunk driving cases. It's the most notorious I've heard and probably the hardest to handle.")[88]

The radical attorney Leonard Weinglass, who had defended Hoffman and the Chicago Seven after their arrest during protests at the 1968 Democratic National Convention, headed up the defense. In a strategy that bore many similarities to that of the Sam Lovejoy trial more than a decade earlier, the defense summoned on behalf of the defendants several high-profile witnesses, including Daniel

Ellsberg (the 1971 *Pentagon Papers* whistle-blower), Ralph McGehee (the former-CIA-agent-turned-agency-critic), Ramsey Clark (the former-attorney-general-turned-radical-activist), and Edgar Chamorro (the former Contra leader), all of whom were to testify to CIA crimes in Central America and around the world. Meanwhile, the C.I.A. on Trial Project raised fifteen thousand dollars for the defense, including seven thousand dollars of Hoffman's own money.[89]

Thomas Lesser, the Northampton lawyer who had defended Lovejoy in 1974 using the necessity defense, joined Weinglass. Their strategy was to use the national press and media attention that now focused on Northampton to put the CIA on trial. Especially damning were the testimonies of the CIA insider Ralph McGehee (who disclosed CIA misinformation) and former Contra Edgar Chamorro (who detailed CIA instructions to the Contras on methods of assassination of local officials that would implicate the Sandinistas in the murders).[90] As Weinglass repeatedly spoke of instances of what he described as CIA crimes around the world, the prosecution followed a strategy of refusing to counter the defense witnesses, arguing that CIA behavior was irrelevant and that the case hinged only on the question of whether trespassing and disorderly conduct had taken place. (After the trial, District Attorney W. Michael Ryan commented that he believed the narrow technical focus to be the best strategy. He added, however, "If it came to defending the C.I.A. or losing, I'd rather lose.")[91]

The case turned the town of Northampton upside down, as news crews from around the country set up their cameras and satellite trucks outside the court and anti- and pro-CIA protestors countered each other with rival chants: "Hey, hey, ho, ho, the CIA has got to go!" was met with "Hey, hey, ho, ho, Amy Carter has got to go!"[92] Carter spent much of her time dodging the national press, but she told a reporter from the *Valley Advocate*, "Whenever someone sacrifices a part of themselves for justice, it aids the cycle of change."[93] In response to a question about when her activism had come to focus on the CIA, the former first daughter explained, "They'd always outraged me, but I guess I decided to make it a priority when I was researching South Africa during my senior year of high school. I found out that the C.I.A. had given information on the African National Congress to the South African government, and that a C.I.A. agent was present when Nelson Mandela was arrested."[94]

On the final day of the trial, Hoffman addressed the jury as part of the closing argument by the defense: "I ask you, is it we, the defendants who are operating outside the system? Or does what you have heard about the C.I.A. activities in Nicaragua and elsewhere mean it is they that have strayed outside the limits of democracy and law?"[95]

In her closing statement, Prosecutor Diane Fernald told the jury of six, "We're talking about crimes that were committed down the road in Hampshire County. We're not talking about illegal activities of the CIA in Central America or elsewhere."[96] On April 15, 1987, however, it was CIA crimes in Central America rather than the activities of the protestors that most moved the six jurors. The panel pronounced the defendants not guilty, acquitting them on all charges. When the jury announced its verdict, the courtroom erupted in cheers and hugs, and only Judge Connon's threat to clear the courtroom calmed the atmosphere.[97] Referring to the jury of six, whose members ranged in age from thirty-four to seventy-seven, Ryan conceded, "If there's a message, it was that the jury was composed of Middle America. It was a great jury for us. They weren't kids. There were a couple of senior citizens. And they believed the defense. Middle America doesn't want the CIA doing what they are doing."[98] Weinglass, soaked with champagne at an after-trial victory party, declared, "It can only be read one way. . . . [T]he jury had to find that the defendants had a right to occupy that building and the illegal activities of the C.I.A. justified a not guilty verdict."[99] A jubilant Amy Carter exclaimed, "A jury of six in Northampton found the C.I.A. guilty of larger crimes than trespass and disorderly conduct and decided that we had a legal reason to protest."[100] When Jimmy Carter learned of the verdict in Northampton, he described himself as a "very proud father tonight" and added, "Amy's been arrested four times, three times protesting apartheid and this last time for what she considers, and I consider, illegal activity of the C.I.A. in Nicaragua."[101]

Post-trial interviews with jurors revealed the miscalculation of the prosecution in its strategy of refusing to counter the testimonies against the CIA given by the witnesses for the defense. Walter LaFreniere, a seventy-seven-year-old cutlery worker and former union shop steward, told a reporter, "We know that these kids [and Hoffman] committed a crime which I'm totally against. But they did it for a reason. These young people, they weren't violent. They were there for a reason and one reason alone, and that's to get rid of that C.I.A. . . . There wasn't one C.I.A. agent that came there to deny these charges."[102] Donna Moody, a thirty-seven-year-old registered nurse from Ware, stated, "I think anybody that would've sat in that courtroom and listened to the expert witnesses, anybody would have felt the same way. . . . It was as if the students had no recourse to speak with the administration [of the University of Massachusetts.]"[103] Anne Gaffney, a sixty-four-year-old clerk at the U.S. Veterans Administration Medical Center in Leeds, was so impressed with the students that she declared, "These young people are doing what perhaps most of us should be doing, but don't have time to."[104]

THE SOLIDARITY MOVEMENT AND THE MEL KING
CAMPAIGN FOR CONGRESS: 1986

Many solidarity activists opposed U.S. policy through civil disobedience; however, many also worked through mainstream political channels to change the direction of U.S. policy. In 1986 the campaign for Congress by the African American activist and former state representative Melvin King became a magnet for solidarity activists in Boston. King had decided to campaign for the Eighth Congressional District, encompassing Cambridge and Somerville, which was to be vacated the following year by Tip O'Neill. The campaign pitted King against the frontrunner, Joseph Kennedy II, and George Bachrach, the state senator from Watertown, who challenged King for the progressive vote.

Born in the South End in 1928, King rose to prominence as head of the Boston Urban League from 1967 to 1971. In one dramatic action that defined King's militant brand of activism in a city that was particularly polarized racially, he dumped a pile of table scraps on a table at a meeting of the United Fund to symbolize the scraps that he believed the organization gave to the black community of Boston. King represented the South End in the Massachusetts House of Representatives from 1973 to 1982. In 1979, after campaigning in jumpsuits and dashikis, he placed third in the Boston mayoral race. In the 1980s, King began to don conventional suits when he campaigned, seeking, like Jesse Jackson, to broaden his political base. In 1983 he placed second in another bid for Boston mayor, losing to Raymond Flynn. King was an important player in both Jackson's Rainbow Coalition and his campaign for the Democratic nomination for president in 1984. In the Massachusetts legislature, King won widespread praise for his 1982 sponsorship of the South Africa Divestment Act.[105]

King's 1986 campaign sought to reassemble the coalition of minorities and progressive whites that had fueled Jackson's 1984 presidential campaign. Leslie Cagan, the Boston-based organizer who had played a central role in the 1983 Central Park rally, joined the King campaign to direct field operations.[106] The King campaign found strong support in Boston-area colleges, especially the Massachusetts Institute of Technology, where King was a professor of urban studies and planning. Students organized a number of block parties and dances, featuring reggae groups and local rock bands to fund-raise for the King campaign. Seeking to appeal to all progressive constituencies in the district, King tailored parts of his campaign to each. He reminded gay and lesbian organizations that in 1973 he had cosponsored the first gay rights bill in Massachusetts with Barney Frank. He met with the local Irish community in pubs such as Paddy's in Cambridge in an effort to forge a Black-Green alliance based on his long-standing support for Irish Republicanism.[107] King denounced the Gramm-

Rudman Deficit Reduction Act, passed by Congress, as a threat to programs that helped the needy, especially minorities, and he continued to call for full U.S. divestment from the apartheid regime in South Africa.[108]

Among the groups that King targeted were the numerous peace and disarmament organizations in the district. King called for a 30 percent reduction in all weapons spending, a nuclear freeze, and an end to the Strategic Defense Initiative (known as Star Wars).[109] King was outspoken in his anti-interventionism, which had come to the fore early in the campaign, when Ronald Reagan ordered an air strike against Libya in response to a recent terrorist bombing in Berlin. King denounced Joe Kennedy for supporting the raid: "A military response to terrorism, one that inflicts damage and death on civilians, is just another form of terrorism."[110]

Solidarity activists could not have expected more from King, who condemned U.S. policy in by far the strongest terms of the three leading candidates. In a draft that Cagan helped prepare, King declared, "On the question of aid to the government of El Salvador . . . [c]an we continue to support a government at war with its own people? Can we continue to support the bombings of civilian populations and the massive dislocation of people from their homes?"[111] On U.S. aid to the Contra army in Nicaragua, King was even more forceful. In the spring of 1986, when Congress voted to send $100 million in aid to the Contras, King inveighed, "Yesterday's vote in the House of Representatives . . . should be seen as a moral and historical equivalent of the Gulf of Tonkin Resolution of 1964. . . . [T]hese Contras are not freedom fighters but instead murderers, torturers and drug dealers. If this language is harsh, it is because the reality in Central America is harsh."[112]

In televised debates and campaign literature, King sought to distinguish himself from his liberal opponents by charging Kennedy with lack of experience and by calling for a nuclear weapons freeze alone (rather than across-the-board defense cuts). King assailed Bachrach for failing to reach out to minorities sufficiently.[113] Late in the campaign—much to the chagrin of King and Bachrach—the popular Tip O'Neill, who had promised not to endorse a candidate, described the district as "Kennedy country."[114] When all was said and done, Kennedy had garnered more than half the vote.[115] For its part, the King campaign had served to energize the Boston-based solidarity movement and encourage the other candidates to take a more forceful stand on the issue of U.S. intervention in Central America.

THE SANCTUARY MOVEMENT COMES TO MASSACHUSETTS

During the 1980s, more than 1,500,000 Central Americans were displaced by the civil wars in the region. Although many settled in refugee camps in their native countries or in neighboring nations, it has been estimated that as many as 750,000 Central Americans made their way to the United States, 400,000 to 500,000 of whom were Salvadorans. Many of the refugees, especially those from El Salvador, claimed that they were seeking asylum from persecution and that death would await them if they returned. In El Salvador such claims carried a good deal of credibility. Yet unlike political refugees from Cuba, Vietnam, the Soviet Union, or the Eastern bloc, who were traditionally welcomed into the United States, those who fled persecution by regimes that were backed by the United States were routinely denied asylum. According to the Reagan administration, the vast majority of the refugees from Central America were motivated by economic factors, and the INS was committed to returning the ever-growing flow of refugees to their countries of origin.[116]

Beginning in 1980, U.S. church groups near the Arizona-Mexico border began to provide sanctuary for Central American refugees fleeing persecution. Tucson became the center of the sanctuary movement, which soon spread to New Mexico and up to the West Coast. By 1983 the movement had exploded, as churches of various denominations throughout the United States began to provide asylum for predominantly Salvadoran and Guatemalan refugees. The sanctuary movement quickly became an embarrassment for the Reagan administration, as refugees shared accounts of terror at the hands of their anticommunist governments and paramilitaries. By 1983, the FBI had infiltrated the growing sanctuary movement with numerous informants, and in 1984—in a high-profile national trial—the Justice Department began prosecution of eleven members of the original sanctuary church in Tucson, Arizona.[117]

The movement had a special appeal to those with religious sensibilities (Protestant, Catholic, and Jewish religious leaders were all well represented), and its resemblance to the nineteenth-century Underground Railroad resonated powerfully with progressive clergy and laypeople alike. The Reverend Peter J. Sammon of St. Theresa's Roman Catholic Church in Sacramento, California, a national spokesman for the movement, declared, "In our view, sending these people back to El Salvador or Guatemala is the same thing as putting Jews on boxcars bound for Dachau."[118]

By early 1985, the sanctuary movement had expanded from churches to whole municipalities. Earlier that year, the Berkeley, California, and St. Paul, Minnesota, City Councils had become the first to vote to declare their municipalities official sanctuaries for Central Americans who were fleeing persecution, and they enjoined municipal officials, as far as legally possible, not to cooperate with federal efforts to deport these refugees. Chicago then followed suit through proclamation by its mayor. The Reagan administration strongly condemned these sanctuary resolutions, warning that word would spread throughout Central America, giving rise to a mass exodus of economic refugees who would falsely believe that these U.S. cities could provide them with legal safe haven.[119]

In April 1985, Cambridge, Massachusetts, which had led the way in the effort to declare itself a nuclear-free zone in 1983, set out to become the next city to declare itself a sanctuary. The campaign was spearheaded by Cambridge solidarity activists, especially those with the Old Cambridge Baptist Church, which had been providing sanctuary for refugees from El Salvador. On May 8, 1985, before what the *Boston Globe* described as a "packed and partisan audience," the nine-member Cambridge City Council considered a resolution to proclaim Cambridge a sanctuary for refugees from El Salvador, Guatemala, and Haiti.[120] Witnesses included sanctuary workers from the Old Cambridge Baptist Church, members of the local academic community, a representative from Centro Presente (a refugee-assistance organization), several Salvadoran and Haitian refugees, and Richard Bell (aide to Senator John Kerry). Estella Ramirez, a Salvadoran trade unionist and refugee, told the city councilors, "It is not for economic reasons that we have come here. We have been forced to come by the political situation in our country. For us, there is no justice and no food. And if we demand them, we are tortured or killed."[121] Speaking for Senator Kerry, Bell denounced the refusal by the administration to grant asylum to Salvadoran refugees as "a stain on this country's honor."[122]

Supporting the resolution, City Councilor Alice Wolfe declared, "We cannot help send people back to countries where they are persecuted and killed."[123] Leonard Russell, mayor of Cambridge, objected to the resolution, arguing that it would mislead Central American refugees into believing that Cambridge could offer more safety than was within its ability. Finally—adding to the national momentum of the sanctuary movement—the Cambridge City Council voted narrowly, five to four, to proclaim itself an official sanctuary.[124]

The sanctuary movement continued to pick up speed during the spring of 1985, as two Guatemalan brothers, known as Joaquin and Pedro, arrived at the Mt. Toby Friends Meeting House in Leverett, Massachusetts, amid great publicity.[125] Ruled by a series of military dictators since the United States–sponsored military overthrow of the democratically elected president Jacobo Arbenz in 1954, Guatemala had an even more egregious human rights record than El Salvador. In 1977 the Carter administration had cut aid to the right-wing government. It was estimated that more than one hundred thousand peasants were massacred between 1954 and the 1980s. In El Salvador, rightist military officials spoke enviously of the "Guatemalan solution," code for all-out war on the population.[126]

Using aliases to protect loved ones who had remained in Guatemala, Pedro and Joaquin were part of a caravan of Central American refugees that had begun that year in Phoenix, Arizona, and had stopped in fifteen cities during its highly publicized cross-country trek. A welcoming ceremony and potluck dinner attended by some 100 to 150 people was held for the brothers upon their arrival at Mt. Toby.[127]

On hand to welcome the Guatemalan brothers was Frances Crowe, who declared, "We choose to give these political refugees not just a measure of safety, but also an opportunity to speak about their lives and experiences."[128] Pedro and Joaquin proceeded to do just that, participating in interviews for the press and media throughout New England (including a Hartford television station and the *Boston Globe*) and giving numerous talks before audiences at Mt. Toby. Wearing masks during their interviews to protect loved ones in Guatemala from government retaliation, the brothers dramatically and personally brought to life for many New Englanders the horrors that confronted so many members of the peasant population in Central America.

Speaking through an interpreter, Joaquin told of his work with a small Christian group that sought to help the economically disadvantaged people of Guatemala. After five members of his group were killed, including a nun who was also raped, Joaquin fled to Honduras. When his wife would not reveal his whereabouts to members of the Guatemalan military, they assembled the children of the household and shot the family dog.[129] Meanwhile—wanted by the military for poetry about the plight of the peasants that he had read over the radio—Pedro had gone into hiding in Guatemala, moving from house to house every night. To a Mt. Toby audience of 150 people, Joaquin explained, "We are tired of the terror....We have a duty to our people to speak out.... [T]he wave of terror unleashed by the army is against the entire people. Only the army and the rich are not suspected of being subversive."[130]

One western Massachusetts resident who was moved by the brothers' accounts was their interpreter, Julie Rappaport, a young activist in her twenties who had recently become involved in the solidarity movement with CAWG. Raised in an educated, nonpolitical, middle-class Jewish home, Rappaport could trace her personal political awareness to the early 1970s, when her older brother was nearly drafted into the armed forces during the Vietnam war and her family began to discuss such options as moving him to Canada. By high school, Rappaport had gained a general political awareness, which had deepened from 1980 to 1984 while she was at Harvard. There she had become involved with feminist groups, including battered women's service organizations, and had participated in Central American and anti-apartheid activism. Rappaport's move to western Massachusetts in 1984, however, shifted her activism to an intense focus on Central America.[131]

Rappaport's role as interpreter for Joaquin and Pedro led her deeper into the movement. "There's nothing like having to repeat atrocities...horrors, in the first person, to really give someone pause," she explained. "It's one thing to ...read a book or a newspaper. It's another thing to be standing next to a person [saying] this is what happened to me, or this is what I saw. And so I became more and more personally affected by what I was hearing, so I decided I wanted to go to Guatemala....I wanted to see what [Joaquin] was telling me."[132] Rappaport thus joined the hundreds of North American and western European internationalists who trekked to Central America in support of the popular and revolutionary movements of the region.

THE INTERNATIONALISTS

During the 1980s, tens of thousands of U.S. internationalists journeyed to Central America as part of a heightened commitment to solidarity activism. El Salvador and Nicaragua were by far the most common destinations for such activists. According to some journalists, more than one hundred thousand U.S. citizens traveled to Nicaragua alone during the decade, many to participate in the coffee harvest for a few weeks or merely to show support for the Sandinistas and protest the policies of the Reagan administration by their presence. Most remained only a few weeks or months; however, by the mid-1980s, a permanent presence of approximately seven thousand internationalists had taken root in a Managua neighborhood that came to be known as Gringolandia.

Many of the most committed internationalists left the relative safety of Managua for the war-ravaged countryside. Among them was the Portland, Oregon, native Benjamin Linder, who became a martyr of the solidarity movement in 1986 when the young engineer, who had been helping remote villages build hydroelectric dams, was killed during a Contra attack in the northern Jinotega province of Nicaragua. Meanwhile, other internationalists traveled to El Salvador, where the Salvadoran armed forces eyed them warily. The murders of the four U.S. church women and two American Federation of Labor and Congress of Industrial Organizations (AFL-CIO) labor organizers at the beginning of the decade made it clear that even U.S. citizens were not safe in that war-torn nation. Later, in 1990, an internationalist named Michael Divine disappeared in Guatemala, a victim of the Guatemalan rightist paramilitary.[133]

The internationalists of the 1980s represented many shades of commitment and drew on different traditions of U.S. activism. After the 1917 Bolshevik Revolution, scores of U.S. citizens, such as the journalist John Reed, traveled to the Soviet Union to witness what many leftists hoped would be a new birth for humanity.[134] The Soviet Union continued to be the revolutionary beacon for much of the Old Left until the late 1930s, when Republican Spain, at the front line of the war against fascism, became the mecca of the Popular Front. More than three thousand U.S. citizens volunteered for the Lincoln Brigades, heading to Spain in what they viewed as an epic struggle that pitted the forces of oppression against the global crusade for democracy and socialism.[135]

As the Soviet Union became a less-appealing focal point for leftist internationalism, many young people in the United States turned to the more religiously influenced civil rights movement of the 1960s as the vehicle for their fight for a more just and humane world. Thousands of idealistic northern college students, black and white, joined the Student Non-violent Coordinating Committee (SNCC) and the Congress of Racial Equality (CORE) and headed into the heart of the Jim Crow South to share the hardships and poverty of oppressed African Americans and fight for freedom and equality. Cuba was the next magnet for international solidarity, with scores of leftists joining the Venceremos Brigade. Among the internationalists of the 1980s were those whose activism was predominantly faith based (such as those who traveled to Nicaragua with Witness for Peace), those whose politics grew out of a broad democratic and secular humanism, and those whose ideology was derived from orthodox Marxism.[136]

By the latter half of the 1980s, Rappaport had formed a more personal connection with the suffering people of Central America through her translation of the first-person accounts and a romantic relationship that had blossomed with Joaquin. Rappaport had hoped to go to Guatemala but had run into complications making the arrangements. As a result, she departed instead for El Salvador, where she spent a year in the Chaletenango province, an FMLN stronghold and the scene of some of the most savage fighting in El Salvador. Rappaport's stay dramatically altered her view of the country and its conflict. She had begun with what she later described as a "facile view" of the war, in which the FMLN guerrillas were the "good guys" and the members of the Salvadoran army the "bad guys." Although her sympathies did not change, they became, in her own words, "more complex." Rappaport recalled, "The civil war wasn't exactly what I had in mind." "Something that became clear the longer I was there was how complicated the situation [was].... [W]ar is a shitty thing. War is bad for everybody.... [I]t doesn't make anybody into good guys.... [I]t's ugly [and] that was hard."[137]

Many of Rappaport's views changed during her stay in El Salvador. The United States–financed Salvadoran military had proved to be worse than she had envisioned in her most Manichean imaginings. Rappaport not only witnessed army atrocities but was also subjected to frequent and humiliating sexual harassment at the point of M-16s by uniformed soldiers of the Salvadoran Army. Describing the army as "hideous," Rappaport summed up her view of the conflict: "This is the pure evil and this is what has to be done to confront a profound, profound, profound evil and it wasn't always admirable...but necessary." Rappaport was especially saddened by the many youths who were impressed into the war by all sides of the conflict. Despite being disheartened by the coercive and sometimes brutal tactics of the rebels, Rappaport believed that the atrocities of the government forces eclipsed any inexpedient actions by the guerrillas. If the members of the FMLN were not the "good guys" she once naïvely held them to be, she nevertheless maintained that "the side that had dignity was clearly the FMLN." Rappaport described the Salvadoran armed forces as led by "horrible evil murderers...and you don't get to be Glenda the Good Witch in the face of that."[138]

Before she left for El Salvador, Rappaport "felt compelled in a weird way to look evil in the face." During her stay, she had many opportunities to do so. One of the many examples that she would later relate to North American audiences took place in a small Salvadoran town where she was doing literacy training. One day a young local man was found dead in the middle of the street, the victim of a right-wing death squad killing. Salvadoran death squads routinely left the tortured and disfigured bodies of their victims in public places as grisly calling cards to remind peasants of their ever-watchful presence. Rappaport recalled, "They beheaded it and just left it there. . . . They made clear to the whole town that no one was to touch his body." In the face of great personal risk, however, a young Salvadoran woman who was working as a literacy volunteer collected the body and took it into the mountains for a furtive burial. Rappaport asked the woman why she put herself in such jeopardy. "People aren't animals to be left dead in the road and he was my friend," responded the woman. Describing the event with the distant stare often associated with combat veterans, Rappaport noted that she was deeply moved by many such examples of "tremendous human dignity in the face of horrible, horrible events." For Rappaport, as for other internationalists who experienced the tragedy of war-ravaged Central America first-hand, it was no longer possible to view the conflict in a detached or abstract manner. "It's one thing to hear the army did x, y, and z," Rappaport observed. "It's another thing to look at it."[139]

Returning to western Massachusetts after her year in El Salvador, Rappaport set out to personalize and humanize the conflict in the region by recounting her experiences at numerous churches and meetinghouses throughout the Pioneer Valley. Rappaport later married Joaquin. The couple had two children, one of whom they named in honor of Sister Gabrielle Victoria de la Roca, Joaquin's friend and fellow activist in Guatemala who had been raped and murdered by members of the Guatemalan armed forces.[140]

Other activists who journeyed to El Salvador came away more unequivocal in their support for the FMLN. Mike Prokosch was born in New York City and raised in Connecticut. In the late 1960s he attended Harvard and was active with Students for a Democratic Society (SDS) until his graduation in 1970. Prokosch then settled in Dorchester, where he put his skills as a graphic designer to use for a left-wing community paper, the *Dorchester Community News*. In the late 1970s Prokosch took a hiatus from activism to focus on family, but he was drawn back in by the escalating U.S. intervention in Central America. "Reagan was repeating the Vietnam War in Central America," Prokosch recalled.[141]

Prokosch was a relative latecomer to the solidarity movement. He began immersing himself in Central American activism during the 1984 referendum campaign, which had won Governor Dukakis's endorsement. Prokosch worked with Boston-based CASA and with local committees, leafleting and going door-to-door on behalf of the referendum. After the success of the referendum, Prokosch spearheaded an effort that put up numerous "car cards" (paid advertisements) about Central America on Boston subways. This impressive campaign caught the attention of Michael Lent, the San Francisco–based national director of CISPES, who recruited Prokosch as the New England regional director of CISPES in 1986.[142]

Prokosch assumed the position as regional director a year after tensions in CISPES had resulted in a national split. Many East Coast chapters of CISPES wanted to move beyond the single-minded focus on cutting U.S. aid to the Salvadoran government to take on broader issues and form a closer alliance with African Americans (especially with Jackson's Rainbow Coalition). The West Coast faction, dominated by Salvadoran émigrés and their North American allies, wished to keep CISPES more focused and closely coordinated with the popular movement in El Salvador. The West Coast faction emerged triumphant but lost a number of East Coast branches in the process.[143]

Prokosch flew out to San Francisco, where he took part in the intensive CISPES organizer training program. According to Prokosch, CISPES was "very good at building up cadres and leadership... organizing from center out.... There was discipline of a positive sort." Back in Boston, Prokosch worked to coordinate existing regional groups behind CISPES-initiated national campaigns and to cultivate new regional groups. CISPES used the union model of organization, Prokosch explained, seeking out respected local activists and then building up the local group through house parties and letter-writing campaigns directed at Congress. Although Boston solidarity groups such as NECAN remained wary of CISPES for its exclusive focus on El Salvador at the expense of Nicaragua, Prokosch helped nurture a strong CISPES chapter in Springfield in the western part of the state and honed his skills at coordinating campaigns among regional solidarity groups.[144]

Prokosch's regional activism led him to join a group of forty North Americans on a trip to war-torn El Salvador in 1986. After what he described as his "hard core" orientation at the Ritz Hotel in San Salvador, Prokosch recalled the air of fear that pervaded the city and the delegation: "It was one of those situations where we sat on the bed and turned the radio up so the spy in the next room couldn't hear us." Prokosch's delegation met mostly with Salvadoran labor activists (especially from the militant telecommunications union) and with prisoners (including inmates of a women's prison). The level of commitment by Salvadoran activists was transformative for Prokosch. He remembered one female activist who responded in Spanish to a question about torture, "If you talk under torture, you can't be a part of the movement anymore, and the movement is my life . . . so I won't talk."[145] The journey to El Salvador deepened Prokosch's commitment to the cause and to CISPES. CISPES activists, Prokosch acknowledges, received updates from the FMLN and coordinated their North American strategy with the rebels. Looking back, he observed, "We were definitely part of the FMLN."[146]

Lois Ahrens, a Northampton resident and one of Julie Rappaport's fellow activists in CAWG, decided after nearly a decade of Central American solidarity activism to travel to the region herself. Well into her thirties, Ahrens viewed herself as a movement veteran less susceptible to the wide-eyed romanticism and naïveté that she believed characterized the views of many younger activists. Although she was deeply committed to a humanist and progressive politics, Ahrens prided herself on her skepticism, which she traced to her family's experience in the Old Left. Born to a working-class, Jewish family in New York City in 1947, Ahrens was raised in the era of Joseph McCarthy and witnessed family friends and relatives cope with the 1950s Red Scare. She had a close relationship with aunts and uncles who, although still committed to leftist politics, had quit the Communist Party in disgust in 1939 after the infamous Hitler-Stalin Pact. Ahrens believed that these family members had helped instill in her a healthy iconoclasm.[147]

For someone so steeped in a left-wing background, Ahrens had been remarkably untouched by the events and political crosscurrents of the 1960s. During most of the decade she had worked for the prestigious New York City publishing firm of McCann Erikson. Eventually, however, the spirit of the sixties caught up with her; Ahrens asked herself, "What am I doing here?"; and in 1970 she quit. Unlike many of her generation, who were led into radical politics through the civil rights or antiwar movement, for Ahrens it was the more personal politics of the gay rights and feminist movements that led her into left-wing activism. After struggling to come to terms with her identity as a lesbian, Ahrens entered a state of deep depression triggered by the death of her grandmother. When she sought counseling, Ahrens—like so many gay men and lesbians of the time—was told that her sexual orientation was a personality disorder akin to alcoholism and drug addiction, which could be "cured" with therapy.[148]

Gradually, Ahrens moved into a growing circle of progressive clergy and psychiatrists who sought to combat the stigma of homosexuality and help gay men and lesbians accept and celebrate themselves. Ahrens thus progressed through the 1970s with a renewed sense of confidence and commitment to political and social change. In 1971 Ahrens moved to Austin, Texas, and became involved in the antiwar movement and in the fast-growing feminist/lesbian community in Austin (including one of the first battered-women's shelters in the nation). Of all her years of activism, Ahrens remembers the 1970s most fondly, as the time of the most exhilarating social change—when women, gay men, and lesbians made their greatest strides.[149]

In 1980 Ahrens moved to Northampton and became involved with the local Necessities/*Necesidades* and other women's groups. Coming from the veteran Austin feminist movement, Ahrens found the incipient Northampton movement "unsophisticated," full of "separatist crap," and stuck at a "terminally early stage."[150] Disillusioned with the militant style of feminism in Northampton, Ahrens moved into the freeze movement and produced a successful local play called *Handy Dandy*, which dealt with the nuclear arms race. Just as in the 1960s and early 1970s many women moved from the antiwar movement into the feminist movement, in the 1980s many women such as Rappaport and Ahrens moved from feminist to more broad-based political activism. Shortly after moving to Northampton, Ahrens was scooped into the Central American solidarity movement by what she describes as the "iron jaws" of Frances Crowe, who discerned in Ahrens a potentially invaluable recruit for the movement. As Ahrens learned more about U.S. policy in Central America, she began to devote increasing amounts of time to the cause, becoming involved in the material aid campaigns and committing acts of civil disobedience during the massive 1985 embargo protests. For Ahrens, as for Rappaport, feminism helped shape the personal focus of her activism. Staying the hand of the male batterer was similar to staying the might of the United States against its weaker, impoverished neighbors to the south.

From this background, Ahrens girded herself for a two-and-a-half-week trip to Central America in 1989. Ahrens spent seven days in El Salvador and eleven days in Nicaragua. In El Salvador, Ahrens took part in a practice known as "accompaniment," in which internationalists "accompanied" threatened Salvadorans in the hope of deterring their abduction or murder. When she returned to the United States, Ahrens sought to share her experiences with local Massachusetts residents as Rappaport had done. To one local reporter, Ahrens offered the following observations on El Salvador after nine brutal years of war: "While there isn't mass slaughter [as there was in the early 1980s], there are incredible amounts of people being killed, tortured, and kidnapped every day. It's like Nazi Germany, except potentially everybody is a Jew."[151] Shortly after Ahrens's visit, El Salvador again became front-page news as the FMLN unleashed another "Final Offensive" in which the guerrilla army entered sections of the capital, San Salvador. During the offensive, pro-government death squads unleashed a wave of terror, which included the widely publicized murder of six Jesuits, their housekeeper, and the housekeeper's young daughter. In a symbolic act that spoke volumes about the mentality of the Salvadoran Right, the death squads meticulously removed the brains of the Jesuits from their skulls.[152]

Although numerous internationalists traveled to El Salvador (and a smaller number to Guatemala) during the 1980s, the most popular destination for U.S. internationalists was revolutionary Nicaragua. Some internationalists did not wholeheartedly support the Sandinista government; however, many others found in Nicaragua an opportunity to go beyond opposition to U.S. policy in the region by actually becoming part of a revolutionary effort to create a new society. One of the many Massachusetts activists drawn to Nicaragua in search of deeper commitment to radical principles and personal fulfillment was John Brentlinger, a philosophy professor at the University of Massachusetts at Amherst. A self-described (small m) "marxist and atheist," Brentlinger embraced a deep humanism that often seemed to verge on the spiritual, as he sought what he described as "the sacred" in a secular world. According to Brentlinger, "Philosophy . . . should move away from the old task of thinking about the self and the world—as if these are finished and there to be known—and toward the task of creative activity and work toward remaking the self and the world." He continued, "It seemed to me that in Nicaragua this work was happening and that it was necessary to join in."[153]

Between 1985 and 1992, Brentlinger made six trips to Nicaragua, each several months in duration. From Nicaragua, Brentlinger wrote, "Many North Americans who come here say they oppose U.S. policies against Nicaragua but do not support the Sandinistas, while I do. I came here with a positive attitude and it continues to grow stronger. When I had personal encounters with right-wing critics of the Sandinistas, I sometimes wondered if I too much identified myself as a supporter of the revolution to be a responsible observer."[154] Despite these reservations, Brentlinger recounted his experiences in a book titled *The Best of What*

We Are: Reflections on the Nicaraguan Revolution, a collection of essays, journal entries, and photographs that documents daily life in Nicaragua and balances the author's idealism with realistic descriptions that do not shy away from showing the Sandinistas or the revolution in a negative light.

Brentlinger first arrived in Nicaragua in the spring of 1985, shortly after the ill-timed trip made by Daniel Ortega, the president of Nicaragua, to the Soviet Union and the imposition of the economic embargo on Nicaragua by President Ronald Reagan. On his first day in Managua, Brentlinger was faced with what he described as "shocking poverty."[155] Only hours into his stay he was robbed;[156] however, Brentlinger soon settled in for an extended stay, befriending many Nicaraguans and speaking to people with very different views of the Sandinistas and the revolution. During his many visits, Brentlinger became more familiar with the land and its people, traveling from urban Managua to remote rural areas. His travels came during the latter half of the decade, as the Contra war, U.S. embargo, and Sandinista missteps had begun to sap the revolutionary enthusiasm of the years during which the Sandinistas had won international acclaim for their successful literacy and inoculation campaigns and had claimed more than 60 percent of the vote in the internationally monitored 1984 elections. The Nicaragua that Brentlinger witnessed was one increasingly exhausted by daily hardships, such as empty store shelves, cuts in social programs, escalating draft calls, draft evasion, tightened social control by the government, flagging revolutionary ardor among a war-weary population, and dogged determination to carry forth the revolutionary struggle.

In *The Best of What We Are*, Brentlinger evokes the appeal of the Sandinista revolution for U.S. radicals. He writes, "The decision to help a foreign country with its revolution looks romantic and quixotic. In the States, I often have the sense of floating in a huge becalmed ocean. Most people do not believe in change. . . . The left is small and fragmented." In contrast, Brentlinger writes, "revolution to Nicaraguans was not a political spectacle or a media event. It was their life. . . . I was made to feel I was part of this revolution, that I had a role to play. Like Brentlinger, many internationalists sought in Nicaragua the promise of community, of brotherhood and sisterhood in a transcendent endeavor. In Nicaragua, observes Brentlinger, "revolutionary spirit breaks down walls that separate us."[157]

Despite Brentlinger's compelling articulation of the communal and religious elements that motivated many internationalists, his descriptions of daily life belie both the glowing accounts of the Sandinista revolution by more starry-eyed internationalists and the sinister depictions of a totalitarian dungeon by the Reagan administration. Brentlinger met Nicaraguans whose lives appeared to be very positively transformed by the revolution A campesino on a cooperative in Corinto, for example, told Brentlinger, "We all think alike...all members of the cooperative.... [I]t is simple. The revolution has taken the power away from the Somocistas and given it to the campesinos.... The big difference [now] is we own land. We have credit at the bank and can build a house for anyone who will move here."[158]

In Managua, Brentlinger spoke frequently with a middle-class woman named Norma, who praised the impact of the revolution on women but decried the on-going sexism in Nicaraguan society. According to Norma, "The revolution builds more schools and needs more teachers. It builds health centers and needs more nurses and doctors. The revolution greatly increases the demand for all kinds of workers. And because of our strength and independence, we Nicaraguan women are ready to study and improve ourselves. We need this revolution. We identify with it."[159] Yet Norma maintained that, as with many leftist revolutions in the twentieth century, machismo and sexism persisted. Brentlinger writes, "Nicaraguan men, including many Sandinistas, continue to lord it over the women they work with, and continue to expect women to serve them in the house, because they don't consider equality in these areas to be a revolutionary necessity."[160]

During his time in Nicaragua, Brentlinger found many more nuanced attitudes between those who openly supported the revolution and those who openly opposed it. In one poignant account, he described one of the increasing number of funerals that occurred throughout Nicaragua in the late 1980s, at which revolutionary rhetoric increasingly rang hollow against the painful realities of a seemingly interminable war:

> The family sat together on a raised grave.... A young man stood by the casket and read a short poem and a statement in a strong, loud voice: "With this death we affirm again, yet again, our commitment to defend Nicaragua from the counterrevolution, and we affirm again, yet again, our unity with the Sandinista National Liberation Front. *Patria Libre*," he shouted, and a few answered, "*O Morir*." After a silence, a man near the grave said, "I have to say you are not speaking for this boy. He had no ideology. He was a boy who died for his country, that is all." After a moment the young man responded again by shouting again, "*Patria Libre*." No one answered, "*O Morir*."[161]

Brentlinger also describes the impact of the ubiquitous internationalists roaming through Nicaragua in the 1980s. He writes of the West German work brigades, young Basque radicals who worked on a cooperative farm, and many more North Americans crisscrossing the country. Brentlinger witnessed positive contributions, misplaced idealism, and even a certain gringo condescension. Although many internationalist projects, such as Linder's electric generators, actually improved the lives of Nicaraguans, in other cases internationalists missed the mark, as with the bread oven built by a West German work brigade in a mountain area where the campesinos ate tortillas. Often, internationalists, especially those who remained only a short time, viewed the revolution through rose-tinted glasses that missed its nuances and complexities. One campesino in the rural North confided to Brentlinger, "Sometimes internationalists come here and talk to people, but the people just tell them what they want to hear, not what they really think. They won't talk to a stranger—they are very independent and suspicious."[162] Despite his self-criticisms and his criticisms of the Sandinistas and the internationalists, Brentlinger remained committed to the Nicaraguan revolution and people (he was one of the few internationalists who returned to Nicaragua after the Sandinistas' fall from power).

When they returned to the United States, Massachusetts internationalists such as John Brentlinger, Michael Prokosch, Lois Ahrens, and Julie Rappaport sought to share their experiences with Bay State audiences to try to convey the complexities of the region and counter the stereotypes that—especially in the mainstream media and in Washington— dominated the U.S. debate on Central America. Like many internationalists, these activists found themselves and their views transformed by the realities that they encountered. Beyond offering alternative perspectives on the region, providing material aid, and helping with harvest work and literacy and health campaigns, the internationalists were an embarrassment to the Reagan administration. Given the outcry that had followed the murders of Ita Ford, Dorothy Kazel, Maura Clarke, Jean Donovan, and Benjamin Linder, moreover, the administration had no desire to confront the reaction that would surely result from the deaths of U.S. citizens in a U.S. invasion of El Salvador or Nicaragua. Thus, the presence of the internationalists acted as a deterrent to an expanded and more direct U.S. military role in the region.

THE SOLIDARITY MOVEMENT UNDER SURVEILLANCE

In 1987 it was revealed that the FBI had conducted widespread infiltration and surveillance of the solidarity movement throughout the 1980s, centered on CISPES and the Maryknoll Order. Beyond secret surveillance, internationalists often complained of being subjected to unfriendly FBI interrogations on their return to the United States. Conservatives defended the investigations, arguing that the two solidarity organizations acted as front groups for the FMLN. The FBI justified the surveillance with the assertion that the targeted solidarity groups represented a potential terrorist threat. Memories of COINTELPRO (FBI counterintelligence programs aimed at neutralizing political dissidents) during the 1960s and revelations of other FBI and CIA abuses in the mid-1970s made by the Church Committee (the U.S. Senate Select Committee to Study Governmental Operations with Respect to Intelligence Activities, chaired by Senator Frank Church), however, caused numerous lawyers, journalists, liberal politicians, and activists to become alarmed at what appeared to be a resurgence of FBI targeting of dissent under the Reagan administration.[163]

When Lois Ahrens of the Northampton CAWG heard about the FBI probe into the solidarity movement, she decided out of curiosity to do a routine Freedom of Information Act (FOIA) request for her files.[164] She was stunned to learn that the FBI did indeed have a file on her but would not release it "for reasons of national security." With the assistance of the local American Civil Liberties Union (ACLU), Ahrens filed suit against the FBI to obtain her files. After more delay and obstruction, in 1990 the FBI finally released Ahrens's twelve-page file, which had so many redactions (blackouts) that the only tangible information that Ahrens could glean from it was the general source of information: a "confidential source who has furnished reliable information in the past." Outraged, Ahrens pressed on with her suit for full release of her files.[165]

In 1990 the case came before U.S. magistrate Michael A. Ponsor of the U.S. District Court in Springfield. The obstruction by the FBI carried over into the court. Before the FBI would allow Ponsor to review Ahrens's file, he would have to undergo an FBI security check. Ponsor initially denounced the FBI demand as "superfluous, time consuming, and intrusive upon the judiciary."[166] Nevertheless, Ponsor eventually gave ground and, although he appeared to be sympathetic toward Ahrens, he ultimately ruled against her. When Ahrens and the ACLU learned that the next judge to hear the case would be a conservative who would be even less likely than Ponsor to order the release of her file, they dropped the suit.[167]

Although Ahrens had initially undertaken the suit out of a sense of outrage, she soon realized the value of the case in terms of drawing the public's attention to federal government spying on people engaged in political dissent in the United States. In this, Ahrens found success. Her suit against the FBI drummed up enormous local publicity in western Massachusetts and was even cited in a Jack Anderson piece for the *Washington Post* that denounced FBI surveillance of U.S. citizens.[168] To one local newspaper, Ahrens declared, "The double standard is the glorification of dissent in other countries [especially Eastern Europe] and the denigration of dissent in this country as being unpatriotic."[169] Another local newspaper article quoted Ahrens as saying, "My political work has included organizing legal demonstrations, public meetings, and educational programs, leafleting, arranging petition campaigns, lobbying, and working in political campaigns. If there is surveillance on me, how many other people doing this sort of work is the FBI watching?"[170] Crowe stated, "What Lois has been doing is [in] the very highest tradition of democratic action. She's extremely responsible, a true patriot."[171]

Support for Ahrens moved beyond the solidarity movement to the community at large. Denouncing FBI surveillance of a respected and well-liked member of the local community, the moderate *Daily Hampshire Gazette* ran an editorial titled "Spying on Citizens," which concluded, "Before we call for democracy in other parts of the world, let's be sure it's practiced here."[172] Letters of support flooded the local press, and Ahrens received letters from local conservatives who expressed shock at the FBI surveillance for exercising her First Amendment rights. Ahrens told the *Valley Advocate*, "I've never had a wider range of people be more supportive than with this effort to force the FBI's hand, to make them reveal what they do and how they do it."[173] The support for Ahrens, like the sympathy of local jurors for Lovejoy in 1974 and for the anti-CIA protestors in 1987, stemmed not just from the progressive political climate in western Massachusetts but also, more broadly, from a strong streak of localism that extended as far back 1786 in the Daniel Shays rebellion. Just as Crowe and others in western Massachusetts had recoiled from the efforts of Boston-based activists to centralize the solidarity movement, Pioneer Valley residents had experienced a visceral reaction to the efforts of Washington, D.C., to spy on their neighbors.

THE DECLINE OF THE SOLIDARITY MOVEMENT

Despite ongoing Central American solidarity activism in Massachusetts in the late 1980s, the movement—which had struggled to emerge from the shadow of the freeze movement in the early 1980s—saw itself increasingly eclipsed by the anti-apartheid and divestment movements. The anti-apartheid movement, tracing its origin as far back as the Chase Manhattan protests in New York City in 1964, had begun gathering steam in 1985, when students on campuses across the nation occupied buildings and constructed makeshift shantytowns in support of the South African liberation struggle. The 1985 anti-apartheid actions coincided with the massive wave of embargo protests that swept the nation that spring.

The solidarity movement, which supported the anti-apartheid movement, welcomed the opportunity that the focus on U.S. support for the white minority regime afforded in their critique of U.S. foreign policy. As the decade progressed, however, the anti-apartheid movement continued to gather momentum as events in South Africa increasingly pushed events in Central America off the headlines. Some solidarity activists drifted into the burgeoning anti-apartheid movement. Ahrens felt somewhat betrayed when, in 1985, Crowe—who had played such a crucial role in her recruitment into the solidarity movement—shifted her focus to the movement against apartheid (according to Ahrens, throughout the 1970s and 1980s, Crowe repeatedly shifted her interest, acting as an unwitting bellwether for the rise and fall of the successive movements of the decades).[174]

Although the rising tide of anti-apartheid activism partly eclipsed the solidarity movement, it was most of all the gradual de-escalation of cold war tensions ushered in by Mikhail Gorbachev and the negotiated end of the civil wars in the region in the early 1990s that marked the end of the solidarity movement. For many solidarity activists, the most important event occurred in 1990, when the unthinkable occurred: Just at the time when the Contra war had all but come to a close, marking the seeming victory of the Sandinistas after a decade of United States–backed counterrevolution, Daniel Ortega and the Sandinistas were defeated in the presidential election by their old foe, Violeta Chamorro and her United Nicaraguan Opposition (UNO). U.S. newspapers had predicted a Sandinista victory in the internationally monitored election. Although the new administration of George H. W. Bush had covertly channeled large funds to Chamorro, it seemed resigned to coexistence with the leftist government in Nicaragua in the event that Ortega won the election. Thus, the defeat, in which the Sandinistas received slightly more than 42 percent of the vote to 58 percent by UNO, sent shock waves through the movement.[175] Demoralization and disillusionment followed the Sandinista defeat. Across Nicaragua, internationalists packed up their backpacks and began an exodus out of what had been, for the better part of a decade, a mecca for the Left.

Among the crestfallen activists was Crowe, who recalled, "People were really sad, let down. Maybe the Sandinistas made some mistakes by going too vigorously."[176] Rappaport, more defiant, viewed the Sandinista defeat as the result of the fact that the Contra war had made it impossible for the Sandinistas to fulfill the promises of the revolution. The Sandinista defeat, said Rappaport, was another example of "the goddamn U.S. just needing to get its way. It made me nuts!"[177] Ahrens was introspective: "After the election in Nicaragua...I remember talking to this friend of mine on the phone who'd been working in Esteli [Nicaragua].... [W]e were crying.... [W]e were on the phone crying. We were shocked.... [W]e were crushed. How could this have happened compared to what we thought was going on?"[178]

John Brentlinger wrote of the day, "I was in Massachusetts the day the Sandinistas lost the election to UNO: February 25, 1990, ten years and eight months after the triumph of the revolution... My friends and I were taken by surprise. We had already circulated posters and fliers and sold tickets for a Sandinista victory dance. We held the dance, but we also held gatherings in friends' houses to talk about our shock and dismay and how to react."[179] Brentlinger tried to be optimistic, noting that, with the Sandinistas in opposition, Nicaragua could never slide back to the days of Somoza and that, even in a more conservative Nicaragua, millions of impoverished Nicaraguans who supported them would have a voice. Unlike most internationalists, Brentlinger, whose bond with the Nicaraguan people survived the defeat of the Sandinistas, continued to visit the country throughout the 1990s. A few years after the Sandinista electoral defeat, the civil war in El Salvador came to a negotiated end, leaving a wasteland of death and destruction.

Even though few leftists identified with Soviet-style communism, the Left suffered another blow in the wake of the demise of the Soviet Union and the proclamation of U.S. victory in the cold war. In *The Best of What We Are*, Brentlinger asks where the decline of revolutionary movements in Central America left solidarity activists and the Left: "The question is made more difficult by the collapse of the so-called socialist regimes in Europe. . . . The world socialist movement . . . for which Nicaragua's revolution signaled a new opening in Latin America and a qualitatively higher form of democracy in the evolution of socialist societies, now seems as devastated as Nicaragua itself. Marxism teaches that hope should base itself on objective conditions. Where is hope to find its way?"[180]

Despite the disillusionment of the Left over the failure to realize its highest dreams in the 1980s, the impact of the solidarity movement on U.S. politics during the decade had been immense. By keeping the specter of Vietnam alive, the solidarity movement had helped reinvigorate liberal opposition to the foreign policy of the Reagan administration, especially in Massachusetts, whose congressional delegation, in tandem with its liberal governor, had transformed the Bay State into the most solid national political block of opposition to Reagan's interventionist policies in Central America.

Throughout the 1980s, Tip O'Neill, Ted Kennedy, Gerry Studds, John Kerry, Michael Dukakis, and Silvio Conte continued to question the policy of the administration, keep the issue of human rights alive, and oppose any sign of direct U.S. military involvement. The illegal Reagan administration circumvention of Edward Boland's 1982 amendment prohibiting military aid to the Nicaraguan Contras had led to the Iran-Contra affair. Thus, just as U.S. policy in Vietnam and the antiwar movement had set in motion the events that led to Watergate, the Reagan administration's obsession with fighting the cold war in Central America and the growing opposition to this foreign policy had led to the chain of events that culminated in the biggest political scandal of the Reagan era.

CHAPTER 6
MASSACHUSETTS POLITICIANS AND CENTRAL AMERICA 1979–1990

A MASSACHUSETTS CONGRESSMAN IN NICARAGUA: JANUARY 1980

In mid-December 1979 Jim Fairchild and George Allen (staff assistants to the House Appropriations Committee) wrote a letter to State Representative Silvio Conte (the moderate Republican from western Massachusetts and ranking Republican on the Foreign Operations Subcommittee) concerning an upcoming fact-finding trip to Nicaragua. Just months into the Sandinista-led revolution that toppled Anastasio Somoza, Jimmy Carter's administration was working to influence the direction of the new government through U.S. economic aid tailored to strengthen the Nicaraguan private sector and promote political pluralism. Carter proposed "reprogramming" (i.e., transferring already appropriated funds from one country to another) $75 million to Nicaragua, thereby reinstituting aid that had been cut in the waning days of the Somoza dictatorship.

Fairchild and Allen wrote Conte that during his trip he should focus on (1) who was in charge in Nicaragua, (2) the status of the economy, (3) who would administer U.S. aid, (4) whom the aid would benefit, and (5) the extent of Soviet and Cuban influence in Nicaragua and what threat that might pose to the United States and the region. The staffers concluded, "Since action on this [aid] request will be based mainly on political impressions of the new government, personal observations would be helpful in forming a position on the issue. We prepare to travel to Nicaragua on or about January 2, 1980, to discuss the situation with United States and Nicaraguan officials and to observe first-hand the physical, economic and political results of the revolution there."[1]

On January 3, the western Massachusetts Republican began his seven-day trip to Nicaragua. Throughout his stay, Conte jotted down his impressions on a yellow-lined notepad. What first struck the congressman was the extent of the damage to Managua and the surrounding countryside. Assessing the political situation, Conte scribbled the notations "S[andinistas] enjoy 90–95% popular support—definitely in command"; "S[andinistas] moving toward total control"; "moderates privately nervous." Regarding the rebel army that had recently deposed Somoza, Conte noted, "S[andinista] Army is the Army" and "Present equipment would delight the American Legion or a World War II buff."[2]

Conte witnessed a Nicaragua that was still swept up in revolutionary fervor and optimism. He observed that the Sandinistas' highly touted literacy campaign was immensely popular, that many captured members of Somoza's despised National Guard had been freed, that the Sandinistas had stayed true to their promise of no executions, and that radio and television aired criticisms of the new government with relative freedom. Although relations with the Sandinista-dominated government were often strained, opposition political parties operated openly.[3]

Conte's verdict on Cuban-Soviet influence was mixed, however. He noted, the "Russians refused aid" and "Nicaragua has few alternatives [to working with the United States]—Russia and Cuba will not spend money—[the Sandinistas] could tighten belts even further based on popular support, [but] how long is questionable." Indeed, given the fact that primary Nicaraguan exports, such as cattle and coffee, did not enjoy much demand in the communist bloc, access to U.S. markets was an imperative for the new government. This gave the United States some influence; however, the long history of U.S. intervention in Nicaraguan affairs played a strong role in the Sandinistas' brand of nationalism. The Soviet Union seemed unwilling to bankroll the Nicaraguan revolution, but Conte observed a large Cuban presence in the country. Cuban arms shipments were meager, but Cuban advisors abounded. The advice from the Cubans was to move in a moderate direction. Conte wrote, "Cuba urging moderation, but 1,200 [Cuban] teachers, 1,000 med[ical personnel], and 300–600 'others' (communications, etc.) present and 600 Nic[araguan] kids in Cuba—[The Cubans were] maybe too visible—Nicaraguan people tell Cuban jokes."[4] Assessing all he had seen, Conte concluded, "We have no choice—support [the new government] or get out." Although "concerned" about the Sandinista trend toward concentrating power and about the Cuban presence, Conte gave a "firm recommendation to grant the loan."[5]

Back in Washington, D.C., before the Foreign Operations Subcommittee, Conte outlined the dilemma that he and the other members of the committee faced: "What this committee must decide is, will this aid help the United States to gain access and influence in the direction of Nicaraguan development, or will this aid assist the eventual economic stability for a Marxist dictatorship? Even for those of us who will probably gamble and vote for this aid, it is a difficult question." Despite these reservations, the committee voted to approve the $75 million loan requested by the Carter administration, with 60 percent earmarked for the Nicaraguan private sector.[6]

The Carter administration modus vivendi with Nicaragua unraveled in the final days of the administration: Reports of alleged Nicaraguan arms shipments to the Farabundo Martí National Liberation Front (Frente Farabundo Martí para la Liberación Nacional [FMLN]) in El Salvador during its Final Offensive in January 1981 led the administration to cut U.S. aid to Nicaragua. By the end of 1981 the new Reagan administration had not only made the cutoff permanent but had also began its secret operations to destabilize the Nicaraguan government.[7]

For Conte, who had generally felt comfortable with the Carter administration approach to Central America, the hard right turn of the incoming Republican administration posed some dilemmas. Although Conte shared Reagan's stated goal of containing communism in Central America, he remained committed to the principle of promoting human rights in the region. The emphatic departure from this policy by the new administration was evidenced by the highly public firing of Ambassador Robert White. Furthermore, Conte shared the concerns of many that Reagan's new, hard-line policy could lead to the introduction of U.S. troops in the region, a proposition that he adamantly opposed. Conte was further torn by dual loyalties: one to his party, which had just reclaimed the White House and was moving farther right and the other to his constituency in the Massachusetts First District, which was fast becoming a hotbed of activism and was moving farther left. Throughout the 1980s, Conte would become increasingly caught in these crosscurrents. As the activist Lois Ahrens commented with respect to the relationship between the solidarity movement and Conte, "We were on his ass."[8]

THE REPUBLICAN: SILVIO CONTE

In early December 1980, Silvio Conte was shocked to learn of the murders of Ita Ford, Maura Clarke, Dorothy Kazel, and Jean Donovan. For Conte, who was Catholic, the fact that three of the women were nuns made the atrocity especially abhorrent. Responding to a letter about the murders from the Reverend Thomas W. Olcott of the Council of Churches of Greater Springfield, Conte outlined his position on human rights in El Salvador:

> I strongly supported the Carter administration's decision to suspend military assistance to El Salvador following the savage murders of American missionary workers. It has been my view that barring massive outside intervention, resumption of such assistance should be contingent upon a full and complete investigation of the recent killings of innocent Americans, an abatement

of violence, the construction of needed social and economic reforms and a moderation of extremist elements within the junta. I have felt that renewed military assistance at this time could exacerbate divisions within El Salvador, contribute to the worsening violence and dangerously escalate U.S. involvement in what is essentially an internal struggle within that strife-torn country.[9]

As Conte responded to constituents in January 1981, events in El Salvador were spiraling out of control. Anticipating the end of the Carter human rights policy after the U.S. election in November, the Salvadoran Right had dramatically escalated its violence. Death squad killings reached a crescendo in January, with murders that included two more U.S. citizens, Michael Hammer and Mark Pearlman (members of the Institute for Free Labor Development [AIFLD], an organization affiliated with the American Federation of Labor and Congress of Industrial Organizations [AFL-CIO] dedicated to the promotion of noncommunist unions in Latin America). Pearlman and Hammer had been meeting with one of the few remaining moderates of the junta, José Rodolfo Viera about an Agency for International Development (AID) project that would help Salvadoran peasants set up cooperatives. On January 3, 1981, masked paramilitaries burst into the restaurant where Pearlman, Hammer, and Viera were meeting and sprayed the three with machine-gun fire.[10]

As right-wing violence grew, the FMLN—hoping to topple the Salvadoran government before Reagan took office—launched its Final Offensive. The strength of the leftist offensive took many by surprise, and the Carter administration responded by reinstating emergency military aid to El Salvador.[11] In a reply to State Representative John Olver, Conte wrote, "I opposed the [Carter] Administration's decision of January 14 to resume military aid to El Salvador. My views were conveyed by telephone to both the White House and the State Department as soon as news of the impending decision reached my office. . . . [T]hese views were reiterated in a telegram to President Carter on January 16."[12] Promising to go even further in the coming session, Conte stated, "Under the new Reagan Administration I am co-sponsoring legislation which would suspend military assistance to El Salvador pending hearings in the House Committee on Foreign Affairs on progress in the investigation of the murders of the six Americans, and on ways to strengthen forces of moderation in El Salvador to bring about reforms and to achieve a negotiated settlement."[13]

By March 1981 Conte's hard line began to soften. The Reagan administration had just authorized $20 million in emergency aid to El Salvador and was now seeking an additional $5 million in reprogrammed aid from the Foreign Operations Subcommittee.[14] As the ranking Republican on the committee, which was controlled by the Democrats, Conte did not relish casting what would have been the deciding vote against the new Republican president. Although the $5 million in aid was a relatively small appropriation, it was a highly symbolic early test of Reagan's policy in El Salvador. Torn, Conte cast the deciding 'yes' vote and then on March 24 justified his action at length before the committee.

Beginning with more rigid cold war rhetoric than was customary for the moderate, he declared, "Mr. Chairman, I will vote for approval solely because of my great concern that the failure to support the President and his policy to stand up to international terrorism and aggression would send the wrong signal to the Soviet Union and Cuba which could have adverse repercussions on the United States and its allies around the world."[15] Having staked out common ground with the administration, Conte then qualified his vote in words more in keeping with his human rights concerns: "However, . . . I will not support any further military assistance for the government of El Salvador unless and until the investigation of the killings of the Americans in El Salvador late last year has been completed and I have assurances that the El Salvador government will no longer permit its military and security forces to inflict violence on innocent civilians in that country."[16]

Members of Conte's staff prepared for the backlash that was sure to follow his March 24 vote. In a memorandum titled "Speaking Points on El Salvador," they set down responses to be included in their replies to letters and phone calls from constituents and to reporters' questions. The "basic position" outlined in the memorandum was that Conte hoped to build up the Salvadoran center against the extreme Left and Right and that he felt compelled to support the new U.S. President on his first major foreign policy test to uphold the credibility of the administration around the world. "Given the situation and my basic position, I was torn over which way to vote last week," the memorandum read.[17]

In a section titled "If Asked Only," Conte's staff set out a response to questions that might arise about "inconsistency between cosponsoring H.Con.Res. 67, which calls for a suspension of military assistance, and [Conte's] March 24 vote." Conte was to respond that the $5 million in military aid was for uniforms, vehicles, communications, and patrol boats, which were "defensive" in nature and that he would "not support sending weapons, ammunition or advisors to that country—barring massive outside intervention."[18]

Conte's subtle distinctions were lost on his constituents, who inundated his offices with letters, telegrams, and phone calls. "I was shocked and saddened to read of your vote in favor of sending additional military aid to El Salvador," wrote one constituent. "What on earth were you thinking? Was it so long ago that the Vietnam War began under almost the exact circumstances?"[19]

Then, on April 11, local solidarity activists printed an advertisement in the *Daily Hampshire Gazette* titled "An Open Letter to Silvio Conte," which stated, "Mr. Conte you cast the determining vote to send $5,000,000 of additional military aid to the governing terrorists in El Salvador. You said you wanted to send a signal to the Soviets and Cuba and to support the administration. You admitted this went against majority sentiment in your district. But we can't blame the Soviets and Cuba for more than 50 years of oppression in El Salvador, Nicaragua and the rest of Latin America. We bear responsibility for that." The advertisement included a photograph of Maryknoll nuns praying over the bodies of the murdered U.S. churchwomen, with the caption "El Salvador Government Terrorism."[20]

As the uproar grew, Conte went on the offensive. Responding to one constituent, he reiterated, "I am convinced that my vote was justified—and is in line with the desires of the majority of the First District—in avoiding potentially high foreign policy costs and in increasing my leverage over the El Salvadoran government and the Administration."[21] In a lengthy letter to Susan Klein-Berndt, the Northampton organizer of the *Daily Hampshire Gazette* signature advertisement, Conte wrote that he was "disappointed" with the piece, which he felt distorted his position. Again he asserted, "I was concerned about misinterpretation that could arise from the failure of Congress to support a new president in his first foreign policy test and which could result in adverse repercussions for the United States and its allies in areas other than El Salvador."[22] Conte also objected to the depiction of him in the advertisement as blindly adhering to cold war dogma. Arguing that he had long held that the problems of the region were rooted in a history of poverty, he wrote, "To imply I 'Blame the Soviets and Cuba for the past 50 years of aggression in El Salvador' . . . is a major distortion."[23]

Conte's assertive defense of his March 24 vote did little to mollify his critics in the First District. Letters, telegrams, and calls continued to pour into the congressman's offices. Despite the occasional note of support, Conte's advocacy of human rights in El Salvador was being lost amid the chorus of criticism. Concerned, Conte's staff sought to get his message out. In an interview with the *Daily Hampshire Gazette*, Bruce Benton, one of Conte's aides, insisted, "[The vote] "is not a reversal of Conte's previous stand against military aid," adding that the equipment to be purchased was "defensive." Benton argued that Conte would not support such aid as weapons or U.S. military advisors, since "that's military."[24] Benton's efforts at damage control included his participation in a panel discussion held by the Northampton Committee on El Salvador at the Unitarian Church before 150 people. He argued that the United States needed to support José Napoleón Duarte not just against the leftist rebels but even more so against the extreme Right, which frequently threatened to topple the junta. A right-wing coup, Benton told the group, would lead to violence "far bloodier than anything that has gone on so far."[25]

After the storm over the $5 million military aid vote subsided, Conte worked hard to assuage his angry constituents. In the spring of 1981, he voted for the Solarz-Bingham amendment sponsored by the New York Democrats Stephen Solarz and Jonathan Bingham. The amendment stipulated that for the president to receive further congressional military aid for El Salvador, he must certify to Congress every 180 days that the Salvadoran government (1) was not carrying out "a consistent pattern of gross violation of internationally recognized human rights, (2) was achieving control over the military, (3) was making progress in land reform, (4) was committed to holding national elections at the earliest date, and (5) was showing a willingness to negotiate an end to the war. Although the amendment lacked the teeth of a legislative veto and required only that the administration claim progress toward the five stated objectives, it kept El Salvador on the congressional agenda and provided a yardstick by which to measure progress in that nation and administration veracity. Proponents further argued that by threatening to stop military aid, the Solarz-Bingham bill provided the administration with a tool for extracting concessions from the recalcitrant Salvadoran government.[26]

Conte embraced the Solarz-Bingham amendment, proclaiming, "I will not vote another nickel until these conditions are met."[27] In early 1982 when the administration issued its first certification, however, he was skeptical: "I was dismayed to learn that the President had certified on January 28 that these five conditions had been complied with. Information as to progress on human rights for El Salvador's citizens, the land reform program, free elections and civilian control over the security and armed forces appears to be ambiguous at best."[28]

Conte continued to walk the tightrope between the Republican administration and his district in 1982. After Jim Fairchild of the House Appropriations Committee had completed another Central American fact-finding trip, Conte issued the following statement to the Foreign Operations Subcommittee: "I reaffirm my position of opposing any increase of military assistance to El Salvador under the present circumstances. However, I continue to support economic and humanitarian assistance to the Duarte government. While support for total withdrawal of U.S. presence from El Salvador may be politically appealing, I must take a responsible position and avoid those steps, which might lead to an increase in the violence in El Salvador."[29]

In the spring of 1982, the president of Mexico, José López Portillo, set forth a peace initiative in what would be the first of many regional efforts to end the bloodshed in Central America. In 1983 Mexico, Venezuela, and Colombia issued the Contadora Peace proposal, which was followed by a peace plan proposed by the president of Costa Rica, Oscar Arias. Many in the U.S. Congress eagerly embraced these regional efforts. Emboldened by López Portillo's initiative, Conte declared, "Above all, a major effort is needed to achieve a negotiated, multilateral political settlement in El Salvador. To this end I have sent a letter . . . to President Reagan expressing my strong support of Mexican President Lopez Portillo's recent peace initiative."[30]

Conte's position distanced him further from the administration, which remained generally skeptical of negotiations. For the Reagan administration, negotiations meant working toward the limited goal of reaching terms under which the rebels would put down their arms and participate in government-run elections. The FMLN and the Democratic Revolutionary Front (Frente Democrático Revolucionario [FDR]) held tight to the position that without power sharing and restructuring of the armed forces, conditions would remain unsafe for the Salvadoran Left. The Reagan administration argued that power sharing would, in effect, allow members of the FMLN-FDR to shoot their way to power.[31]

Like many of his colleagues and much of the U.S. press and media, however, Conte was enthusiastic about the March 1982 Salvadoran elections. Duarte's Christian Democrats squared off against a coalition of conservative parties led by the newly formed National Republican Alliance (Alianza Republicana Nacionalista [ARENA]), an extreme right-wing party founded by the former army major Roberto D'Aubuisson (a man reputed to have ties to many death squads and believed by Robert White to have ordered the assassination of Archbishop Romero).[32] Leftist parties (who cited the impossibility of open campaigning without putting their members' lives in jeopardy) boycotted the election, and the FMLN (which denounced the election as illegitimate) sought to disrupt the proceedings.[33]

In the United States, the elections were hailed as a triumph of democracy in which voter turnout was unexpectedly high and many Salvadorans braved rebel sabotage and gunfire in order to vote (left-liberal periodicals in the United States pointed out that voting was mandatory and that failing to vote was a criminal offense). The results, however, left some, including Conte, uneasy. A right-wing coalition that included ARENA won a narrow majority, and as its first order of business set about dismantling modest efforts at land reform made by the previous government. Meanwhile, death squad killings continued unabated, and the war dragged on.[34]

By early 1983, Conte had become more vocal in his criticism of administration policy. This was primarily the result of two factors: an escalating level of constituent pressure and a legal impasse in the cases of the murdered U.S. citizens. In the spring of 1983, the previously heavy shower of constituent mail on El Salvador became a flood. One assistant sent Conte a memorandum stating, "The office—and district offices—has been swamped with letters, phone calls and telegrams. All are opposed to further military aid. In recent times, the letters have come outside of the traditional liberal hotbeds of Amherst and Northampton."[35]

As concern from the district increased, the case against the accused murderers of the four U.S. churchwomen ground to a halt. In May 1981 six members of the Salvadoran National Guard one of whom was subsequently released, had been arrested for the slayings. In November 1981—despite compelling ballistic, fingerprint, and polygraph evidence obtained by the Federal Bureau of Investigation (FBI) that linked the Guardsmen to the murders and despite reports that the Guardsmen had acted on orders from above—the U.S. Embassy and the Salvadoran government declared the investigation at an impasse.[36] Despite strong evidence that the deaths of Pearlman and Hammer had been ordered by two high-ranking military officers and a prominent, wealthy businessman with close ties to D'Aubuisson, a similar impasse had been reached in that case.[37]

The Lawyers Committee for International Human Rights, which pursued the case in close cooperation with the victims' families, took up the search for justice in the murders of the four U.S. churchwomen. Heading the case for the Lawyers Committee was Michael H. Posner, who publicly declared that the difficulty was that, fearing reprisal by the military, no Salvadoran judge would agree to hear the case. Writing to L. Craig Johnstone of the State Department, Posner stated, "Lawyers in El Salvador have grave, and probably justified fears that if they become involved in this case their lives may be jeopardized.... In part because of these fears, no lawyer appears willing to help conduct a thorough investigation of the possible involvement of higher authorities in ordering the killings or covering them up."[38]

Largely because of the persistent efforts of the Lawyers Committee, Deane Hinton, the U.S. ambassador to El Salvador, pressured the Salvadoran government to reopen the case. Finally, in late November 1982, a Salvadoran court agreed to try the four accused National Guardsmen, but—backed by the U.S. Embassy— refused to consider evidence that orders for the murders had come from higher up the chain of command. Posner complained to Johnstone, "A number... of [Salvadoran] lawyers have stated to us that they do not believe the U.S. Embassy in San Salvador supports a more thorough investigation of the case."[39] The limited focus of the trial divided the relatives of the victims, some of whom described it as "only a first step."[40]

In the early spring of 1983, the renewed case bogged down further when the Salvadoran judiciary announced that ballistic, fingerprint, and polygraph evidence provided by the FBI would be inadmissible under Salvadoran law. As a result, the court announced, there was insufficient evidence to try the case.[41] The ruling set off a storm of protest in the United States. Meanwhile, citing Conte's "longtime interest in the case" and his statement that he would support "no more aid till [the case was] resolved," Posner asked Johnstone at the State Department to inquire whether Conte would "act as a 'good faith broker.'" Conte agreed and began corresponding with the Lawyers Committee, receiving regular updates on the case.[42]

Appearing at hearings before Conte's Foreign Operations Subcommittee in March 1983, Posner described the obstacles the Lawyers Committee were encountering in the pursuit of justice for the churchwomen. During a trip to El Salvador with William Ford (brother of Ita Ford) the previous January, he had encountered a "shocking pattern of official indifference, incompetence and ill will" toward the case on the part of Salvadoran officials. The highest Salvadoran judicial figure, Prosecutor General Mario Adalberto Rivera "and his staff," Posner reported, "are both shockingly uninterested and wholly unprepared for trial . . . [and] . . . continue to ignore existing evidence that there were orders from superiors to apprehend the women."

Posner also complained, "Salvadoran judges—those who survive—seem to find ways to avoid bringing homicide charges to trial. As of last summer, we were told that Judge [Bernardo] Rauda [Marcia] had sixty murder cases pending before him and not one had been closed. Each week he inspects five or six bodies—new murders in which no investigation is even opened."[43] Posner concluded his testimony with an impassioned plea to the committee:

> Mr. Chairman, in the two years since the deaths of the four women, their case has taken on a special significance. To be sure, only a narrow parochialism could judge these murders worse or even more important than the tens of thousands of murders of Salvadoran citizens by government forces. But . . . [t]hese killings . . . have also become symbolic because in a period when 30,000 civilians, including the country's Archbishop, have been murdered, many by government armed forces, only the cases of the North Americans are being investigated. For this reason, the demand to fix responsibility in this case becomes part of a far wider demand, that elementary respect for human life and human rights may be restored and recognized as obligations by those who govern El Salvador.[44]

Outside the hearings, at Posner's request, Conte agreed to contact Rivera, about the stalled case. In a formal letter, Conte expressed his concerns to El Salvador's top judicial official: "I am not an expert in Salvadoran law, by any means, but I am concerned about vital evidence apparently ignored and put aside. Progress in this trial was cited by an act of Congress as a criterion for further United States assistance to your country. . . . I urge you to use the powers of your good office to admit this valuable information. The fair and proper conduct of this trial is extremely important to many people in the United States, including myself."[45]

Rivera replied to Conte's letter, "I feel honored to have received from you the letter in which you refer to the case under investigation concerning the death of the American nuns." Rivera went on to blame the "formalities" of the Salvadoran justice system for the difficulties in pursuing the case, explaining, "Our investigative system suffers from a certain rigidity."[46]

Conte sought to pressure not only the Salvadoran government but the Reagan administration as well. During the Foreign Operations Subcommittee hearings, Conte politely but firmly confronted Secretary of State George Schultz, declaring, "[This] single case probably causes you more difficulty in selling [the administration's proposal for additional aid] . . . than any other issue. . . . The only conclusion I can personally draw is that we haven't got . . . [the Salvadoran government's] attention on this issue."[47] Schultz—who shunned the confrontational style of his predecessor, Alexander Haig, in favor of a more conciliatory approach to Congress—responded to Conte's remarks, "Before I can sell you, I have to sell myself. Some of these cases are deeply troubling to me; there just has to be a better job done on it."[48]

In June 1983 Conte took to the floor of the House of Representatives and announced his support for a resolution by the Massachusetts Democrat Gerry Studds, adding to the certification requirements for U.S. military aid to El Salvador the requirement that a verdict be reached in the cases of the murdered U.S. citizens. In his most impassioned remarks on the case to date, Conte declared, "Mr. Speaker, this depressing story of the six brutally murdered Americans is not a new chapter in the unfolding saga of El Salvador. . . . Two and a half years have passed since these events took place and little measurable progress has been made to resolve the case. . . . How can a close and well-supported ally apparently ignore the cry of outrage by the American public and Congress?"[49] Echoing a point made repeatedly by the Lawyers Committee and those in the solidarity movement, Conte asked, "If the treatment of this highly publicized and crucial case is any indication of the administration of justice in El Salvador, what chance do campesinos have?"[50]

For constituents in the First District, Conte's staff amplified the congressman's new outspokenness by issuing press releases. In a piece titled "Conte Toughens Stance," the Daily Hampshire Gazette summed up Conte's trajectory on El Salvador over the course of the three previous years: "The unresolved murders have been a concern of Conte's since 1981.... After coming under fire for casting a subcommittee vote that allowed military aid to continue to El Salvador, Conte promised he would vote for no further aid until the murderers were brought to justice.... [Y]esterday's remarks represent another step by Conte to distance himself from the administration's policy in Central America and to appease constituents who have pressured him since January to stop military aid to El Salvador."[51]

In November 1983 Conte voted with a majority of Congress to withhold a larger, $19 million military aid package until a verdict was reached. The case was reopened, and in May 1984 a five-member jury found the four Guardsmen guilty. The court subsequently sentenced them to thirty years in jail (El Salvador, ironically, had no death penalty). An attorney for the Lawyers Committee for International Human Rights expressed ambivalence over the outcome: "I don't want to undermine what has happened but almost everything about this case makes me uncomfortable.... It's an American show. We... have nudged them and shoved them every step of the way."[52] Four years later, all but one of the convicted Guardsmen admitted that the orders to kill the churchwomen had come from high up the military chain of command. Later that year, three of the Guardsmen were released.

THE LIBERAL CRUSADER: STATE REPRESENTATIVE GERRY STUDDS

The popular amendment to reinstate the verdict requirement—which had been part of the Solarz-Bingham amendment but had lapsed—was the work of Gerald ("Gerry") E. Studds, a passionate liberal who represented the Massachusetts Twelfth District (including Cape Cod, Martha's Vineyard, and Nantucket). From the outset of the debate on Central America, Studds had emerged as one of the most outspoken critics of Reagan's Central American policies, joining other liberal Democrats—including John Conyers of Michigan, Ron Dellums of California, Michael Barnes of Maryland, and Christopher Dodd of Connecticut—in leading the opposition to the new direction the administration had taken. As a member of the House Foreign Affairs Committee, Studds was strategically positioned to contest the new policy, and he had earned a reputation for challenging the president on both the arms race and Central America.[53]

Studds's political views were shaped in the cauldron of the 1960s. After graduating from Yale University in 1960, he went directly into the Foreign Service Offices and then transferred to the staff of President John Kennedy, where he remained from late 1962 through 1963. Studds worked as a legislative assistant for Harrison A. Williams, Jr., the Democratic congressman from New Jersey in the mid-1960s and, as a delegate in the Convention Hall, was witness to the mayhem of the 1968 Democratic National Convention. Over the course of the next few years, Studds taught history and served in the office of the president of the University of Massachusetts. In 1972 Studds won election to Congress from the Twelfth District, a bastion of liberalism in the only state to stand behind George McGovern. Thereafter, Studds continued to win reelection, even when, in 1978, his opponent leveled charges of homosexuality against him. Studds went on to become one of the first openly gay members of Congress.[54]

Studds became an ardent proponent of post-1960s liberalism, seeking to change the cold war policies and ideology that had led the United States into the Vietnam War. His unflagging liberalism remained unchanged after the conservative resurgence of 1980. Relatively secure in his district, Studds did not undergo the doubts and soul searching that many liberals experienced in the demoralizing aftermath of the 1980 election. The election had seen the defeat of such liberal standard bearers as Senators Frank Church and George McGovern and had left the Democrats on the defensive. Senator Paul Tsongas of Massachusetts observed at the time, "The last election changed things. Not only did we lose Democrats and liberals, but those who are left are so weary. Everyone is running for cover from Reagan and the conservative trend."[55] Studds emerged from the debacle zealously committed to rallying liberal opposition to the new administration.

Before Ronald Reagan took office, Studds was involved in the Central American crisis. Between January 9 and 19, 1981, he had traveled to Central America with State Representatives Barbara Mikulski and Robert Edgar on a fact-finding mission sponsored by the Boston-based Unitarian Universalist Service Committee. In a report for the House Foreign Affairs Committee, chaired by Clement Zablocki, Studds had summarized the information he had gathered on Costa Rica, Honduras, Guatemala, Nicaragua, and El Salvador during his trip. Despite the fact that Zablocki introduced the report with a foreword in which he stated, "The findings and recommendations contained in this report are those of Representative Studds and do not necessarily reflect the views of the members of the Committee on Foreign Affairs,"[56] the document became a benchmark emblem of left-leaning liberalism. Frequently quoted by liberals and radicals alike, it was cited in the 1981 Daily Hampshire Gazette advertisement that assailed Conte's vote in support of $5 million in military aid for El Salvador.[57]

Studds's report, which was a combination of information summaries and policy recommendations, was especially concerned with events in Nicaragua. Studds began his section on Nicaragua as follows: "Rising from the ashes of a devastating earthquake and civil war, Nicaragua's future political course remains as yet unclear. The air and airwaves continue to crackle with the exhilaration of revolution, the boundless energy of an entire society set free at last to determine its own fate. Able now to make their own mistakes, the Somozaless segments of Nicaragua have forged a mixed record of social progress, economic ups and downs and festering political discord." Like Conte, Studds perceived that most Nicaraguans supported the revolution: "Their accomplishment has been to create within Nicaragua a universal commitment to greater social equity and concern for the country's multitude of poor, ill-clothed, ill-fed, and sick people. There is a fully shared sense the revolution is necessary and just."[58]

During its sojourn in Nicaragua, the delegation made the usual rounds among Sandinistas, political and business opposition leaders, and the Nicaraguan population. One issue of concern to Studds, which had been expressed to him in interviews with a number Costa Rican and Honduran officials, was the rapidly expanding size of the Nicaraguan Army (which stood at the time at more than thirty thousand troops). Sandinista officials had responded to his inquiries about the issue that they feared a counterrevolution backed by the United States. Studds reported, "Nicaraguan junta members and those in the Sandinista party . . . argue they must prepare for the counterrevolutionary attacks which they believe will inevitably occur. They point to the precedent of the Bay of Pigs."[59] Many seemed braced for the incoming Reagan administration, according to Studds: "The entire Nicaraguan leadership is aware of the rhetoric used by candidate Reagan," which called for "'the removal of the government in Managua.'"[60] One Sandinista official anticipated a Vietnam scenario: "One junta member told us that the size of the armed forces was predicated on the need to hold off invading American forces long enough to cause U.S. public opinion to mobilize in opposition to the intervention."[61]

Like Conte, Studds was convinced that the nature of the Nicaraguan export economy moved the country toward cooperation with the United States and maintenance of a mixed economy: "Nicaragua seeks aid from, and friendship with, all nations of the world. Elementary economics permit them no choice. Fidel Castro's demeaning and frustrating dependence on the Soviet Union is not seen by Nicaragua's new leadership as a desirable model for their country." In an argument that would be echoed in the coming years, the report contended that a U.S. economic embargo would force Nicaragua to "rely on Cuba and the Soviet Union for the assistance they must have to rebuild."[62]

The "Studds Report," which was generally sympathetic to the Nicaraguan revolution, criticizes the new government on several issues. Studds cited anger over an opposition rally canceled by the Sandinistas as an example of harassment of the opposition; the possibility of Sandinista involvement in the assassination of Jorge Salazar, an opposition business leader; the indefinite postponement of elections; and the precarious freedom of the press. Pointing to the selective concern over human rights that permeated the cold war era, Studds wrote, "Nicaragua has become a litmus test ideally suited for the separation of human rights hypocrites of both the left and right from those with a true commitment to social and civil justice. There are many who now express great anger and shock at the shortcomings of the FSLN [Frente Sandinista de Liberación Nacional (Sandinista National Liberation Front)] who never uttered a whimper of concern during the Somoza era.... Others exist, however, who accept all too willingly the rationalizations of the FSLN, despite a propensity to criticize the same type of arguments bitterly when put forth by regimes perceived as right wing."[63]

Studds advocated what amounted to a liberalized version of the earlier Carter policy, advising, "The United States must be objective, patient, and restrained.... The United States needs to keep the Nicaraguan revolution in perspective. It is, after all, a revolution different from any other; far different, certainly, from Castro's. There is no single charismatic leader, there was no single force which won the victory."[64]

The report concluded with a plea for the United States to respect Nicaraguans' right to self-determination: "The most important result is that the people who fought, and whose friends were bombed, and whose children and wives were wounded or crippled or ripped apart, are now the ones that count in determining the future political life of their own country. This is, after all, what revolutions are fought for, and this is why revolutions are won."[65]

Studds's ten-day trip coincided with the fiercest period of the Salvadoran civil war, during which the FMLN launched its Final Offensive and right-wing death squad killings reached a new high. The U.S. State Department therefore advised Studds and his entourage not to enter El Salvador.[66] The delegation did, however, arrange to meet in Honduras with several Christian Democratic representatives of the Salvadoran government, non-Marxist members of the FDR, and campesino war refugees.[67]

Included in the report were verbatim transcripts of interviews conducted by Congresswoman Mikulski with Salvadoran women who had recently fled the war zones into what became a refugee camp in neighboring Honduras. The women recounted horrific acts of savagery by the Salvadoran military that were, by then, becoming all too familiar. At one point, the interviews were disrupted; the report quoted Mikulski speaking into her tape recorder: "While we were doing these interviews, an airplane flew overhead, and the village immediately is upset because they are afraid that some harm is going to come to them."[68]

Although Studds was unable to enter El Salvador, Mikulski's interviews supported his strong antipathy toward offering aid to the Salvadoran military.

His recommendations with respect to El Salvador, which were stronger than those for any other country in his report, staked out a position from which the Massachusetts Democrat would not swerve in the coming years: "The United States should suspend military sales, training and assistance to the security forces of El Salvador on the grounds that those forces are operating independent of responsible civilian control, and are conducting a systematic campaign of terrorism directed against segments of their own population."[69]

In the spring of 1981, Studds proposed the first of many amendments, including one (House Resolution 1509) that called for an unconditional end to all future U.S. aid to the Salvadoran military. Many opponents of Reagan's policy, uncomfortable with this overt challenge to the new president, sought instead to influence administration policy through the certification requirements of the Solarz-Bingham amendment. In response to one of the many letters that urged support for the Studds amendment, Conte replied, "I have decided not to cosponsor H.R. 1509 (Studds Bill) because . . . the prohibition against U.S. military assistance at any time in the future, as called for by H.R. 1509, would send a signal that the United States would be powerless to deter outside intervention, thereby inviting external forces to fill the power vacuum."[70] Many liberal Democrats had similar concerns about the degree to which the Studds amendment tied the president's hands on a foreign policy issue. By staking out the left flank on opposition to Reagan's policy in El Salvador, however, Studds provided cover for less radical proposals that aimed to influence administration policy and established his own reputation as one of the most inveterate foes of the Reagan administration.[71]

In December 1981, the Reagan administration issued its first certification that El Salvador was meeting the requirements set forth by Congress—seemingly in direct defiance of reports by the press, human rights groups, and first-hand witnesses that pointed to meager land reforms and ongoing human rights violations. Among the recent examples of atrocities in El Salvador that December was the El Mozote massacre, in which (according to church and press sources) the army had massacred between seven hundred and one thousand peasants.[72] Studds took it upon himself to challenge Undersecretary of State Thomas Enders at a certification hearing: "The president has just certified that up is down, and in is out, and black is white. I anticipate his telling us that war is peace at any moment."[73] Later that year, when the administration again certified progress on the five conditions, Studds and thirty-three cosponsors introduced a bill (House Joint Resolution 552) that declared "the president's July certification with respect to El Salvador to be null and void" and imposed a two-year suspension of military aid. Nevertheless, concerns about the political consequences of a collapse of the Salvadoran government deterred moderates and many liberals from backing the bill.[74]

In 1983, opposition to Reagan administration policy in Central America gathered momentum for several reasons: (1) The Democrats had gained seats in the November 1982 elections, deflating Reagan's aura of invincibility and encouraging reinvigorated congressional efforts to support a nuclear weapons freeze resolution and oppose administration policy on Central America. (2) The legal impasse in the prosecution of the accused murderers of the churchwomen in El Salvador slowly strengthened opponents of administration policy. (3) The solidarity movement continued to expand and redouble efforts to end U.S. support for the Salvadoran military, including spearheading a massive letter-writing campaign to Congress.[75] Once again Studds sought to mobilize more determined opposition to Reagan's policies by introducing a bill—this time to make "null and void" the most recent certification by the administration and to exercise the congressional power of the purse by terminating U.S. military aid to El Salvador. At the first certification hearing of the year, Studds declared, "At some point we must be willing to cut off aid."[76]

Beginning with the case of the U.S. churchwomen, Studds denounced the recent certification: "Nowhere in the certification documents is there a determination by the President that the government of El Salvador has made good faith efforts to investigate and bring to justice those responsible for the murders of the four churchwomen and two agrarian reform workers in El Salvador two years ago." He then went on to raise the cases of Michael Kline, a U.S. citizen who had been found executed at point-blank range, and John Sullivan, a U.S. journalist who had recently disappeared in El Salvador. In response to the administration assertion of human rights progress based on a reduction of death squad murders from an average of four hundred per month in 1980 to two hundred per month in 1983, Studds stated, "The Reagan Administration has accepted a ludicrously low standard of performance in the area of human rights." He concluded, "It is not ordinarily the role of Congress both to enact and also to enforce the law, but with respect to El Salvador and the certification process, that time has come."[77]

Studds solicited cosponsors for his nullification bill to add to the thirty-three he had recruited in his 1982 effort. Circulating a "Dear Colleague" letter throughout the House of Representatives, in which he detailed the evidence against the claims made by the administration, he argued that Congress was now forced to reassert itself: "The Reagan administration is unwilling to sacrifice its other policy goals in order to confront directly the extremists in that country with whom it has chosen to deal. . . . It is up to Congress, therefore, to act aggressively and to guarantee that the legal conditions placed on our aid to El Salvador are taken seriously—both by the government of El Salvador and by our own executive branch."[78]

The new nullification effort attracted almost one hundred cosponsors. Admitting to the press that his bill had no chance of passing, Studds pressed on nonetheless.[79] Despite a Democratic majority in the House and the sympathy of Speaker of the House Tip O'Neill, Studds once again ran into the obstacle of Democratic moderates (especially those from the South and Southwest) who feared an open challenge to the president on what they regarded as a national security issue. Given the strong anticommunist sentiment in many districts, they were unwilling to embrace any policy that might entail the charge of being soft on communism. Powerful Democrats such as James Wright of Texas and David Boren of Oklahoma supported administration policy in El Salvador by and large.[80]

In late spring of 1983, Studds told an interviewer for the *New York Times*, "It eludes me why people search for bipartisanship at all costs.... Bipartisanship is the code word that lets members go the other way on the MX [missile and] duck the problems of Central America."[81] In June, Studds decided to take on the advocates of moderation publicly in an op-ed piece in the *New York Times* titled "Bipartisan Consensus? A Mirage." Studds argued that in spite of polls that showed public apprehension about the Reagan nuclear arms buildup and intervention in Central America, too many Democrats were willing to support administration policy in these areas. Commenting on the MX missile, Studds asserted that despite the fact that most Democrats "hope to kill it before it kills us," moderates in the party were supporting the missile in the hope that in exchange for their support Reagan would take steps toward arms control negotiations. He also observed, "A number of Congressional Democrats seem to feel that President Reagan's personal popularity makes it unwise or unsafe to oppose his policies directly. The President has effectively conveyed to the American people a nostalgic and simplistic view of the world. Mr. Reagan strikes a responsive chord in us all, because most of us have held similar views—until the clearly contrasting blacks and whites of youth gave way to the complex grays of adulthood."[82]

With a presidential election coming the following year, Studds argued, Democratic bipartisanship was a mistake, and the party must accentuate, not blur, its differences with Reagan. Defying conventional wisdom, which saw national security policy as playing to Reagan's strengths, Studds called on Democrats to challenge the president head on: "Barring further economic collapse, if the Democrats don't win on the issues of war and peace in 1984, they will not win at all. The polls indicate quite clearly that a majority of the American people oppose

Administration policy in Central America and desire a far more vigorous effort to control the nuclear arms race. The personal popularity of the President does not extend to his policies. Democrats can only lose, therefore, by blurring the real distinctions between their principles and judgments and those of the President."[83]

Shortly after Studds undertook his public campaign to push the Democratic Party in a more confident and confrontational direction, a sex scandal seriously slowed his efforts and exacted a painful political price. Widespread rumors of sexual impropriety between members of Congress and congressional pages and of drug use on Capitol Hill in the early 1980s prompted the House Ethics Committee to establish a commission to investigate. The investigation revealed far less misconduct than had been expected, but its report singled out two members of Congress: Daniel B. Crane, an Illinois Republican, who was charged with having had sexual relations with a seventeen-year-old female page and Gerry Studds, who was charged with having had an affair with a seventeen-year-old male page in 1973 and having made advances toward two other pages.[84]

Studds argued that the affair was consensual, private, and not improper; however, in order to protect the identity of the page, he waived his right to an Ethics Committee trial. Consequently, the House Ethics Committee recommended official reprimands for both Crane and Studds. Although Studds had been openly gay since the 1970s, the taint of impropriety left him politically wounded and tarnished his reputation as someone who staked out the moral high ground on Central America and other issues.[85] Although Newt Gingrich of Georgia—the rising star of a more brash, ideologically committed brand of right-wing Republicanism—moved to have Studds expelled from Congress, Speaker of the House Tip O'Neill squelched the effort.[86]

Although Studds survived the scandal and continued to win reelection in the Twelfth District, the events of 1984 reshaped the issue of El Salvador: Reagan's resounding reelection, the election of Duarte as president of El Salvador, and the growing stability of the Salvadoran government as the war settled into a stalemate transformed El Salvador into a less-debated and less-divisive topic in the halls of Congress.[87] Moreover, by mid-decade, U.S. support for the Nicaraguan Contras had supplanted El Salvador as the major source of debate over administration policy in Central America. Although Studds continued to speak out on both El Salvador and Nicaragua, his early 1980s exemplification of opposition to Reagan's policy on the region was slowly fading. As the U.S. proxy war against Nicaragua shifted to center stage and as the Central American solidarity movement increasingly emerged from the shadows of the freeze movement, Democratic heavyweights began to take up the mantle of opposition.

THE SPEAKER: TIP O'NEILL

Speaker of the House Tip O'Neill came from a very different school of politics from that of Gerry Studds. O'Neill was one of the last great New Deal–style liberals, a self-proclaimed champion of the little guy, who unabashedly advocated redistributing wealth toward low-income and working-class people. Reared in the backslapping milieu of Boston ethnic politics, O'Neill—who was a master of parliamentary maneuver and cloakroom compromise—was never completely comfortable with the new breed of issue-driven Democratic crusaders who began to flood the party in 1972. In 1988 O'Neill spoke bluntly to Senator Gary Hart of Colorado, a candidate for the Democratic nomination for president in both 1984 and 1988: "You're not my cup of tea. . . . [Y]ou're this new type of liberal. I'm the old work and wages, take care of the poor and the hungry [kind of liberal]. I don't like your kind of politics."[88]

Although he was a product of the cold war, in many ways O'Neill became a bridge between the old and new Democrats in the 1960s, when—relatively early on—he came out against the Vietnam War (which he saw as a tragic mistake that took its worst toll on low-income and working-class people). "Of all the votes I cast during thirty-four years in the House of Representatives [the Gulf of Tonkin resolution, which gave President Lyndon Johnson the authority to conduct military operations in Southeast Asia without a declaration of war] is the only one I regret," recalled the O'Neill in 1986.[89]

Despite the central role that Vietnam played in shaping O'Neill's views, his main interest lay in domestic affairs (and when it came to foreign affairs, he displayed little savvy). In the 1970s, O'Neill supported détente and the Carter human rights policy in general; however, after the Soviet invasion of Afghanistan in 1979, he became a staunch supporter of the Carter push for arms buildup, including the MX missile.[90] Although O'Neill—whose Cambridge district was a stronghold of the nuclear freeze movement—supported a freeze resolution and helped shepherd it through the House, he worked assiduously to win missile contracts for Massachusetts. In the early Reagan years O'Neill worked to create an image of bipartisanship in foreign affairs. Much to the chagrin of liberal party members, he supported both Reagan's dispatch of U.S. marines to Lebanon and his invasion of Grenada in 1983. According to John A. Farrell, an O'Neill biographer, "If he did not share Reagan's vision, neither did he employ his powers to foil it. With a few key exceptions—most notably U.S. intervention in Central America—the Speaker approached the President's foreign policy from the mushy bi-partisan center."[91]

As the 1980s progressed, however, O'Neill's opposition to the Reagan administration policies in El Salvador and Nicaragua became increasingly adamant.

Like many Americans, O'Neill feared that Reagan's policies could embroil U.S. troops in a Vietnam War—-type quagmire. As one aide put it, "There's a sense of déjà vu here for the Speaker.... To him, the question isn't 'Who lost Vietnam?' but 'Who got us into Vietnam in the first place?'"[92] Moreover, although O'Neill was never completely comfortable with Quakers, academic radicals, or others he regarded as middle-class reformers, the participation of so many nuns and Jesuits in the Cambridge solidarity movement greatly influenced the devoutly Catholic congressman.[93]

In the early 1980s, a Cambridge-based women's solidarity organization called the Nicaraguan Action Group tried to move O'Neill into more forceful opposition against Reagan's Central American policies by occupying his congressional office on two separate occasions. Half of the group consisted of nuns who were deeply influenced by both liberation theology and the murders of Ita Ford, Dorothy Kazel, Maura Clarke, and Jean Donovan. In 1984 Sister Jeanne Gallo of the Sisters of Notre Dame de Namur told a reporter for the *New York Times*, "We realized Mr. O'Neill was key to what happened in the House. Many of us were in his district. The group decided to work on educating him about Central America and work on him to move things through Congress to help end human rights abuses."[94] Anne Shumway, another Nicaraguan Action Group member, noted, "We've been very pleased that he listens to us. He is a good Catholic and trusts people in the church who give him information. He's also a humanitarian and feels he should act on the things he learns."[95]

Since he was a young man, the church had played an important role in shaping O'Neill's outlook. He had attended Dominican primary and secondary schools in Boston and graduated from Boston College, a Jesuit institution. O'Neill was perhaps most influenced by Eunice ("Annie") Tolan, an aunt who was a nun in the Maryknoll Order (who died in 1981 at the age of ninety-one).[96] Through Tolan, O'Neill developed a profound respect for the Maryknoll sisterhood and eventually for the faith-based solidarity movement. "I have a connection with the Maryknoll Order.... I have great trust in that order, O'Neill told the *New York Times*. "When nuns and priests come through, I ask them questions about their feelings, what they see, who the enemy is, and I'm sure I get the truth. I haven't found any of these missionaries who aren't absolutely opposed to [Reagan's] policy."[97]

O'Neill's skepticism about U.S. intervention came from another personal source as well. Growing up in Boston, O'Neill had a friend named Eddie Kelly, who became a Marine and was shipped to Nicaragua in the late 1920s to fight the nationalist Augusto César Sandino. Kelly returned wheelchair bound (as a result of a knife wound) and embittered by his experience. In response to O'Neill's inquiry about what the U.S. Marines were doing in Nicaragua, Kelly had replied, "We're taking care of the United Fruit Company."[98]

In the early years of the Reagan administration, O'Neill spoke out on the subject of Central America but took a relatively hands-off approach toward divisions in the Democratic Party over the issue. Southern Democrats led by Jim Wright of Texas, who tended to view Central America much as Reagan did, generally supported the Republican president's policies (especially in El Salvador). O'Neill's early laissez-faire attitude toward Central America grew out of his determination to maintain as much unity as possible between centrists and liberals in the fierce budget battles of 1981 and 1982. During this time, members of the solidarity movement and Democratic Party liberals such as Gerry Studds worked to push O'Neill into a more assertive role with respect to Central America.[99]

Beginning in 1983, O'Neill slowly began to exert more influence. On April 27, 1983, as debate on military aid to El Salvador became heated in Congress, Reagan made a televised address to a joint session of Congress given exclusively to the topic of Central America that took his message directly to the American people. He called on Congress to put aside "passivity, resignation and defeatism" and meet "this challenge to freedom and security in our hemisphere."[100] Comparing himself to President Harry Truman in 1947, but eerily reminiscent of Lyndon Johnson in 1965, Reagan declared, "The national security of all the Americas is at stake in Central America. If we cannot defend ourselves there, we cannot expect to prevail elsewhere. Our credibility would collapse, our alliances would crumble and the safety of our homeland would be put in jeopardy."[101]

It fell to O'Neill and Senate Minority Leader Robert Byrd of West Virginia to choose which Democrat would give the ten-minute televised response to the president's speech. Despite opposition by southern moderates, O'Neill and Byrd chose the liberal Connecticut senator Christopher Dodd—who had been a driving force behind the certification requirements and a frequent critic of administration policy—to represent the party's response.[102] Traditionally, such opposition responses showcase a rising talent in the party, are relatively innocuous, and are quickly forgotten. Dodd's televised response to the president's April address, in contrast, created an uproar. Denouncing the president's policy as "a formula for disaster,"[103] Dodd insisted that rather than pour endless amounts of military aid into Central America with the risk of U.S. troops to follow, the administration must adopt a policy that targeted "the factors which breed revolution" through economic aid. "We must make violent revolution preventable by making peaceful revolution possible," Dodd declared.[104] Challenging the cold war paradigm invoked by Reagan, Dodd continued:

If Central America were not racked with poverty, there would be no revolution. If Central America were not racked with hunger, there would be no revolution. If Central America were not racked with injustices, there would be no revolution.[105]

Dodd went on to detail his first-hand experiences in El Salvador: "I know about the morticians who travel the streets each morning to collect the bodies of those summarily dispatched the night before by Salvadoran security forces—gangland style—the victim on a bended knee, thumbs wired behind the back, a bullet in the brain." Although the bulk of Dodd's response focused on El Salvador, he also denounced the covert operations carried out by the administration against Nicaragua, which, he argued, would drive the Sandinistas into the arms of the Soviets and the Cubans. Dodd's impassioned conclusion set off a wave of anger among most Republicans and a number of southern Democrats. He quoted Senator Edward Kennedy, who had called the president's policy a "prescription for a wider war," and then inveighed, "When that day comes—when the 'dogs of war'—are loose in Central America, when the cheering has stopped, we will know where the President's appeal for more American money and a deeper American commitment has taken us."[106]

What soon became known as Dodd's Dogs of War speech created a good deal of controversy. Several prominent Democrats, including State Representative Jim Wright of Texas, Senator Lloyd Bentsen of Texas, and Senator Henry ("Scoop") Jackson of Washington, made it known to reporters that they were unhappy with O'Neill's choice of respondent and with Dodd's speech. Jeane Kirkpatrick of the State Department denounced Dodd's speech as "demagoguery," adding, "I know many Democrats didn't think it represented mainstream Democratic positions." O'Neill, for his part, stood solidly behind his choice.[107]

O'Neill's bipartisan cooperation with Reagan on foreign policy continued to erode throughout 1983. From 1984 through his retirement in 1986, O'Neill not only became increasingly outspoken in challenging Reagan's Central American policies but also pushed the Democratic Party to oppose what was quickly taking center stage as the major foreign policy battlefield of the mid-1980s: the U.S. government–directed Contra war against the Sandinista government in Nicaragua.[108]

THE BOLAND AMENDMENTS

From the time he took office, Reagan worked to subvert and destabilize the government in Managua. Beginning in early 1981, the Central Intelligence Agency (CIA) worked to put together an anti-Sandinista guerrilla army from the remnants of Somoza's old National Guard. In mid-1981 the new Contra army began making forays into Nicaragua from its bases in neighboring Honduras, attacking isolated villages in Nicaragua and scurrying back across the border. Slowly, the covert war grew, as the Contra army expanded and penetrated deeper into the Nicaraguan interior. Soon the northern Contras were joined by a southern Contra army operating out of Costa Rica (led by a flamboyant former Sandinista named Eden Pastora) and a rebellion by Mosquito natives on the remote eastern Atlantic coast of Nicaragua.[109] William Casey, who headed the CIA, met secretly with the Senate and House Intelligence Committees and assured their respective chairmen—the Arizona Republican Barry Goldwater and the Massachusetts Democrat Edward Boland—that the Contra army numbered fewer than fifteen hundred soldiers and that its covert operations were limited to the goal of interdicting Sandinista arms supplies to the guerrillas in El Salvador. In no way was it U.S. policy, Casey affirmed, to foment efforts to topple the government in Nicaragua.[110]

Elected to Congress in 1952, Ed Boland was hardly a crusader like Gerry Studds or an old school liberal like Tip O'Neill. Boland had a reputation as a moderate who shunned publicity, a foreign policy traditionalist who deferred to presidents but believed strongly in the rule of law. As the *New York Times* observed, Boland was "not known for rocking many boats."[111] Boland was the type of circumspect member of Congress ideally suited to chair an Intelligence Committee; he was an establishment figure who commanded respect on Capitol Hill. Boland had been a personal friend of John F. Kennedy's and shared a Washington, D.C., apartment with Tip O'Neill. When William Casey assured Boland of the limited scope of the covert operations in Nicaragua, Boland took the CIA chief at his word; he authorized secret funds for the operation, with the understanding that the goal was only to interdict arms supplies.[112]

In February 1982, the *Washington Post* published the first press reports that emanated from Honduras covering the covert raids into Nicaragua.[113] The story remained low key, however, until November 1982, when *Newsweek* published detailed reports of Contra operations that put the counterrevolutionary army at four thousand troops (Casey had told Boland they numbered no more than fifteen hundred) and included reports of atrocities that would grow increasingly common in the coming years.[114] In response to the reports, Tom Harkin, the liberal State Representative from Iowa, denounced the Contras as "vicious cutthroat murderers ... [and] remnants of the evil, murderous National Guard" and proposed legislation to ban all U.S. support for any group undertaking military activities against Nicaragua.[115] To head off what he regarded as a drastic response, Boland offered a substitute measure, which (carrying the same language as the classified bill) specified that U.S. support for the operation be limited to the goal of arms interdiction and not "for the purpose of overthrowing the government of Nicaragua." The first Boland amendment passed in December 1982 by a vote of 411 to 0 and was accepted in conference by the Republican-controlled Senate.[116]

Reports of widening Contra attacks and Contra cruelty continued to grow in early 1983. Both the House and Senate Intelligence Committees sent fact-finding delegations to Honduras and Nicaragua to determine exactly what was taking place. Their reports were not reassuring. Congressman Berkley Bedell, the Democrat from Iowa, declared, "If the American people could have talked with the common people of Nicaragua, whose women and children are being indiscriminately kidnapped, tortured and killed by terrorists financed by the American taxpayers, they would rise up in legitimate anger and demand that support for criminal activity be ended at once."[117] Robert Torricelli, the Democrat from New Jersey, reported that U.S. officials with whom he had met privately in Central America had told him that they regarded the Boland amendment as a "legal triviality."[118] Senator Patrick Leahy—whose findings were seconded by the House Democrat Wyche Fowler of Georgia—reported that the Contra operations were far broader than anything the Intelligence Committees had been led to believe.[119]

Despite protestations by Republicans such as Barry Goldwater and Senator Howard Baker of Tennessee, the cautious Boland declared, "It is my judgment that there has been an apparent violation of the law. If you look at the stories that have come out of there, from reporters and members [of Congress] who have gone down there, the evidence is very strong."[120] Reporters pressed President Reagan for a response to Boland's comments. "We are complying with the law," insisted Reagan. "Anything that we're doing in that area is simply trying to interdict the supply lines which are supplying the guerrillas."[121] "But Mr. President," asked another reporter, "what is the American public to think if Congressman Boland, who as you know is chairman of the House Intelligence Committee, says there's strong evidence that we are violating the law?" Reagan responded by attacking the press: "Well, maybe some of you people misled him."[122]

Boland and Zablocki proceeded to put forth a bill that would deny funds for the purpose of destabilizing the government of Nicaragua and replace the Contras' "interdiction" money with $80 million in interdiction aid for regional governments. Over the summer Boland's determination grew, when the administration announced military exercises in Honduras called Big Pine II, which lasted six months and involved more than five thousand U.S. Army troops and a huge naval flotilla off the coast of Nicaragua. Administration saber rattling during Big Pine II convinced many members of Congress not only that Reagan sought to overthrow the Sandinista government but also that the military exercises might be intended as a precursor to a U.S. invasion of Nicaragua.[123] The House approved the Boland-Zablocki amendment, but the Republican-controlled Senate voted for $50 million in aid for the Contras. Tip O'Neill urged the House not to budge, but the joint conference committee settled on a compromise $24 million for the Contras.[124]

The full scope of the covert CIA activities came to light in the spring of 1984, when international reports confirmed that the agency had been mining Nicaraguan harbors and blowing up coastal oil refineries. More than two dozen international ships from around the world suffered damage from the CIA mine strikes. Moreover, the oil refinery fires covertly set by U.S. special forces at Corinto necessitated the evacuation of more than twenty thousand residents and sent millions of gallons of fuel into the environment. Few believed the Reagan administration claims that the widespread sabotage was the work of the Contras. The government of Nicaragua took the case to the World Court in the Hague, and the administration quickly announced that it did not recognize the jurisdiction of the World Court. Even the most stalwart defender of Contra aid, Barry Goldwater, denounced the administration for engaging in illegal activities and for keeping the Intelligence Committees in the dark.[125]

Boland submitted yet another amendment to cut off Contra funding and "end this deadly war." In May 1984, the House passed the third Boland amendment by a vote of 241 to 177. The Senate voted for $28 million in aid, which was held up in conference. This time the compromise tipped in favor of the House. Although the conference committee approved $14 million, the funds were to remain frozen until March 1985 and could then be dispersed only by a joint resolution of Congress. Furthermore, the new Boland amendment forbade the channeling of aid to the Contras through any government agency. For the first time, the Boland amendment of May 1984 cut off all U.S. funds for the Contras. As a result, Marine Major Oliver North began to seek alternative sources of funding for the Contras, who now numbered more than ten thousand. Working under National Security Council advisors Robert McFarland and later John Poindexter, North was confident that he was carrying out the president's wishes. In 1985, as part of his secret Contra funding operations, North illegally sold missiles to Iran and diverted the profits to the Contras.[126]

The debates on Contra aid during the spring of 1984, which represented the apex of opposition to Reagan's policy toward Nicaragua, forced the issues of Central America onto the floor of the Republican-controlled Senate, where no floor debate had occurred since 1981. Throughout the early 1980s, Senator Ted Kennedy had spoken out against Reagan's policies on Central America but had directed his focus more toward the campaign for a nuclear freeze resolution. The waning of the freeze movement and the escalation of the Reagan administration campaign to destabilize Nicaragua in 1983 and 1984 led Kennedy to turn his attention to the Central America debates.[127]

On March 28, 1984, Kennedy opened Senate debate on additional aid for El Salvador and the Contras with a strong denunciation of administration policies in Central America as "interventionist" and "imperialistic." "The time is long overdue for pursuing the path of negotiations," he declared.[128] Working closely with Senators Leahy and Dodd, Kennedy proposed a series of amendments. Although doomed in the Republican-controlled Senate, the amendments kept the floor open to a sustained debate on Central America. The proposals included amendments to (1) limit aid to El Salvador to $21 million, (2) make all future aid to El Salvador contingent on the resolution of the cases against the accused murderers of the U.S. churchwomen and labor advisors, (3) delete all funds to the Contras, and (4) ban the introduction of U.S. combat forces into Central America without an explicit vote of approval by Congress. Kennedy pushed especially hard for the last amendment;[129] when it failed in a vote of seventy-two to twenty-three, he sought to put a positive face on the outcome: "There were only two Senators courageous enough to vote against the Gulf of Tonkin resolution. We did considerably better than that."[130]

The Reagan administration revived the issue of Contra aid in early 1985. Although Reagan had won a landslide victory over Walter Mondale the previous November, winning forty-nine of fifty states, the popular president's coattails were shorter than expected. The Republicans picked up fourteen seats in the House and lost two in the Senate, neither of which changed hands. Nevertheless, hard-liners in the administration encouraged Reagan to go all out over the issue of Contra aid. The vast, secret, illegal funding network of the National Security Council was only enough to keep the Contras in the field, not enough to topple the Sandinista government. Thus, in the spring of 1985, the administration sought the release of the $14 million in suspended aid set aside by the House-Senate compromise of 1984.[131]

Liberals in the House were determined to defeat even the most innocuous-sounding bill for fear that a conference committee compromise would restore military aid to the Contras. The liberals received encouragement from Speaker of the House Tip O'Neill, who had grown increasingly outspoken about his opposition to Contra aid. The previous year, O'Neill had denounced the Contras: "These people have been down there as murderers, marauders, and rapists.... What are we going to do? Reward them? What are they? Paid Hessians?"[132] Although the Senate voted fifty-three to forty-six to release the $14 million in "humanitarian" aid, the House kept the restrictions of the Boland amendment in place by preventing any such bill from passing.[133]

The tide seemed to be running against the administration, when it received help from an unexpected quarter. Just days after the votes that killed Contra aid in late April 1985, Daniel Ortega, the president of Nicaragua, embarked on an ill-timed journey to the Soviet Union. Reagan administration supporters pointed to the trip as proof of their claims that Nicaragua was moving into the communist bloc. Ortega's mission put opponents of Contra aid on the defensive. Commenting on the Nicaraguan president, O'Neill told a reporter, "He's embarrassed us, to be perfectly truthful." One of O'Neill's aides told another reporter, "We're in a damaging limiting situation."[134]

The Ortega trip opened up a floodgate of red-baiting. The White House communications director, Patrick Buchanan, declared, "The Speaker and the House Democrats, I think, have an obligation to tell the American people why they trusted the words of Nicaraguan communists over the President of the United States, why they put faith in the promises of a man who heads a regime that is admittedly Marxist-Leninist."[135] Although embarrassed by Ortega's action, O'Neill stood his ground in opposing Contra aid, insisting, "[Ortega's] visit to Moscow does not justify an American attempt to overthrow the government of Nicaragua. It does not justify aid to the Contras."[136]

Before the furor over Ortega's April trip to the Soviet Union died down, President Reagan issued an executive order imposing a U.S. economic embargo on Nicaragua. In response, O'Neill asserted that the United States "must stop acting like the elephant that reels in terror every time the mouse scoots across the floor."[137] Meanwhile, the embargo set off a massive wave of Pledge of Resistance protests and sit-ins across the country. Although the embargo sparked an explosion of activist protest and sharpened liberal opposition to Reagan's policies, however, the fallout from Ortega's trip had turned the tide, and the administration moved to have Congress reconsider Contra aid.

On June 1, 1985, O'Neill took to the airwaves to respond to President Reagan's Saturday morning radio address. He dedicated his radio time to two topics close to the hearts of left-leaning activists and liberal reformers: apartheid in South Africa and U.S. intervention in Central America. O'Neill blasted the president's policies in Central America as "a retread version of gunboat diplomacy" and declared that apartheid had become "a symbol of our policy in Africa." He called on the United States to stand "tall in support of the right of every nation to seek its own national destiny and the right of every people to choose their own form of government," and added, "Unfortunately in Central America and South Africa, our policies fall short of that standard. What we are doing contradicts what America stands for."[138]

Although O'Neill's radio address received a good deal of attention and stimulated a significant amount of commentary, it was not enough to defeat renewed Contra aid. In early June, the House of Representatives voted 232 to 196 against renewing the Boland amendment and passed a $27 million "nonlethal" aid bill identical to one that was passed by the Senate. Congressionally funded aid to the Contras, which the 1984 Boland amendment had cut for more than a year, began to flow once again. Because the aid was nonmilitary and could not be delivered through the CIA, O'Neill argued that he had won a partial victory. This view did not take into account the millions of dollars in illegal covert funds, which were now available for increased arms purchases. Moreover, the $27 million kept the Contra army in the field and held the door open to future U.S. military aid. The injection of aid was felt almost immediately as the Contra war against Nicaragua again intensified.[139]

The entire Massachusetts delegation—including Conte, who was one of only seven Republicans to buck the president—voted against nonlethal aid.[140] Shortly after the vote, Conte learned that the administration was closing the Agricultural Stabilization Office in Amherst and planned to relocate it to Providence, Rhode Island. Although the office—which served farmers in Massachusetts, Rhode Island, and Connecticut—employed only six people, its closing was a clear expression of Reagan's displeasure with the maverick Republican. In response to the slap on the wrist, Conte quipped, "Maybe they'll take my beekeeper's office away."[141]

Other members of the Massachusetts delegation were more serious in the wake of the vote. Senator Edward Kennedy believed that the embargo and the renewed Contra aid presaged a heightened commitment to the overthrow of Nicaragua that might well lead to a U.S. military invasion. In a speech before an audience from the American Stock Exchange, Kennedy warned, "In short, our present course is taking the United States toward unilateral intervention in Nicaragua—toward a war which, whether we like it or not, will inevitably involve American forces in combat... [an invasion that] would plunge us into the most unwanted, unnecessary and unjustified war in our history."[142]

Invoking memories of Vietnam, at home as well as abroad, Kennedy stated, "Domestically some of the greatest damage would be inflicted on our own society, which would be bitterly divided. Do we really want to relive an earlier decade of angry protest and the tragic days of Kent State?"[143] The embargo protests of the spring made this scenario credible, and by calling to mind Vietnam, Kennedy touched on a theme that permeated the debate over Central America throughout the 1980s.

THE LONG SHADOW OF THE VIETNAM WAR

Throughout the 1980s, the debates over Central America fluctuated between two poles that had come to delineate the boundaries of U.S. cold war foreign policy. The first was the lingering fear of "losing" a country to communism. As the Texas Democrat Jim Wright observed in 1985, "Nobody wants to be portrayed as friendly toward communism. That's been true for forty years."[144] Especially during the debates over El Salvador, few congressional critics of administration policy wished to risk the political backlash that would result if the country fell to the Marxist rebels because they had cut aid. This fear counterbalanced the distaste with which many liberal and moderate members of Congress viewed the repressive Salvadoran regime. Conte summed up the dilemma succinctly: "It's a Catch-22 situation. Congress doesn't want to see El Salvador go down, but they don't want to further the killings [through military aid] either.... There's no doubt about it, it's a very difficult, thorny issue."[145]

The other pole that shaped the debate was the Vietnam War, which had left deep and lasting scars in the national psyche but had impressed upon conservatives, liberals, and radicals in vastly different ways. For many conservatives, the lesson learned was that political leaders should not limit the military in its pursuit of victory. For those on the Right, the war in Vietnam was not so much won by the North Vietnamese and the Viet Cong as it was lost by the Americans. For many liberals, the lesson was to resist turning every regional conflict into an East-West showdown in which the United States overextends itself by committing its power, prestige, and the lives of its youth to preserving a corrupt and unpopular government. For the Left, the U.S. war in Vietnam was proof of the imperialist and militarist dynamics of U.S. foreign policy that could be stopped only through mass movements and ultimately through social change on our own shores.

Throughout the 1980s, the Vietnam War haunted the debates over Central America, with the comments of Reagan's critics replete with references to the Indochina war. Ted Kennedy invoked the specter of the Gulf of Tonkin resolution in 1984 and Kent State in 1985. In 1983 he echoed a phrase from the Vietnam War era when he charged, "The president's overall policy is a prescription for a wider war." When Dodd spoke of "unleashing the dogs of war," he meant to conjure up the image of U.S. troops sloshing through Central American jungles. Many liberals found themselves caught between the fear of "losing" a nearby nation to communism and the fear of failing to prevent another Vietnam War. Commenting on El Salvador in 1983, O'Neill stated, "There's a strong feeling around here that it's another Vietnam situation. . . . At the same time nobody wants to see that country go Marxist."[146]

Just as the fear of appearing soft on communism put opponents of Reagan's policies on the defensive, the Vietnam syndrome forced Reagan to deny repeatedly that it was headed in that direction. The administration went to great lengths to sidestep language that might conjure up the conflict in Southeast Asia. U.S. advisors, who had played a role in drawing the military deeper into the war in Vietnam, were referred to as "trainers" in El Salvador.[147] With the Vietnam War in mind, Congress capped the number of U.S. advisors in El Salvador at fifty-five. In response to the question of whether the administration was basing its policies in Central America on the "domino theory," Secretary of State Alexander Haig described Soviet designs in Central America instead as a "priority hit list."[148] For his part, Reagan maintained, "Let me say to those who invoke the memory of Vietnam: There is no thought of sending American combat troops to Central America."[149] Again he sought to move beyond the Vietnam syndrome in a 1984 speech at Georgetown University, when he criticized those in Congress who believed that the United States was "still in the troubled waters of Vietnam" whose reluctance to use force abroad had hamstrung U.S. policy. Alluding to the policies of the Carter years, Reagan declared, "We will not return to the days of hand-wringing, defeatism, decline and despair."[150]

Reagan's defensiveness over comparisons with Vietnam was well founded. Throughout the 1980s, opinion polls revealed the lingering impact of the Vietnam War on public opinion, with poll after poll showing opposition to Reagan's policies in Central America and fear that U.S. troops would end up there.[151] A 1984 *New York Times* poll showed that only one in three people supported Reagan's policies in Central America and that more than half feared that his policies would lead to the introduction of U.S. combat troops.[152] Polls also revealed that many Americans were not well informed about Central America and that opposition to administration policies increased as one became more informed. Edward R. Tufte, a Yale University public opinion expert, noted a major shift in public attitudes since the time of the Vietnam War. Whereas before Vietnam, "uninformed loyalty" was not uncommon with respect to foreign affairs, in the post–Vietnam War era "uninformed skepticism and informed hostility" were the rule.[153]

The solidarity movement appealed to these widespread public doubts. Although relatively few Americans shared the enthusiasm of the Left for the revolutionary forces of Central America, they shared their fear of U.S. military intervention. Among the slogans of the movement were "El Salvador is Spanish for Vietnam." Unlike the Vietnam War resistance, however, in which opposition grew slowly, the solidarity movement hoped to stop direct U.S. intervention before it began. In many ways, the Pledge of Resistance hoped to keep the threat of Vietnam War–era mass protest in reserve as a deterrent to a U.S. military invasion of Nicaragua or El Salvador.

In fact, the movement against U.S. intervention in Central America included many veterans of the Vietnam War.[154] Among them was Charles Clements, a U.S. Air Force pilot during the war in Vietnam who, after becoming a Quaker and a physician, went into Salvadoran rebel "zones of control" to treat victims of the war. Clements, who documented his experiences in El Salvador in his book *Witness to War*, was a frequent witness at congressional hearings.[155] Another veteran, S. Brian Willson, was a guard at a U.S. Air Force base during the Vietnam War. In the 1980s he received a special commendation from Governor Michael Dukakis for his work with veterans in Massachusetts. After becoming active in the solidarity movement, he went to Nicaragua. In 1987 he and three other veterans attempted to block a naval troop train carrying weapons bound for El Salvador. When the engineer refused to stop the train, he lost both of his legs.[156]

In June 1985, when Congress voted for $27 million in "nonlethal" aid to the Contras, six Vietnam veterans—apparently unaware of Senator John Kerry's strong opposition to Contra aid—occupied his Boston office. When he learned of the occupation, Kerry, a fellow veteran, placed a call from Washington to his office in the Boston Federal Building and spoke with the protestors for more than an hour. According to Jim Packer, a forty-one-year-old participant, "We spoke to Kerry in a conference call and ... realized that many of our goals are similar. ... We agreed to leave peaceably at 11 p.m." Packer explained to a reporter, "We are not connected with the Pledge of Resistance. ... The idea was that we were upset at the Senate vote and what we see as an escalation toward war in Central America. We did this as a protest against the Senate vote and the road to war. ... We've had the experience and we don't want another generation of vets."[157]

THE VIETNAM WAR VETERAN: SENATOR JOHN F. KERRY

John Forbes Kerry was born to a career diplomat father and a blue-blooded mother. His mother hailed from the Forbes family, one of the most prestigious and elite in Boston, and Kerry grew up in affluence. Like many of his generation, Kerry was inspired by President John F. Kennedy in the early 1960s, and he took great pride in the fact that the two shared a first name and middle initial. Educated first at St. Paul's School, Kerry began to speak out against the Vietnam War in debates while he was a student at Yale University. After graduation, when Kerry learned that he was to be drafted, he enlisted in the navy to avoid combat as an army infantryman. Because he enlisted at a time when the use of patrol boats, or "swift boats," was being expanded in the rivers of South Vietnam, however, he soon found himself in command of a patrol boat on the Mekong Delta. The young lieutenant was wounded in fierce combat in February 1969 and went on to receive three Purple Hearts, a Bronze Star, and a Silver Star during his tour of duty.[158]

In January 1970 Kerry received an early discharge in order to run for Congress. The Massachusetts Fourth District seat was held by a prowar Democrat, who Kerry (who had always harbored political ambitions) hoped to unseat by running as an antiwar candidate. When Father Robert Drinan of Boston College, an antiwar activist, decided to run, however, Kerry joined Father Drinan's campaign, which went on to win the seat.[159]

In 1970 Kerry joined the fast-growing group Vietnam Veterans against the War (VVAW). Kerry's outstanding oratorical abilities, his political connections, and his skill as a fund-raiser resulted in his meteoric rise in the organization. He appeared on the *Dick Cavett Show* and on *Meet the Press*, where he criticized the war and the treatment of veterans under Richard Nixon's administration.[160] Kerry became a leader of the liberal wing of VVAW, which sought a single-issue focus on opposing the war by working within the system. Meanwhile, the smaller, revolutionary wing of VVAW, which believed that only sweeping social change could end this war and prevent another, pushed for more confrontational tactics.[161]

During the April 1971 VVAW protests in Washington, D.C., the young veteran rose to national prominence. At the last minute, William Fulbright, chairman of the House Foreign Relations Committee, asked Kerry to appear as a witness at its hearings. Speaking passionately and eloquently against the war, Kerry asked the senators, "How do you ask a man to be the last to die in Vietnam? How do you ask a man to be the last one to die for a mistake?"[162] After his testimony, Kerry put his name to a compilation of stories by VVAW members titled *The New Soldier*,[163] but within a year he had left the organization. To his VVAW supporters, Kerry had helped establish the national reputation of the group, conferring upon it a mainstream respectability with his moving Senate testimony and his many speeches.[164] To his critics, Kerry was merely using VVAW as a launching pad for a political career. One radical VVAW critic commented, "He came, he saw, he conquered, and he split."[165]

In 1972, an election year that saw McGovern win Massachusetts and Studds ride an antiwar message to victory, Kerry ran for Congress and lost. Throughout much of the 1970s, Kerry worked quietly as a district attorney in Middlesex County, Massachusetts. Then, in 1982, Dukakis tapped the Vietnam veteran as lieutenant governor in his second run for the governorship.[166] In 1984 Kerry ran for the Senate seat vacated by the popular centrist Democrat Paul Tsongas. His Republican opponent was the conservative businessman Raymond Shamie, who positioned himself as an ideological twin to Ronald Reagan. The race was contentious, and Kerry fared better than expected. In a national election that witnessed the landslide reelection of Reagan, Kerry won 56 percent to 44 percent.[167]

Kerry quickly took up the issue of Central America, frequently invoking the lessons of Vietnam: "One of the greatest errors of Vietnam was our inability to read history. We were unwilling to look at the long-term process that was playing itself out between North and South and among Vietnam, Cambodia, Laos, and other areas. Today, in the same way, we are not looking at the history of American involvement in Central America as well as the aspirations of the indigenous population."[168]

In his first months as a U.S. senator, Kerry focused on opposing aid to the Contras. He worked to cultivate ties to the Massachusetts solidarity movement by having one of his aides, Richard Bell, read statements of support to solidarity protestors (including the building occupiers) during the spring embargo protests. Kerry voted twice against "nonlethal" aid, and in April 1985 he went on a peace mission to Managua with the Democratic freshman senator from Iowa, Tom Harkin. The senators met personally with the Nicaraguan president, Daniel Ortega, who asked Harkin and Kerry to bring back a ceasefire proposal in exchange for bilateral talks with the United States and an end to U.S. funding of the Contras. The State Department denounced the proposal as propaganda and demanded that the Sandinista government open direct talks with the Contras (whom the Sandinistas regarded as U.S. puppets). Harkin, for years one of the most outspoken critics of Reagan's Central American policies, commented, "It became clear that they [members of the Nicaraguan government] desire peace and not only normal but friendly relations with the United States."[169]

Kerry's foray into international peacemaking was a bold move so early in his career as a U.S. senator. The Reagan administration denounced Kerry and Harkin as tools of Sandinista propaganda, Senator Barry Goldwater accused them of breaking the law, and conservatives from the far Right decried them as traitors. Still, Kerry remained unruffled. When a reporter for the Valley Advocate asked him whether the administration was more interested in a military solution than in negotiations, Kerry answered, "That's exactly why they reacted the way they did. It's a case of if you don't like the message, kill the messenger. We put them in a very embarrassing position because we exposed their policy.... We wanted to stop the killing, to bring about some stabilization."[170] When he returned from Nicaragua, Kerry declared, "We are treating the nations of Latin America as our Eastern Europe. Pluralism of views in our hemisphere apparently has no place in this administration's policies, just as pluralism in the Eastern Bloc is not allowed by the Soviets."[171] In May 1985 Kerry denounced the embargo, stating, "This unilateral display of arrogance is unpardonable.... The action will only weaken our position in the hemisphere. We are undermining the very hemispheric institutions which are so vital to our ability to marshal solidarity in the face of any real threat of Soviet intrusion into our sphere of influence."[172] Despite Kerry's arduous efforts, Congress voted for $27 million in nonlethal aid.

In the spring of 1986, Contra aid again came before Congress. This time, the Reagan administration hoped to take advantage of the growing congressional hostility toward the Sandinistas (who had taken increasingly repressive measures in response to the escalating war) to push for $100 million in lethal aid. Toward this end, the administration employed new levels of red-baiting and the president feverishly lobbied a handful of centrist Democrats and Republicans. Meanwhile, Tip O'Neill had recently announced his retirement at the end of the year and had made clear his wish to see as part of his legacy an end to the Contra war. Democrats rallied to "win one for the Tipper" in what many in the press billed as a final showdown between the president and the Speaker of the House. In the first test of strength, O'Neill prevailed, with the House narrowly defeating the Contra aid bill by a vote of 222 to 210.[173]

Shortly thereafter, the Sandinista army followed the Contras several miles into Honduras, as it had on several previous occasions. This time, however, the Reagan administration magnified the incident to the level of an invasion and in the ensuing hysteria managed to turn enough swing votes to procure House passage of Contra aid by a vote of 221 to 209. The fate of the Contras now fell to the Republican-controlled Senate, where the energetic newcomers Kerry and Harkin launched a filibuster soon joined by Ted Kennedy and others. Fearing that they would be tarred as obstructionists, however, some liberal senators worked to end the filibuster and focus on winning back the Senate in 1986.[174]

Kerry's crusade against the Contras was not limited to his 1985 visit to Managua and his 1986 filibuster. In the spring of 1986, Kerry urged the Republican chairman of the Foreign Affairs Committee, Richard Lugar, to allow him to conduct hearings to investigate allegations of Contra drug smuggling and gunrunning. According to Richard McColl, a Kerry aide who stated that the staff had found "no smoking gun," there were nevertheless "enough people telling the same story" to warrant hearings.[175] Arguing that the best way to eliminate any Contra corruption was to make sure the Contras were fully funded, Lugar continued to deny Kerry the hearings.[176]

Continuing their research, Kerry and his staff stumbled on a secret arms supply network; at the end of 1986, the scope of the network became apparent when a Lebanese newspaper broke the news of a vast covert operation being run out of the National Security Council in which missiles were being sold to Iran in exchange for promises of the release of U.S. hostages, with the profits from the sales then diverted to the Contras. Further evidence had emerged in October 1986 when a military cargo plane shot down by the Nicaraguan military was discovered to have a cargo of arms and boots. These illicit operations had grown in direct response to the 1984 Boland amendment cutoff of Contra aid.

In late 1986, under public pressure, Attorney General Edmund Meese appointed Lawrence E. Walsh as independent prosecutor to investigate the illegal arms sales to Iran and the diversion of profits to the Contras. In 1987, when the House and Senate set up a joint Iran-Contra Committee, Oliver North, Robert McFarland, Richard Secord, and John Poindexter became household names as members of Congress investigated the scope of the operations and the extent of the president's involvement. Although much of the public embraced North as a hero during his televised testimony before the committee, the popularity of the marine did not extend to support for Reagan's Contra policies. As the extent of high-level involvement within the administration became evident, Reagan's poll ratings reached all-time lows.[177]

The Iran-Contra scandal and the 1986 elections, which turned the Senate over to Democratic control, opened the door for Kerry to pursue his allegations of Contra drug smuggling. In the spring of 1988, Kerry began holding several weeks of one-man hearings on the Senate Foreign Relations Subcommittee on Terrorism, Narcotics, and International Operations. The committee interviewed numerous witnesses and took video-recorded affidavits from people in Central America. Richard J. Brenneke, an arms smuggler, told Kerry that he had been approached by Israeli Mossad agents to coordinate a drug smuggling and gun-running scheme with the Medellin cartel in Colombia and with the Panamanian dictator, Manuel Noriega. According to Brenneke, the Israelis assured him that Vice President George H. W. Bush's national security advisor, Donald Gregg—who, they claimed, was coordinating the efforts to arm the Contras—had full knowledge of the plan.

Brenneke's testimony was corroborated by the former Panamanian consul José Blandon, who described drug-laden planes owned by the Medellin cartel receiving safe transit from Noriega in Panama in return for kickbacks and promises of better relations with Washington. Blandon claimed that he had secret information that "could affect the [1988] elections of the United States."[178] The drug smugglers Michael Palmer, George Morales, and Gary Betzner told the Kerry committee that they would regularly refuel at Contra camps in Costa Rica. Morales and Betzner claimed that they took drugs out of Colombia and returned with arms, which they delivered to the southern Contras by landing at the private airstrip of the rancher John Hull, a U.S. citizen with well-known ties to the CIA. The convicted Medellin cartel money launderer Ramón Milian Rodriguez testified that he had delivered approximately $10 million to the Contras.[179]

Kerry's hearings were rife with problems. First, the majority of his testimony came from crime figures, most of whom were convicts, and despite the similarities in their stories, there was no smoking gun to prove the sensational charges. Second, since the hearings were public, Kerry could not divulge classified information that might have been in his possession. As one aide told *The Nation*, "The issue is how Kerry can get the maximum amount of information out without generating a political reaction that will cause everything to end up with the Intelligence Committee and closed hearings."[180] Kerry had to abandon many leads that led to classified CIA fronts and assets. He had gone out on a limb. To be sure, a number of the allegations made at the hearings had first appeared in the press, and some reporters continued to follow up on charges made at the hearings. Most members of Congress, however, kept Kerry's investigation at arm's length. Despite Kerry's efforts to avoid a partisan image, in an election year, the hearings carried that risk. Some of the allegations that emerged led to the office of Vice President Bush, then the front-runner in the race for the Republican nomination for president. No one stood to gain more from such allegations than the man who had made Kerry his running mate in 1982, the front-runner in the Democratic race for president, the governor of Massachusetts, Michael Dukakis.

THE PRESIDENTIAL CANDIDATE: MICHAEL S. DUKAKIS

After generating a stir in the spring of 1988, Kerry's hearings quietly wound down. As the 1988 presidential campaign took on momentum, however, suspicions of inappropriate ties between the Republican nominee, George H. W. Bush, and the Panamanian strongman Manuel Noriega continued to surface. The issue of Central America remained in the headlines, but Reagan's drive to topple the Sandinistas had suffered a serious setback with the Iran-Contra affair. Furthermore, a peace proposal made by the Costa Rican president, Oscar Arias, had grown into a peace process known as Esquipulas, in which Guatemala, Nicaragua, El Salvador, Honduras, and Costa Rica agreed to work toward regional stability and internal reconciliation. In 1987 Congress vastly reduced Contra aid and limited appropriation to lists of nonlethal items. In 1988 Congress failed to pass even a modest proposal for humanitarian aid, and the Contras began peace talks with the Sandinistas, who wished to put the war behind them to try to revive the ailing Nicaraguan economy in anticipation of the 1990 elections required by Esquipulas.[181]

Michael Dukakis succeeded in winning the 1988 Democratic nomination in a race against several prominent Democrats, including Senator Al Gore, Jr., of Tennessee; State Representative Richard Gephardt of Missouri; and the Reverend Jesse Jackson (who campaigned against Dukakis from the Left and proved to be his most serious challenger). Dukakis portrayed himself as a good government progressive and a skilled technocrat rather than a traditional liberal. In many ways, this was an accurate description. As governor, between 1973 and 1979, Dukakis had rooted out a good deal of corruption but had infuriated old school liberals, who accused him of balancing the budget on the backs of low-income people through draconian welfare cuts. In his second term, he softened his image but made his name nationally through the success of modest job training programs for the unemployed and a program that increased the collection of delinquent taxes. His image as a skillful economic administrator benefited from a high-tech boom, especially around the Route 128 corridor near Boston, that helped fuel his much ballyhooed "Massachusetts Miracle."[182]

It was in other areas, however, that Dukakis earned his reputation as a liberal, virtually all of which—including his opposition to the Seabrook Nuclear Power Station and his support of a nuclear weapons freeze—were the focus of grassroots activism in the 1970s and 1980s. During the 1988 campaign, the area in which Dukakis stood closest to his past liberalism was Central America. His opposition to Reagan's policies in Central America, which had grown out of personal experience and was reinforced by the solidarity activism that flourished in the Bay State during the 1980s, was strongly and deeply rooted.

Much of Dukakis's outlook on politics had been shaped during his student years at Swarthmore College in Pennsylvania in the early 1950s. The Quaker college was an oasis of liberalism, pacifism, and tolerance during the age of McCarthyism. Dukakis generally gravitated toward good government politicians such as Adlai Stevenson, but a trip to Latin America in 1954 moved his views on U.S. foreign policy considerably toward the Left. After receiving a summer fellowship to study at the University of San Marcos in Peru, Dukakis found himself in a hotbed of politics. As Dukakis recalled, "It just so happens that 1954 was the year the United States government overthrew the popularly-elected government in Guatemala."[183]

Dukakis watched the overthrow of Jacobo Arbenz from a very different vantage point than those who resided in the United States, many of whom were influenced by the anticommunist fulminations of Secretary of State John Foster Dulles and the publicity campaign of the United Fruit Company. According to Dukakis, "Everyone in Latin America knew that the United States was in the process of overthrowing the democratically-elected government of Guatemala."[184] During his presidential campaign, Dukakis discussed this formative experience on various occasions. In a speech titled "Building a New Partnership for the Americas" at the City Club of Chicago, Dukakis recounted:

> During the summer of 1954, I had the opportunity to live with a wonderful family in Lima, Peru.... [I]t's where I first confronted the inconsistencies in our policies towards our neighbors to the south. For it was in 1954 that the United States government, operating right out of the Embassy in Guatemala City, engineered the overthrow of the democratically-elected government of Guatemala.... The result of the U.S.-directed military coup in Guatemala was thirty years of the most brutal repression any country in this hemisphere has ever endured. In this century, the United States has mounted nineteen major military expeditions to Latin America.... And we helped overthrow a democratically-elected government... in Chile in 1973. Every time, we did so in the name of democracy and freedom. And almost without exception, the legacy of our intervention has been tyranny, not freedom.[185]

In the 1980s, Dukakis was not persuaded in the least by the Reagan administration argument that Soviet subversion was the main source of unrest and revolution in Central America. In fact, Dukakis believed that what he described as Reagan's "trigger-happy, reach-for-your gun, communist-under-every-bed ideology" would lead the United States to war,[186] and he condemned Reagan's Contra policy as "illegal and immoral."[187] He denounced the Contras as "thugs and mercenaries," and he charged, "Our tax dollars [have been] used to blow up health clinics and farm cooperatives."[188] Dukakis argued that the United States would achieve its objectives "not by overthrowing governments we don't happen to agree with, not by cozying up to Latin American dictators as we have so often done over the past century, but by demonstrating every day... the powerful force of our ideals."[189]

As governor, Dukakis expressed his opposition to U.S. policy in the region directly to the Reagan administration. In 1985, amid the Nicaraguan embargo crisis, Dukakis wrote to Jayne Plank, Reagan's director of intergovernmental affairs, "I believe that what the Administration is trying to do in Nicaragua is both morally and legally indefensible and I think you and the President are entitled to know why." He drew attention to the 1947 Rio Treaty: "The Rio Treaty was not an insignificant event. Coming after decades of U.S. interventionism... it was a major event in the history of U.S.-Latin American relations." He pointed out that Article 18 of the Organization of American States prohibited the use of armed force to intervene in the internal affairs of member states, adding, "The language of Article 18 is clear and unequivocal. It does not say that it can be waived when we don't like the government of a particular Latin American nation. It does not say that it applies in the case of a right-wing dictatorship, but has no effect if the dictatorship is of the left." He denounced the interventions in Guatemala and Chile, declaring, "Today, Guatemala has one of the most repressive regimes in the hemisphere—one, I might add, so brutal that it makes Sandinista violations of civil liberties look like a Sunday School picnic by comparison." He concluded, "I hope the Administration will abandon this foolhardy and lawless course. I hope it will consider seriously the proposals for peace with which Senators Harkin and Kerry returned from Nicaragua."[190] Dukakis sent copies of the letter to President Reagan, Secretary of State Schultz, and each member of the Massachusetts congressional delegation.

By early 1986, Dukakis was confronting an issue faced by a growing number of governors: whether to send his state National Guard to Honduras to take part in military exercises. The Defense Department argued that the exercises were held to acclimate National Guard troops to an environment in which they might one day have to do combat; however, many critics of administration policy argued that the deployment of the National Guard was part of an ongoing campaign to intimidate the Sandinistas and that much of its work in Honduras consisted of building roads near the Nicaraguan border that might be used for a U.S. invasion. Dukakis asked his staff to look into legal grounds for refusing to comply with the federal order. An aide reported to the governor that "except in time of war or national emergency, a member of the National Guard may not be ordered to active duty without the consent of the Governor."[191] The memorandum pointed out that for the president to federalize the National Guard of any state, one of three conditions had to be met: (1) an invasion or danger of invasion by a foreign nation, (2) rebellion or danger of rebellion against the government of the United States, or (3) the inability of the president to execute the laws of the United States with regular forces.[192]

Dukakis and several other governors, including Bruce Babbitt of Arizona and Joseph E. Brennan of Maine, decried what they saw as an "unwarranted politicization of the National Guard."[193] In 1986 Dukakis decided to refuse to send the Massachusetts National Guard to Honduras. A Dukakis spokesperson stated, "These are citizen-soldiers, and they ought not to be placed into a potentially dangerous situation on allegedly friendly training exercises. . . . If the U.S. wants to send troops into Central America, that ought to be something that the president asks the Congress and the Congress debates and votes on. . . . Barring that, I don't think there ought to be this subterfuge of sending Guard units down from the various states."[194]

In late 1986, Congress passed an amendment by the Mississippi Democrat G. V. Montgomery, which held that governors could not withhold troops from exercises except in the case of an emergency in the state. Taking on a federal-versus-states-rights dimension, the National Guard dispute created tension between state governors and Congress. The 1986 National Governors' Association meeting adopted a resolution that reaffirmed their right to control their own National Guard training in peacetime.[195] The Democratic governor of Minnesota, Rudy Perpich, then determined to challenge the new law in court, arguing that although the federal government could call out the militia, the training of the National Guard was still vested in the states. Massachusetts, Maine, Arkansas, Colorado, Delaware, Hawaii, Kansas, Ohio, Rhode Island, Vermont, and Iowa joined Minnesota in its suit. When a U.S. District Court upheld the Montgomery amendment, Dukakis appealed the decision, declaring, "Today's decision is unfortunate but it is not the end of the battle to reaffirm the right of each governor to be responsible for the training of his or her state militia in peacetime."[196] He added, "The Reagan Administration is using National Guard training in Central America as part of an ill-advised and illegal strategy to overthrow the Nicaraguan government."[197] Dukakis and other governors lost the appeal. In the summer of 1987, Federal District Court Judge Donald Alsop ruled that states had no right to withhold the National Guard and that Congress could exercise authority over state National Guards, including training, as part of the federal reserve system.[198] The governors had lost their case, but government resistance to Reagan's Central American policies, which had begun with sanctuary laws passed in various cities had now reached a state level.

When Dukakis announced his intention to run for president, he was better known nationally for his innovative economic policies as governor than for his stands on nuclear power, the arms race, or U.S. intervention in Central America. Nevertheless, his liberal positions on these issues helped him in the primaries, with his stand on Central America appealing especially to activist elements in the party. At Marquette University, Dukakis proclaimed, "I want to build a Central America that is free from civil wars and secret wars...where our energy and our resources are devoted to building and educating and investing, not killing and sabotaging and tearing down."[199] Dukakis quickly became the Democratic front-runner.

By early summer in 1988, every contender except Jesse Jackson had dropped out of the race. On July 20, 1988, Governor Bill Clinton of Arkansas nominated Dukakis for president at the Democratic National Convention in Atlanta. Even though Jackson had no chance of winning the nomination, William Winpisinger, head of the International Association of Machinists, nominated the civil rights veteran for president.[200] For many social activists on the Left, Jackson was the Democrat who most embodied their ideals. Throughout the 1980s, Jackson's Rainbow Coalition worked to build bridges between the civil rights and minority empowerment movements and the predominantly white environmental and peace movements.[201] In 1988 Jackson called for an end to U.S. intervention in the Third World and a five-year freeze on military spending.[202]

Dukakis, by contrast, moved toward the center of the foreign policy spectrum. The governor continued to oppose numerous weapons systems and called for deep cuts in the Reagan administration Strategic Defense Initiative (SDI) program (Star Wars); however, Dukakis surrounded himself with "defense Democrats" such as Madeleine Albright and Joseph Nye, endorsed the D-5 Trident missile and the Stealth and B-1 bombers, and called for an expansion of conventional forces.[203] In a speech in Dallas, Texas, titled "Building a Strong Conventional Defense," Dukakis sought to synthesize his advocacy of a strong conventional defense with his opposition to the nuclear arms race: "We know if it is necessary to use military force, it will almost certainly be our conventional forces, rather than our nuclear forces that will be tested.... We need a strong nuclear deterrent. We have a strong nuclear deterrent. But we also need strong conventional forces if we are serious about reducing the risk of nuclear war."[204]

With respect to Central America, however, Dukakis rarely distanced himself from his positions, weaving references to the issue throughout his campaign speeches. Early in his acceptance speech in Atlanta, the Democratic nominee proclaimed, "It's time to understand that the greatest threat to our national security in this hemisphere is not the Sandinistas—it's the avalanche of drugs that is pouring into this country and poisoning our kids ... [b]ecause this election is not about ideology. It's about competence. It's not about overthrowing governments in Central America; it's about creating jobs in middle America."[205]

When it came to choosing a running mate, Dukakis followed a traditional ideological and geographical ticket-balancing strategy, naming the moderate Texas senator Lloyd Bentsen. On several issues, most notably Central America, there was a large ideological chasm between the two. Bentsen had called the Sandinistas "violent revolutionaries ... dedicated to spreading their brand of communism anywhere they can reach."[206] The Republican ticket candidates, George H. W. Bush and the Indiana congressman Dan Quayle, sought to accentuate the difference between the Democratic running mates, but the effort was somewhat encumbered as a result of their advisors' counsel to downplay the unpopular issue of Contra aid.[207]

The 1988 presidential campaign was one of the most negative in recent memory. Bush's campaign manager, Lee Atwater, undertook an aggressive strategy to paint Dukakis as a card carrying member of the ACLU [American Civil Liberties Union] who had furloughed the black rapist Willie Horton, had banned the Pledge of Allegiance, and was weak on the issue of defense.[208] Fully anticipating the Bush campaign strategy, the Dukakis's staff scoured the previous three decades of *Boston Globe* articles in search of anything that could be used against the Massachusetts governor. In one memorandum, an aide wrote, "Terry Bergman told us that our aim should be to uncover or shed new light on incidents in Michael Dukakis's career that might help members of the Bush campaign typecast the governor as a radical liberal, as she believed they would."[209] The staff member who covered the early 1970s reported "very little . . . about the future governor, and certainly nothing that could be cited as support for the view that Dukakis is a dangerous left-leaning radical."[210]

Still, the Dukakis campaign expected trouble when it came to the governor's second term and the issue of Central America. Staffers put together charges anticipated and proposed responses. The practice charges pulled no punches:

CHARGE: Mike Dukakis's collection of leftist causes includes American groups like CISPES, which has openly endorsed the Salvadoran guerrillas' agenda, and even a Salvadoran labor union almost certainly tied to the guerrillas. RESPONSE: Mike Dukakis has always made a point of talking with many different groups and organizations to get a thorough view of any issue. These groups were among the organizations involved in Latin American policy in Massachusetts. . . . In no case has there been illegal activity. The same cannot be said of Vice-President Bush, whose government paid out $200,000 to a drug-smuggling Panamanian dictator.[211]

The Bush campaign generally sought to distance itself somewhat from the position of the current administration on Central America. Lawrence Walsh had not directly implicated the vice president in the Iran-Contra affair, but leads had indicated that Bush might have been more involved than he claimed.[212] The Bush campaign challenges of Dukakis's Central American policies were half-hearted at best. Americans were fatigued by a decade of proxy war in Central America that had shown few results and had led to the biggest political scandal since Watergate.

The race between Bush and Dukakis came to hinge far more on symbolism than on issues. Dukakis's failure to counter aggressively the Bush campaign attacks left its mark. His continued insistence that the campaign was about competence rather than ideology alienated the Democratic Party base and left uncommitted voters cold. Dukakis acquitted himself well in the debates, but his technocratic demeanor came across as aloof and distant to an electorate accustomed to the charisma of Reagan.

Just as the 1984 Mondale campaign marked the demise of the old blue-collar New Deal liberalism, many saw the ill-fated Dukakis 1988 campaign as the last hurrah of post-1960s Massachusetts liberalism. By 1988, the moniker "liberal" had become stigmatized. After 1988 the conservative, South-based wing of the party led by Al From's Democratic Leadership Council increasingly took control of the Democratic Party. In 1992 the self-proclaimed New Democrat Bill Clinton took back the White House for the Democrats for the first time in twelve years.

If Dukakis tried to distance himself from the liberal label during the campaign, however, Bush similarly tried to distance himself from the zealous ideological conservatism of his predecessor. By 1988, the "Reagan revolution" had run out of steam. As early as 1986, ideological conservatives in the Republican Party grumbled as Reagan undertook serious arms control negotiations with Mikhail Gorbachev. It was the Iran-Contra affair, however, that gave the coup de grâce to the rightward thrust of the Reagan years.

Popular use of the term "Contragate" conjured up memories of Watergate. Both Watergate and the Iran-Contra affair ultimately came down to a clash between the imperial presidency and a left-liberal opposition movement. Just as the illegal wiretaps that grew into Watergate began with Nixon's desire to conceal illegal U.S. military incursions into Cambodia in the face of a powerful antiwar movement, the illegal arms sales to Iran and the money transfers to the Contras grew out of the impact of the solidarity movement on Congress, which had resulted in the Boland amendment. Like the Nixon administration, the Reagan administration witnessed the conviction of its officials—John Poindexter, Robert McFarland, Oliver North, and Defense Secretary Caspar Weinberger, to name a few—for illegal activity, including deceiving Congress.

As one of his final acts as president, Bush pardoned every convicted and accused conspirator in the Iran-Contra affair.[213]

CONCLUSION

THE END OF A DECADE

In 1989 Alfredo Cristiani of the National Republican Alliance (Alianza Republicana Nacionalista [ARENA]) party in El Salvador assumed the presidency. During the election, Cristiani had tried to distance the ARENA party image from association with Roberto D'Aubuisson and the death squads. While Cristiani's efforts earned growing U.S. congressional support for the Salvadoran government, solidarity activists charged that the democratic makeover of the ARENA party merely masked its death squad apparatus. In Boston, solidarity activists targeted Senator John Kerry for his recent support of military aid for the Cristiani government. On May 31, accompanied by a small group of solidarity activists, Rebecca Pierce—a forty-five-year-old mother, rock climber, and member of the Boston Committee in Solidarity with the People of El Salvador (CISPES)—surreptitiously made her way toward Senator Kerry's regional office on the eighth floor of the State Transportation Building. As her associates distracted security, Pierce used ropes and hooks from her rock climbing gear to step off the indoor balcony overlooking the plaza and fasten and then unfurl a twenty-five-foot banner that read, "Senator Kerry, Stop Funding Death Squads in El Salvador." As she swung, suspended above the plaza, Pierce tossed fliers to the gathering crowd of some two thousand onlookers below. Within an hour, police and firefighters had hooked Pierce, pulled her onto the balcony, and placed her under arrest.[1]

According to Mike Prokosch—the Boston-based regional director of CISPES, who helped run interference for Pierce—members of Senator Kerry's staff attempted to make contact with Pierce during the action. For Kerry—who had cultivated an image as a steadfast opponent of Republican policy in Central America throughout the 1980s, especially in Nicaragua—Pierce's protest was a source of embarrassment. Activists who had accused Kerry of inconsistency over the years focused on his recent vote for Salvadoran military aid to illustrate the charge. Kerry responded to Pierce's protest by commenting, "I appreciate the woman's concern and I'm very sensitive to the passion she and others display on this issue. We are working on a policy that will hold all sides accountable."[2] In retrospect, as Prokosch sees it, Kerry's waffling on military aid to El Salvador obscured his more positive work on Central American issues. "I am sympathetic to Kerry for his work on Nicaragua," he reflected. "He stuck his neck out and should have gotten more credit than he did."[3]

The 1980s ended in El Salvador almost exactly as the decade had begun. In November 1989 the Farabundo Martí National Liberation Front (Frente Farabundo Martí para la Liberación Nacional [FMLN]) launched a massive Final Offensive and, for the first time since early 1981, held several large sectors of San Salvador. The offensive revealed more support for the Marxist rebels in the capital than the United States or the Salvadoran government had expected but not enough, as the rebels had hoped, to spark an uprising that would topple the government. The Salvadoran military extricated the FMLN from their positions in the city by means of massive and indiscriminate artillery barrages that caused widespread casualties among the civilian population.[4]

The offensive also triggered a paroxysm of death squad killings, which had leveled off since 1984. During the offensive, the world learned that at the University of Central America on the outskirts of San Salvador, six Jesuit priests, their cook, and the cook's fifteen-year-old daughter had been murdered. They had been pulled from their beds, shot execution style, and their brains had been removed from their skulls and displayed on the grounds outside their dormitory. The Jesuits had openly sympathized with the impoverished population, had embraced liberation theology, and had worked to promote a negotiated end to the war. President Cristiani responded by implying that the killings were the work of the leftist rebels, who sought to discredit the government. William Walker, the U.S. ambassador, gave credit to the insinuations.[5]

The murders propelled one final Massachusetts congressman to the fore on the subject of Central America. Tom Foley, the Democratic Speaker of the House from the state of Washington, appointed a Special Task Force on El Salvador to investigate the killings, with State Representative Joe Moakley as chairman. Moakley represented the Catholic, working-class district of South Boston.[6] Although throughout the 1980s he had kept a low profile on foreign affairs, Moakley now played a key role in helping to end the decade-long civil war in El Salvador.[7]

Moakley, who had known two of the murdered Jesuit priests personally, set out on his investigation with a zeal that was fueled by his Catholic faith. "Up until their murders, I never personally knew anyone who was killed in El Salvador," he stated. "Because they were friends, I am especially outraged at the brutal nature of their deaths. I grieve for them."[8] Moakley's Task Force proceeded to visit El Salvador, interview witnesses, and face obstruction by the Salvadoran government and a reluctance to cooperate on the part of the U.S. Embassy. All evidence pointed toward Colonel Guillermo Alfredo Benavides. In May, Moakley denounced what he described as a cover-up by the Salvadoran military and declared that the investigation was at a "virtual standstill." On South Boston streets, constituents yelled their support to Moakley: "Don't let those guys murder priests and get away with it!"; "Get the Jesuit killers!" Moakley told a *New York Times* reporter, "It used to be there wasn't half a vote in the El Salvador issue. Then they killed the Jesuits."[9]

As the investigation reached an impasse, Moakley enlisted the aid of Christopher Dodd (the Democrat from Connecticut) and Patrick Leahy (the Democrat from Vermont) to cut military aid to El Salvador by 50 percent. In an effort to promote negotiations, the Dodd-Leahy bill required the elimination of the remaining military aid if the Salvadoran government refused to negotiate and the restoration of the eliminated aid if the FMLN launched an offensive. Moakley took to the floor of the House, proclaiming, "Enough is enough. The time to act has come. They killed six priests in cold blood. I stood on the ground where my friends were blown away by men to whom the sanctity of human life bears no meaning."[10] To the astonishment of the Salvadoran military, the House voted 250 to 163 in support of the Dodd-Leahy bill. After the vote, Moakley commented, "You know what really bothers me? If some Speaker had organized a task force when Archbishop [Oscar] Romero was killed to challenge the administration, the aid could have been cut a long time ago."[11]

In 1991 the Cristiani government and the FMLN began negotiations under the auspices of the United Nations. As the cold war drew to a close, pressure by Congress on the Salvadoran military and pressure by Latin American governments on the rebels kept the negotiations moving. In early 1992 a peace accord was signed. The Salvadoran military would be cut in half and purged of human rights violators. The FMLN would be disarmed under U.N. supervision and integrated into the Salvadoran police force. An appointed U.N. Commission on the Truth for El Salvador would investigate atrocities that had occurred during the decade of civil war. In early 1992 a Salvadoran court convicted two officers for the murder of the Jesuit priests, their cook, and the cook's daughter. Colonel Benavides was convicted of issuing the command for the murders. The convicted officers were sentenced to thirty years in prison. Seven other officers who were suspected of involvement were acquitted. The convictions marked the end of the era of military impunity in El Salvador.[12]

The negotiated settlement in El Salvador brought to a close one of the darkest chapters of the final decade of the cold war. The report by the U.N. Commission on the Truth for El Salvador, "From Madness to Hope: The Twelve-Year War in El Salvador," documented the savage atrocities and estimated that more than seventy-five thousand Salvadorans, mostly civilians, had died in the conflict.[13] More than thirty thousand Nicaraguans had died during the Contra war sponsored by the United States. Tens of thousands of people had died in Guatemala.[14] By keeping alive the fears of a Vietnam War–like conflict and the civil unrest that would result at home, the solidarity movement had helped to prevent full-scale U.S invasions of El Salvador and Nicaragua.

The Massachusetts congressional delegation had mounted the strongest of any state delegation opposition to the policies of the Reagan administration in Central America. Constrained by the Vietnam syndrome allegations, the Reagan administration pursued a policy of proxy and low-intensity warfare. The Sandinistas survived the Contra war, but—with the help of massive covert U.S. financial support for their political opposition—they went down in narrow defeat in the 1990 elections. In the end, the United States failed to achieve its sought-after military victory over the Marxist rebels in El Salvador; only negotiations could end the deadly stalemate in that long-suffering land. As the cold war came to a close, the United Stated lost interest in and disengaged from Central America, dramatically cutting all forms of aid to the region throughout the 1990s and leaving it to recover from a decade of war largely on its own.[15]

THE END OF AN ERA AND A NEW WORLD ORDER

In 1989 President George H. W. Bush ordered an invasion of Panama to topple the dictator Manuel Noriega. The official charge against Noriega, a long-time U.S. client, was drug smuggling, but the reason was more likely that the erratic dictator was now viewed as an unreliable custodian of the Panama Canal. In August 1990 the Iraqi dictator Saddam Hussein invaded Kuwait. During the Iran-Iraq war in the 1980s, the United States had worked to build up the Iraqi regime as a bulwark against the Islamic fundamentalism of Iran, which was viewed as a threat to the oil kingdoms of the Persian Gulf. Now President Bush deployed five hundred thousand U.S. troops to Saudi Arabia as the bulk of an international coalition to oust Iraq from Kuwait.[16]

A large activist movement grew in the United States in opposition to the impending war in the Persian Gulf, taking up the rallying cry, "No Blood for Oil!" Bush had set a January 15, 1991, deadline for Iraq to pull out of Kuwait, vowing to go to war with or without congressional approval if Iraq did not comply. Three days before the deadline, the many days of impassioned congressional debate on whether to continue economic sanctions on Iraq or endorse a war resolution came to an end. Echoing the sentiments of the antiwar movement, Senator Edward Kennedy proclaimed, "Not a single American life should be sacrificed in a war for the price of oil."[17] The House approved the war resolution by a vote of 250 to 183, and the Senate passed the resolution by a vote of 52 to 47. The only member of the Massachusetts delegation whose position had remained in question going into the vote was Silvio Conte. On the day of the vote, Conte joined the rest of the Massachusetts delegation and only two fellow Republicans in voting against the authorization to go to war. Massachusetts thus became, fittingly, the only state whose delegation cast all its votes against the war. It would be one of the last votes that Conte would cast in his four decades in Congress.[18] On February 8, 1991, Silvio Conte died from a blood clot in the right side of his brain. His vote against the war resolution helped cement the affection that some western Massachusetts activists had begrudgingly developed for the Republican.[19]

The successful war against Iraq, especially at the cost of fewer than 150 U.S. lives, led to a tidal wave of patriotism. Yellow ribbons and U.S. flags adorned front yards across the United States, and Bush's popularity ratings exceeded 80 percent. The president proclaimed a New World Order, one in which the United States would shape the post–Cold War world. In early March, still basking in the glow of victory, President Bush declared, "By God, we've kicked the Vietnam syndrome once and for all."[20] For a decade and a half, advocates of an interventionist foreign policy chafed at the constraints that the Vietnam syndrome placed on the ability of U.S. presidents to deploy troops around the world. As the Latin American affairs specialist William LeoGrande has observed, "We went to war in Central America to exorcise the ghosts of Vietnam and renew the national will to use force abroad."[21] Although the American public would not countenance the cost in U.S. lives that had occurred during the Vietnam War, the 1991 Gulf War opened up a new era of willingness to assert U.S. military might around the world.

The Vietnam syndrome, however, entailed far more than the fear that the use of military force abroad would incur numerous casualties. The war in Vietnam had broken the cold war consensus and had called into question U.S. institutions. To be sure, the civil rights movement was the progenitor of 1960s activism and the training ground for a whole generation of activists. Unlike the civil rights movement—which was in many ways the culmination of post–World War II liberalism—the war in Vietnam, by legitimating the Left, effected a split in cold war liberalism. The Vietnam War produced a whole new generation of liberals who came to Congress in the early 1970s determined to steer the nation in a new direction and prevent any replay of the Vietnam experience. In 1982, during hearings on El Salvador held by the House Foreign Affairs Committee, Congressman Gerry Studds took part in one of his many adversarial exchanges with Secretary of State Alexander Haig. The dialogue, like so many before, turned to Vietnam:

Haig: Were you there, Mr. Studds, in Vietnam?
Studds: No. I was here trying to get us out of there.
Haig: Where were you at the time, just for my personal interest?

Studds: Where was I when?

Haig: During the Vietnam conflict?

Studds: Which part of it?

Haig: Start to finish.

Studds: That, unfortunately, is how I got myself in my current mess. I ran for this institution because I thought it was a tragic mistake.[22]

The Vietnam War made it possible for many mainstream Americans and politicians to question and consider alternatives to the dominant institutions and premises of U.S. society. The war had discredited the U.S. political establishment, had raised doubts about the "best and brightest" in government, and had helped to legitimate grassroots progressive activism. During the 1970s and 1980s, movements of the Left—in opposition to nuclear power, nuclear weapons, and U.S. intervention in Central America—all percolated up (to use the term coined by the national freeze movement activist Randall Forsberg) to influence mainstream politics.

The Vietnam War had also accentuated the cataclysmic potential of the cold war. During the post–Vietnam War era, nuclear power, nuclear weapons, and U.S. involvement in Central America all held enough threat of apocalypse to fuel the search for an alternative world order based on a global humanity that transcended the cold war dualities of modern capitalism and Soviet-style authoritarian socialism. Activists sought to create a new world free of the shadow of self-destruction. Many members of the Left continued to pursue the ideals of participatory democracy, international self-determination, world peace, racial and gender equality, and the liberation of humankind from economic exploitation. In 1968 many believed that an alternative world order was on the verge of sweeping the globe. In the 1970s and 1980s, activists moved in that direction from the bottom up, in what the activist and historian Barbara Epstein calls "prefigurative politics." Activists summed up the post–Vietnam War era with the words "Think Globally; Act Locally."

The 1960s opened up space not only for movements of the Left but also for movements of the Right. The 1970s and 1980s witnessed a bifurcation of U.S. politics. Exploiting the social and cultural alienation that many Americans felt toward the movements of the 1960s, the economic dislocations of the 1970s, and anger over the decline of U.S. global power, the New Right gained a slow ascendancy after 1980. Although liberals and activists of the Left could not stop the rightward shift of the nation, they blunted the trajectory of nuclear energy expansion, helped move a reluctant conservative president back toward arms control negotiations, and prevented more-direct U.S. military action in Central America.

When President Bush pronounced the death of the Vietnam syndrome, he hoped his victory in Iraq would end not only a national self-doubt that inhibited the full assertion of U.S. military power abroad but also the alternative vision for the United States and the world embodied by the left-liberal movements of the 1960s and beyond. It was these movements, and the alternative path they represented, that for a decade and a half after the Vietnam War had most inhibited the Right from realizing its vision of a New World Order.

The end of the cold war had a profound effect on the U.S. Left. Although few leftist activists were anxious to follow the Soviet model, many hoped that revolutions such as the one in Nicaragua might provide a new model that would lead to social justice. The failure of revolutionary movements in the developing world left many disillusioned. The end of the cold war removed the frame of reference for many activists, who—after the seeming disorientation of the 1990s— slowly regrouped around the movement against corporate globalization later in the decade. Although much of the new anti–corporate globalization movement pursued nonviolent tactics rooted in the strategies of the 1970s and 1980s, the protests against the World Trade Organization in Seattle and against the International Monetary Fund and the World Bank elsewhere witnessed a return of the street-fighting militancy of the late 1960s. The anti–corporate globalization movement was sidelined by the terrorist acts that took place on September 11, 2001. The attacks on the Pentagon and the World Trade Center towers accelerated the neoconservative unilateralist policies of the George W. Bush administration. In 2003, however, in response to the impending war in Iraq and the new doctrine of "preventive war," the world witnessed an unprecedented wave of peace demonstrations around the globe. Not since the mass peace marches against the Euromissiles in the early 1980s had Europe experienced such large-scale protest, and not since the freeze movement had so many Americans from all walks of life participated in a peace movement. The communications revolution of the 1990s set in place the tools for the coordination of global protests on a scale that was unimaginable during the previous three decades. As global power continues to drift rightward, the activism of the Left, which appears to be redefining itself once again, shows every likelihood of playing an important role on the world stage.

NOTES

INTRODUCTION

1. Taylor Branch, *Parting the Waters: America in the King Years, 1953–1963* (New York: Simon and Schuster, 1988); Clayborne Carson, *In Struggle: SNCC and the Black Awakening of the 1960s* (Cambridge, Mass.: Harvard University Press, 1981).

2. Maurice Isserman, *If I Had a Hammer: The Death of the Old Left and the Birth of the New Left* (Urbana: University of Illinois Press, 1987).

3. Terry Anderson, *The Movement and the Sixties* (New York: Oxford University Press, 1995); Alexander Bloom and Wini Breines, *Takin' It to the Streets: A Sixties Reader* (New York: Oxford University Press, 1995); Morris Dickstein, *Gates of Eden: American Culture in the Sixties* (New York: Basic, 1977); David Farber, *The Age of Great Dreams* (New York: Hill and Wang, 1994); Todd Gitlin, *Sixties: Years of Hope, Days of Rage* (New York: Bantam, 1987); James Miller, *Democracy Is in the Streets: From Port Huron to the Siege of Chicago* (New York: Simon and Schuster, 1987); Douglass Rossinow, *Politics of Authenticity: Liberalism, Christianity, and the New Left in America* (New York: Columbia University Press, 1998); Kirkpatrick Sale, *SDS* (New York: Random House, 1973); Irwin Unger, *The Movement: A History of the American New Left, 1959–1972* (New York: Dodd, Mead, 1974).

4. Ronald Fraser, ed., *1968: A Student Generation in Revolt: An International Oral History* (New York: Pantheon, 1988).

5. Terry Anderson, *The Sixties* (New York: Longman, 1999); Stephen A. Kent, *From Slogans to Mantras: Social Protest and Religious Conversion in the Late Vietnam Era* (New York: Syracuse University Press, 2001); Max Elbaum, *Revolution in the Air: Sixties Radicals Turn to Lenin, Mao, and Che* (New York: Verso, 2002).

6. Michael Herr, *Dispatches* (New York: Alfred A. Knopf, 1978).

7. Hunter S. Thompson, *Fear and Loathing in Las Vegas: A Savage Journey to the Heart of the American Dream* (New York: Random House, 1971).

8. Two 1970s works have especially reinforced the gulf between the 1960s and 1970s. One is Tom Wolfe's famous essay "The Me Decade and the Fourth Great Awakening," in *Mauve Gloves and Madmen, Clutter and Vine* (New York: Farrar, Straus and Giroux, 1976). The other is Christopher Lasch's *The Culture of Narcissism: American Life in an Age of Diminishing Expectations* (New York: Warner, 1979). Both are penetrating works that illuminate a good deal of American culture in the 1970s but downplay continuities with the 1960s and virtually ignore post-1960s activism. For this view, see also Edwin Schur, *The Awareness Trap: Self-Absorption instead of Social Change* (New York: Quadrangle, 1976). Peter Clecak refutes their views in *America's Quest for the Ideal Self: Dissent and Fulfillment in the 60s and 70s* (New York: Oxford University Press, 1983). Clecak emphasizes the themes that unify the 1960s and 1970s both culturally and politically. He argues that the pursuit of personal fulfillment and social justice are themes that unify both decades. His appraisal of the 1970s is far more generous than Wolfe's or Lasch's. Peter Carroll shares Clecak's more positive assessment of the 1970s in *It Seemed like Nothing Happened: America in the 1970s* (New Brunswick, N.J.: Rutgers University Press, 1982).

9. The prominence of women in the antinuclear struggles of the 1970s continued the trajectory begun in the movements of the 1960s. See Sara Evans, *Personal Politics: The Roots of Women's Liberation in the Civil Rights Movement and the New Left* (New York: Vintage, 1979).

10. The historian Barbara Epstein called these cultural changes in the movements of the 1970s and 1980s "pre-figurative politics" in *Political Protest and Cultural Revolution: Non-violent Direct Action in the 1970s and 1980s* (Berkeley: University of California Press, 1991). Wini Breines argues the importance of community organizing in the New Left in *Community and Organization in the New Left, 1962–1968: The Great Refusal* (New York: Praeger, 1982).

11. On the 1960s counterculture and technology, see Theodore Roszak, *The Making of a Counterculture: Reflections on the Technocratic Society and Its Youthful Opposition* (1969; Berkeley: University of California Press, 1995).

12. Epstein, *Political Protest and Cultural Revolution*. For a direct-witness account, see Harvey Wasserman, *Energy War: Reports from the Front* (Westport, Conn.: Hill, 1979).

13. Diane McWhorter, *Carry Me Home: Birmingham, Alabama: The Climactic Battle of the Civil Rights Revolution* (New York: Simon and Schuster, 2001). For an account of the mass detentions of 1971, see the last chapter of Lucy Barber, *Marching on Washington: The Forging of an American Political Tradition* (Berkeley: University of California Press, 2002).

14. Paul Boyer discusses the cycles of the movement against nuclear weapons in "Epilogue: From the H-Bomb to Star Wars: The Continuing Cycles of Activism and Apathy," in *By the Bomb's Early Light: American Thought and Culture at the Dawn of the Atomic Age* (Chapel Hill: University of North Carolina Press, 1985).

15. About nine hundred thousand people participated in the march.

16. David S. Meyer, *A Winter of Discontent: The Nuclear Freeze and American Politics* (New York: Praeger, 1990).

17. Frances FitzGerald most persuasively makes this argument for the political impact of the freeze movement in *Way Out There in the Blue: Reagan, Star Wars, and the End of the Cold War* (New York: Simon and Schuster, 2000). FitzGerald also argues, however, that the power of the freeze movement helped cause Reagan to push more aggressively for his missile defense system, the Strategic Defense Initiative (SDI).

18. William M. LeoGrande, *Our Own Backyard: The United States in Central America, 1977–1992* (Chapel Hill: University of North Carolina Press, 1998); Robert Kagan, *A Twilight Struggle: American Power and Nicaragua, 1977–1990* (New York: Free Press, 1996); Thomas Walker, ed., *Reagan versus the Sandinistas: The Undeclared War on Nicaragua* (Boulder, Colo.: Westview Press, 1987).

19. For the roots of Latin American solidarity movements in the 1950s and 1960s, see Van Gosse, *Where the Boys Are: Cuba, Cold War, and the Making of the American Left* (New York: Verso, 1993).

20. Daniel L. Migliore, *Called to Freedom: Liberation Theology and the Future of Christian Doctrine* (Philadelphia: Westminister Press, 1980); Margaret Randall, *Christians in the Nicaraguan Revolution* (Vancouver, Canada: New Star, 1983); Phillip Berryman, *Liberation Theology: Essential Facts about the Revolutionary Movement in Latin America—and Beyond* (Philadelphia: Temple University Press, 1987).

21. Van Gosse, "'The North American Front': Central American Solidarity Activism in the Reagan Era," in *Reshaping the U.S. Left: Popular Struggles in the 1980s*, ed. Mike Davis and Michael Sprinker (New York: Verso, 1988).

22. Allen J. Matusow, *The Unraveling of America: A History of Liberalism in the 1960s* (New York: Harper and Row, 1984).

23. Kevin Boyle, ed., *Organized Labor and American Politics, 1894–1994: The Labor-Liberal Alliance* (Albany: State University of New York Press, 1998); Peter Levy, *The New Left and Labor in the 1960s* (Urbana: University of Illinois Press, 1994).

24. Sale, *SDS*; Miller, *Democracy Is in the Streets*.

25. Carson, *In Struggle*.

26. Robert Weisbrot, *Freedom Bound: A History of America's Civil Rights Movement* (New York: Plume, 1991); Anderson, *Sixties*; Farber, *Age of Great Dreams*.

27. Sale, *SDS*; Miller, *Democracy Is in the Streets*; Gitlin, *Sixties*.

28. David Farber, *Chicago '68* (Chicago: University of Chicago Press, 1988); Theodore White, *The Making of the President, 1968* (New York: Atheneum, 1969).

29. James Reichley, *Conservatives in an Age of Change: The Nixon and Ford Administrations* (Washington, D.C.: Brookings Institution, 1981); Stephen E. Ambrose, *Nixon* (New York: Simon and Schuster, 1987).

30. Charles DeBenedetti, *An American Ordeal: The Antiwar Movement of the Vietnam Era* (Syracuse, N.Y.: Syracuse University Press, 1990).

31. In *Power and Protest: Global Revolution and the Rise of Détente* (Cambridge, Mass.: Harvard University Press, 2003), Jeremi Suri argues that the motive for détente by U.S., Soviet, and Chinese leaders was to counter domestic unrest among their respective populations.

32. Theodore White, *The Making of the President: 1972* (New York; Bantam, 1973); Hunter S. Thompson, *Fear and Loathing on the Campaign Trail, '72* (New York: Fawcett Popular Library, 1973).

33. Carroll, *It Seemed like Nothing Happened*.

34. Jerome L. Himmelstein, *To the Right: The Transformation of American Conservatism* (Berkeley: University of California Press, 1990).

35. Jerry W. Sanders, *Peddlers of Crisis: The Committee on the Present Danger and the Politics of Containment* (Boston: South End Press, 1983).

36. Carroll, *It Seemed like Nothing Happened*.

37. Thomas Edsall, *Chain Reaction: The Impact of Race, Rights, and Taxes on American Politics* (New York: Norton, 1991); Jonathon Rieder, *Canarsie: The Jews and Italians of Brooklyn against Liberalism* (Cambridge, Mass.: Harvard University Press, 1985). See also Gary Gerstle and Steve Fraser, eds., *The Rise and Fall of the New Deal Order* (Princeton, N.J.: Princeton University Press, 1989).

38. Lawrence E. Walsh, *Firewall: The Iran-Contra Conspiracy and Cover-Up* (New York: Norton, 1997); Peter Kornbluh and Malcolm Byrne, eds., *The Iran-Contra Scandal: The Declassified History* (New York: New Press, 1993); Theodore Draper, *A Very Thin Line: The Iran-Contra Affairs* (New York: Hill and Wang, 1991).

39. For a discussion of Americanism on the Left and Right, see Gary Gerstle, *Working-Class Americanism: The Politics of Labor in a Textile City, 1914–1960* (Cambridge, England: Cambridge University Press, 1989).

40. Ross Gelbspan, "Hundreds Arrested in Boston Protest," *Boston Globe*, May 8, 1985.

41. Burton Hersh, *The Shadow President: Ted Kennedy in Opposition* (South Royalton, Vt.: Steerforth Press, 1997). For Ted Kennedy's early years, see Burton Hersh, *The Education of Edward Kennedy: A Family Biography* (New York: Morrow, 1972).

42. Edward M. Kennedy and Mark O. Hatfield, *Freeze! How You Can Help Prevent Nuclear War* (New York: Bantam, 1982).

43. Vincent O'Connor, interview by the author, Amherst, Mass., April 3, 2003.

44. John A. Farrell, *Tip O'Neill and the Democratic Century* (Boston: Little, Brown, 2001).

45. Gerald Nicosia, *Home to War: A History of the Vietnam Veterans Movement* (New York: Three Rivers Press, 2001). See also Michael Kranish, Brian C. Mooney, and Nina J. Easton, *John F. Kerry: The Complete Biography by the Boston Globe Reporters Who Know Him Best* (New York: Public Affairs, 2004), and Douglass Brinkley, *Tour of Duty: John Kerry and the Vietnam War* (New York: William Morrow, 2004).

46. Charles Kenney and Robert L. Turner, *Dukakis: An American Odyssey* (Boston: Houghton Mifflin, 1988); Richard Gaines and Michael Segal, *Dukakis and the Reform Impulse* (Boston: Quinlan Press, 1987).

CHAPTER 1

1. Peter Carroll, *It Seemed like Nothing Happened: America in the 1970s* (New Brunswick, N.J.: Holt, Rinehart and Winston, 1990).

2. Ibid., 83. See also David Boulton, *The Making of Tania: The Patty Hearst Story* (London: New English Library, 1975).

3. John Kifner, "Toppler of A-Plant Tower Shocks New England Town with Protest," *New York Times*, March 1, 1974.

4. Quoted in Studs Terkel, *American Dreams: Lost and Found* (New York: Ballantine, 1980), 460–61.

5. Carroll, *It Seemed like Nothing Happened*; Jerome Price, *The Antinuclear Movement* (Boston: Twayne, 1982); Anna Gyorgy, ed., *No Nukes: Everyone's Guide to Nuclear Power* (Boston: South End Press, 1979); Harvey Wasserman, *Energy War: Reports from the Front* (Westport, Conn.: Lawrence Hill, 1979).

6. Carroll, *It Seemed like Nothing Happened*, 123.

7. Elliot Eisenberg and John Schidlovsky, "Twin Nuclear Plants: Blessing or Curse?: Montague Dilemma," *Springfield Union and Sunday Republican*, January 6 1974.

8. "Basis for Northeast Utilities Commitment to Nuclear Power," NU Study, International Brotherhood of Electrical Workers Locals 36, 161, 707, and 710 Records (1929–1985) (hereafter cited as IBEW), August 6, 1974, box 7, folder 97, series 1: Local 36 (1969–1985), subseries 4: Nuclear Energy, MS 107, Special Collections and University Archives, W.E.B. Du Bois Library, University of Massachusetts, Amherst.

9. Quoted in Eisenberg and Schidlovsky, "Twin Nuclear Plants: Blessing or Curse?: Montague Dilemma."

10. "The Way It Is," NU Information Bulletin, July 1975; "Montague Nuclear Power Station Fact Sheet," circa 1974; "Nuclear Power: Issues and Answers," NU pamphlet, IBEW, box 7, folder 97.

11. Eisenberg and Schidlovsky, "Twin Nuclear Plants: Blessing or Curse?: Montague Dilemma," and "Twin Nuclear Plants: Blessing or Curse?: Workers' Families and Friends Have Confidence in Plant Safety," *Springfield Morning Union*, January 10, 1974; Wasserman, *Energy War*, 31; Gyorgy, *No Nukes*, 399.

12. Quoted in Dorothea Katzenstein, "Montague: NU's Ground Zero," *Valley Advocate*, September 19, 1973, 10–11.

13. Quoted in ibid., 11.

14. MASSPIRG, "Preliminary Report on Nuclear Power Plants," *Frances Crowe Papers*, Sophia Smith Collection, Smith College, Northampton, Massachusetts (hereafter cited as FCP, Sophia Smith Collection). (The Crowe Papers in the Sophia Smith Collection are distinguished from the Frances Crowe Private Papers, Northampton, Massachusetts, which are in the personal possession of Frances Crowe and were made available to the author.)

15. On the national commune movement, see Terry Anderson, *The Sixties* (New York: Longman, 1999), chaps. 5 and 7; Richard Fairfield, *Communes, USA: A Personal Tour* (Baltimore: Penguin, 1977); Gilbert Zicklin, *Countercultural Communes: A Sociological Perspective* (Westport, Conn.: Greenwood Press, 1983); and Timothy Miller, *The 60s Communes: Hippies and Beyond* (Syracuse, N.Y.: Syracuse University Press, 1999).

16. Harvey Wasserman, telephone interview by the author, March 15, 2007.

17. The story of the LNS is told in Raymond Mungo, *Famous Long Ago: My Life and Hard Times with the Liberation News Service* (Boston: Beacon Press, 1970). The founding of the Packers Corner Farm in Vermont is described in Raymond Mungo, *Total Loss Farm* (New York: Dutton, 1970). The founding of the Montague Farm is recounted in Stephen Diamond, *What the Trees Said: Life on a New Age Farm* (New York: Dell, 1970). For an account of the FBI infiltration of the Liberation News Service and efforts to disrupt the underground press across the United States in the late 1960s and early 1970s, see Angus Mackenzie, "Sabotaging the Dissident Press: The Untold Story of the Secret Offensive Waged by the U.S. Government against Antiwar Publications," *Columbia Journalism Review* (March/April 1981).

18. Randy Kehler, telephone interview by the author, May 5, 2003. Kehler had become acquainted with the communes through his life partner Betsy Corner, a member of the Wendell commune who was known as Cornwoman. "I was an in-law. Betsy was one of the family," Kehler recalled. Ibid.

19. Vince O'Connor, interview by the author, May 13, 2003, Amherst, Massachusetts.

20. Sam Lovejoy, interview by the author, May 24, 2003 Montague, Massachusetts.

21. Wasserman interview. Wasserman told of an occasion when members of the commune played against the Greenfield Police Department in a softball game: "Half of our team was on acid. It was 'Tim Leary meets Dunkin' Donuts." Ibid.

22. Leonard L. Richards, *Shays's Rebellion: The American Revolution's Final Battle* (Philadelphia: University of Pennsylvania Press, 2002).

23. Edene Stetson and Linda David, *Glorying in Tribulation: The Lifework of Sojourner Truth* (East Lansing: Michigan State University Press, 1994); Jacqueline Bernard, *Journey toward Freedom: The Story of Sojourner Truth* (New York: Feminist Press at the City University of New York, 1990); Paul E. Johnson and Sean Wilenz, *The Kingdom of Matthius* (New York: Oxford University Press, 1994).

24. O'Connor interview.

25. Lovejoy interview.

26. Wasserman, *Energy War*, 27–32; Gyorgy, *No Nukes*, 393–95.

27. Elliot Eisenberg and John Shidlovsky, "Twin Nuclear Plants: Blessing or Curse?: Backers Cite Need for Progress, Prospect of Big Cut in Tax Rate," *Springfield Union and Sunday Republican*, January 7, 1974.

28. Lovejoy interview.

29. Lovejoy interview.

30. Mungo, *Famous Long Ago*, 71; Diamond, *What the Trees Said*, 44–45.

31. Kehler interview.

32. Quoted in Kent Robinson, "An Interview with Samuel Lovejoy," *The Saboteur*, March 15, 1975, MS 224, 55, Special Collections and University Archives, W.E.B. Du Bois Library, University of Massachusetts, Amherst.

33. Quoted in ibid., 5.

34. Quoted in ibid., 54.

35. Quoted in ibid., 8, 12.

36. Quoted in ibid., 13–18.

37. Quoted in ibid., 13.

38. Dan Keller and Charles Light, *Lovejoy's Nuclear War*, a documentary film by Green Mountain Post Film Co-op, Turners Falls, Mass., 1974.

39. Quoted in Robinson, "Interview with Samuel Lovejoy," 14.

40. Quoted in ibid., 14.

41. Quoted in ibid., 25.

42. Kifner, "Toppler of A-Plant Tower Shocks New England Town with Protest,"

43. Ibid.

44. Quoted in Robinson, "Interview with Samuel Lovejoy," 52, 22, 21, 22.

45. Quoted in ibid., 25.

46. Quoted in ibid., 27, 29–31.

47. Quoted in ibid., 31.

48. Quoted in ibid., 45, 41.

49. Lovejoy interview. According to Lovejoy, "The SLA was a cult [that] twisted the rhetoric [of the movement]." Ibid. Lovejoy had a more favorable attitude toward the Weathermen, however. He recalled that he was with fifty Weatherpeople (as they began to call themselves) in Cuba when the news arrived about the police murder of the Black Panther Fred Hampton in Chicago; shortly thereafter the announcement came that the Weatherpeople would become the Weather Underground.

50. Quoted in Robinson, "Interview with Samuel Lovejoy," 47.

51. Quoted in ibid., 50.

52. Quoted in ibid., 45. See also Keller and Light, *Lovejoy's Nuclear War*.

53. Quoted in Robinson, "Interview with Samuel Lovejoy," 45.

54. Editorial, "Freedom Threatened," *Greenfield Recorder*, February 22, 1974.

55. Quoted in Don Saint-Pierre, "Utility Tower Toppler Freed," *Greenfield Recorder*, Feb. 22, 1974.

56. Neil R. Perry, "Jack and the Nuclear Beanstalk," *Greenfield Recorder*, February 23, 1974.

57. Quoted in St. Pierre, "Utility Tower Toppler Freed," *Greenfield Recorder*, February 23, 1974.

58. Quoted in "'Not My Style,' Says Nader," *Greenfield Recorder*, March 19, 1974.

59. Lovejoy interview.

60. Frances Crowe, interview by the author, April 24, 1996, Northampton, Mass.

61. Kehler interview.

62. Kehler interview.

63. Kifner, "Toppler of A-Plant Tower Shocks New England Town with Protest." .

64. Quoted in Arthur Cohen, "Tower Toppler Tells Why," *Valley Advocate*, March 20, 1974, 3.

65. Quoted in Robinson, "Interview with Samuel Lovejoy," 55.

66. Kifner, "Toppler of A-Plant Tower Shocks New England Town with Protest.".

67. Quoted in "Statement Tells Why Tower Was Wrecked," *Greenfield Recorder*, February 22, 1974.

68. Gary Gerstle, *Working Class Americanism: The Politics of Labor in a Textile City, 1914–1960* (Cambridge, England: Cambridge University Press, 1989), 5.

69. Kifner, "Toppler of A-Plant Tower Shocks New England Town with Protest," *New York Times*, March 1, 1974.

70. Quoted in ibid.

71. Quoted in "Statement Tells Why Tower Was Wrecked."

72. Quoted in ibid.

73. Quoted in ibid.

74. Official copies of the referendum questions are located in IBEW, box 7, folder 93.

75. *Montague Muse*, no. 1 (Summer 1974), FCP, Sophia Smith Collections.

76. Kehler interview.

77. Samuel Lovejoy, editorial, *Montague Muse*, no. 1 (Summer 1974), FCP, Sophia Smith Collections.

78. Robert Strachota, "Dear Friend," AEC letter, August 28, 1974, FCP, Sophia Smith Collections.

79. "Wendell Votes Against Nukes," *Greenfield Recorder*, May 13, 1974;; Ralph Gordon, "Third Town Calls for Nuclear Plant Moratorium," *Springfield Morning Union*, May 18, 1974.

80. Quoted in Gordon, "Third Town Calls for Nuclear Plant Moratorium."

81. Undated and unidentified newspaper clipping, IBEW, box 7, folder 95.

82. Crowe interview.

83. Mary Wentworth, interview by the author, December 4, 2007, Longmeadow, Mass.

84. Charles L. Keller, "Tower Toppling Trial Begins Preliminaries," *Greenfield Recorder*, September 10, 1974 Although Judge Smith failed to dissuade Lovejoy from representing himself, he persuaded him to retain council for occasions when Lovejoy would take the stand. Wasserman, *Energy War*, 22.

85. John Gofman, *Poisoned Power: The Case against Nuclear Power Plants* (Emmaus, Pa.: Rodale Press, 1971).

86. Keller and Light, *Lovejoy's Nuclear War*.

87. Ibid.

88. Wasserman, *Energy War*, 27–38.

89. Quoted in ibid., 37.

90. Keller and Light, *Lovejoy's Nuclear War*.

91. Ibid.

92. Ibid. See also Wasserman, *Energy War*, 27–38.

93. Keller and Light, *Lovejoy's Nuclear War*.

94. Ibid. Bell went on to become a committed antinuclear and environmental activist and a crucial bridge between the countercultural activists and mainstream members of the community. The antinuclear activists centered on the Montague Farm brought a wealth of experience from the 1960s, including community organizing. O'Connor said of Bell,

"Well, you're the librarian for a little town, you know everybody and everybody knows you, and when you come out and say this nuclear power thing doesn't sound like a good idea to me and are willing to do things with a bunch of hippies, that becomes the most dangerous combination. They got farmers involved." O'Connor interview.

95. Linda Matys, "Lovejoy: 'They Went for Broke,'" *Valley Advocate*, October 2, 1974, 3.

96. Keller and Light, *Lovejoy's Nuclear War*. See also Wasserman, *Energy War*, 27–38.

97. Crowe interview.

98. Keller and Light, *Lovejoy's Nuclear War*.

99. Ibid.

100. Ibid.

101. Ibid.

102. Ibid.

103. Kehler interview.

104. "Anna's Report from California," *AEC News* (April 1976), FCP, Sophia Smith Special Collections.

105. Quoted in Wasserman, *Energy War*, 38. Official copies of the referenda are located in IBEW, box 7, folder 93.

106. Charles Bragg to J. Z. Souvenie, "Manpower Estimates," IBEW, box 7, folder 97.

107. George O'Brien, interview by the author, April 27, 1996, Florence, Mass.

108. Ibid.

109. Ibid.

110. Unidentified newspaper clipping, *Hartford Times*, December 23, 1974, IBEW, box 7, no. 95.

111. IBEW antimoratorium pamphlets, IBEW, box 6, folder 77.

112. O'Brien interview.

113. Quoted in undated and unidentified newspaper clipping, IBEW, box 6, folder 82.

114. Quoted in ibid.

115. O'Brien interview. The 1974 western Massachusetts moratorium campaign became a model of a strategy that the nuclear industry used with increasing effectiveness throughout the 1970s. By putting organized labor out front as the public face of a pronuclear campaign while industry representatives orchestrated strategy behind the scenes, the nuclear industry was able to elicit far more public sympathy than they would have if corporate presidents and industry experts had taken the lead. Union workers and their families effectively countered the grassroots image of the antinuclear movement with one of their own. Furthermore, the confluence of interests between labor and capital allowed the nuclear industry to mobilize the vast human resources, energy, and experience of the labor movement in waging public campaigns with the formidable nuclear industry financial resources. This strategy was most widely and effectively used in the 1976 nuclear referendum campaign in California. See Thomas R. Wellock, *Critical Masses: Opposition to Nuclear Power in California, 1958–1978* (Madison: University of Wisconsin Press, 1998).

116. O'Brien interview. Barrett and Semanie, for the most part, allowed O'Brien to debate in his own inimitable style. An exception was in 1977 when a local television station asked O'Brien to participate in a series of televised debates on the Montague Twin Nuclear Power Station. The station went to great lengths to advertise the upcoming debates. One promotion for the series stated, "The issue has broken the community into interest groups

reminiscent of the Vietnam War era. Jobs are in high demand, and many labor unions have allied themselves with the utilities and other industries who see the plant as an example of economic progress for the region. Students, older progressives, members of the peace and ecology movements see the plant as a threat to life and nature." CCATV promotional news release, IBEW, box 6, folder 77. When Barrett and Semanie learned that the station had invited some "heavy hitters" from New York to participate in the debates, they told O'Brien, "Stay the hell out of that." They were worried, recalled O'Brien, "that I'd get my ass handed to me" and that "I might embarrass the whole crowd." O'Brien interview.

117. O'Brien interview.

118. Quoted in General Electric newsletter, Fall 1975, IBEW, box 7, folder 95.

119. Paul R. Snoop to George O'Brien, memorandum, October 15, 1974, IBEW, box 7, folder 93.

120. Charles H. Pillard to all international officers, all representatives, all local unions and councils, memorandum, circa Fall 1974, IBEW, box 7, folder 93.

121. O'Brien interview.

122. Lelan F. Sillin, Jr., to the Colony Club of Springfield, Massachusetts, address, February 26, 1975, IBEW, box 7, folder 97.

123. Quoted in George O'Brien, draft speech, circa 1974, IBEW, box 6, folder 80.

124. Quoted in Robinson, "Interview with Samuel Lovejoy," 60–61.

125. George O'Brien, draft speech #1, undated, IBEW, box 6, folder 78.

126. George O'Brien, draft speech #2, undated, IBEW, box 6, folder 78.

127. Joshua B. Freeman, "Hardhats, Construction Workers, Manliness and the 1970 Pro-war Demonstrations," *Journal of Social History* (Summer 1993): 725–44; David Halle, *America's Working Man: Work, Home, and Politics among Blue-Collar Property Owners* (Chicago: University of Chicago Press, 1984); Peter Carroll, "No One Calls It the Working Class," in *It Seemed like Nothing Happened*. In the 1970s, *The Tonight Show* with Johnny Carson also lampooned the image of the backward, blue-collar superpatriot through the host's regular character Floyd R. Turbo, who (in a 1977 show) defended nuclear power: "Put me down as an American who favors building nuclear plants. I say nuclear energy plants are safe.... So what if people begin to glow a little bit? At least we won't be faced with the question of not knowing where our children are at night. I say we should trust science.... [S]cience has given us cyclamates, saccharine and DDT.... So what if an atomic plant blows up? The people who say that, they are afraid to die. I'm not afraid to die because all my life I have lived by the good book, the American Legion magazine.... What do they expect us to use for fuel, buffalo chips. Now, these jerks want to use solar energy for electricity. Doesn't that take the cake? How do they expect me to plug my drill into the sun? I'd need a very big step-ladder." Quoted in "Johnny Carson Sets Us Straight," *The Nation*, June 18, 1977, 746.

128. Crowe interview.

129. O'Connor interview.

130. George O'Brien, draft speech #2, undated, IBEW, box 6, folder 80.

131. George O'Brien, draft speech #1, undated, IBEW, box 6, folder 80.

132. George O'Brien, draft speech #3, undated, IBEW, box 6, folder 80.

133. Quoted in Environmentalists for Full Employment bulletin, circa 1977, IBEW, box 7, folder 91.

134. Harvey Wasserman, "Environmentalists, Labor Joining Hands," undated and unidentified article, circa 1977, IBEW, box 7, folder 95. The EFE fought an uphill battle. At its October 1975 convention, the American Federation of Labor and Congress of Industrial Organizations (AFL-CIO) issued a nuclear energy endorsement stating, "Government action is required to promote public acceptance of nuclear power. Steps should be taken to reduce lead time for getting plants into production." *AFL-CIO American Federationist* (July 1975): 3. One labor leader wrote to O'Brien that unions such as the United Mine Workers and the railroad unions "cannot be expected to take an active interest in nuclear power, nor is support expected from white collar workers. The fact that specific jobs are at stake for the construction trades is sufficient to command an endorsement from these unionists, however, since, as one seasoned observer recently pointed out, 'If one union has a major "guts job" problem, other unions provide support for them. . . . [T]he amount of work even the construction trades can devote to nuclear lobbying in Washington should not be underestimated.'" Gene Sturgeon to George O'Brien, memorandum, September 22, 1975, IBEW, box 6, folder 85. Yet in 1975 the United Autoworkers began reaching out to environmentalists by hosting a conference at its Black Lake, Michigan, retreat, which brought together unions representing machinists, sheet metal workers, miners, and farm workers to support environmental initiatives and work toward alliances with environmental groups. The conference gave Wasserman hope. Commenting on environmentalism and labor, he wrote, "Both movements are in a critical state of flux right now and important segments of the two are working toward a mutual understanding. When they reach it, we can look forward to breathing some clean air again." Wasserman, "Environmentalists, Labor Joining Hands."

135. Unidentified newspaper clipping, *Hartford Times*, December 23, 1974, IBEW, box 7, no. 95. Cindy Weiss, undated and unidentified newspaper clipping, circa November 6, 1974, IBEW, box 7, folder 97. The total was 22,464 votes for the moratorium and 25,806 votes against. A total of 15,301 residents supported dismantling the existing plants in Rowe, Massachusetts, and Vernon, Vermont, with 31,948 against. In Montague increasing opposition to the plants was evident in the 1,091 votes for the moratorium compared to 1,948 votes against. Weiss, undated and unidentified newspaper clipping. See also *Hartford Times*, December 23, 1974.

136. Quoted in Robinson, "Interview with Samuel Lovejoy," 66.

137. Quoted in unidentified newspaper clipping, *Hartford Times*, December 23, 1974, box 7, no. 95.

138. Quoted in ibid.

139. Sillin to the Colony Club of Springfield, Massachusetts, address, February 26, 1975.

140. Unidentified newspaper clipping, *Hartford Times*, December 23, 1974, IBEW, box 7, no. 95.

141. O'Connor interview.

142. "Olver: A Professor of Liberal Arts," *Boston Globe*, May 1, 1991; Chris Black, "1st District, Left to Right Bipartisan Consensus: Olver Is a True Liberal," *Boston Globe*, May 26, 1991.

143. Crowe interview.

144. O'Connor interview.

145. Price, *Antinuclear Movement*, 9, 11.

146. Quoted in *Hartford Times*, December 23, 1974.

147. Weiss, undated and unidentified newspaper clipping, circa November 1974.

148. Laurie Gullion, "Nuclear Hearings End," *Greenfield Recorder*, June 3, 1977.

149. Crowe interview. Recalling her experiences with public participation at NRC hearings, Crowe stated, "They don't really let anyone say very much." Ibid.

150. David Kaplan, Thomas Lesser, William Newman, "To: Citizens Concerned about the Proposed Montague Nuclear Plant, Re: Analysis of Proposed Intervention in EFSC Hearings," October 11, 1977, FCP, Sophia Smith Collection.

151. Robert Barrett, NU Consultant, "Reasons Why Hearings for Montague Nuclear Power Station Should Not Be Postponed," memorandum, June 23, 1975, IBEW, box 7, folder 94.

152. Sillin to the Colony Club of Springfield, Massachusetts, address, February 26, 1975.

153. Ibid.

154. "Impact of Power Plant Deferrals to Construction Workers, Manufacturing Workers, Utility Workers," IBEW Utility Department Study, January 1975, IBEW, box 7, folder 93.

155. Quoted in Northeast Utilities, "In the Wake of the Three Mile Island Accident . . ." advertisement, *Daily Hampshire Gazette*, May 14, 1979.

156. Beu Eaton and Gary Nielson, "Interview: Sam Lovejoy and Harvey Wasserman," *Valley Advocate*, January 21, 1981, 6–7.

157. Quoted in ibid., 6.

CHAPTER 2

1. Christian Joppke, *Mobilizing against Nuclear Energy: A Comparison of Germany and the United States* (Berkeley: University of California Press, 1993), 97–101.

2. Quoted in ibid., 79.

3. Ibid., 102–11.

4. Ibid.

5. Ibid., 116–20.

6. Barbara Epstein, *Political Protest and Cultural Revolution: Nonviolent Direct Action in the 1970s and 1980s* (Berkeley: University of California Press, 1991), 84.

7. Ibid., 58.

8. Harvey Wasserman, "Nuclear War by the Sea," *The Nation*, September 11, 1976. Reprinted in *Energy War: Reports from the Front*, ed. Wasserman (Westport, Conn.: Lawrence Hill, 1979), 49.

9. Henry F. Bedford, *Seabrook Station: Citizen Politics and Nuclear Power* (Amherst: University of Massachusetts Press, 1990), 64–93.

10. Joppke, *Mobilizing against Nuclear Energy*, 33; Robert J. Duffy, *Nuclear Politics in America: A History and Theory of Government Regulation* (Lawrence: University of Kansas Press, 1997), 59–61.

11. Bedford, *Seabrook Station*, 64–93.

12. Steve Varnum, "The Voice of Protest," *Concord Monitor Online*, August 22, 1999. Available at www.cmonitor.com/stories/top100/0822chichester.shtml. Accessed May 15, 2003.

13. Ibid., 74–75.

14. Quoted in Wasserman, "Nuclear War by the Sea"; idem, *Energy War*, 50.

15. Ibid. The New Hampshire towns were Hampton, Hampton Falls, North Hampton, Exeter, Kensington, Durham, and Rye. They were joined by Salisbury, Massachusetts.

16. Harvey Wasserman, "Opening Battle of the Eighties," *Mother Jones*, August 1977; idem, *Energy War*, 83.

17. Quoted in Wasserman, *Energy War*, 82.

18. Quoted in Steve Varnum, "The Voice of Protest," *Concord Monitor Online*, August 22, 1999, 5. Available at www.cmonitor.com/stories/top100/0822chichester.shtml. Accessed May 15, 2003.

19. Bedford, *Seabrook Station*, 74–76.

20. Epstein, *Political Protest and Cultural Revolution*, 62–63; Wasserman, "Nuclear War by the Sea"; Wasserman, *Energy War*, 53.

21. Epstein, *Political Protest and Cultural Revolution*, 63–65. One of Boardman's sons had been a draft resister in the 1960s. Vince O'Connor, interview by the author, May 13, 2003, Amherst, Massachusetts.

22. O'Connor interview, May 13, 2003.

23. Ibid.

24. Epstein, *Political Protest and Cultural Revolution*, 63–65.

25. Ibid., 76–78; Harvey Wasserman, "Resistance Gets Set for the Spring," *The Nation*, February 11, 1978; Wasserman, *Energy War*, 112.

26. Quoted in Joppke, *Mobilizing against Nuclear Energy*, 80.

27. Epstein, *Political Protest and Cultural Revolution*, 59.

28. Wasserman, *Energy War*, xii.

29. Wasserman, "Nuclear War by the Sea"; idem, *Energy War*, 49.

30. Wasserman, "Opening Battle of the Eighties"; idem, *Energy War*, 79.

31. Wasserman, *Energy War*, 79.

32. Quoted in Wasserman, *Energy War*, 49. See also idem, "Nuclear War by the Sea."

33. Quoted in Wasserman, *Energy War*, 79. See also idem, "Opening Battle of the Eighties."

34. Robbie Leppzer, *Seabrook 1977*, a 16mm, 86-minute documentary film by Turning Tide Productions, Wendell, Massachusetts, 1977; Daniel Keller and Charles Light, *The Last Resort*, a documentary film by Green Mountain Post Films Co-op, Turners Falls, Massachusetts, 1978.

35. Wasserman, "Nuclear War by the Sea"; idem, *Energy War*, 53.

36. Epstein, *Political Protest and Cultural Revolution*, 64–65.

37. Wasserman. *Energy War*.

38. Wasserman, "Nuclear War by the Sea"; idem, *Energy War*, 53.

39. Wasserman, "Nuclear War by the Sea"; Wasserman, *Energy War*, 53; Epstein, *Political Protest and Cultural Revolution*, 65.

40. Wasserman, "Nuclear War by the Sea"; Wasserman, *Energy War*, 53; Epstein, *Political Protest and Cultural Revolution*, 65.

41. Dan Keller and Charles Light, *Lovejoy's Nuclear War*, a documentary film by Green Mountain Post Film Co-op, Turners Falls, Mass., 1974.

42. Ibid.

43. Quoted in Joppke, *Mobilizing against Nuclear Energy*, 70.

44. Quoted in Wasserman, *Energy War*, 54. See also idem, "Nuclear War by the Sea." Carter's reply gave the Green Mountain Post filmmakers the name for their Seabrook documentary: *The Last Resort*.

45. Wasserman, *Energy War*, 54. See also idem, "Nuclear War by the Sea." See also Epstein, *Political Protest and Cultural Revolution*, 65.

46. Wasserman, "Nuclear War by the Sea"; idem, *Energy War*, 55.

47. Wasserman, "Trial of the Seabrook Ten," *Valley Advocate*, September 8 and 15, 1976; idem, *Energy War*, 55–58.

48. Wasserman, *Energy War*, 55–59.

49. Ibid., 56, 58.

50. Quoted in ibid., 58.

51. Ibid.

52. Ibid.

53. Bedford, *Seabrook Station*, 5–6.

54. Charles Kaiser, *1968 in America: Music, Politics, Chaos, Counterculture, and a Generation* (New York: Weidenfeld and Nicolson, 1988), 90–91.

55. Bedford, *Seabrook Station*, 5–6.

56. Wasserman, *Energy War*, 80 and 123. See also idem, "Opening Battle of the Eighties"; idem, "Power at the Polls," *Valley Advocate*, December 6, 1978.

57. Bedford, *Seabrook Station*, 21.

58. Wasserman, *Energy War*, 111. See also idem, "Resistance Gets Ready for the Spring."

59. Wasserman, *Energy War*, 112.

60. Quoted in ibid., 111.

61. Wasserman, *Energy War*, 69–70. See also idem, "High Tension in the Energy Debate—The Clamshell Response," *The Nation*, June 18, 1977.

62. Wasserman, *Energy War*, 69.

63. Quoted in John Kifner, "Occupation of Atomic Plant Site Scheduled Today," *New York Times*, April 30, 1977.

64. O'Connor interview, May 13, 2003.

65. Wasserman, "High Tension in the Energy Debate"; idem, *Energy War*, 70.

66. Quoted in Wasserman, *Energy War*, 70.

67. "Leftist Groups Hope for Violence," *Manchester Union Leader*, April 29, 1977.

68. "The Siege of Seabrook," *Time*, May 16, 1977, 59; Wasserman, "High Tension in the Energy Debate"; idem, *Energy War*, 70.

69. Quoted in Joppke, *Mobilizing against Nuclear Energy*, 80.

70. Leppzer, *Seabrook 1977*.

71. John Kifner, "2,000 Occupy Nuclear Plant Site in New Hampshire, Vow to Stay," *New York Times*, May 1, 1977.

72. Ibid. See also Wasserman, "High Tension in the Energy Debate"; Wasserman, *Energy War*, 71.

73. Wasserman, *Energy War*, 71–74.

74. Ibid. See also Bedford, *Seabrook Station*, 70.

75. Quoted in Wasserman, "Resistance Nears a Critical Mass," *The Nation*, October 8, 1977, 329.

76. Bedford, *Seabrook Station*, 157–58. Ironically, few antinuclear activists voted for Dukakis in 1974. They opted instead for the liberal Republican Francis Sargent, who—unlike Dukakis (who gave qualified support for nuclear power during his campaign)—openly opposed nuclear power. With respect to Dukakis's decision to withhold Massachusetts state police, electoral politics might have factored in. Noting the numerous Massachusetts contingents at the site, O'Connor observed, "Arresting your voters is not the coolest thing to do, especially if you don't have to do it." O'Connor interview, May 13, 2003.

77. John Kifner, "Hundreds Arrested in New Hampshire Atom Protest," *New York Times*, May 2, 1977. See also Richard Asinof, "No-Nukers Demonstrate Their Strength at Seabrook," *Valley Advocate*, May 11, 1977.

78. Wasserman, *Energy War*, 71. See also idem, "High Tension in the Energy Debate."

79. Quoted in Wasserman, *Energy War*, 72.

80. Ibid., 72; John Kifner, "Atom Plant Protest Is Being Prolonged," *New York Times*, May 5, 1977.

81. Wasserman, *Energy War*, 72.

82. Quoted in ibid., 74.

83. Quoted in ibid., 72.

84. Ibid., 74; John Kifner, "Atom Protesters Tell U.S. Judge That Armory 'Jails' Are Unhealthy," *New York Times*, May 10, 1977.

85. Kifner, "Atom Plant Protest Is Being Prolonged."

86. Quoted in ibid.

87. Quoted in Wasserman, *Energy War*, 74. See also idem, "High Tension in the Energy Debate."

88. O'Connor interview, May 13, 2003.

89. Wasserman, *Energy War*. See also idem, "High Tension in the Energy Debate"; idem, "People against Power," *The Progressive* (April 1978): 16–19.

90. Quoted in John Kifner, "New Hampshire Governor Asks Public for Funds to Help Pay Cost of Jailing Protesters," *New York Times*, May 7, 1977.

91. Quoted in ibid.

92. Epstein, *Political Protest and Cultural Revolution*, 68.

93. John Kifner, "Arrested Antinuclear Protesters Allow to Play on Armory Lawn," *New York Times*, May 9, 1977.

94. O'Connor interview, May 13, 2003.

95. Quoted in Wasserman, *Energy War*, 74–75. See also idem, "High Tension in the Energy Debate."

96. Kifner, "Arrested Antinuclear Protesters Allow to Play on Armory Lawn."

97. O'Connor interview, May 13, 2003.

98. Ibid.

99. Quoted in Kifner, "Arrested Antinuclear Protesters Allow to Play on Armory Lawn."

100. O'Connor interview, May 13, 2003.

101. Ibid.

102. Asinof, "No-Nukers Demonstrate Their Strength at Seabrook," 7.

103. Mary Wentworth, interview by the author, December 4, 2007, Longmeadow, Massachusetts.

104. Mary L. Wentworth, *Discovering America: A Political Journey* (Philadelphia, Pa.: Xlibris, 2003), 370–71, 374.

105. Quoted in Asinof, "No-Nukers Demonstrate Their Strength at Seabrook," 8.

106. Ibid. Lovejoy ran into trouble when he tried to dominate meetings during the Montague protests as well. On one occasion he was asked to stop repeating points that had been made by women in the group. Vince O'Connor, telephone interview by the author, April 3, 2003.

107. Anna Gyorgy and Nesta King, "Turning Tide: The Time for Safe, Local and Renewable Energy Has Come," program, circa 1977–1978, FCP, Sophia Smith Collection.

108. Kifner, "Atom Protesters Tell U.S. Judge That Armory 'Jails' Are Unhealthy."

109. Wasserman, *Energy War*, 75. See also idem, "High Tension in the Energy Debate."

110. Quoted in Wasserman, *Energy War*, 75. See also idem, "High Tension in the Energy Debate."

111. O'Connor interview, May 13, 2003.

112. Quoted in Wasserman, *Energy War*, 103–4. See also idem, "Resistance Gets Set for the Spring."

113. Quoted in Wasserman, *Energy War*, 104.

114. Quoted in ibid.

115. Ibid., 104–5.

116. "Anti-Atom Alliance," *Newsweek*, June 5, 1978.

117. Wasserman, "High Tension in the Energy Debate," 748.

118. Quoted in Joppke, *Mobilizing against Nuclear Energy*, 66–67. See also Thomas R. Wellock, *Critical Masses: Opposition to Nuclear Power in California, 1958–1978* (Madison: University of Wisconsin Press, 1998), 72, 147; Harvey Wasserman, "New Battle Looms in Nuclear Controversy," *Valley Advocate*, November 17, 1976.

119. Quoted in Joppke, *Mobilizing against Nuclear Energy*, 67.

120. Quoted in George O'Brien, Notes from Northeast Nuclear Advocates Workshop, circa 1977, IBEW, box 6, folder 83, subseries 4: Nuclear Energy, MS 107.

121. George O'Brien, Notes, September 9, 1977, IBEW, box 7, folder 97.

122. Wasserman, *Energy War*, 88.

123. Quoted in Wasserman, *Energy War*, 88–89. See also idem, "The Lyndon Johnson of the Seventies," *Valley Advocate*, June 29, 1977.

124. Quoted in Wasserman, *Energy War*, 88–89.

125. Ibid., 88–89.

126. Environmentalists for Full Employment bulletin, July 27, 1977, IBEW, box 7, folder 93; Philip Shaberoff, "Tensions Increase Between Labor And Environmentalists Over Jobs," *New York Times*, May 28, 1977; Joppke, *Mobilizing against Nuclear Energy*, 76.

127. Quoted in "Workers, Energy, and Jobs," Clamshell Alliance newsletter, circa 1977, IBEW, box 6, folder 85.

128. Ibid.

129. Resolution Adopted by AFL-CIO Executive Council, May 4, 1977, IBEW, box 6, folder 85.

130. Wasserman, "Resistance Gets Set for the Spring"; idem, *Energy War*, 112.

131. Paul Langner, "Seabrook Protesters Settle in for 3-Day Rally," *Boston Globe*, June 24, 1978.

132. O'Connor interview, May 13, 2003. See also Joppke, *Mobilizing against Nuclear Energy*, 79–80.

133. Joppke, *Mobilizing against Nuclear Energy*, 79.

134. Epstein, *Political Protest and Cultural Revolution*, 68–75, 80–84.

135. Ibid. See also Wasserman, "Resistance Gets Set for the Spring"; Wasserman, *Energy War*, 105–10.

136. Quoted in Gary Nielson, "Seabrook: Another Kent State?" *Valley Advocate*, June 14, 1978, 10.

137. Quoted in ibid., 17.

138. Quoted in ibid., 14.

139. Quoted in ibid., 14.

140. Gary Nielson, "Seabrook Protest Largest Anti-nuke Rally in the U.S.," *Valley Advocate*, July 5, 1978, cover.

141. Epstein, *Political Protest and Cultural Revolution*, 76; Wasserman, *Energy War*, 113.

142. Harvey Wasserman, "Seabrook Occupation 1978," *WIN*, June 22, 1978, 14.

143. Epstein, *Political Protest and Cultural Revolution*, 33.

144. Wasserman, "Resistance Gets Set for the Spring"; idem, *Energy War*, 108.

145. Wasserman, "Resistance Gets Set for the Spring"; Wasserman, *Energy War*, 109–10; Epstein, *Political Protest and Cultural Revolution*, 6–8.

146. Wasserman, *Energy War*, 110.

147. Ibid., 113; Epstein, *Political Protest and Cultural Revolution*, 68–75, 80–84.

148. Quoted in Wasserman, *Energy War*, 113.

149. Ibid.

150. Quoted in unidentified newspaper clipping, *New Times*, July 24, 1978, 19, Frances Crowe Private Papers (hereafter cited as FCPP.).

151. Epstein, *Political Protest and Cultural Revolution*, 75–76.

152. Ibid., 76.

153. Ibid., 84–85.

154. Quoted in ibid.

155. Wasserman, "Seabrook Occupation, 1978," 14. Wasserman later expressed regret for having lodged these charges. Harvey Wasserman, telephone interview by the author, March 15, 2007.

156. Wasserman, "Seabrook Occupation, 1978," 14.

157. Quoted in Gary Nielson, "Seabrook: Another Kent State?" 14.

158. Quoted in unidentified newspaper clipping, *New Times*, July 24, 1978, 19, FCPP.

159. Epstein, *Political Protest and Cultural Revolution*, 73.

160. Quoted in Wasserman, *Energy War*, 113. See also idem, "Resistance Gets Set for the Spring."

161. Quoted in Cathy Wolff, "Media Madness and the Myth of the Mollusk," *Peacework* (July/August 1996), 9.

162. Quoted in Eaton and Nielson, "Interview: Sam Lovejoy and Harvey Wasserman," 8.

163. Joppke, *Mobilizing against Nuclear Energy*, 100–130.

164. Quoted in Michael Knight, "Protesters Convene Near Nuclear Plant," *New York Times*, June 25, 1978.

165. Paul Langner, "Seabrook Protesters Settle in for 3-Day Rally"; Michael Kenney

and Tony Pearson, "3,000 Mass for Protest at N-Plant," *Boston Globe*, June 25, 1978; Paul Langner, Seabrook Pros, Antis Have Their Say: Thousands Swell Protest," June 26, 1978; "We Did It Again," *Clamshell Alliance News*, July 1978; Wasserman, *Energy War*, 116–21.

166. Joppke, *Mobilizing against Nuclear Energy*, 71–77.

167. Amory Lovins, *Soft Energy Paths: Toward a Durable Peace* (San Francisco: Friends of the Earth International, 1977).

168. Quoted in Langner, "Seabrook Pros, Antis Have Their Say."

169. Quoted in Kenney and Pearson, "3,000 Mass for Protest at N-Plant."

170. Quoted in Nielson, "Seabrook Protest Largest Anti-nuke Rally in U.S.," 10. Out-of-state participants, many coming hundreds of miles, were particularly outraged. One told a reporter, "I suppose I would have been scared by Thomson and his Blue Meanies, but I would have come anyhow. . . . I can't get over the thought that this is only going to be a fun fair, and my husband and I didn't come 200 miles to camp out at a fair for the weekend." Another sighed, "I came up from Louisiana. It wasn't until I got here that I found out this occupation has been called off." Quoted in ibid.

171. Langner, "Seabrook Pros, Antis Have Their Say."

172. Quoted in *New York Times*, June 27, 1978, 10.

173. Quoted in Richard Higgins, "'Closet Clams' Come Out: Exuberant Air Prevails at Protest," *Boston Globe*, June 26, 1978.

174. Quoted in ibid.

175. Quoted in ibid., 20–21.

176. Quoted in Michael Knight, "20,000 Gather at Site of Seabrook Nuclear Protest," *New York Times*, June 26, 1978, 14.

177. Quoted in Stephen Zunes, Seabrook: A Turning Point," *The Progressive* (September 1978): 28–31.

178. Quoted in "Nuclear Demonstrators End Rally with March in Manchester, N.H.," *New York Times*, June 27, 1978.

179. Alan P. Henry, "Flexing for the Showdown at Seabrook," *Boston Herald American*, October 5, 1979.

180. Quoted in ibid.

181. "Some Important Questions and Answers," CDAS flier, circa summer/fall 1979, FCP, Sophia Smith Collection.

182. "Join the Occupation to Shut Down Seabrook, October 6," SCANN flier, circa summer/fall 1979, FCP, Sophia Smith Collection.

183. "Let's Shut Down Seabrook!" handbook for the October 6, 1979, direct action at Seabrook, circa summer/fall 1979, FCP, Sophia Smith Collection.

184. One of the few important exceptions was Tony and Louisa Santasucci, who allowed more than fifteen hundred protestors to camp on their property during the October 1979 action. Paul Langner, Seabrook: Push . . . Shove; Protesters Forced Back," *Boston Globe*, October 9, 1979.

185. "Seacoast New Hampshire Clamshell Position on the October 6 Occupation," circa fall 1979, FCP, Sophia Smith Collection.

186. "Let's Shut Down Seabrook!"

187. Quoted in Igal Roodenko, "Pros and Cons—The October 6 Occupation," *WIN*, September 27, 1979, 14–16.

188. "Let's Shut Down Seabrook!" In her copy of the handbook, the only marks made by Frances Crowe were where she underlined that passage.

189. "Statement of the American Friends Service Committee of New Hampshire Concerning the October 6 Demonstration at Seabrook," September 24, 1979, FCP, Sophia Smith Collection.

190. Ibid.

191. Citizens for Nonviolence at Seabrook, card, circa fall 1979, FCP, Sophia Smith Collection.

192. Robert J. Rosenthal, "Seabrook Demonstrators Retreat After Skirmishing: Protesters Were Set for Anything," Boston Globe, October 7, 1979.

193. Ben Bradlee and Robert Rosenthal, "N-Site Protest Was Sum of Several Incidents," Boston Globe, October 10, 1979.

194. Rosenthal, "Seabrook Demonstrators Retreat After Skirmishing"; Paul Langner, "Seabrook Protesters Rebuffed Twice More," Boston Globe, October 7, 1979.

195. Ben Bradlee, "The People. . . And Why They Came," Boston Globe, October 8, 1979.

196. Quoted in Bradlee and Rosenthal, "N-Site Protest Was Sum of Several Incidents."

197. Ibid.

198. Daniel F. Ford, Three Mile Island: Thirty Minutes to Meltdown (New York: Viking Press, 1981); John G. Fuller, We Almost Lost Detroit (New York: Ballantine, 1975).

199. Quoted in Joppke, Mobilizing against Nuclear Energy, 62.

200. Quoted in ibid., 78.

201. Wasserman, Energy War, 249. See also Joppke, Mobilizing against Nuclear Energy, 140.

202. "Hell No We Won't Glow," Time, May 21, 1979, 17. See also Tom Matthews, Mary Lord and Eleanor Clift, "Fallout from the Nuke-In," Newsweek, May 21, 1979, 34–35.

203. "Activist Confronts the President," Greenfield Recorder, May 18, 1979.

204. "Clams Blast Carter for Nuclear Position at Seabrook," Clamshell Alliance News 2, no. 1 (June 1977), FCP, Sophia Smith Collection.

205. Quoted in "The Activist Confronts the President," Greenfield Recorder, May 18, 1979.

206. Quoted in Beu Eaton and Gary Nielson, "Interview: Sam Lovejoy and Harvey Wasserman," Valley Advocate, January 21, 1981, 10.

207. Joppke, Mobilizing against Nuclear Energy, 84; Danny Goldberg, Julian Schlossberg and Anthony Potenza, No Nukes: The MUSE Concerts for a Non-nuclear Future, Madison Square Garden, September 19–23, 1979, a film distributed by Warner Brothers, September 1980, 103 minutes.

208. David Sokol, "Rockin' down the Nukes: MUSE-ings from the Musicians," Valley Advocate, October 3, 1979, 14, 16, 19; Greenfield Recorder, November 29, 1980. Some critics charged that the media/press focus on the celebrities detracted from the antinuclear message of the concerts, whereas others believed that the Green Mountain Post Films antinuclear documentary seemed out of place amidst the music. Still others charged that the Warner Brothers distribution of the No Nukes concert film was erratic; the company responded that the political title of the concert film may have scared people away. The concert became perhaps best known for the high-energy performance of Springsteen, which overshadowed not only the performances of other musicians at the event but also the antinuclear cause. Many theaters refused to show the film because of the numerous

instances in which audiences took to dancing in the aisles. Debbie Schafer, "'No Nukes' Film Opens," *Greenfield Recorder*, November 29, 1980.

209. Quoted in Charles G. Smith, "Rockin' Down the Nukes: The Biggest Demonstration Yet," *Valley Advocate*, October 3, 1979, 20.

210. Joppke, *Mobilizing against Nuclear Energy*, 142.

211. Duffy, *Nuclear Politics in America*, 118; Jerome Price, *The Antinuclear Movement* (Boston: Twaine, 1982), 10–11, 45.

212. Matthews et al., "Fallout from the Nuke-In"; Leslie Bennett, "Nuclear Power Program Condemned by Kennedy," *New York Times*, February 16, 1980.

213. Duffy, *Nuclear Politics in America*, 142–43.

214. Bedford, *Seabrook Station*, 125–61.

215. Ibid.

216. Ibid., 141, 157–58; Duffy, *Nuclear Politics in America*, 206–8; Price, *Antinuclear Movement*, 89–90.

217. Quoted in Brad Pokomy, "Dukakis Says No to Seabrook," *Boston Globe*, September 21, 1986, Metro Section.

218. Bedford, *Seabrook Station*, 157–58; Duffy, *Nuclear Politics in America*, 206–8; Price, *Antinuclear Movement*, 89–90; Ben A. Franklin, "Officials Deride Proposal on Nuclear Evacuations," *New York Times*, February 25, 1987.

219. Quoted in Bedford, *Seabrook Station*, 157.

220. Larry Tye, "Election May Settle Future of Seabrook," *Boston Globe*, May 2, 1988.

221. Quoted in ibid.

222. Quoted in David Mehegan, "Dukakis Villain in Sununu's Tale of Two States," *Boston Globe*, September 10, 1988.

223. Quoted in John Milne, "Dukakis Courts Seabrook Foes in N.H.," *Boston Globe*, August5, 1987. When asked if he supported closing existing operational nuclear plants, Dukakis replied, "I don't think as a practical matter you can do that." Quoted in ibid.

224. Quoted in John Milne, "Fighting Words; Race for Presidency May Get Personal Here; Dukakis-Sununu Grudge Match Seen," *Boston Globe*, July 24, 1988.

225. Bedford, *Seabrook Station*, 201.

226. Ibid., 162–65.

227. Joppke, *Mobilizing against Nuclear Energy*, 52.

228. Ibid., 53.

229. Quoted in ibid., 148.

CHAPTER 3

1. Peter Carroll, *It Seemed like Nothing Happened: America in the 1970s* (New Brunswick, N.J.: Rutgers University Press, 1982), 339–50. See also Daniel Horowitz, *Jimmy Carter and the Energy Crisis of the 1970s: The "Crisis of Confidence" Speech of July 15, 1979* (New York: Bedford/St. Martins, 2005).

2. Carroll, *It Seemed like Nothing Happened* 185–231.

3. Quoted in Harvey Wasserman, *Energy War: Reports from the Front* (Westport, Conn.: Hill, 1979), 67. See also idem, "Carter's Choice and Ours," *New Age*, January 1977.

4. Wasserman, *Energy War*, 85–89. See also idem, "The Lyndon Johnson of the Seventies," *Valley Advocate*, June 29, 1977.

5. Carroll, *It Seemed like Nothing Happened*, 194, 214–15.

6. Jerry W. Sanders, *Peddlers of Crisis: The Committee on the Present Danger and the Politics of Containment* (Boston: South End Press, 1983).

7. Steve Breyman, *Why Movements Matter: The West German Peace Movement and U.S. Arms Control Policy* (New York: State University of New York Press, 2001), 35–36.

8. Frances FitzGerald, *Way Out There in the Blue: Reagan, Star Wars, and the End of the Cold War* (New York: Simon and Schuster, 2000), 186–87; David S. Meyer, *A Winter of Discontent: The Nuclear Freeze and American Politics* (New York: Praeger, 1990), 36–38; Carroll, *It Seemed like Nothing Happened*, 342.

9. Carroll, *It Seemed like Nothing Happened*, 340–41.

10. Ibid., 340–42.

11. Ibid., 212.

12. FitzGerald, *Way Out There in the Blue*, 19–71.

13. Quoted in Carroll, *It Seemed like Nothing Happened*.

14. Carroll, *It Seemed like Nothing Happened*, 345–46.

15. Meyer, *Winter of Discontent*; Douglass C. Waller, *Congress and the Nuclear Freeze: An Inside Look at the Politics of a Mass Movement* (Amherst: University of Massachusetts Press, 1987).

16. Paul Boyer, *By the Bomb's Early Light: American Thought and Culture at the Dawn of the Atomic Age* (Chapel Hill: University of North Carolina Press, 1994), 352, 355. See also idem, "From Activism to Apathy: The American People and Nuclear Weapons, 1963–1980," *Journal of American History* (March 1984). For a comprehensive account of the anti–nuclear weapons movement in the final decades of the cold war, see Lawrence S. Wittner, *Toward Nuclear Abolition: A History of the World Nuclear Disarmament Movement, 1971 to the Present* (Palo Alto, Calif.: Stanford University Press, 2003).

17. Boyer, *By Bomb's Early Light*, 352–67.

18. Frances Crowe, "A Journey of Conscience," draft speech, circa 1981–1982, FCP, Sophia Smith Collection.

19. Meyer, *Winter of Discontent*, 137–52.

20. Ibid., 157–58.

21. Quoted in Michael Feinsilber, "Seed Planted in WMass Spreads Across Nation," *Greenfield Recorder*, May 25, 1982.

22. Randall Forsberg, "Call to Halt the Nuclear Arms Race: Proposal for a Mutual U.S.- Soviet Nuclear Weapons Freeze," FCP, Sophia Smith Collection.

23. Meyer, *Winter of Discontent*, 162.

24. Ibid., 171–73.

25. Ibid., 173–75.

26. Quoted in undated and unidentified newspaper clipping, circa February 1980, "Traprock Peace Center Records, 1979–1985," MS 80, series 5, box 5, folder 32, Special Collections and University Archives, W.E.B. Du Bois Library, University of Massachusetts, Amherst (hereafter cited as TPCR).

27. Quoted in ibid.

28. Randy Kehler, telephone interview by the author, May 5, 2003.

29. Ibid.

30. Ibid.

31. Quoted in Cori Fugere, "Protesters Talk About Resistance," *Greenfield Recorder*, July 3, 1980.

32. Ibid.

33. Quoted in undated and unidentified newspaper clipping, circa February 1980, TPCR, MS 80, series 5, box 5, folder 32.

34. Ibid.

35. *An Act of Conscience*, a documentary film by Robbie Leppzer, Turning Tide Productions, Wendell, Massachusetts, 1997.

36. Kehler interview.

37. Kehler interview. See also, Stephen Frank, "Traprock Peace Center to Explore Disarmament 'Myths,'" *Greenfield Recorder*, December 3, 1979.

38. Kehler interview.

39. Quoted in "Peace Groups Encouraged," *Greenfield Recorder*, November 6, 1980.

40. Quoted in *Traprock Report* 1, no. 5 (November 1980), TPCR 1, box 1, folder 1, MS 80,

41. *Berkshire Eagle*, circa October 1982, Frances Crowe Private Papers, Northampton, Massachusetts (hereafter cited as FCPP).

42. Quoted in ibid.

43. Quoted in Amherst Bulletin, circa June 1982, TPCR, MS 80, box 5, series 5, folder 31.

44. Kehler interview.

45. Quoted in undated and unidentified newspaper clipping, November 1980, TPCR, MS 80, series 5, box 5, folder 32.

46. Kehler interview.

47. *Traprock Report* 1, no. 1 (February/March 1980), TPCR, series 1, box 1, folder 1, MS 80.

48. *Traprock Report* 3, no. 11 (September 1983), TPCR, series 1, box 1, folder 4, MS 80.

49. Alexander Cockburn and James Ridgeway, "The Freeze Movement versus Reagan," *New Left Review* 137 (January/February 1983): 20.

50. Peter McGrath, "Does Civil Defense Make Sense?" *Newsweek*, April 26, 1982, 31.

51. Quoted in Feinsilber, "Seed Planted in WMass Spreads Across Nation."

52. *Traprock Report* 1, no. 2 (April/May 1980), TPCR, series 1, box 1, folder 1, MS 80.

53. Quoted in *Daily Collegian* (University of Massachusetts at Amherst) circa 1981, FCPP.

54. For the role of Massachusetts women activists in the Seneca Fall Women's Encampment, see Deborah McDermott, "An Encampment for Peace; Four Area Women Arrested in Protest over Nuclear War," *Greenfield Recorder*, September 6, 1983. For a definitive analysis of the maternalist approach in the peace movement, see Amy Swerdlow, *Women Strike for Peace: Traditional Motherhood and Radical Politics in the 1960s* (Chicago: University of Chicago Press, 1993).

55. Quoted in Traprock fund-raiser, TPCR, series 1, box 1, folder 1, MS 80.

56. Kehler interview.

57. "Thinking Globally, Acting Locally," Traprock flier, TPCR, series 5, box 5, folder 32, MS 80.

58. Albert Einstein, "The Real Problem Is in the Hearts of Men," *New York Times Magazine*, June 23, 1946, 44. Quoted in Boyer, *Winter of Discontent*, 59.

59. Randy Kehler and Gordon Faison, memorandum, "To: Active Participants in the Nuclear Freeze Campaign," July 22, 1981, TPCR, series 1, box 1, folder 2, MS 80.

60. *Traprock Report* 2, no. 1 (February 1981), TPCR, series 1, box 1, folder 2, MS 80.

61. Quoted in J. P. Powers, *Post Standard*, undated and unidentified newspaper clipping, TPCR, series 5, box 5, folder 31, MS 80.

62. Quoted in Meyer, *Winter of Discontent*, 174.

63. Quoted in *Traprock Report* 1, no.1 (February/March 1980), TPCR, series 1, box 1, folder 1, MS 80.

64. Quoted in undated and unidentified newspaper clipping, circa November 1980, TPCR, MS 80, series 5, box 5, folder 32.

65. For a detailed summation of Forsberg's philosophy and strategy, see Meyer, *Winter of Discontent*, 157–63.

66. *Traprock Report* 1, no. 2 (April/May 1980), TPCR, series 1, box 1, folder 1, MS 80.

67. Quoted in Meyer, *Winter of Discontent*, 176.

68. *Traprock Report* 1, no. 2 (April/May 1980), TPCR, series 1, box 1, folder 1, MS 80.

69. Quoted in Beu Eaton, "Peace on the Ballot; Valley Voters Take On the Arms Race," *Valley Advocate*, October 1, 1980.

70. Meyer, *Winter of Discontent*, 173–75. Undated and unidentified newspaper clipping, circa fall 1980, Frances Crowe Private Papers, Northampton, Massachusetts (hereafter cited as FCPP).

71. "Tips for Petitioners," memorandum, FCP, Sophia Smith Collection.

72. Kehler interview.

73. Undated and unidentified newspaper clipping (probably from the *Valley Advocate*), circa fall 1980, FCPP.

74. Quoted in "Yes on 7" flier, circa fall 1980, FCPP.

75. Paul Dunphy, "Nation May Note Area Vote," *Daily Hampshire Gazette*, October 3, 1980.

76. Quoted in ibid.

77. Quoted in "Missile Protesters Asked to Leave Fair," *Daily Hampshire Gazette*, September 2, 1980.

78. Some of the "Arms Race Survey" cards with answers and comments are housed in the FCP, Sophia Smith Collection. The questions were as follows: (1) With our present nuclear stockpile, government officials estimate that we can kill every Soviet citizen: (a) once, (b) ten times over, (c) forty times over, (d) sixty times over. (2) Which nation has forged all of the major advances in the arms race? (a) the Soviet Union, (b) the United States, (c) both led some advances. (3) About 40 percent of our federal budget is used for military spending. How does a large military budget affect the economy? (a) stops unemployment, (b) aids free enterprise, (c) creates unemployment and inflation, (d) lowers taxes. (4) Over the next five years, the average family of four will spend at least how much on nuclear weapons? (a) about $500, (b) about $1,000, (c) about $5,000, (d) about $8,000. Ibid.

79. "Saneworld: A Newsletter of Action on Disarmament and the Peace Race," January 1981, FCPP.

80. Quoted in "A Christian Response of 'Yes' to Question 7," pamphlet, FCPP.

81. Quoted in ibid.

82. Steve Turner, "War Destroys, Peace Employs," *Valley Advocate*, October 1, 1980, 10, 12–13.

83. Ibid. The IAM report also concluded that between 1975 and 1978, the top one

hundred defense contractors with IAM contracts received an increase of $5 billion from the Pentagon, whereas the IAM suffered a net loss of twelve thousand jobs.

84. Quoted in ibid., 10.

85. Quoted in undated and unidentified newspaper clipping (probably from the *Valley Advocate*), circa October 1980, TPCR, box 5, folder 33, MS 80.

86. *Traprock Report* 2, no. 2 (April 1981), TPCR, series 1, box 1, folder 2, MS 80.

87. Quoted in undated and unidentified newspaper clipping, circa October 1980, FCPP.

88. Quoted in ibid.

89. Quoted in undated and untitled clipping, *Daily Collegian*, circa October 1980, FCPP.

90. "Health Care Providers in Support of Proposition 7," *Daily Hampshire Gazette*, advertisement, October 31, 1980.

91. Carroll, *It Seemed like Nothing Happened*, 324–25.

92. Meyer, *Winter of Discontent*, 173–75.

93. *Springfield Morning Union*, circa November 1–3, 1980, FCPP.

94. Quoted in Meyer, *Winter of Discontent*, 147.

95. Ibid., 173–75. Kehler informed western Massachusetts activists that national leaders saw the November referendum as a "bellwether of the whole moratorium movement." Traprock fund-raising letter, October 15, 1980, TPCR, series 1, box 1, folder 1, MS 80.

96. Kehler interview.

97. Quoted in "Ellsberg Urges an End to Nuclear Madness," *Valley Advocate*, October 15, 1980.

98. Quoted in ibid. See also Phyllis Anderoni, "Mideast Policy Could Lead Us Into War, Says Ellsberg," *Springfield Morning Union*, October 7, 1980.

99. Quoted in "Ellsberg Urges an End to Nuclear Madness."

100. Quoted in Turner, "War Destroys, Peace Employs," 10.

101. Quoted in "Missile Protesters Asked to Leave Fair."

102. Quoted in untitled clipping, *Greenfield Recorder*, February 9, 1980, TPCR, MS 80, series 5, box 5, folder 32.

103. "Behind the Scenes: The Myth of the Soviet Threat," pamphlet, FCPP.

104. "But What about the Russians?" pamphlet, FCPP. A copy of the pamphlet is also available in the FCP, Sophia Smith Collection.

105. *Traprock Report* 4, no. 1 (January 1984), TPCR, series 1, box 1, folder 5, MS 80.

106. Meg Gage, a Traprock member, was among those who visited the Soviet Union. Gage met with an "unofficial" Soviet disarmament group, which, although it was not antigovernment, was viewed with suspicion by Soviet officials. Gage described the group as "rhetorical and guarded" during official meetings and "candid" during unmonitored breaks. She found her Soviet hosts friendly but noted the "lack of information available to the Soviet people." Nevertheless, she believed that her peace mission met with "some success." Quoted in *Traprock Report* 3, no. 10 (July 1983), TPCR, series 1, box 1, folder 4, MS 80. One example of a nationally circulated letter signed by U.S. peace activists and sent to the Soviet leadership was an appeal for the release of Sergei Batrovin in 1982. The letter read in part, "We welcome the recent Soviet renunciation of first use of nuclear weapons. However, it belies the Soviet claim to be 'peace loving' when independent Soviet peace activists—our brothers and sisters in the movement—are labeled as 'provocative,'

'illegal' and 'anti-social.' ... As activists opposed to actions by the Reagan administration that would escalate the arms race, we the undersigned call upon you to release SERGEI BATOVRIN, now interned in a psychiatric hospital, and to cease harassment of other independent activists and allow their voices to be heard on this most vital of issues—the issue of survival in the shadow of nuclear war." Quoted in *Traprock Report* 3, no. 5 (September 1982), TPCR, series 1, box 1, folder 3, MS 80.

107. Quoted in *Traprock Report* 2, no. 1 (February 1981), TPCR, series 1, box 1, folder 2, MS 80.

108. *Traprock Report* 1, no. 5 (November 1980), TPCR, series 1, box 1, folder 1, MS 80.

109. Quoted in Traprock Peace Center, "Supports Nuclear Moratorium," *Daily Hampshire Gazette*, letter to the editor, October 30, 1980.

110. Randy Kehler and Gordon Faison, memorandum, "To: Active Participants in the Nuclear Weapons Freeze Campaign," July 22, 1981, TPCR, series 1, box 2, folder 1, MS 80.

111. "Voters Split Over Two Nuclear Issues," *Daily Hampshire Gazette*, November 5, 1980.

112. Meyer, *Winter of Discontent*, 173–75.

113. Quoted in Paul Dunphy, "Nation May Note Area Vote."

114. Frances Crowe, "A Journey of Conscience," draft speech, circa 1983, FCP, Sophia Smith Collection.

115. Quoted in C. Duncan Harp, "Local Option," *The Nation*, December 6, 1980, 597.

116. Quoted in Traprock fund-raising letter, October 15, 1980, TPCR, series 1, box 1, folder 1, MS 80.

117. Quoted in *Traprock Report* 1, no. 5 (November 1980), TPCR, series 1, box 1, folder 1, MS 80.

118. Mark O. Hatfield to Western Massachusetts "Yes on 7" Committee, c/o Traprock, March 9, 1981, FCP, Sophia Smith Collection.

119. Frances Crowe, "A Journey of Conscience," draft speech, circa 1983, FCP, Sophia Smith Collection.

120. Anne Willard to Frances Crowe, letter, circa November/December 1980, FCPP.

121. Ruth Sanders to AFSC Western Massachusetts Regular Office, letter, circa November/December 1980, FCPP.

122. *Traprock Report* 2, no. 2 (April 1981), TPCR, series 1, box 1, folder 2, MS 80; Beu Eaton, "Traprock Peace Center Pushes Senate on Resolution Against Nuclear Weapons," *Valley Advocate*, March 18, 1981.

123. Charles E. Claffey, "Massachusetts; Nuclear Free Zone Issue Stirs Cambridge; Arms Control Advocates Split Over Referendum's Effect on Research," *Boston Globe*, October 16, 1983. The article reviews the movement in Cambridge from 1981 through 1984.

124. *Traprock Report* 2, no. 1 (February 1981), TPCR, series 1, box 1, folder 2, MS 80.

125. *Traprock Report* 1, no. 5 (November 1980), TPCR, series 1, box 1, folder 1, MS 80.

126. John Olver to Traprock Peace Center Staff and Colleagues, letter, November 25, 1980, FCP, Sophia Smith Collection.

127. Undated and unidentified newspaper clipping, circa December 1980, FCPP.

128. Quoted in ibid.

129. Quoted in David Shea, "House Approves Nuclear Resolution," *Greenfield Recorder*, June 11, 1981.

130. *Traprock Report* 2, no. 1 (February 1981), TPCR, series 1, box 1, folder 2, MS 80.

131. Ibid.

132. Ibid.

133. Quoted in *Traprock Report* 2, no. 2 (April 1981), TPCR, series 1, box 1, folder 2, MS 80.

134. Ibid.

135. Quoted in "Excerpts of Testimony," From Persons Who Submitted or Presented Testimony in Support of Massachusetts Senate Resolution #455 to the Joint Legislative Committee on Federal Financial Assistance, Gardner Auditorium, State House, Boston, March 30, 1981, FCP, Sophia Smith Collection.

136. Shea, "House Approves Nuclear Resolution."

137. Quoted in ibid.

138. Massachusetts Coalition for a Nuclear Weapons Freeze, "Massachusetts Legislature Adopts a Nuclear Weapons Freeze Resolution," press release, June 9, 1981, FCP, Sophia Smith Collection.

139. Quoted in *Amherst Bulletin*, July 8, 1981.

140. "A Welcome Freeze," *Boston Globe*, March 15, 1982.

141. Meyer, *Winter of Discontent*, 184–91.

142. Kehler interview.

143. "Minutes: Western Massachusetts Coalition Steering Committee," May 19, 1982, FCP, Sophia Smith Collection.

144. *Traprock Report* 3, no. 6 (November 1982), TPCR. See also Meyer, *Winter of Discontent*, 111–13.

145. Quoted in Glenn A. Briere, "Olver Urges Nuke Freeze," *Springfield Morning Union*, May 27, 1982.

146. Meyer, *Winter of Discontent*, 217.

147. Debi McDermott, "Freeze Referendum Held Up on Beacon Hill," *Greenfield Recorder*, July 3, 1982.

148. Quoted in ibid.

149. Quoted in "Olver Pushes Freeze Vote," *Greenfield Recorder*, August 4, 1982.

150. Quoted in McDermott, "Freeze Referendum Held Up on Beacon Hill."

151. Ibid.

152. Quoted in "Dukakis Urges Support for Nuclear Freeze Resolution," Michael Dukakis gubernatorial campaign press release, August 3, 1982, FCP, Sophia Smith Collection.

153. Associated Press, "Nuclear Weapons Question to Be on Ballot," *Greenfield Recorder*, September 24, 1982.

154. Quoted in ibid.

155. Quoted in ibid.

156. Quoted in ibid.

157. Quoted in ibid. On the King administration, see Richard Gaines and Michael Segal, *Dukakis and the Reform Impulse* (Boston: Quinlan Press, 1987), 125–36.

158. Waller, *Congress and the Nuclear Freeze*, 101–59.

159. Ibid.

160. *Traprock Report* 3, no. 6 (November 1982), TPCR, series 1, box 1, folder 3, MS 80.

161. Quoted in ibid.

162. Meyer, *Winter of Discontent*, 72–73; Breyman, *Why Movements Matter*, 54–55; Fitz-Gerald, *Way Out There in the Blue*, 89–90.

163. Quoted in Breyman, *Why Movements Matter*, 55.

164. Quoted in ibid. See also Meyer, *Winter of Discontent*, 73.

165. Quoted in Breyman, *Why Movements Matter*, 55.

166. Peter McGrath, "Does Civil Defense Make Sense?" *Newsweek*, April 26, 1982, 31–33.

167. "Federal Officials Shelve Nuclear Evacuation Plan," *Morning Union*, March 5, 1985.

168. Claffey, "Massachusetts; Nuclear Free Zone Issue Stirs Cambridge."

169. Quoted in "County Residents Join in N.Y. Arms Control Rally, "*Greenfield Recorder*, June 11, 1982.

170. *Amherst Bulletin*, May 23, 1984.

171. Quoted in "Federal Officials Shelve Nuclear Evacuation Plan."

172. Quoted in Alice Warner, "Nuclear Disaster Plan Criticized in Amherst," *Daily Hampshire Gazette*, February 9, 1982.

173. Breyman, *Why Movements Matter*, 101–2.

174. Nancy Newcombe, "Passage of Nuclear Bylaw Only First Step," *Amherst Bulletin*, May 23, 1984.

175. "Federal Officials Shelve Nuclear Evacuation Plan."

176. Undated and unidentified newspaper clipping, circa June 1984, FCPP.

177. *The Sentinel*, circa May 1984, FCPP.

178. Quoted in Richard Schreuer, untitled editorial, *Boston Globe*, April 16, 1983.

179. *The Sentinel*, circa May 1984, FCPP.

180. Ibid. See also Schreuer, untitled editorial.

181. Quoted in undated and unidentified newspaper clipping, circa June 1984, FCPP.

182. Ibid.

183. Quoted in "Massachusetts New Executive Order on Civil Defense," press packet, June 28, 1984, Michael S. Dukakis Presidential Campaign Papers, University Libraries, Archives and Special Collections Department, Northeastern University, Boston, Massachusetts, box 5, folder 71, MS 32 (hereafter cited as MSDPCP).

184. Quoted in ibid.

185. "Governor Michael S. Dukakis: Background and Accomplishments," circa 1988, MSDPCP, box 4, folder 71, MS 32.

186. On Michael Dukakis's political career, see Gaines and Segal, *Dukakis and the Reform Impulse*, and Charles Kenney and Robert L. Turner, *Dukakis: An American Odyssey* (Boston: Houghton Mifflin, 1988).

187. Gaines and Segal, *Dukakis and the Reform Impulse*, 163.

188. Ibid.

189. *Traprock Report* 3, no. 10 (May 1983), TPCR, series 1, box 1, folder 4, MS 80.

190. *Traprock Report* 4, no. 6 (October 1984), TPCR, series 1, box 1, folder 5, MS 80.

191. Maureen Goggin and Susan Jacobson to John DeVillars, memorandum on the subject of arms control, February 23, 1987, MSDPCP, box 5, folder 283, MS 32.

192. Executive Order No. 242, by His Excellency, Michael S. Dukakis, Governor, June 28, 1984, MSDPCP, box 4, folder 231, MS 32.

193. Quoted in undated and unidentified newspaper clipping, circa June 1984, FCPP.

194. Quoted in *Associated Press*, circa June 1984, FCPP.

195. Quoted in *Traprock Report* 4, no. 4 (July 1984), TPCR, series 1, box 1, folder 5, MS 80.

196. Quoted in "Federal Officials Shelve Nuclear Evacuation Plan."

197. *Traprock Report* 4, no. 6 (October 1984), TPCR, series 1, box 1, folder 5, MS 80.

198. Executive Order No. 254, by His Excellency Michael S. Dukakis, April 25, 1985, MSDPCP, box 5, folder 283, MS 32.

199. Ibid.

200. "Talking Points for Announcement of Governor's Advisory Committee on the Impact of the Nuclear Arms Race on Massachusetts," April 25, 1985, MSDPCP, box 5, folder 283, MS 32.

201. *First Year Report of the Governor's Advisory Committee on the Impact of the Nuclear Arms Race on Massachusetts*, June 20, 1986, MSDPCP, box 5, folder 283, MS 32.

202. Maureen Goggin and Susan Jacobson to John DeVillars on the subject of arms control, February 23, 1987, MSDPCP, Box 5, Folder 283, MS 32.

203. *Traprock Report* 6, no. 4 (July/August 1986), TPCR, series 1, box 1, folder 5, MS 80.

204. *First Annual Report of the Governor's Advisory Committee on the Impact of the Nuclear Arms Race on Massachusetts*, June 20, 1986, MSDPCP, box 5, folder 283, MS 32, 10.

205. Kenney and Turner, *Dukakis*, 213–14.

206. Quoted in *Traprock Report* 6, no. 4 (July/August 1986), TPCR, series 1, box 1, folder 5, MS 80.

207. Quoted in ibid.

208. Quoted in Andrew J. Dabilis, "30,000 Jobs in Mass. Tied to Nuclear Industry," *Boston Globe*, March 24, 1986.

209. Quoted in "Talking Points for Meeting with Governor's Advisory Committee on the Impact of the Nuclear Arms Race on Massachusetts," June 26, 1986, MSDPCP, box 5, folder 283, MS 32.

210. Quoted in ibid.

211. Ibid.

212. Quoted in ibid.

CHAPTER 4

1. Steve Breyman, *Why Movements Matter: The West German Peace Movement and U.S. Arms Control Policy* (Albany: Sate University of New York Press, 2001), 1–9.

2. Frances FitzGerald, *Way Out There in the Blue: Reagan, Star Wars, and the End of the Cold War* (New York: Simon and Schuster, 2000), 72–113; David S. Meyer, *A Winter of Discontent: The Nuclear Freeze and American Politics* (New York: Praeger, 1990), 49–60.

3. Quoted in Breyman, *Why Movements Matter*, 53.

4. Ibid., 9.

5. Ibid., 53.

6. Ibid., 120, 125.

7. Ibid., 100.

8. Meyer, *Winter of Discontent*, 229–30.

9. On the role of Massachusetts activists in direct action protests against the Euromissiles in the United States, see Deborah McDermott, "Four Area Women Arrested in Protest Over Nuclear War," *Greenfield Recorder*, September 6, 1983. See also *Traprock Report* 3, no. 8 (March 1983), TPCR, series 1, box 1, folder 1, MS 80. The U.S. media did not begin substantive coverage of the European movement until quite late in 1981. The *Traprock Report* announced, "Because of the news blackout on disarmament activities in Europe,

we will, in each newsletter, share some highlights on the large and growing disarmament movement in Europe." *Traprock Report* 2, no. 4 (September 1981), TPCR, series 1, box 1, folder 2, MS 80.

10. For the vantage point of the Reagan administration, see Paul Lettow, *Ronald Reagan and His Quest to Abolish Nuclear Weapons* (New York: Random House, 2006), and Lou Cannon, *President Reagan: The Role of a Life Time* (New York: Simon and Schuster, 1991).

11. *Traprock Report* 2, no. 2 (April 1981), TPCR, series 1, box 1, folder 2, MS 80; Traprock fund-raising letter, October 15, 1980, TPCR, series 1, box 1, folder 2, MS 80; Meyer, *Winter of Discontent*, 176–77.

12. Quoted in Traprock fund-raising letter, October 15, 1980, TPCR, series 1, box 1, folder 1, MS 80.

13. Meyer, *Winter of Discontent*, 176–77.

14. Randy Kehler and Gordon Faison, "To: Active Participants in the Nuclear Weapon Freeze Campaign," memorandum, July 22, 1981, TPCR, series 1, box 1 folder 2, MS 80.

15. 'Strategy for Stopping the Nuclear Arms Race," Nuclear Weapons Freeze Campaign, March 1981, FCP, Sophia Smith Collection.

16. Executive Committee to the National Committee, "Insuring Strong Task Forces," memorandum, December 11, 1981, FCP, Sophia Smith Collection.

17. Ibid., 181.

18. Quoted in ibid., 181.

19. Quoted in "Call for a Nuclear Weapons Freeze," National Committee summary of the National Conference in St. Louis, December 11–13, 1981, FCP, Sophia Smith Collection.

20. Randy Kehler, "Comments on the Strategy-Related Papers Distributed at October 30, 1981, East Coast Meeting," memorandum, November 9, 1981, FCP, Sophia Smith Collection.

21. Ibid.

22. Randy Kehler and Gordon Faison, "To: Active Participants in the Nuclear Weapon Freeze Campaign," memorandum, July 22, 1981, TPCR, series 1, box 1 folder 2, MS 80 (emphasis in original).

23. Ibid.

24. Ibid.

25. Thomas Raymond Wellock, *Critical Masses: Opposition to Nuclear Power in California, 1958–1978* (Madison: University of Wisconsin Press, 1998). Christian Joppke, *Mobilizing against Nuclear Energy: A Comparison of Germany and the United Sates* (Berkeley: University of California Press, 1993), 65–69.

26. Harry C. Boyte, "The Formation of the New Peace Movement: A Communitarian Perspective," *Social Policy* (Summer 1982), 4.

27. Meyer, *Winter of Discontent*, 79.

28. Alexander Cockburn and James Ridgeway, "The Freeze Movement versus Ronald Reagan," *New Left Review* 137 (January/February 1983): 11.

29. Meyer, *Winter of Discontent*, 123, 125.

30. Ibid., 128–29.

31. Quoted in David M. Alpern, "Who's Who in the Movement," *Newsweek*, April 26, 1982, 22.

32. Meyer, *Winter of Discontent*, 99.

33. Quoted in Douglas C. Waller, *Congress and the Nuclear Freeze: An Inside Look at the Politics of a Mass Movement* (Amherst: University of Massachusetts Press, 1987), 39.

34. Meyer, *Winter of Discontent*, 102; Waller, *Congress and the Nuclear Freeze*, 67.

35. Cockburn and Ridgeway, "Freeze Movement versus Reagan," 9. See also Meyer, *Winter of Discontent*, 100.

36. Cockburn and Ridgeway, "Freeze Movement versus Reagan," 17–18.

37. Ibid.

38. Waller, *Congress and the Nuclear Freeze*, 38–39.

39. Cockburn and Ridgeway, "Freeze Movement versus Reagan," 10; Meyer, *Winter of Discontent*, 110–11.

40. Mike Feinsilber, "Seed Planted in WMass Spreads across Nation," *Greenfield Recorder*, May 25, 1982.

41. Meyer, *Winter of Discontent*, 88. Similar polls showed that, when it came to nuclear weapons policy, 38 percent of Americans distrusted Reagan. Meyer, *Winter of Discontent*, 87.

42. Meyer, *Winter of Discontent*, 183.

43. Waller, *Congress and the Nuclear Freeze*, 76.

44. Quoted in *Freezeletter* (July 1981), FCP, Sophia Smith Collection.

45. Coalition for a Nuclear Weapons Freeze, "Western Massachusetts Steering Committee Minutes," March 17, 1982, FCP, Sophia Smith Collection.

46. Coalition for a Nuclear Weapons Freeze, "Western Massachusetts Steering Committee Minutes," February 24, 1982, FCP, Sophia Smith Collection.

47. Western Massachusetts Coalition for a Nuclear Weapons Freeze, "Strategy Ideas for November 1982: Steering Committee Minutes," November 1982, FCP, Sophia Smith Collection.

48. Ibid. In 1983 Massachusetts freeze proponents worked closely with several Bay State legislators to delay a vote on the MX. A Massachusetts Coalition for a Nuclear Weapons Freeze memorandum noted, "This was accomplished by the Massachusetts delegation—Speaker [Tip] O'Neill, Representatives [Ed] Markey and [Nick] Mavroules—to give us more time to marshal our forces. It had a great deal to do with the effects of Coalition members." Joanne Duhle, Massachusetts Coalition for a Nuclear Weapons Freeze, to Coalition Members, memorandum, June 17, 1983, FCP, Sophia Smith Collection.

49. Ben Senturia to Local Organizers, memorandum on freeze lobbying preparation, Nuclear Weapons Freeze Campaign, circa 1983, FCP, Sophia Smith Collection.

50. Randy Kehler, telephone interview by the author, May 5, 2003.

51. Feinsilber, "Seed Planted in WMass Spreads across Nation."

52. Quoted in Judith Miller, "Effort to 'Freeze' Nuclear Arsenals Spreads in U.S.," *New York Times*, March 15, 1982. See also Meyer, *Winter of Discontent*, 128.

53. Meyer, *Winter of Discontent*, 184–86.

54. Leslie Cagan, "Being Left: It Should Be Possible, It Has to Be Possible," *ZMag* (June 1998): 1, available at www.org/ZMag/articles/caganjune1998.htm, retrieved December 5, 2006.

55. Ibid., 1–3.

56. Leslie Cagan, draft statement, circa 1981, *Leslie Cagan Papers* Tamiment 138, Tamiment Library/Robert F. Wagner Labor Archives, Elmer Holmes Bobst Library, New York University Libraries (hereafter cited as LCP).

57. Leslie Cagan to Special Session on Disarmament (SSD) Working Group on August 24 Meeting, minutes, September 9, 1981, LCP, Tamiment 138.

58. "Call to the June 12th Rally," circa spring 1982, LCP, Tamiment 138.

59. Meyer, *Winter of Discontent*, 184–86; Robin Herman, "Protesters Old and New Forge Alliance for Antinuclear Rally," *New York Times*, June 4, 1982; "War in Peace," *WIN*, August 15, 1982, 6–7.

60. Leslie Cagan to the Reverend Herbert Dougherty, letter, April 14, 1982, LCP, Tamiment 138.

61. Meyer, *Winter of Discontent*, 184–86; *New York Times*, June 4, 1982; "War in Peace," 6–7.

62. Greater Boston Campaign for the United Nations Second Special Session on Disarmament (SSD-II), letter, June 1982, LCP, Tamiment 138.

63. Hope Abramson and Peg Carter, "Dear Sisters," letter, Feminist Task Force of the Greater Boston June 12 Campaign, circa spring 1982, LCP, Tamiment 138.

64. Undated and unidentified newspaper article, Frances Crowe Private Papers, Northampton, Massachusetts (hereafter cited as FCPP); City of Cambridge in City Council Resolution, March 20, 1982, LCP, Tamiment 138.

65. City of Cambridge in City Council Resolution, March 20, 1982, LCP, Tamiment 138.

66. New York City Police Department Report, May 25, 1982, LCP, Tamiment 138.

67. Meyer, *Winter of Discontent*, 187.

68. Quoted in *Amherst Bulletin*, circa June 1982, TPCR, MS 80, box 5, series 5, folder 31.

69. *Morning Union*, circa May 1982, TPCR, MS 80, box 5, series 5, folder 31.

70. Quoted in ibid.

71. Quoted in Meyer, *Winter of Discontent*, 187–88.

72. Cockburn and Ridgeway, "Freeze Movement versus Reagan," 11.

73. Meyer, *Winter of Discontent*, 186.

74. Quoted in *Amherst Bulletin*, June 23, 1982.

75. There were, however, some undercurrents of tension at the event. A week before the rally, Israel had invaded Lebanon in a move that drew a good deal of criticism, some of it from within Israel itself. Some rally participants wished to denounce the Israeli invasion and emphasize the fact that Israel was also a nuclear power. In the end, Professor Noam Chomsky of the Massachusetts Institute of Technology and the veteran activist David Dellinger were the only two speakers to broach the potentially divisive issue. Cockburn and Ridgeway, "Freeze Movement versus Reagan," 12.

76. Quoted in Meyer, *Winter of Discontent*, 210–11. See also Alexander Cockburn and James Ridgeway, "Peace in Central Park," *Village Voice*, June 22, 1982.

77. Quoted in Waller, *Congress and the Nuclear Freeze*, 108.

78. Quoted in Meyer, *Winter of Discontent*, 187.

79. Waller, *Congress and the Nuclear Freeze*, 35.

80. Quoted in *Traprock Report* 3, no. 2 (March 1982), TPCR, series 1, box 1 folder 3, MS 80.

81. Quoted in Waller, *Congress and the Nuclear Freeze*, 87.

82. Quoted in ibid., 47.

83. Quoted in Meyer, *Winter of Discontent*, 224.

84. Waller, *Congress and the Nuclear Freeze*, 66–67.

85. Ibid.

86. Cockburn and Ridgeway, "Freeze Movement versus Reagan," 21.

87. Edward M. Kennedy and Mark O. Hatfield, *Freeze! Or How You Can Help Prevent Nuclear War* (New York: Bantam Books, 1982), v.

88. *Traprock Report* 3, no. 3 (May 1982), TPCR, series 1, box 1, folder 3, MS 80.

89. Meyer, *Winter of Discontent*, 224.

90. Waller, *Congress and the Nuclear Freeze*, 175–79.

91. Edward Markey, United States Committee against Nuclear War, A Political Action Committee for a Nuclear Freeze, fund-raising letter, circa 1983, FCP, Sophia Smith Collection.

92. Meyer, *Winter of Discontent*, 206.

93. "Beginner's Luck," cover letter accompanying freeze advertisement kit, FCP, Sophia Smith Collection. The FCP also holds all twelve advertisements, whose creators claimed to be nonprofessional volunteers, although they were clearly quite familiar with modern marketing theories.

94. Ibid.

95. Kehler interview. Commenting on the saturation coverage, Kehler said, "In the end that hurt us." Ibid.

96. Quoted in W. Dale Nelson, "Full House Freeze Vote Seen As Close," *Greenfield Recorder*, March 9, 1983.

97. Quoted in Waller, *Congress and the Nuclear Freeze*, 79.

98. Quoted in Joanne Omang "Magazine Articles Cited in KGB-Freeze Link," *Washington Post*, November 13, 1982.

99. "Minutes of the Executive Committee Meeting," Nuclear Weapons Freeze Campaign, September 28, 1982, FCP, Sophia Smith Collection.

100. June 12 Rally Committee, press release, November 12, 1982, LCP, Tamiment 138.

101. Quoted in Omang "Magazine Articles Cited in KGB-Freeze Link." Certainly, pro-Soviet organizations, including the American Communist Party and the World Peace Council, endorsed the freeze. These groups seem merely to have attached themselves to a popular movement, and in the U.S. movement their influence was marginal. In Europe, in contrast, various communist parties played a more prominent role; even so, however, they usually advocated tactics more conservative than those of the rest of the European peace movement. See Breyman, *Why Movements Matter*.

102. Ibid., 78.

103. Meyer, *Winter of Discontent*, 227–28.

104. Quoted in "Nuclear Freeze Narrowly Fails in House of Representatives," Nuclear Freeze Foundation, circa August 1982, FCP, Sophia Smith Collection.

105. Quoted in ibid.

106. Quoted in ibid.

107. Meyer, *Winter of Discontent*, 227–28.

108. Quoted in "Nuclear Freeze Narrowly Fails in House of Representatives," Nuclear Freeze Foundation, circa August 1982, FCP, Sophia Smith Collection.

109. Quoted in ibid.

110. Cockburn and Ridgeway, "Freeze Movement versus Reagan," 11.

111. Waller, *Congress and the Nuclear Freeze*, 164–65.

112. Randall Forsberg, chairman of the National Advisory Board, press release, Nuclear Weapons Freeze Campaign, November 1982, FCP, Sophia Smith Collection.

113. Ibid.

114. *Traprock Report* 3, no. 8 (March 1983), TPCR, series 1, box 1, folder 4, MS 80.

115. Quoted in Waller, *Congress and the Nuclear Freeze*, 258.

116. Ibid.

117. Quoted in ibid., 78.

118. Quoted in ibid., 258.

119. Ibid., 286. See also Meyer, *Winter of Discontent*, 231.

120. Quoted in Waller, *Congress and the Nuclear Freeze*, 285.

121. Quoted in Meyer, *Winter of Discontent*, 231.

122. Ibid., 232.

123. Breyman, *Why Movements Matter*, 193–96.

124. "Decisions Made by the Third National Conference of the Nuclear Weapons Freeze Campaign," St. Louis, Missouri, February 4–6, 1983, FCP, Sophia Smith Collection.

125. Quoted in McDermott, "Four Area Women Arrested in Protest Over Nuclear War."

126. NWFC, "Dear Local Organizer," September 14, 1983, FCP, Sophia Smith Collection.

127. Ibid. In mid-October, Kehler discussed the impact of the KAL 007 incident in a letter to freeze organizers, FCP, Sophia Smith Collection.

128. *Traprock Report* 3, no. 12 (October 1983), series 1, box 1 folder 4, MS 80, TPCR.

129. Quoted in undated and unidentified newspaper clipping, TPCR, MS 80, box 5, folder 33.

130. Quoted in "Missile Delay Sought by Conte, Other Freeze Backers," *Daily Hampshire Gazette*, November 21, 1983.

131. Randy Kehler, "Where We've Been and Where We're Going," NWFC letter, October 1983, FCP, Sophia Smith Collection.

132. Quoted in *Traprock Report* 3, no. 12 (October 1983), TPCR, series 1, box 1, folder 4, MS 80.

133. Breyman, *Why Movements Matter*, 204–5.

134. *Traprock Report* 3, no. 12 (October 1983), TPCR, series 1, box 1, folder 4, MS 80.

135. Ibid.

136. Meyer, *Winter of Discontent*, 198–201.

137. *Amherst Record*, circa July 1981, FCPP.

138. Quoted in *Amherst News*, circa June 1981, FCPP.

139. *Valley Advocate*, circa June 1981, FCPP.

140. Quoted in *United Methodist Reporter*, circa June 1981, FCPP.

141. Frances Crowe, draft speech, circa 1982, FCP, Sophia Smith Collection.

142. Quoted in undated and unidentified newspaper clipping, circa 1983, FCPP.

143. Frances Crowe, "Journey of Conscience," draft speech, circa 1982, FCP, Sophia Smith Collection.

144. Quoted in *Valley Advocate*, circa March 1982, TPCR, MS 80, box 5, folder 33.

145. Quoted in ibid.

146. Quoted in Bill Babel, "Quaker Protests with a Purpose," *Springfield Union and Sunday Republican*, November 16, 1980.

147. Ibid.

148. Quoted in ibid.

149. Ibid.

150. Frances Crowe, draft speech, circa 1978–1979, FCP, Sophia Smith Collection.

151. Ibid. On one occasion, when she believed that military recruiters who were addressing students in an auditorium were taking more than their allotted five minutes, she interrupted to say, "This isn't working. . . . I suggest [to] those . . . opposed to war in any form [who] want to know about your legal options to military service, move to this side of the room." According to Crowe, all but five people did. Ibid.

152. Frances Crowe, interview by the author, December 3, 1996, Northampton, Massachusetts.

153. Quoted Babel, "Quaker Protests with a Purpose."

154. Frances Crowe, "Keynote Speech to the First New Jersey Conference on the Freeze, 1981," draft speech, FCP, Sophia Smith Collection.

155. Ibid.

156. Frances Crowe, draft speech, August 8, 1982, FCP, Sophia Smith Collection.

157. Crowe, "Keynote Speech to the First New Jersey Conference on the Freeze, 1981."

158. Frances Crowe, interview by the author, December 3, 1996, Northampton, Massachusetts.

159. "Crowe; Acting on Principles," *Daily Hampshire Gazette*, January 11, 1984.

160. Undated and unidentified newspaper clipping, circa December 1983 to January 1984, FCPP.

161. Quoted in undated and unidentified newspaper clipping, FCPP.

162. Quoted in Sarah van Arsdale, "Crusader 'Learned' in Prison," *Springfield Union*, February 6, 1984.

163. Ibid.

164. Quoted in ibid.

165. Undated and unidentified clippings, FCPP.

166. *Traprock Report* 4, no. 2 (March 1984), TPCR, series 1, box 1, folder 5, MS 80.

167. Meyer, *Winter of Discontent*, 242–46.

168. Mary L. Wentworth, *Discovering America: A Political Journey* (Philadelphia, Pa.: Xlibris, 2003).

169. Ibid., 589, 588.

170. Ibid., 610, 613.

171. Quoted in Frances FitzGerald, *Way Out There in the Blue: Reagan, Star Wars, and the End of the Cold War* (New York: Simon and Schuster, 2000).

172. FitzGerald, *Way Out There in the Blue*.

173. Quoted in Meyer, *Winter of Discontent*, 222.

174. FitzGerald, *Way Out There in the Blue*, 180, 200, 203.

175. Ibid., 199.

176. Quoted in "Dukakis Assails Reagan Administration Arms Control Policy," Michael Dukakis press release, October 20, 1984, MSDPCP, box 5, folder 283, MS 32.

177. Meyer, *Winter of Discontent*, 250.

178. *Traprock Report* 4, no. 3 (May 1984), TPCR, series 1, box 1 folder 5, MS 80.

179. *Traprock Report* 4, no. 2 (March 1984), TPCR, series 1, box 1, folder 5, MS 80.

180. Waller, *Congress and the Nuclear Freeze*, 292–33.

181. Meyer, *Winter of Discontent*, 271.

182. Ibid., 255–56.

183. Ibid., 272.

184. Kehler interview.

185. Ibid.

186. Ibid. Based on their experience with the power of the nuclear weapons industry, many freeze activists later led the movement for campaign finance reform.

CHAPTER 5

1. Timothy M. Phelps, "For Two Nuns, Needs of the Poor Hid the Danger," *New York Times*, December 7, 1980, 1.

2. Marvin E. Gettleman, ed., *El Salvador: Central America in the New Cold War* (New York: Grove Press, 1981); William M. LeoGrande, *Our Own Backyard: The United States and Central America, 1977–1992* (Chapel Hill: University of North Carolina Press, 1998), 34.

3. LeoGrande, *Our Own Backyard*, 47–48.

4. Thomas P. Anderson, *Matanza: El Salvador's Communist Revolt of 1932* (Lincoln: University of Nebraska Press, 1971).

5. LeoGrande, *Our Own Backyard*, 59–60.

6. Phelps, "For Two Nuns."

7. LeoGrande, *Our Own Backyard*, 18–27; Bernard Dietrich, *Somoza and the Legacy of U.S. Involvement in Central America* (New York: Dutton, 1981).

8. LeoGrande, *Our Own Backyard*; Phelps, "For Two Nuns."

9. Phelps, "For Two Nuns."Gettleman, *El Salvador*, 140.

10. Quoted in Phelps, "For Two Nuns."

11. Quoted in ibid.

12. Ibid.

13. Quoted in Gettleman, *El Salvador*, 135–36.

14. Quoted in ibid. (Quoted in full in "Romero," available at www.icomm.ca/carecen/page25.html, retrieved November 25, 2002.)

15. Quoted in Phelps, "For Two Nuns." See also Gettleman, *El Salvador*, 140, and Leo-Grande, *Our Own Backyard*, 60–61.

16. Phelps, "For Two Nuns."

17. LeoGrande, *Our Own Backyard*, 16–17, 43–46. Carter's new policy in Central America was further underscored by his 1977 declaration "Being confident of our future, we are now free of that inordinate fear of Communism which once led us to embrace any dictator who joined us in that fear." Quoted in Gettleman, *El Salvador*. On the Carter human rights policy, see (in addition to William LeoGrande's excellent overview) Richard Thornton, *The Carter Years: Toward a New Global Order* (New York: Paragon House, 1991); Joshua Muravchic, *The Uncertain Trumpet: Jimmy Carter and the Dilemmas of Human Rights Policy* (Lanham, Md.: Hamilton Press, 1986); and Hamilton Jordon, *Crisis: The Last Year of the Carter Presidency* (New York: Putnam, 1982).

18. LeoGrande, *Our Own Backyard*, 58, 76, 82.

19. Quoted in Larry Rohter, "4 Salvadorans Say They Killed U.S. Nuns on Orders of Military," *New York Times*, April 3, 1998.

20. LeoGrande, *Our Own Backyard*, 52–71. See also Jeff McMahan, *Reagan and the World: Imperial Policy in the Cold War* (New York: Monthly Review Press, 1985), and Thomas Walker,

ed., *Reagan versus the Sandinistas: The Undeclared War on Nicaragua* (Boulder, Colo.: Westview Press, 1987).

21. Lou Cannon, *Reagan: The Role of a Life Time* (New York: Simon and Schuster, 1991).

22. LeoGrande details the early Reagan administration debate between those who wished to disregard human rights concerns completely and those, such as Undersecretary of State Thomas Enders, who pushed to support Duarte and the Christian Democrats against a right-wing military coup and to make at least nominal genuflections in the direction of human rights. LeoGrande, *Our Own Backyard*, 72–103.

23. LeoGrande, *Our Own Backyard*, 104–24; Walker, *Reagan versus the Sandinistas*; Robert Kagan, *A Twilight Struggle: American Power and Nicaragua, 1977–1990* (New York: Free Press, 1996).

24. LeoGrande, *Our Own Backyard*, 152–58.

25. Van Gosse, *Where the Boys Are: Cuba, Cold War, and the Making of the American Left* (New York: Verso, 1993). Gosse further traces the interest of the Left in Latin America to activism surrounding Chile in the 1970s. See idem, "Unpacking the Vietnam Syndrome: The Coup in Chile and the Rise of Popular Anti-Interventionism," in *The World the Sixties Made: Politics and Culture in Recent America*, ed. Gosse and Richard Moser (Philadelphia: Temple University Press, 2003).

26. Gettleman, *El Salvador*.

27. Walker, *Reagan versus the Sandinistas*; Kagan, *Twilight Struggle*.

28. Quoted in Van Gosse, "'The North American Front': Central American Solidarity in the Reagan Era," in *Reshaping the U.S. Left: Popular Struggles in the 1980s*, ed. Mike Davis and Michael Sprinker (New York: Verso, 1988), 11–49.

29. Ibid. For background on the role of Salvadorans in the movement, see also Van Gosse, "'El Salvador Is Spanish for Vietnam': A New Immigrant Left and the Politics of Solidarity," in *The Immigrant Left*, ed. Paul Buhle and Dan Georgakas (Albany: State University of New York Press, 1996), 302–29.

30. Ibid. 25.

31. Ibid., 15.

32. Quoted in William Pohl, "Rallying Point; Marching Protesters Urge End of U.S. Involvement in El Salvador," *Daily Hampshire Gazette*, April 27, 1981.

33. Ibid.

34. Quoted in ibid.

35. Quoted in ibid.

36. Barton Meyers and Jean Weissman, "The Solidarity Movement in the U.S.," in Gettleman, *El Salvador*, 379–91. See also Gosse, "'North American Front.'"

37. Barton and Meyers, "Solidarity Movement," 371–91.

38. Lois Ahrens, interview by the author, December 8, 1996, Northampton, Massachusetts.

39. Francis X. Clines, "U.S. Acting Legally About Nicaragua, President Asserts," *New York Times*, April 15, 1983; LeoGrande, *Our Own Backyard*, 89, 114–15, 144–45.

40. Quoted in *Boston Globe*, circa December 1983, Frances Crowe Private Papers, Northampton, Massachusetts (hereafter cited as FCPP). See also Frances Crowe, interview by the author, December 3, 1996, Northampton, Massachusetts.

41. Stephen Lyons, "Two City Women Back Home; They Say Trip to Nicaragua Shows Errors in U.S. Policy," *Daily Hampshire Gazette*, November 26, 1983.

42. Walker, *Reagan versus the Sandinistas*. See also Kagan, *Twilight Struggle*.

43. Walker, *Reagan versus the Sandinistas*; Martin Tolchin, "U.S. Aide Defends Mining Without Acknowledging It," *New York Times*, April 12, 1984.

44. Michael S. Dukakis to Rebecca Cunningham, letter, December 12, 1983, MSDPCP, box 5, folder 282, MS 32.

45. Dan Petegorsky to Michael S. Dukakis, letter, September 8, 1983, MSDPCP, box 5, folder 282 MS 32.

46. "A Proclamation by His Excellency Michael S. Dukakis, Governor," 1983, MSDPCP, boxes 4 and 5, folders 282 and 229, MS 32.

47. "The Working People of Central America: Marta Alicia Rivera," undated and unidentified newspaper clipping, circa 1984,. MSDPCP, box 4, folder 229, MS 32; Michael S. Dukakis, "Letter of Endorsement," March 28, 1984, MSDPCP, box 4, folder 229, MS 32. Dukakis's staff put together practice charges so that the governor could rehearse responses to expected charges by the George H. W. Bush campaign in 1988. In one, the charge read, "MSD endorsed with a signed proclamation the 1984 U.S. tour by Marta Alicia Rivera, a leading member of a Salvadoran labor organization. She had been kidnapped and tortured by the Salvadoran military, and she was touring the U.S. speaking about it. The Massachusetts Association of Teachers asked MSD to back [the] tour. Judging from the group's literature and its activities inside El Salvador, it's almost certainly tied to the guerrillas. The connection is immediately recognizable from the literature. However, there's never any proof of these ties." Dukakis's response was to affirm his confidence in the Massachusetts Teachers Association and denounce the Reagan-Bush administration for its illegal donation of two hundred thousand dollars to "a drug-smuggling Panamanian dictator," Manuel Noriega. "Central American Groups," circa summer 1988, MSDPCP, box 4, folder 229, MS 32.

48. Quoted in "Remember Vietnam?" flier, circa October 1984, MSDPCP, box 4, folder 282, MS 32.

49. "A Proclamation by His Excellency, Michael S. Dukakis, Governor," 1985, MSDPCP, box, 4, folder 229, MS 32.

50. LeoGrande, *Our Own Backyard*, 316–18.

51. "Latin American Policies Are Protested in U.S.," *New York Times*, May 8, 1985; Ross Gelbspan, "Hundreds Arrested in Boston Protest," *Boston Globe*, May 8, 1985; Crowe interview.

52. Quoted in Mitchel Zemel, "Scores Arrested in Protests Against Nicaraguan Policy," *Springfield Daily News*, May 8, 1985. See also Crowe interview.

53. Crowe interview.

54. Ibid.

55. Quoted in undated and unidentified newspaper clipping, circa May 8, 1985, FCPP.

56. Quoted in ibid.

57. "Latin American Policies Are Protested"; Gelbspan, "Hundreds Arrested in Boston Protest."

58. Gelbspan, "Hundreds Arrested in Boston Protest."

59. Quoted in ibid.

60. Quoted in ibid.

61. Quoted in Ross Gelbspan, "500 Charged in Protest Over Embargo," *Boston Globe*, May 9, 1985.

62. Quoted in ibid.

63. "Embargo Spurs Protests and Arrests across State," *Daily Hampshire Gazette*, May 8, 1985, 11.

64. For an overview of the South African divestment movement in the spring of 1985, see Todd Gitlin, "Divestment Stirs a New Generation," *The Nation*, May 9, 1985.

65. Steven V. Roberts, "House Reverses Earlier Ban on Aid to Nicaragua; Passes $27 Million Aid Package," *New York Times*, June 13, 1985.

66. Ibid.

67. LeoGrande, *Our Own Backyard*, 426–28.

68. "93 Protesters Arrested in WMass," *Springfield Morning Union*, June 13, 1985, 1, 17.

69. Quoted in Philip Bennet, "Boston Demonstrators Join Thousands; In Protest of U.S. Policy on Nicaragua," *Boston Globe*, June 13, 1985, 31.

70. Quoted in ibid.

71. Quoted in ibid.

72. Quoted in Andrew Torchia, "500 Protest U.S. Policy in Central America," *Boston Globe*, June 14, 1985, 75.

73. Gosse, "'North American Front.'"

74. Ahrens interview.

75. Ibid.

76. Crowe interview.

77. Ibid.

78. Bernard Weinraub, "Hundreds Arrested at C.I.A. Protest on Foreign Policy," *New York Times*, April 28, 1987.

79. "Eleven Arrested at UMass," *Daily Hampshire Gazette*, November 15, 1986; Stephanie Kraft, "The Triumph of Necessity," *Valley Advocate*, April 20, 1987, 6.

80. "Eleven Arrested at UMass."

81. Ibid.

82. Marty Jezer, *Abbie Hoffman: American Rebel* (New Brunswick, N.J.: Rutgers University Press, 1992).

83. Quoted in Michael James, "CIA Protest at UM Ends in Arrests, Legal Moves," *Daily Hampshire Gazette*, November 25, 1986.

84. Ibid.

85. Quoted in ibid.

86. Matthew L. Wald, "Amy Carter Tells Court She Sat In Road to Alter C.I.A. Policy," *New York Times*, April 14, 1987; Matthew L. Wald, "Amy Carter Acquitted Over Protest," *New York Times*, April 16, 1987.

87. Kraft, "Triumph of Necessity," 6.

88. Quoted in Deborah McDermott, "The CIA Trial Verdict: Judge Kept Control of Courtroom," *Daily Hampshire Gazette*, April 16, 1987.

89. Wald, "Amy Carter Tells Court"; Wald, "Amy Carter Acquitted."

90. Kraft, "Triumph of Necessity," 6.

91. Quoted in Deborah McDermott, "Trial, Verdict Send a Message: Freeing Protesters Seen As Statement Against CIA," *Daily Hampshire Gazette*, April 16, 1987.

92. Quoted in Kraft, "Triumph of Necessity," 6.

93. Quoted in ibid., 7.

94. Quoted in ibid.

95. Quoted in *The Best of Abbie Hoffman*, ed. Daniel Simon and Abbie Hoffman (New York: Four Walls Eight Windows, 1989), 387.

96. Quoted in Wald, "Amy Carter Acquitted."

97. McDermott, "Trial, Verdict Send a Message."

98. Quoted in Wald, "Amy Carter Acquitted." Ryan told another journalist, "It was a great jury. It was a conservative jury. The moment they were empanelled I thought we had it won." Quoted in McDermott, "Trial, Verdict Send a Message."

99. Quoted in McDermott, "Trial, Verdict Send a Message."

100. Quoted in ibid.

101. Quoted in Wald, "Amy Carter Acquitted."

102. Quoted in Paul Oh, "Jurors Discuss Protestors; 'They did it for a reason,'" *Daily Hampshire Gazette*, April 16, 1987, 1.

103. Quoted in ibid.

104. Quoted in ibid.

105. "Mel King for Congress," biography, circa 1986, LCP, Tamiment 138; "Mel King or Joe Kennedy?" Mel King for congress campaign literature, circa 1986, LCP, Tamiment 138; "King Blending Politics, Activism in 8th District," *Boston Globe*, August 5, 1986. See also Mel King, *Chain of Change: Struggles for Black Community Development* (Boston: South End Press, 1981), and Mel King and James Jennings, eds., *From Access to Power: Black Politics in Boston* (Cambridge, Mass.: Schenkman, 1986).

106. Leslie Cagan, "Being Left. It Should Be Possible, It Has to Be Possible," *ZMag* (June 1998), available at www.org/ZMag/articles/caganjune98.htum, retrieved December 5, 2006.

107. Leslie Cagan to field organizers, memorandum, March 3, 1986, LCP, Tamiment 138. See also Kenneth J. Cooper, "Candidates in 9th District Woo the Irish Vote," *Boston Globe*, August 22, 1986.

108. "Mel King Calls for Repeal of Gramm-Rudman," press release, February 12, 1986, LCP, Tamiment 138.

109. "Mel King and Peace Issues," Mel King for congress campaign literature, circa 1986, LCP, Tamiment 138.

110. Quoted in "Mel King Condemns Attack on Libya," press release, April 15, 1986, LCP, Tamiment 138.

111. Mel King, draft speech on Central America, March 18, 1986, LCP, Tamiment 138.

112. Quoted in "Mel King Condemns Contra Aid Vote," press release, June 26, 1986, LCP, Tamiment 138.

113. Barry Weisberg, "Report to [Mel King for Congress] Campaign Committee," August 23, 1986, LCP, Tamiment 138.

114. Quoted in Paul Sullivan, "'Tip' Calls 8th 'Kennedy Country' & Draws Fire," *Boston Herald*, July 26, 1986.

115. Matthew L. Wald, "Joseph Kennedy's Margin Makes Him a Favorite," *New York Times*, September 18, 1986.

116. Robert Lindsey, "Aid to Aliens Said to Spur Immigration," *New York Times*, December 23, 1985; Renny Golden and Michael McConnel, *Sanctuary: The New Underground Railroad* (Maryknoll, N.Y.: Orbis Books, 1986); Ann Crittenden, *Sanctuary: A Story of American Conscience and Law in Collision* (New York: Weidenfeld and Nelson, 1988).

117. Crittendon, *Sanctuary*.

118. Quoted in Lindsey, "Aid to Aliens."

119. Ibid.; Ross Gelbspan, "Cambridge Votes to Be a Sanctuary," *Boston Globe*, April 9, 1985.

120. Ibid.

121. Quoted in ibid.

122. Quoted in ibid.

123. Quoted in ibid.

124. Ibid.

125. *Transcript-Telegram*, circa April 1985, FCPP.

126. Stephen Schlesinger and Stephen Kinzer, *Bitter Fruit: The Untold Story of the American Coup Attempt in Guatemala* (Garden City, N.Y.: Anchor, 1983).

127. *Transcript-Telegram*, circa April 1985, FCPP.

128. Quoted in ibid.

129. Keith Stone, "Seeking Sanctuary; Guatemalan Refugees to End Cross-Country Trip Here," *Daily Hampshire Gazette*, June 17, 1985; Julie Rappaport, interview by the author, December 10, 1996, Amherst, Massachusetts.

130. Quoted in *Springfield Daily News*, circa July 1985. FCPP.

131. Rappaport interview.

132. Ibid.

133. Paul Berman, "In Search of Ben Linder's Killers," *New Yorker*, September 23, 1996; John Brentlinger, *The Best of What We Are: Reflections on the Nicaraguan Revolution* (Amherst: University of Massachusetts Press, 1995). See also Ron Ridenour, *Yankee Sandinistas: Interviews with North Americans Living and Working in the New Nicaragua* (Willimantic, Conn.: Curbstone Press, 1986).

134. John Reed, *Ten Days That Shook the World* (New York: International, 1919).

135. Peter Carroll, *The Odyssey of the Abraham Lincoln Brigade* (Palo Alto, Calif.: Stanford University Press, 1994).

136. Berman, "In Search of Ben Linder's Killers."

137. Rappaport interview.

138. Ibid.

139. Ibid.

140. Ibid.

141. Michael Prokosch, telephone interview by the author, February 22, 2007.

142. Ibid.

143. Ibid.

144. Ibid.

145. Quoted in ibid.

146. Ibid.

147. Ahrens interview.

148. Ibid.

149. Ibid.

150. Ibid.

151. Quoted in Kitty Axelson, Lois Ahrens; Witness in El Salvador," *Valley Advocate*, August 28, 1989.

152. Ahrens interview; LeoGrande, *Our Own Backyard*, 569–74.

153. Brentlinger, *The Best of What We Are*, 68.

154. Ibid., 41. Emphasis in original.

155. Ibid., 17.

156. Ibid., 18.

157. Ibid., 67.

158. Quoted in ibid., 251.

159. Quoted in ibid., 143.

160. Ibid., 151.

161. Ibid., 222.

162. Quoted in ibid., 226.

163. Gary Stern, *The FBI's Misguided Probe of CISPES*, Center for National Security Studies, Report No. 11, June 1988.

164. Ahrens interview.

165. Ibid.; Diane Gonzalez, "Activist Says Inked-Out Files Prove FBI Spies on Citizens," *Daily Hampshire Gazette*, July 11, 1990.

166. Quoted in Judith Kelliner, "FBI Ordered to Produce Records on Activist," *Daily Hampshire Gazette*, November 27, 1990.

167. Ahrens interview.

168. Jack Anderson undated and unidentified newspaper clipping, circa 1991, FCPP.

169. Quoted in Douglas Clark, "Activist; FBI Probe Represents Double Standard," *Daily Hampshire Gazette*, January 6, 1990.

170. Quoted in "Suing the FBI," *Valley Advocate*, January 22, 1990, 4.

171. Quoted in Clark, "Activist; FBI Probe Represents Double Standard."

172. "Spying on Citizens," editorial, *Daily Hampshire Gazette*, January 10, 1990.

173. Quoted in "Suing the FBI," 4.

174. Ahrens interview.

175. Mark A. Uhlig, "Election in Nicaragua; Nicaragua is Calm in Heavy Turnout for Critical Vote," *New York Times*, February 27, 1990.

176. Crowe interview.

177. Rappaport interview.

178. Ahrens interview.

179. Brentlinger, *The Best of What We Are*, 285.

180. Ibid., 2–3.

CHAPTER 6

1. Jim Fairchild and George Allen to Silvio O. Conte, "Re: Nicaraguan Travel Request," letter, December 13, 1979, Silvio O. Conte Congressional Papers, 1950–1991, series 3e, box 64, folder: "Nicaragua—Contra Aid, 1980–86," MS 371, subgroup II, Special Collections

and University Archives, W.E.B. Dubois Library, University of Massachusetts, Amherst (hereafter cited as SOC).

2. Silvio O. Conte, handwritten notes, January 3, 1980, SOC, series 3e, box 64, folder: "Nicaragua: Contra Aid, 1980–86," MS 371, subgroup II.

3. Ibid.

4. Ibid.

5. Ibid.

6. Silvio O. Conte, "Nicaragua and Honduras Supplemental, FY 1980," draft statement, SOC, series 3e, box 64, folder: "Nicaragua—Contra Aid, 1980–86," MS 371, subgroup II.

7. William LeoGrande, *Our Own Backyard: The United States in Central America, 1977–1992* (Chapel Hill: University of North Carolina Press, 1998), 29–32, 69.

8. Lois Ahrens, interview by the author, December 8, 1996, Northampton, Massachusetts.

9. Silvio O. Conte to Ray Miller and the Reverend Thomas W. Olcott, letter, January 19, 1981, SOC, series 3e, box 64, folder: "El Salvador: Letters and Statements," MS 371, subgroup II.

10. LeoGrande, *Our Own Backyard*, 66–67.

11. Ibid., 69–70, 95.

12. Silvio O. Conte to the Honorable John Olver, letter, February 17, 1981, SOC, series 3e, box 64, folder: "El Salvador: Letters and Statements," MS 371, subgroup II.

13. Ibid.

14. LeoGrande, *Our Own Backyard*, 96.

15. "Remarks of the Honorable Silvio O. Conte before the Foreign Operations Subcommittee of the Full House Appropriations Committee," March 24, 1981, SOC, series 3e, box 64, folder: "El Salvador: Letters and Statements," MS 371, subgroup II.

16. Ibid.

17. "Speaking Points on El Salvador," circa April 1981, SOC, series 3e, box 64, folder: "El Salvador: Letters and Statements," MS 371, subgroup II.

18. Ibid.

19. David J. Hoey to Silvio O. Conte, letter, received April 24, 1981, SOC, series 3e, box 64, folder: "El Salvador: Letters and Statements," MS 371, subgroup II.

20. "An Open Letter to Silvio Conte," *Daily Hampshire Gazette*, advertisement, April 11, 1981, 5.

21. Silvio O. Conte to David J. Hoey, letter, April 27, 1981, SOC, series 3e, box 64, folder: "El Salvador: Letters and Statements," MS 371, subgroup II.

22. Silvio O. Conte to Susan Klein-Berndt, letter, April 26, 1981, SOC, series 3e, box, 64, folder: "El Salvador: Letters and Statements," MS 371, subgroup II.

23. Ibid.

24. Quoted in *Daily Hampshire Gazette*, circa April 1981, SOC, series 3e, box 64, folder: "El Salvador: Letters and Statements," MS 371, subgroup II.

25. Quoted in ibid.

26. LeoGrande, *Our Own Backyard*, 130–32.

27. Silvio O. Conte, undated statement criticizing President Ronald Reagan's January 28, 1982, certification of El Salvador, circa January 1982, SOC, series 3e, box 64, folder: "El Salvador: Letters and Statements," MS 371, subgroup II.

28. Ibid.

29. "Statement of U.S. Rep. Silvio O. Conte (R-Mass.) on the Completion of a Fact-Finding Mission in Central America of Foreign Operations Appropriations Subcommittee Staff Member Jim Fairchild," March 8, 1982, SOC, series 3e, box 64, folder: "El Salvador: Letters and Statements," MS 371, subgroup II.

30. Ibid.

31. LeoGrande, *Our Own Backyard*, 189.

32. Ibid., 49.

33. Ibid., 48–50, 149–73.

34. Ibid., 149–73.

35. "Tim to Silvio O. Conte Re: El Salvador Nuns Case," memorandum, March 23, 1983, SOC, series 3e, box 64, "El Salvador: Fourth Certification, 1983–84" folder, MS 37, subgroup II.

36. Stephen Kinzer, "Salvador Judge Delays Trial of 3 in Nuns' Slaying," *New York Times*, March 17, 1983.

37. "Salvador Arrest Reported in Killing of Americans," *New York Times*, Dec. 20, 1983, 1982.

38. Michael H. Posner to L. Craig Johnstone, letter, November 30, 1982, SOC, series 3e, box 64, folder: "El Salvador—Nun Slaying, 1982–1983," MS 371, subgroup II.

39. Ibid.

40. Quoted in "Ari L. Goldman, "For Relatives of the 4 Churchwomen, It's Only a 'First Step,'" *New York Times*, May 25, 1984.

41. "Salvadoran Court Delays Trial of Soldiers Accused in U.S. Women's Death," *Washington Post*, March 17, 1983.

42. Michael H. Posner. handwritten notes, circa February/March 1982, SOC, series 3e, box 64, folder: "El Salvador: Nun Slaying, 1982–83," MS 371, subgroup II.

43. Ibid.

44. Ibid.

45. Silvio O. Conte to Dr. Mario Adalberto Rivera, Fiscal General, La Republica de El Salvador, letter, March 23, 1983, SOC, series 3e, box 64, folder: "El Salvador: Nun Slaying, 1982–1983," MS 371, subgroup II.

46. Dr. Mario Adalberto Rivera to Silvio O. Conte, letter, June 20, 1983, SOC, series 3e, box 64, folder: "El Salvador: Nun Slaying, 1982–1983," MS 371, subgroup II.

47. Quoted in *Washington Times*, circa March 1983, SOC, series 3e, box 64, folder, "El Salvador—Nun Slaying, 1982–1983."

48. Quoted in ibid.

49. "Remarks of the Hon. Silvio O. Conte in Support of H.R. 1271," draft, SOC, series 3e, box 64, folder: "El Salvador: Fourth Certification, 1983–84," MS 371, subgroup II. The Studds amendment was intended to reinstate the requirement, which had lapsed.

50. Ibid.

51. "Conte Toughens Stance," *Daily Hampshire Gazette*, June 7, 1983.

52. Quoted in Lydia Chavez, "5 Salvadorans Are Found Guilty in Slaying of U.S. Churchwomen," *New York Times*, May 25, 1984.

53. LeoGrande, *Our Own Backyard*, 92, 156–57; Lyons, "Conte Toughens Stance."

54. Andrew Blake, "Studds: A Liberal Democrat from a Conservative District," *Boston Globe*, July 15, 1983.

55. Quoted in LeoGrande, *Our Own Backyard*, 92.

56. Clement Zablocki, foreword to "Central America, 1981: Report to the Committee on Foreign Affairs, United States House of Representatives," by Gerry E. Studds (Washington, D.C.: U.S. Government Printing Office, 1981), 5.

57. Ibid.; "An Open Letter to Silvio Conte," 5.

58. Studds, "Central America, 1981," 5.

59. Ibid., 7.

60. Ibid., 8.

61. Ibid., 7.

62. Ibid., 12.

63. Ibid., 9.

64. Ibid.

65. Ibid., 15.

66. Ibid., 22.

67. Ibid., 24.

68. Quoted in ibid., 28.

69. Ibid., 29.

70. Silvio O. Conte to Edwin Gabler, letter, March 31, 1981, SOC, series 3e, box 64, folder: "El Salvador: Legislative Action," MS 371, subgroup II.

71. LeoGrande, *Our Own Backyard*, 2.

72. Mark Danner, *El Mozote: A Parable of the Cold War* (New York: Vintage Books, 1994).

73. Quoted in LeoGrande, *Our Own Backyard*, 156.

74. "Draft: H.J. Res. 552 Declaring the President's July Certification with Respect to El Salvador to Be Null and Void," July 1982, SOC, series 3e, box 64, folder: "El Salvador: Legislative Action," MS 371, subgroup II.

75. Conte's aides noted the surge in mail in early 1983. "Memo: To Mr. Conte. From: Tim. Re.: El Salvador Certification—District Response," February 2, 1983, SOC, series 3e, box 64, "El Salvador: Third Certification Report" folder, MS 371, subgroup II. See also *Daily Hampshire Gazette*, June 7, 1983.

76. Quoted in LeoGrande, *Our Own Backyard*, 172.

77. "Statement of U.S. Representative Gerry Studds regarding the Third Certification Affecting El Salvador," February 4, 1983, SOC, series 3e, box 64, folder: "El Salvador: Third Certification Report, 1983," MS 371, subgroup II.

78. Gerry Studds to Members of the House of Representatives, "Dear Colleague," letter, January 21, 1983, SOC, series 3e, box 64, folder: "El Salvador: Legislation, 1983," MS 371, subgroup II.

79. Lyons, "Conte Toughens Stance."

80. LeoGrande, *Our Own Backyard*, 157, 588.

81. Quoted in Martin Tolchin, "Democrats' Fear: They'll Get the Blame for 'Losing' Central America," *New York Times*, May 30, 1983.

82. Gerry Studds, "Bipartisan Consensus? A Mirage," *New York Times*, June 13, 1983.

83. Ibid.

84. "News Summary," *New York Times*, July 15, 1983.

85. Ibid.

86. John A. Farrell, *Tip O'Neill and the Democratic Century* (Boston: Little, Brown, 2001), 631.

87. LeoGrande, *Our Own Backyard*, 260–82.

88. Quoted in Farrell, *Tip O'Neill and the Democratic Century*, 679.

89. Quoted in Leo Grande, *Our Own Backyard*, 455.

90. Farrell, *Tip O'Neill and the Democratic Century*, 609–11. O'Neill later opposed the MX missile. Ibid., 620.

91. Ibid., 609.

92. Quoted in Tolchin, "Democrats' Fear.".

93. Farrell, *Tip O'Neill and the Democratic Century*, 607–25.

94. Quoted in Philip Taubman, "The Speaker and His Sources on Latin America," *New York Times*, September 12, 1984.

95. Quoted in ibid.

96. Ibid.

97. Quoted in ibid.

98. Quoted in Farrell, *Tip O'Neill and the Democratic Century*, 612.

99. LeoGrande, *Our Own Backyard*, 92, 157–58, 169.

100. Quoted in "Transcript of Democrat's Response to Reagan Speech on Central America," *New York Times*, April 28, 1983.

101. Quoted in ibid.

102. Ibid.

103. Quoted in ibid.

104. Quoted in ibid.

105. Quoted in ibid.

106. Quoted in ibid.

107. Bernard Weinraub, "Mrs. Kirkpatrick Critical of Dodd," *New York Times*, May 1, 1983.

108. Farrell, *Tip O'Neill and the Democratic Century*, 607–25; LeoGrande, *Our Own Backyard*, 324–25, 454–56.

109. LeoGrande, *Our Own Backyard*, 285–305.

110. Ibid., 300.

111. Philip Taubman, "The Ferment Over Central America," *New York Times*, April 25, 1983.

112. LeoGrande, *Our Own Backyard*, 300, 312.

113. Don Oberdorfer, "Reagan Backs Action Plan for Central America," *Washington Post*, February 14, 1982; Christopher Dickey, "Nicaraguan Moderates Assail U.S. for Alleged 'Destabilization' Plan," *Washington Post*, March 18, 1982.

114. John Brecher, John Walcott, David Martin and Beth Nissen, "A Secret War for Nicaragua," *Newsweek*, November 8, 1982.

115. Quoted in LeoGrande, *Our Own Backyard*, 306.

116. Ibid., 304.

117. Quoted in Martin Tolchin, "Key House Member Fears U.S. Breaks Law on Nicaragua," *New York Times*, April 14, 1983.

118. Quoted in ibid.

119. Taubman, "The Ferment Over Central America."; LeoGrande, *Our Own Backyard,* 312.

120. Quoted in Tolchin, "Key House Member Fears U.S. Breaks Law on Nicaragua.".

121. Quoted in ibid.

122. Quoted in ibid.

123. LeoGrande, *Our Own Backyard,* 317, 320–21. For an overview of Contra aid through the late spring of 1984, see Hedrick Smith, "Reagan Fighting to Win Aid for Anti-Sandinistas," *New York Times,* May 27, 1984.

124. LeoGrande, *Our Own Backyard,* 324.

125. Ibid., 330–40.

126. Ibid., 343–45; Lawrence E. Walsh, *Firewall: The Iran-Contra Conspiracy and Cover-up* (New York: Norton, 1997); Peter Kornbluh and Malcolm Byrne, eds., *The Iran-Contra Scandal: The Declassified History* (New York: New Press, 1993).

127. LeoGrande, *Our Own Backyard,* 243.

128. Quoted in Eileen McNamara, "Kennedy Ties Salvador Aid, Rights Progress," *Boston Globe,* March 29, 1984.

129. Hedrick Smith, "Democrat Says Senate Will Approve Salvador Aid," *New York Times,* March 29, 1984; Hedrick Smith, "Senate Defeats Attempts to Limit U.S. Troop Use in Latin America," *New York Times,* March 30, 1984.

130. Quoted in Eileen McNamara, "Reagan Backed in Latin Aid Vote," *Boston Globe,* March 30, 1984.

131. LeoGrande, *Our Own Backyard,* 397–413.

132. Quoted in Smith, "Reagan Fighting to Win Aid."

133. LeoGrande, *Our Own Backyard,* 423–26.

134. Quoted in Associated Press, "House May Revive Aid to the Contras," *Springfield Morning Union,* May 9, 1985.) One of the reasons for Ortega's trip was to cement an oil deal with the Soviet Union. Nicaragua had received the bulk of its oil from Mexico, until— under pressure from the United States—it had stopped extending oil credits to Nicaragua. LeoGrande, *Our Own Backyard,* 426–28.

135. Quoted in Richard Cohen, "Buchanan's Line . . . Or Reagan's?" *Washington Post,* March 12, 1986.

136. Quoted in Walter V. Robinson, "Debate Sharpens Over Contra Aid," *Boston Globe,* May 8, 1985.

137. Quoted in ibid.

138. Quoted in Adam Pertman, "O'Neill Launches Bid Against U.S. Policies on Latins, S. Africa," *Boston Globe,* June 1, 1985.

139. LeoGrande, *Our Own Backyard,* 31–38.

140. Steven V. Roberts, "House Reverses Earlier Ban on Aid to Nicaraguan Rebels; Passes $27 Million Package," *New York Times,* June 13, 1985.

141. Quoted in Robert LaRussa, "Behind the Nicaragua Vote," *Valley Advocate,* June 19, 1985, 6.

142. Quoted in Associated Press, "Nicaragua; Kennedy Condemns Reagan's Policies," *Daily Hampshire Gazette,* June 12, 1985.

143. Quoted in ibid.

144. Quoted in Roberts, "House Reverses Earlier Ban."

145. Quoted in Martin Tolchin, "Congress is Skeptical on Salvadoran Aid," *New York Times*, March 12, 1983.

146. Quoted in ibid.

147. LeoGrande, *Our Own Backyard*, 95.

148. Quoted in Bernard Gwertzman, "Haig Cites 'Hit List' for Soviet Control of Central America," *New York Times*, March 19, 1981.

149. Quoted in "President Reagan's Address on Central America to Joint Session of Congress," *New York Times*, April 28, 1983.

150. Quoted in "Excerpt from President Reagan's Speech on Foreign Policy and Congress," *New York Times*, April 7, 1984. In the conclusion of his in-depth study of the United States and Central America in the 1980s, William LeoGrande writes, "We went to war in Central America to exorcise the ghosts of Vietnam and to renew the national will to use force abroad. These imperatives, more than the Soviet threat, Fidel Castro's menace, or the Nicaraguan and Salvadoran revolutions, shaped U.S. policy." LeoGrande, *Our Own Backyard*, 590.

151. Lindsey Gruson, "Poll Reveals Fear of El Salvador as a New Vietnam," *New York Times*, July 24, 1983.

152. David Shribman, "Poll Finds a Lack of Public Support for Latin Policy," *New York Times*, April 29, 1984.

153. Quoted in *New York Times*, circa July 1983, FCPP.

154. Gerald Nicosia, *Home to War: A History of the Vietnam Veterans Movement* (New York: Crown Publishers, 2001).

155. Charles Clements, *Witness to War* (Toronto: Bantam, 1984). A 1985 documentary on Clements's life, "Witness to War: Dr. Charlie Clements," won the 1985 Academy award for best short subject documentary.

156. "Autobiography of S. Brian Willson," available at www.brianwillson.com/bio.html, accessed March 20, 2008; *New York Times*, September 2, 1987.

157. Quoted in Associated Press, "Nicaragua; Kennedy Condemns Reagan's Policies."

158. Nicosia, *Home to War*, 70–71. John Kerry's 2004 bid for the presidency produced two excellent works on his career. For a comprehensive overview, see Michael Kranish, Brian C. Mooney, and Nina J. Easton, *John F. Kerry: The Complete Biography by the Boston Globe Reporters Who Know Him Best* (New York: Public Affairs, 2004); for an account of his years in Vietnam and his rise as a leading opponent of the Vietnam War, see Douglas Brinkley, *Tour of Duty: John Kerry and the Vietnam War* (New York: William Morrow, 2004).

159. Nicosia, *Home to War*, 72; Kranish, Mooney, and Easton, *John F. Kerry*, 114; Brinkley, *Tour of Duty*, 339–40.

160. Nicosia, *Home to War*, 72, 108.

161. Ibid., 114.

162. Quoted in ibid., 133.

163. John Kerry and Vietnam Veterans Against the War, David Thorne, and George Butler, eds., *The New Soldier* (New York: Macmillan, 1971).

164. Nicosia, *Home to War*, 136; Kranish, Mooney, and Easton, *John F. Kerry*, 110–40; Brinkley, *Tour of Duty*, 346–411.

165. Quoted in Nicosia, *Home to War*, 211.

166. Fox Butterfield, Massachusetts Senate Race Narrows," *New York Times*, October 30, 1984.

167. Fox Butterfield, "The 1984 Election: Each State Has its Own Battles; Democratic Victor in Massachusetts," *New York Times*, November 7, 1984.

168. Quoted in Kenneth T. Walsh, Seven New Senators Take Their Stands," *U.S. News and World Report*, April 15, 1985, 37.

169. Quoted in Bernard Weinraub, "U.S. Rejects Nicaraguan Offer of Conditional Truce," *New York Times*, April 22, 1985.

170. Quoted in Stephanie Kraft, "Kerry on the Sandinista Peace Proposal," *Valley Advocate*, May 1, 1985, 12.

171. Quoted in Robert LaRussa, "Kerry Breaks with the Pack," *Valley Advocate*, May 8, 1985, 11.

172. Quoted in ibid., 11.

173. LeoGrande, *Our Own Backyard*, 454–57.

174. Ibid.

175. Quoted in Sarin Fritz, "Democrats to Probe Alleged Contras Corruption," *Los Angeles Times*, April 23, 1986.

176. Ibid.

177. LeoGrande, *Our Own Backyard*, 456–504; Walsh, *Firewall*; Kornbluh and Byrne, *Iran-Contra Scandal*.

178. Quoted in Robert Parry and Rod Nordland, "Guns for Drugs?" *Newsweek*, May 23, 1988.

179. David Corn, "Kerry's Drug Hearings: Can He Lift the C.I.A. Veil?" *The Nation*, April 30, 1988.

180. Quoted in ibid., 94.

181. LeoGrande, *Our Own Backyard*, 514–32.

182. Richard Gaines and Michael Segal, *Dukakis and the Reform Impulse* (Boston: Quinlan Press, 1987).

183. Quoted in Charles Kenney and Robert L. Turner, *Dukakis: An American Odyssey* (Boston: Haughton Mifflin, 1988), 38.

184. Quoted in Morton M. Kondracke, "Carter Redux?" *New Republic*, May 23, 1988, 14.

185. Michael Dukakis, "Building a New Partnership for the Americas," City Club of Chicago, September 17, 1987, MSDPCP, box 6, folder 324, MS 32.

186. Quoted in Kenney and Turner, *Dukakis*, 39.

187. Quoted in Susan F. Rasky, "Democrats Chided on Aid to Contras," *New York Times*, August 3, 1988.

188. Quoted in Kondracke, "Carter Redux?" 14.

189. Quoted in ibid.

190. Michael S. Dukakis to Jayne Plank, letter, April 23, 1985, MSDPCP box 5, folder 282, MS 32.

191. Timothy Barnicle to Governor Michael S. Dukakis, memorandum, February 18, 1986, MSDPCP, box 5, folder 282, MS 32.

192. Ibid.

193. Quoted in Fred Hiatt, "Governors Wary of Sending Guard Troops to Honduras," *Washington Post*, April 5, 1986.

194. Quoted in ibid.

195. Mark Gearan, Pat Branch, and Susan Jacobson to Michael S. Dukakis, October 30, 1986, MSDPCP, box 6, folder 342, MS 32.

196. Quoted in "Dukakis and Shannon to Appeal National Guard Decision," news release from the office of Governor Michael S. Dukakis, May 6, 1988, MSDPCP, box 6, folder 342, MS 32.

197. Quoted in ibid.

198. "States Lose Suit on the Guard's Latin Missions," New York Times, August 5, 1987.

199. Michael S. Dukakis, "A Partnership for Peace and Democracy in Central America," speech at Marquette University, March 30, 1988, MSDPCP, box 6, folder 324, MS 32.

200. "The Democrats in Atlanta: Nomination Speeches for 2 Top Contenders," New York Times, July 21, 1988.

201. Sheila D. Jackson, The Jackson Campaign and the Future of U.S. Politics (New York: Monthly Review Press, 1986).

202. Andrew Kopkind, "The Rainbow and the Democrats," The Nation, July 1988, 48–53.

203. Kondracke, "Carter Redux?" 13.

204. Michael S. Dukakis, "Building a Strong Conventional Defense," speech, Dallas, Texas, November 13, 1987, MSDPCP, box 4, folder 248, MS 32.

205. Quoted in "The Democrats in Atlanta: Transcript of the Speech by Dukakis Accepting the Democrats' Nomination," New York Times, July 22, 1988.

206. Quoted in Rasky, "Democrats Chided on Aid to Contras."

207. Ibid.

208. Richard Ben Cramer, What It Takes: The Way to the White House (New York: Random House, 1992).

209. Jim Schwartz, "Report on My Research on Old Issues of the Boston Globe," July 8, 1988, MSDPCP, box 6, folder 362, MS 32.

210. Ibid.

211. Quoted in "Central American Groups," circa July 1988, MSDPCP, box 4, folder 229, MS 32; this and several similar documents with anticipated charges against Dukakis and proposed responses can be found in MSDPCP, boxes 4 and 6, folders 229 and 326, MS 32.

212. Walsh, Firewall.

213. Walsh, Firewall; Kornbluh and Byrne, Iran-Contra Scandal. Oliver North's conviction was overturned on a technicality.

CONCLUSION

1. Kathryn Marchoki, "Protest Reaches Dangerous Heights; Rock-Climbing Mom Rips U.S. Aid to El Salvador," Boston Herald, June 1, 1989, 7; Mike Prokosch, telephone interview, February 22, 2007.

2. Quoted in Marchoki, "Protest Reaches Dangerous Heights."

3. Prokosch interview.

4. William LeoGrande, Our Own Backyard: The United States in Central America, 1977–1992 (Chapel Hill: University of North Carolina Press, 1998), 568–72.

5. Ibid.; Lindsey Gruson, "6 Priests Killed in a Campus Raid in San Salvador," New York Times, November 17, 1989.

6. Robert Pear, "Salvador Evidence Escaped U.S. Envoy," *New York Times*, January 16, 1990, 8.

7. LeoGrande, *Our Own Backyard*, 571–75.

8. Quoted in John Aloysius Farrell, "Moakley Remembers Slain Jesuit Friends," *Boston Globe*, November 14, 1990.

9. Quoted in Clifford Krauss, "Washington at Work; Religion and Politics Become Fused in Congressman's District, and Heart," *New York Times*, August 23, 1990.

10. Quoted in LeoGrande, *Our Own Backyard*, 574.

11. Quoted in Krauss, "Washington at Work."

12. LeoGrande, *Our Own Backyard*, 575–79.

13. "From Madness to Hope: The Twelve-Year War in El Salvador," Report of the U.N. Commission on the Truth for El Salvador, Belisario Betancur, chairman, 1993.

14. LeoGrande, *Our Own Backyard*, 582–83.

15. Ibid., 585.

16. Walter LaFeber, *America, Russia, and the Cold War, 1945–2000* (New York: McGraw Hill, 2002).

17. Quoted in Michael K. Frisky, "Congress, After Emotional Debate, Authorizes Use of Force in the Gulf," *Boston Globe*, January 13, 1991.

18. Ibid.

19. David Nyhan, Martin F. Nolan, Michael Frisby, and Stephen Kurkjian, "Silvio Conte Dies at Age 69," *Boston Globe*, February 9, 1991.

20. Quoted in Ann McDaniel, Evan Thomas, and Howard Fineman, "The Rewards of Leadership," *Newsweek*, March 11, 1991.

21. LeoGrande, *Our Own Backyard*, 590.

22. Quoted in U.S. Congress, House of Representatives, Committee on Foreign Affairs, "East-West Relations—U.S. Security Assistance," 97th Cong., 2nd sess., March 2, 1982, 18.

INDEX